Assessment for Regular
and Special Education Teachers

Assessment for Regular and Special Education Teachers

A Case Study Approach

Edited by

Anthony F. Rotatori

and

Robert Fox

5341 Industrial Oaks Blvd.
Austin, Texas 78735

Printed in the United States of America

Library of Congress Cataloging in Publication Data
Main entry under title:
Assessment for regular and special education teachers.
   Includes bibliographies and index.
   1. Educational tests and measurements—
United States—Case studies.   2. Psychological
tests—United States—Case studies.   3. Ability—
Testing—Case studies.   I. Rotatori, Anthony F.
II. Fox, Robert, 1951–
LB3051.A768   1985   371.2′6   85-572
ISBN 0-936104-43-0

5341 Industrial Oaks Boulevard
Austin, Texas 78735

10 9 8 7 6 5 4 3 2 1   85 86 87 88 89

Contents

5

Assessment of Reading Skills / 109

John Wills Lloyd, Norma A. Cameron, Patricia A. Lloyd

6

Assessment of Oral Language Skills / 141

Blanche Podhajski

7

Assessment of Arithmetic Performance / 183

Terry Rose

8

Assessment of Written Expression and Handwriting Skills / 213

Sandra B. Cohen, Michael M. Gerber

9

Assessment of Spelling Skills / 249

Michael M. Gerber, Sandra B. Cohen

10

Assessment of Behavior Disorders / 279

Douglas Cullinan, Herbert Root

11

Assessment of Adaptive Behavior / 311

Harvey N. Switzky, Anthony F. Rotatori, Robert fox

12

Assessment of Vocational Skills / 335

13

Assessment of Visually Handicapped Students / 361

14

Assessment of Hearing-Impaired Students / 383

15

Assessment of Giftedness, Talent, and Creativity   /   407

John O. Schwenn

Contributors

Shirin Antia, PhD
Assistant Professor
Department of Special Education
University of Arizona
Tucson, Arizona

Paul Bates, PhD
Associate Professor
Department of Special Education
Southern Illinois University
Carbondale, Illinois

Norma A. Cameron, EdD
Assistant Professor
Department of Special Education
University of Virginia
Charlottesville, Virginia

Sandra B. Cohen, PhD
Associate Professor
Department of Special Education
University of Virginia
Charlottesville, Virginia

Douglas Cullinan, EdD
Associate Professor
Department of Learning,
  Development, and Special
  Education
Northern Illinois University
DeKalb, Illinois

Robert Fox, PhD
Associate Professor
School of Education
Marquette University
Milwaukee, Wisconsin

Michael M. Gerber, PhD
Assistant Professor
Special Education Program
University of California
Santa Barbara, California

Toni Henize, EdD
Associate Professor
Department of Learning,
  Development, and Special
  Education
Northern Illinois University
Dekalb, Illinois

S. J. LaGrow, EdD
Assistant Professor
Department of Blind Rehabilitation
Western Michigan University
Kalamazoo, Michigan

John Wills Lloyd, PhD
Assistant Professor
Department of Special Education
University of Virginia
Charlottesville, Virginia

Patricia A. Lloyd, MEd
Head Teacher
Child Development Center
University of Virginia
Charlottesville, Virginia

Georgia Faye Macklin, PhD
Assistant Professor
Department of Special Education
Gallandet College
Washington, DC

Ernest Pancsofar, PhD
Assistant Professor
Department of Special Education
Bowling Green State University
Bowling Green, Ohio

Blanche Podhajski, PhD
Departments of Neurology and
  Communication Science
  and Disorders
University of Vermont
Burlington, Vermont

Reese Price, MA
Doctoral Student
Department of Psychology
Ohio State University
Columbus, Ohio

J. E. Prochnow-LaGrow, EdD
Instructor
Department of Learning,
  Development, and Special
  Education
Northern Illinois University
DeKalb, Illinois

Herbert Root, EdD
Assistant Professor
Division of Education and
  Psychology
Wayne State College
Wayne, Nebraska

Terry Rose, EdD
Associate Professor
Department of Educational
  Leadership and Instruction
University of North Carolina
Charlotte, North Carolina

Anthony F. Rotatori, PhD
Full Professor
Department of Special Education
University of New Orleans
New Orleans, Louisiana

John O. Schwenn, PhD
Associate Professor
Department of Special Education
Delta State University
Cleveland, Mississippi

Harvey N. Switzky, PhD
Full Professor
Department of Learning,
  Development, and Special
  Education
Northern Illinois University
DeKalb, Illinois

Ellen Weinhouse, PhD
Nisonger Center
Ohio State University
Columbus, Ohio

Preface

As early as 1957 Lee J. Cronbach, then president of the American Psychological Association, encouraged his colleagues at their annual convention to join efforts in a search for aptitude-treatment interactions. His plea was supported by research literature indicating that people learn in different ways. Certainly Cronbach's statement that people learn differently did not shock his audience in 1957, nor would it be likely to surprise most contemporary teachers, parents, or students. However, the implication of accepting this notion requires us also to consider that different individuals will use different strategies for learning the same information. Consequently, adapting these ideas to education, we should be striving constantly to achieve a carefully balanced match between the unique learner characteristics each child brings to the classroom setting and our choices of classroom environments, student-teacher ratios, curriculum content, and teaching methods. Fortunately, most children educated today thrive in a variety of different classroom settings. The majority learn to read and write, spell, work math problems, and successfully acquire additional information in several other academic areas (e.g., history, geography, literature). However, when significant mismatches occur between a child's particular learning characteristics and our teaching methods or materials, learning may fail to occur or at least fall far short of teacher and parent expectations. It is for these children who fail to thrive in our present educational system that much of our past and present work in assessment and intervention is directed.

Historically, researchers and practitioners in the assessment field focused on obtaining accurate and valid measures for a number of children's characteristics related to learning. Assessment texts were devoted largely to describing and evaluating the technical adequacy of this expanding battery of testing instruments. This work represented a necessary and important step toward the next, more ambitious goal of establishing better links between assessment findings and educational efforts. Teachers today are constantly faced with the dilemma of making sense out of the variety of assessment information frequently available for a given child and its usefulness for helping them decide on educational programs and methods. This present state of affairs certainly engenders feelings of frustration and leads teachers often to ask whether we are simply testing for testing's sake. With increasing frequency, teachers and parents are challenging the usefulness of tests for offering specific educational directions. For example, how will knowing that a child scored poorly on a test of visual-motor perception help a teacher to plan for the same child's reading problems? What relevance does a significant verbal IQ–performance IQ discrepancy in a given child have for classroom programming?

These concerns and an infinite number of others represent legitimate questions for which our current state-of-the-art technology in education has no definitive answers. Consequently, we are forced to be pragmatic and rely heavily on common sense for making education decisions. However, by critically examining what we currently do in individual classrooms that works for at least some individuals, we might begin to create a data base for such educational discoveries. Linking these discoveries to specific child-learning characteristics would help develop over time a large number of significant assessment-educational interactions. As this data base accumulates, perhaps the needed theory or theories linking assessment information to intervention decisions will emerge.

Chapters 1, 2, and 3 in this book cover important standard background information relating to the development of testing instruments, including their technical attributes, interpretation, bias, and use. Chapters 4 through 15 address the development of specific assessment skills in fairly circumscribed areas. Each of these chapters covers areas in which knowledge has increased over the past several years. We are fortunate to have experts in these areas who have contributed chapters in their specialized fields of study.

This textbook has a number of educational features that will facilitate the reader's understanding of the content. Each of the assessment skills chapters includes a discussion of both formal and informal assessment instruments with specifics on matching the type of procedure to the assessment purpose. At the beginning of each chapter, objectives are listed to prepare the reader for the specific content in the chapter. Case studies are used throughout the text to illustrate the application of each assessment area. The case study is placed within the chapter at key points to accent specifics of the chapter. At the end of each chapter, educational suggestions delineate practical concerns regarding the utilization of the assessment information contained in the chapter. Study questions at the end of each chapter encourage the reader to examine and review his or her comprehension of the chapter content. Each chapter also has suggested readings that provide the reader with a valuable reference list for more comprehensive study of the chapter's content.

This book was written with the upper undergraduate and beginning graduate student as the main audience. We encourage readers of this book to continually challenge the information provided in terms of (1) its usefulness in helping understand the unique characteristics that each child brings to the classroom and (2) its helpfulness in providing educational direction. As Cronbach (1957) wrote, "The greatest social benefit will come . . . if we can find for each individual the treatment (education) to which he can most easily adapt" (p. 679). If our assessment knowledge, instruments, and practices help in this noble endeavor, their continued existence will be justified.

Reference

Cronbach, L. J. (1957). The two disciplines of scientific psychology. *American Psychologist, 12,* 671–684.

1

Assessment Considerations

Anthony F. Rotatori
Robert Fox
Faye Macklin

OBJECTIVES

After completing this chapter the teacher should be able to:

1. List three major purposes of testing students.
2. Discuss the merits of assessment via a multidisciplinary team approach.
3. List common guidelines for assessment practices.
4. List the useful aspects of norm-referenced testing.
5. List the useful aspects of criterion-referenced assessment.
6. Discuss five procedures for collecting observational data.
7. List the essential elements for organizing the individualized educational program.
8. Define the terms *special education, related services, least restrictive environment, mainstreaming,* and *due process.*

Aim of Assessment

The field of assessment is one of the most controversial areas in education. Psychometric properties of popular assessment instruments, including their reliability, validity, and norms, are constantly scrutinized and frequently reported as being inadequate. Even when the technical adequacy of an instrument has been established, there continue to be arguments over its usefulness in the educational system. A major educational goal of assessment is to provide information about a child or a group of children that will foster the creation of the best possible circumstances to facilitate or enhance their learning and development. Simply stated, our assessments should tell us how to facilitate a child's optimal learning.

The topic of assessment is not only an academic one. Assessment practices that lead to discrimination, wrong educational placements, and inappropriate choices of curriculum or teaching strategies *can* and *do* have a very detrimental impact on children. For example, Williams (1971) reported the dangers involved when standardized tests are used with black children. Courts have ruled on the inappropriateness of relying on IQ scores for placement of minority students (e.g., *Larry P. v. Riles*, 1979). IQ testing was outlawed in San Francisco, and group intelligence test measures have been banned in the New York City schools (Bersoff, 1973). These real-life outcomes of educational assessment point to the serious nature of this field and its potential impact on the lives of children. Even when one goes beyond the more publicly visible problems in testing, such as the IQ controversy, we must seriously question to what degree our assessment practices have contributed to improved learning in children. At present, one would be forced to give a very modest reply to this question. If assessment is to lend specific direction to teachers for improving their student's learning, then the aim of assessment should not be to *explain* or *predict* a child's behavior but to carefully *describe* the phenomena. This aim can be achieved if a teacher attends to some basic premises that are common to most traditional theoretical assessment orientations. These premises are described below.

Premise 1: Each Child Is Unique

Teachers have to recognize and accept the notion that each child is unique. We have seen that even at the research level we run into trouble when we try grouping children for our programs based on gross assessment findings. Obviously if researchers are still wrestling with this problem, it is folly for teachers to group children using measures such as an IQ as the basis for educational decisions. Children are much too complex to be forced into homogeneous diagnostic categories, such as minimally brain damaged. The individual child simply does not benefit from these practices. As Forness (1981) states, our ever increasing knowledge about the complexities involved for children with learning and behavior problems has "dissuaded educators and related professionals from the idea that homogeneous diagnostic categories exist for handicapped children; such research argues the need for individual educational planning for each child receiving special education" (p. 57). It would not be hard to make a similar case for *all* children.

Premise 2: The Developing Child

The child's brain changes dramatically over time, especially during the early years. This development produces important changes in the child that are less dependent on environmental influences than the physiological changes occurring within the child. We see influences of this development in all areas of the child's functioning—from basic motor skill maturation to displaying increasingly complex language and cognitive skills. We also see the outcome when this maturational process is delayed or interrupted, as in children with serious prenatal problems leading to very reduced levels of behavior (e.g., profoundly retarded). Thus, taking into account the child's developmental status in our assessment efforts is critical for maintaining reasonable expectations and goals for a child's progress.

Premise 3: A Contemporary Focus

The child is who he or she is due to dynamic interaction between a unique physiological makeup and the environment in which he or she develops. It is within the context of these historical interactions that the causes of concerns such as a cognitive delay, a behavior disorder, or a learning problem are investigated. However, historical data often become obscured by people's changing perceptions of what happened years ago. Also the event(s) originally responsible for a child's problem no longer may be helpful for understanding contemporary problems. Knowing, for example, that a child who is aggressive has lived in a very stormy home environment may have little bearing on the child's present behavioral repertoire in the classroom. That is, the child's aggressive behavior may have served a quite different historical function in the home (gaining parental attention) than it presently serves in the classroom (getting him removed from an academic lesson). Certainly, in cases where the historical data enhance our contemporary knowledge about and interactions with an individual, this data source should obviously be considered. However, a teacher can proceed quite effectively with children using only a contemporary perspective.

Premise 4: The Child's Physical Status

Teachers are well aware of the fact that children will not perform optimally if they are sick, tired, or hungry. We also know from the fields of psychology and psychiatry that a number of cognitive, affective, and behavior problems may have underlying physical causes. Headaches, for example, may be the result of tension or, in rare instances, be caused by a tumor. A child's unusual behavior (such as running wildly around the classroom for a brief period of time) may be maintained by the attention it produces or, in exceptional instances, be the result of a psychomotor seizure. Another child may lack toileting skills because he was never consistently taught or because of an unusually small bladder or weak sphincter muscle control. In cases involving physical correlates or causes, providing educational or psychological intervention alone is inappropriate and may even be dangerous. Therefore, a necessary prerequisite to assessment is cognizance of the potential impact of the child's physical status on his or her present functioning. When physical concerns exist, appropriate professionals need to be consulted.

Premise 5: Maintain an Empirical Perspective

An objective description of the assessment process must be maintained throughout the entire process. An assessment orientation that relies heavily on constructs (e.g., socially maladjusted; ego) quickly becomes lost in confusion and practical usefulness. In contrast, an assessment orientation that instead relies on observable behavior (performance on a math sheet) or indirectly observable behavior (learning strategies used to solve math problems as assessed in a teacher-student interview) will be more functional for the classroom teacher.

Premise 6: Assessment as a Continuous Process

Assessment should not be conceived as an activity that is done at the beginning or the end of a school year, or even quarterly. Assessment should be an ongoing process. As the assessments yield specific teaching interventions, they also should be used to evaluate our chosen interventions and, if necessary, suggest appropriate modifications.

Premise 7: Usefulness

The ultimate benchmark for any assessment is its practical usefulness. Can teachers provide better instruction and/or curriculum to a child based on the assessment findings? Is the educational program tailored to meet the child's needs? Are assessments and interventions perceived as logically compatible activities by teachers? If we can answer yes to these questions, the assessment process will begin to serve its function.

Purposes of Testing

There are five general purposes for teacher assessment of their students. They include collecting data (1) to meet administrative requirements; (2) to assist in classification concerns; (3) to provide input for placement decisions; (4) to furnish information to make program decisions; and (5) to specify meaningful and realistic curriculum objectives (Rotatori, Galloway, & Rotatori, 1980).

Administrative Requirements

Traditionally, school systems have required teachers to assess their students at the beginning and at the end of the school year. The information is used as a gross measure of the effectiveness of texts and curriculum used during the year as well as the efficacy of pilot educational programs that may have been implemented. Also, the reporting of pretest and posttest results to parents, to the board of education, and/or to state and federal regulators of educational grants to the schools appears to be a practical way of summarizing overall student progress. Lastly, assessment data are collected to update the files of special education students as required by state and federal regulations.

Classification Decisions

Before a student receives special education services, assessment data must be gathered and evaluated to determine whether a student is eligible for such services (e.g., speech therapy, resource room assistance, physical therapy). In most cases eligibility involves the classification of the student according to some special education category (e.g., mentally retarded, behavioral disorder, learning disabled). Classification should not be for the sole purpose of labeling students. The classification decision should lead to an opportunity for meeting the specialized education needs of the individual within the least restrictive setting.

Placement Decisions

Most school systems have an array of placement options (e.g., self-contained classroom, specialized learning center, live-in residential-educational facility) for students who have special education needs. Assessment data can be evaluated to match the students' needs with the least restrictive educational environment. The placement decision is most meaningful and appropriate when a multidisciplinary group of educators and professionals are involved in the process.

Program Decisions

The diversity and vastness of programs within a school system are accented by directories listing the directors and coordinators of such programs. The specified educational philosophy and/or orientation, as well as criteria for acceptance into the program are described. Teachers collect assessment data on student skills and characteristics that are then analyzed by responsible program administrators regarding the merits of the student who is entering their program. Once within a program, assessment data are used to move the student toward the attainment of specific program goals.

Curriculum Objectives

Specifying curriculum objectives is the most important purpose for assessing students. The assessment data collected allow the teacher to plan a meaningful and appropriate instructional environment. The instructional plan is formalized by the specification of long- and short-term curriculum objectives. The teacher then uses certain instructional material and specific techniques to provide the opportunity for the student to reach criteria mastery of the objectives. Assessment data allow the teacher to locate starting points within the curriculum and/or specific task mastery skills for each student in the classroom.

Multidisciplinary Team Approach in Assessment

Who should collect data? The advent of Public Law 94–142 has broadened the area and scope of assessment for a referred student. Prior to the law, assessment, classification, eligibility, and placement

TABLE 1.1 Collectors/Providers of Data in a Multidisciplinary Team Approach to Assessment

Team Member	Data
Teacher	Academic performance
	Social/emotional/adaptive status
	Classroom/academic progress
	Effectiveness of various educational interventions
	Special skills areas
School Psychologist	Intellectual level interpretation
	Personality description
	Integrating and interpreting child's behavior in school and home
	Emotional/social growth from counseling
School Nurse	Vision/hearing screening
	Health problems
	Present medical treatment
Social Worker	Social history
	Services in community
	Counseling with family/student
Administrator	Knowledge of programs
	Service options
	Follow-up of meeting
Parents	Past and current status of child
	a. health and medical history
	b. social/emotional
	c. school progress
	d. developmental history
	Results of counseling
	Dynamics of family patterns
Physical Therapist	Gross motor
	Fine motor
	Interpretation of motor disabilities
Speech Therapist	Speech difficulty
	Language disability
	Progress in speech therapy

decisions were the responsibility of two or three professionals (e.g., school psychologist, school social worker, and learning disability diagnostician). Since the implementation of the law, the professional responsibility for the above decisions has increased and has truly become multidisciplinary in nature (e.g., school psychologist, social worker, school nurse, classroom teacher, learning disability diagnostician, speech therapist, reading specialist, parents, and a school administrator). Additionally, observational data concerning the student's academic performance in the classroom must be included in the assessment process.

This multidisciplinary approach to evaluation and decision making has structured the assessment such that each individual member of the team is responsible for generating data about a specific area. Table 1.1 delineates the type of data each team member can collect in a comprehensive multidisciplinary team approach to assessment and decision making. At times it may not be possible or necessary for all personnel listed in Table 1.1 to be involved. The members available must decide who will collect the needed information.

Guidelines for Assessment

The assessment procedure should be well-structured and organized. Typically the procedure is divided into three parts: (1) planning the assessment, (2) conducting the assessment, and (3) analyzing and summarizing the assessment data. Initially the planning of assessment begins with the referral question. In most cases the referral question is initiated by the classroom teacher; however, others (parents, social worker, or school counselor) typically make referrals. The referral question should be specific enough to give an overall direction to the focus of the assessment data to be generated. Many times the referral question may only allude to the need for special services. In this case, assessment data may have to be generated to determine whether the student is eligible for special service.

Many schools have an assessment planning committee composed of a small group of teachers who meet and discuss referrals on students within their school. The committee then outlines an assessment plan that would include: (1) the assessment data that have to be collected in order to answer the referral question, (2) the data to be collected by the classroom teacher, (3) the other professionals (e.g., school psychologist, school nurse) who may be needed to generate specific data (e.g., IQ level, visual skills, auditory skills), and (4) the information that is needed from the parents.

Before conducting the actual assessment, permission to test must be obtained from the student's parent or guardian. Typically the school principal is the one who communicates to the parents the need for assessment, the outlined stages of assessment that will occur, and an explanation of the permission forms to be signed.

The actual assessment should be conducted in an atmosphere that will elicit representational behavior of the student. When standardized tests are administered, assessment should be carried out in an examination room that minimizes extraneous sources of distraction while maximizing the student's performance and motivation. Whenever classroom behavior has to be observed and collected, the teacher must ensure that behavior is sampled from a variety of representational activities and situations in which the student is typically involved.

Assessment data must be analyzed and summarized in an atmosphere of objectivity. Objectivity is necessary to answer the referral question with the intent of identifying the needs of the student and of making recommendations for meeting those needs. Certainly some subjectivity of the team members may be unavoidable; however, each member should operate with a spirit of fairness and sense of ethics. Lastly, the team members must adhere to the principle of confidentiality of the assessment data collected and reported.

CASE STUDY

Part I

Name: Marie
Date of Birth: June 10, 1970
Date of Evaluation: August 10, 1983

Age: 13 years, 2 months
Grade Placement: Junior High, Trainable mentally retarded

Background Information

Marie is a pretty, pleasant 13-year-old girl who has Down's syndrome. She comes from a middle-class family. Her father is a car salesman and her mother is a clerk at a large department store. Both parents have a high school degree. Marie has two older sisters and a younger brother. Her family lives in a small rural town.

Marie was institutionalized by her parents shortly after her birth based upon the recommendations of the family physician, who felt that Marie would benefit more from the educational system at the state hospital for the retarded. At the age of nine she was transferred to a nonprofit, small private residential facility for the retarded that was closer to her family.

Presently, Marie is bused to the local public school for her education. Staff at the school feel that Marie has made a number of academic gains the past school year and requested a current educational evaluation to assist in planning for the coming school year.

Observations

Marie was observed during a 70-minute observation period. During this time she was involved in (1) speech, (2) prevocational activities, (3) story reading at the library, (4) lunch, (5) game playing, and (6) coin identification. Throughout the observation Marie's attention to task was adequate, even when teacher attention was being directed at another student. Instruction was mostly verbal with only occasional modeling. Marie did well with the above instructional format. There were a few instances of being overly affectionate, but a verbal comment and modeling were used to correct this behavior. At lunch, Marie was quite verbal and social, and her teacher reinforced her for this.

Past Testing

Test	Date	Results
Carrow Test of Auditory Comprehension of Language	1/79	Language Age 3-5 years
Stanford-Binet Intelligence Scale	4/7/79	Mental Age 5-3 years IQ—52
Carrow Test of Auditory Comprehension of Language	5/80	Language Age 5-4 years
Carrow Test of Auditory Comprehension of Language	3/82	Language Age 5-8 years

Formal versus Informal Assessment

A major consideration of a teacher gathering assessment data is whether to use informal or formal tests. In general, the purpose of the assessment influences the type of tests to be used. Formal and informal tests have both advantages and disadvantages (see Table 1.2

TABLE 1.2 Advantages of Formal and Informal Assessment Testing

Formal Tests	Informal Tests	
Norm-Referenced	Criterion-Referenced	Teacher-Constructed
1. Results in variability and ranking	1. Allows for individualized pacing of student during instruction	1. Provides immediate feedback to teacher on students' level of performance
2. Allows for comparisons of scores between students	2. Quite helpful in writing objectives for IEPs	2. Provides feedback to students on their progress in curriculum areas
3. Traditional methods can be used to establish reliability	3. Helpful in providing day to day feedback to student	3. Test item closely approximates the skills and objectives of classroom teaching programs

TABLE 1.2 *(cont'd)*

Formal Tests	Informal Tests	
Norm-Referenced	Criterion-Referenced	Teacher-Constructed
4. Gives relative standing of student on content of test	4. Compares student to a standard of performance	4. Data is easily adapted to classroom materials and programs
5. Standardized	5. Objective scoring	5. The tests frequently are similar to instructional activities
6. Objective scoring	6. Tells whether a student has a skill	6. Almost always given by teacher who has more rapport with student than any other professional that student comes in contact with
7. Used often as data for placement classification decisions	7. Provides feedback on whether student can go on to next level of skill sequence	7. Easy to administer, score, and interpret
8. Allows for comparison of student against a regional norm	8. Provides feedback in regard to altering instruction during school year	8. Inexpensive
9. Highly structured in regards to administration, scoring and interpretation	9. Since items are sequential, it suggests what to teach next	9. Provides direct input for planning and altering teaching during school year
	10. Data gives an absolute mastery of content of test	10. Data are helpful in parent conferences
	11. Generally standardized	
	12. Explicit administration, scoring and interpretation	
	13. Generally easy to interpret	

TABLE 1.3 Disadvantages of Formal and Informal Assessing Testing

Formal Tests	Informal Tests	
Norm-Referenced	Criterion-Referenced	Teacher-Constructed
Measures what has happened rather than what is happening	Data does not rank students	Selecting and sequencing test items can be difficult at times
Provides limited data to teacher for instructional changes	Test does not lead to variability in student scores	Tends to be more sensitive to teacher subjectivity in regards to scoring and interpretation
Student's data is treated as numerical index of position	Cannot use traditional procedures for collecting reliability	Less structured
Limited input in writing IEPs	There may be disagreement on what constitutes the standard of performance	Not standardized
Provides limited feedback for students on their day-to-day progress	Results do not inform teachers whether students achieve what they should when they should	Does not allow for comparison of students to regional or national norms
Test items are often remotely connected to the content and the skills being taught in the school program	Failure to master an objective may be due to instruction, the test items, the standard of mastery, or the objective itself	
May need specific training to make interpretation		
Can be expensive		

and 1.3), but the crucial difference between the two is the interpretation that is to be derived from the score. If a teacher is interested in comparing a student's score on a test to others (norm group) on whom the test was standardized, then a formal norm-referenced test is selected. In contrast, if a teacher is interested in comparing the student's performance to a specified behavior standard of performance or as a measure of a student's performance in specific curricular areas, an informal test is selected. The informal test can be either teacher-constructed (weekly math quiz) or standardized criterion-referenced.

The results of formal testing (norm-referenced) allow the teacher to rank students in the class based upon their scores. The ordering implies that a student who is listed above another student performed better on the test. The results of informal testing allow the teacher to decide the level of behavior that a student has attained.

Uses for Norm-Referenced Tests

Teachers can employ norm-referenced tests to make decisions about students. For example, the tests can determine which students should be counseled to enter the college curriculum at the high school level. The scores are also used to accept students into a program with a limited enrollment. For example, a student must have a sufficiently high Graduate Record Examination (GRE) score even to be considered for a doctoral program at most major universities. Scores are often used for placement of students in certain special education programs. For example, a student must have an IQ well within the mentally retarded range to be placed in a trainable mentally handicapped classroom in the public schools. Norm-referenced tests are often used as part of the certification process in a number of professions (e.g., dietician, psychologist, social worker, teacher) in which the individual must score at or above an established cutoff point to be considered for certification. Norm-referenced tests are also used for program evaluation. For example, a school may have initiated a particular reading program, and the school principal wants to know whether this program resulted in higher reading grades than the traditional reading program used by the school.

Uses for Criterion-Referenced Tests

A teacher most frequently uses criterion-referenced tests to assess whether a student has mastered a daily instructional assignment or a unit of instruction. The test score indicates the mastery of instructional objectives, which have been sequentially arranged. The teacher can decide whether to take up the next module or unit depending upon the mastery level attained. If the student has performed adequately on the sequenced objectives, the student moves onto the next unit of objectives. In contrast, if the student has not attained a specified mastery level, restudy of the sequenced objectives is necessary.

Criterion-referenced tests can also be employed to evaluate instructional programs. The tests determine whether the teacher's instructional format, materials, and procedures have assisted the student in attaining mastery of the instructional objectives that were originally specified in the program.

Uses for Teacher-Constructed Tests

Informal assessment by a teacher involves the use of nonstandardized, teacher-constructed tests that assess a student's performance on a teacher's curriculum. The tests are used when norm-referenced tests do not provide the teachers with enough specific data to assess a student's progress on the curriculum being used. The informal test may measure a wide range of student skills after exposure to a unit of instruction or may measure a student's specific skill on a subunit of instruction. Informal tests are less structured than norm-referenced and criterion-referenced tests. Furthermore, the scoring of informal tests can be influenced by a teacher's subjectivity. A major difference between informal tests and criterion-referenced tests is that criterion-referenced testing evaluates a student's progress with regard to an absolute standard of performance. Thus, if a teacher wants to estimate a student's present level of performance, an informal test can be used. However, if the teacher wants to determine present level of performance according to a specific mastery standard, a criterion-referenced test should be used.

Procedures for Collecting Observational Data

At times the teacher will find it necessary to collect observational data on a student in order to answer an assessment concern (e.g., is the student's rate of talk-outs greater than that of the typical student in this grade?). Observational procedures allow the teacher to collect a systematic record of specific behaviors of concern. Five procedures typically used by teachers are: (1) continuous recording, (2) event recording, (3) duration recording, (4) interval recording, and (5) time sampling.

Continuous Recording
When using the continuous recording procedure, the teacher writes down everything that the student is doing as well as the events that are happening around the student. A time period is chosen by the teacher that allows him or her to observe and record without having to play an active role in teaching. This procedure allows for the collection of a large class of behaviors. Unfortunately, continuous recording is quite time-consuming. Also, the teacher may find it difficult at times to write down everything that is occurring.

Event Recording
When a teacher is interested in collecting data on discrete events, event recording is typically used. Basically, it is a frequency calculation of discrete events as they occur during an observation period. For example, a teacher may count the number of times a student talks out

loud to a fellow student without permission during reading. A tallying device (e.g., note pad, wrist counter) is generally used to make this procedure more convenient for the teacher. In most situations the procedure allows the teacher to continue with an active teaching role.

Duration Recording

When a teacher is concerned with how long a behavior lasts because of its interference with instruction or learning, duration recording is often used. The procedure allows the teacher to record the elapsed time of an identified behavior during a specified observation period. For example, a teacher may want to know how long it takes a mildly retarded 14-year-old child to start working at the commencement of each academic assignment. When using this procedure, it is necessary to have a timing device (e.g., stopwatch, watch with a second hand) to allow for accurate recording. At times it may be inconvenient for the teacher to use this procedure while engaged in an active teaching role.

Interval Recording

When a teacher wants to know the patterns of a student's behaviors over a period of time, interval recording can be used. Generally, a number of observation periods are arranged over a time period that is reflective of the student's day. The observation session is divided into equal time periods. For example, suppose a teacher wanted to know whether a student's inattentiveness to the teacher's verbal instructions occurred throughout the lecture period. The teacher could arrange for three 1-minute observation periods that are divided into 10-second intervals. The three observation periods could be at the beginning, the middle, and the end of the lecture period. The teacher would then record whether the student was attentive or inattentive during each 10-second interval. This procedure requires that the teacher not have an active teaching role while collecting data.

Time Sampling

When a teacher does not have time to provide undivided attention to carry out interval recording but wants information on the patterns of a student's behavior over a period of time, time sampling can be used. This procedure allows the teacher to record the occurrence or nonoccurrence of behaviors immediately following specified time intervals. For example, suppose a teacher who is supervising study hall wants to know whether a student is attending to classroom assignments throughout the period. The teacher could divide the one-hour study hall period into three five-minute periods that are further divided into five one-minute intervals. The teacher would then record whether the student was attentive or inattentive when the one-minute interval timed out. This procedure allows the teacher to observe the student while having an active role in the supervision of the study hall. It must be remembered that a decision on the student's behavior is made at the instant the one-minute interval timed out.

CASE STUDY

Part II

Present Testing

Intelligence

The *Stanford-Binet Intelligence Scale* (Form L-M), 1972 revision, was administered to measure Marie's present intellectual functioning level. She attained a Mental Age of 5-2 years and an IQ of 44. She passed all the items at the 3-6 year level and failed all the items at the 7-0 year level. Her best skills were on nonverbal items (e.g., visual motor or discrimination items). Her speech was distorted and at times difficult to understand. Also noted was a decrease in speech clarity with the more difficult and abstract verbal items. Marie's work pattern was persistent and confident on the easy items; however, on the more abstract tasks she tended to stall and look to the examiner for assistance and reassurance. Emotionally, Marie was quite shy and her responsiveness and spontaneity was not as high when compared with her interactions with teacher and peers. The test scores indicate a maintenance of her intellectual capabilities when compared with the 1979 testing on the Stanford-Binet.

Academic

The *Peabody Individual Achievement Test* (PIAT) was given to assess Marie's present academic skill levels. She attained first-grade level scores in Reading Recognition and Spelling. She is achieving at about a middle kindergarten level in math. A summary of her grade and age scores follows:

Test	Raw Score	Grade Score	Age Score
Mathematics	12	.4	5-5 years
Reading Recognition	19	1.3	6-6 years
Spelling	19	1.5	6-8 years
General Information	5	below .1	below 5-4 years

Psychomotor

The *Bender-Gestalt Test* was given to measure Marie's psychomotor skill level. According to the Koppitz scoring system, her drawings resulted in a Developmental Age of 5 years to 5 years, 5 months. The drawings did not indicate any significant visual-motor deficits.

Adaptive

The *Vineland Social Maturity Scale* was given to assess Marie's self-care skill level. A calculation of the scale items resulted in a Social Age of 7-4 years and a Social Quotient of 56. Marie has independent skills in eating, dressing, buttoning, and toileting. She is able to carry out with supervision household chores, such as dusting, vacuuming, and setting the table. The administration of the *Community Living Skills Assessment Inventory*, a criterion-referenced adaptive scale, revealed that Marie is deficient in the following skills but could benefit from training sessions in these areas.

I. Small group living skills
    A. Food preparation
        1. Sandwiches
        2. Salads
        3. Hot dishes
        4. Cook eggs, hot dogs
        5. Jello
        6. Open cans
        7. Cook vegetables
II. Leisure time
    A. Crafts/hobbies/games
        1. Bingo
        2. Checkers
        3. Crossword puzzles
        4. Darts
        5. Jacks
        6. Lotto
        7. Ping-Pong
        8. Tic-tac-toe
        9. Cycling
        10. Play pool
        11. Play pinball
III. Community living skills
    A. Calendar functions
        1. Year
        2. Work days
        3. School days
        4. School year
        5. Vacation time
        6. Weekends
    B. Time Functions
        1. Tell time by hour and half hour
    C. Travel
        1. Obey street lights
        2. Cross streets looking both ways
        3. Use sidewalks when walking
    D. Prepare for emergencies
        1. Fire in home or store
        2. Lost
        3. Injured
        4. Spells name, knows phone number, knows address

Reinforcement

The *Reinforcement Survey Hierarchy for Retarded Individuals* was administered to Marie's teachers and aides in the residential facility to identify preferred rewards that could be used during educational and training sessions. It was reported that Marie has a high preference for the following reinforcers:

Listening to: radio, sing-along, story telling, tapes, records, musical and rhythm
     instruments
Looking at: catalogs, magazines, films, TV, picture books, mirrors, picture of
     self
Playing with/on/in: dress-up clothes, wearing jewelry
Academic activities: coloring book, pasting pictures in scrapbook, running
     errands, drawing, teacher helper, finger painting
Touching/feeling of: pat on back, holding hands, petting animals
Social: verbal praise, first in line, hugs, applause, kisses, smiling, shaking hands,
     laughing, medals, ribbons, plaques, and smelling of perfume, hand lotion,
     soap

Summary and Recommendations

Marie is a 13-year-old Down's syndrome individual who has a pleasant affect.
Intellectual testing on the Stanford-Binet revealed cognitive skills in the moderately retarded range. Adaptive assessment testing revealed daily living skills
similar to a 7- to 8-year-old child. Academically, as measured by the PIAT, Marie
has reading and spelling skills similar to a 6½-year-old child. In contrast, her math
skills are similar to a 5½-year-old child.

1. For the upcoming school year Marie's social and prevocational development
   should be the main academic areas stressed. She is receiving some good
   experiences at school in these areas. One must be concerned with the fact that
   Marie might function more optimally in these areas of development if she were
   living in another type of home setting such as a foster home, a group home, or
   with her family. Inquiries into such a placement should be made.
2. Marie appears to be ready for a school program with trainable retarded
   children that are more similar to her skill levels. Presently she is doing well, but
   in general her peers are functioning lower than her socially and academically.
   This at times leads to bossiness in Marie.
3. Continuation in learning manual signs appears warranted due to Marie's
   distorted speech. She should be able to learn many more functional signs.
   Also, Marie could be used as a peer tutor for signing. This would give her more
   status and an opportunity to practice her signs.

IEP, Public Law 94-142, and Assessment

The individualized educational program (IEP) required by Public Law
94-142, the Education of All Handicapped Children Act, recognizes
differences among students, including different rates of learning, and
provides a sense of direction for maximal use of resources to ensure
that students attain the required minimum competencies. The rules
and regulations for developing the IEP are specific and draw a
distinction between the IEP and instructional plans (i.e., lesson plans).
The purpose of the IEP is to provide "the general direction to be taken
by those who will implement the IEP and serve as the basis for

developing detailed instructional plans" (*Federal Register*, 1977, p. 5470).

Developing the IEP requires drawing relationships and making associations between various sources of assessment data and fashioning information into a format that can provide perspective and direction for formulating educational goals. Thus, the IEP would include annual goals and short-term objectives that lead to the accomplishment of those goals. The IEP is to serve as a guide to teachers for the development of detailed instructional plans for achieving specific educational and personal goals.

The processes for the development of the IEP provide a scheme that can be considered a systematic approach to instruction for the handicapped learner. It shows the relationship of all the elements to each other even though it does not portray the fine details of each element. The IEP is a guideline and should be used as a checklist in planning for teaching. Detailing of the elements would be encompassed in the broader context of teaching and lesson planning for providing individualized instruction for the handicapped learner.

Elements of an IEP

The basic tenet of Public Law 94-142, which requires an IEP, is to ensure an educational program designed on the basis of the specific child's needs and a working relationship between the assessment of learner needs and instructional treatment. The regulations governing Public Law 94-142 acknowledge the assessment process as an integral part of appropriate educational planning. The emphasis is on the need for multifaceted assessment and not just intelligence measures. Therefore, the areas identified for the content of the IEP are reflective of educational appraisal as well as test data. Figure 1.1 illustrates the sequence for development of the IEP and the interrelationship of the elements with assessment and instructional planning.

The IEP for each child must include:

1. A statement of the child's present levels of educational performance, including academic achievement, social adaptation, prevocational and vocational skills, psychomotor skills, and self-help skills.
2. A statement of annual goals describing the educational performance to be achieved by the end of the school year under the child's IEP.
3. A statement of short-term instructional objectives, which must be measurable, intermediate steps between the present level of educational performance and the annual goals.

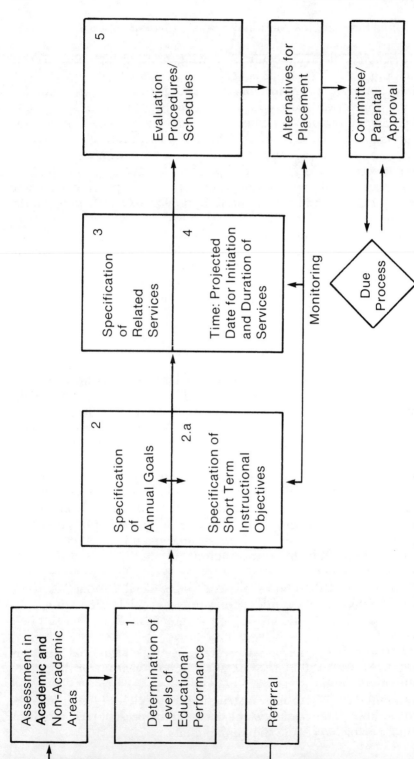

Figure 1.1. Sequence for development of the IEP and the interrelationship of the elements with assessment and instructional planning.

4. A statement of specific educational services to be provided, including a description of all special education and related services that are needed to meet the unique needs of the child, including the type of physical education program in which the child will participate (and any specific instructional media and materials needed).
5. The date when those services will begin and length of time the services will be given.
6. A description of the extent to which the child will participate in regular education programs.
7. A justification for the type of educational placement the child will have.
8. A list of the individuals who are responsible for implementation of the IEP.
9. Objective criteria, evaluation procedures, and schedules of determining, on at least an annual basis, whether the short-term instructional objectives are being achieved (Torres, 1977).

Level of Performance

The first step essential to individualized instructional planning is assessment of entry-level skills of the learner in academic areas (e.g., reading, math, history) as well as nonacademic areas (vocational, psychomotor, art, music, developmental skills). The child's current level of performance establishes the basis for formulating annual goals and short-term instructional objectives. Discrepancies between the child's entry-level skills and those required in the classroom should be identified, thereby defining an educational need. These discrepancies should then be addressed under both (1) goals and objectives and (2) resources required and related services to be provided to the child.

The child's performance should be evaluated within the total context of the settings in which he or she functions (i.e., home, school, community, and peer groups). Assessment of the child should be comprehensive and reflect areas specific to the child's disability. For instance, audiological and communication skills evaluations would be warranted for the hearing impaired.

The IEP should include each subject or skill area in which instruction will be adapted to meet the special needs of the handicapped student. Criteria to use in determining the curriculum areas include the student's identified strengths and weaknesses as indicated by assessment data, the general curriculum being taught in the school setting, and the relevance of the subject-matter content for the student's successful adaptation to the school and home environment (Turnbull, Strickland, & Brantly, 1982).

Goals and Objectives

A goal is a measurable statement that describes the educational performance to be achieved by the end of the school year. Short-term objectives are measurable, intermediate stops that must be attained to ensure the likelihood that the long-term goals will be achieved. Short-term instructional objectives should:

1. Reflect a hierarchical and sequential relationship to the goal.
2. Show congruence between goal statements and skill areas targeted by assessment data.
3. Be contiguous with curriculum being taught in the school setting.
4. Be practical, relevant, and manageable for both student and teacher(s).
5. Reflect an orderly progression through the skill to meet the desired goal.
6. Be written in unambiguous terms.
7. Reflect the following criteria: (a) describe something which the learner does or produces; (b) state a behavior or a product of the learner's behavior; (c) state the conditions under which the behavior is to occur; (d) specify the criteria for measurement of the desired behavior or product.

The task of writing objectives has been traditionally delegated to special education teachers, who have elected to use school districts' lists of instructional objectives, commercially produced curriculum objectives, school-based objectives, scope and sequence charts, or their own goals and objectives. Whatever the preference of teachers may be, goals and objectives should be properly defined and formulated based on assessment information provided by individuals who comprise the IEP committee. Therefore, the writing of objectives should be a joint effort of the IEP team and reflect multifaceted and diverse needs of the special student based on the assessment information.

Assessment, both formal and informal, is to aid the IEP team and implementing teachers in specifying goals and objectives for instructional programs, classroom management, instructional strategies, selection and modification of materials and media, and evaluation of student's progress. The classroom teacher is in a key position to collect a vast amount of specific assessment data relevant to a particular child's school performance and instructional needs. It is assumed that the teacher who is working with the child is in the best position to assess the child in his or her current learning situation and is knowledgeable about the skills and behaviors necessary for appropriate performance in academic areas and the techniques for assessing those skills and behaviors.

Evaluation is the measure of the degree to which the student has attained the objectives. Evaluation serves to ascertain the progress of an individual student in relation to his or her own starting point. The use of the IEP on a continuous basis can simplify the process of evaluation in that the child can be examined in terms of where he or she started, what instructional strategies and resources were used, and what was achieved. Evaluation should be ongoing (formative) in addition to reporting end results (summative). Monitoring on a systematic and regular basis can provide feedback on the progress an individual student is making toward specified goals and objectives, thereby permitting intervention and modification of the individualized program if warranted.

Teachers who coordinate the IEP for an individual student must evaluate the student across curriculum areas. Such evaluations should reflect progress in cognitive, affective, and psychomotor skill areas. Various methods of evaluation may be used such as curriculum checklists, anecdotal notes, daily progress records, parent-teacher conferences, observational records, case staffings, criterion-referenced testing, standardized testing, and reports for related service areas. In order for evaluation to be useful, it is important to report not only the *expected* but also the *unexpected* outcomes or behaviors.

Special Education and Related Services

The law requires that not only must annual goals and instructional objectives be stated on the IEP but also the related services that are required. In evaluating the instructional program and placing the handicapped student, it is important to describe how the various resources were used to help accomplish the goals and objectives. Such information can be used to determine the effectiveness of the overall program.

Public Law 94-142 defines three terms that parents and teachers should be knowledgeable about:

1. *Handicapped*. This term refers to those children identified as being mentally retarded, hearing impaired, speech impaired, visually handicapped, seriously emotionally disturbed, orthopedically impaired, or other health impaired, deaf-blind, multihandicapped, or having specific learning disabilities.
2. *Special Education*. The law defines special education as specially designed instruction, at no cost to parents or guardians, to meet the unique needs of a handicapped child, including classroom instruction, instruction in physical education, home instruction, and instruction in hospitals and institutions.

3. *Related Services.* The term related services means transportation
   and such developmental, corrective, and other supportive services—including speech pathology and audiology, psychological
   services, physical and occupational therapy, recreation, and medical and counseling services (except that such medical services shall
   be for diagnostic and evaluation purposes only)—as may be
   required to assist a handicapped child to benefit from special
   education, and includes the early identification and assessment of
   handicapping conditions in children (*Federal Register*, 1977, pp.
   42479–42480).

The expectation of Public Law 94-142, which requires an IEP for
each handicapped learner, is that there will be an interrelatedness
between assessment data, the specially designed instruction, and the
related services provided to meet the unique needs of the child.

Special education and related services should be directed to the
achievement of the annual goals and short-term instructional objectives as specified in the student's written IEP. Handicapped students
should have access to participation in academic and nonacademic
areas, including extracurricular, intramural, and interscholastic activities like sports, recreation, and social activities.

The Least Restrictive Environment

Once special education and related services have been specified,
alternatives for placement must be considered.

> PL 94-142 requires that each local education agency shall insure to the
> maximum extent appropriate, that handicapped children are educated
> with children who are not handicapped, and that special classes, separate
> schooling or other removal of handicapped children from the regular
> environment occurs only when the nature of the severity of the handicap
> is such that an education in regular classes with the use of supplementary
> aids and services cannot be achieved satisfactorily (*Federal Register*, 1977,
> p. 42497).

The key word in the provision for an appropriate education is
"appropriate." Educators, in considering alternatives for educational
placement, tend to use the terms *least restrictive environment* and
mainstreaming interchangeably. However, a distinction must be made
between the two terms.

Mainstreaming is the placement of handicapped students in
classes and schools with nonhandicapped students for all or portions
of their education with varying degrees of specialized support services.
Under this system, handicapped students may be assigned to the
following alternative instructional settings:

1. Regular classes, with or without supporting services.

2. Regular class plus supplementary instructional services (such as resource room, itinerant instruction, diagnostic/consultative services, interpreter-tutors, etc.).
3. Part-time special class.
4. Full-time special class.
5. Special schools in the local education system.

The intent of the law is to provide an appropriate education but not necessarily in mainstreamed settings. The least restrictive environment is the placement of the handicapped student in an educational setting that is most appropriate based on the assessment of the child's needs, services required, and alternatives available.

In selecting the least restrictive environment, consideration must be given to any potentially harmful effect on the child or on the quality of services he or she needs (i.e., for some children, placement in regular classes with nonhandicapped students could be the more restrictive environment). Unless a handicapped child's IEP requires some other arrangements, the child should be educated in the same school that he or she would attend if not handicapped (*Federal Register*, 1977, p. 42497).

Variations on the theme of mainstreaming and least restrictive environment have been reported with the difference in educational programming being reflected by the goals and objectives and by the way resources are directed to meet individual needs, according to disability. Some examples of these variations are:

1. Regular class placement for hearing-impaired students with interpreter-tutors and notetakers (Holcomb & Corbett, 1975).
2. Regular class placement for behaviorally disordered students with provisions for an Intervention Now Classroom staff by a crisis teacher (Beare, 1981; Cullinan & Epstein, 1982; Wood & Lakin, 1979).
3. Primary placement of students in classes for the learning disabled, but mainstreaming these students into regular classes for certain academic subjects (Maher, 1981; Siegel & Gold, 1982).
4. Providing opportunities for interaction between severely handicapped and nonhandicapped students through cooperative work projects, prearranged joint play, some vocational training activities, birthday parties, art, music, and physical education (Stainback, Stainback, & Jaben, 1981).
5. Providing opportunities for nonhandicapped students to teach playground skills to their mentally retarded peers (Donder & Nietupski, 1981; Sternberg & Adams, 1982).
6. Use of nonhandicapped peers as tutors for autistic children (McHale, Olley, Marcus, & Simeonson, 1981).

The fundamental questions that must be asked are these. For whom is this type of placement appropriate? What resources are required? How are the resources to be used? What are the expected educational goals?

Summary

Assessment is a process that involves gathering and interpreting information about an individual student for use in educational decision making. The process is usually multisourced so as to define precisely the entry-level behaviors of handicapped students. Today the array of diagnostic assessment information and services made available to classroom teachers has increased the complexity of decisions they must make in determining student needs and instructional planning. Therefore, it is imperative that teachers play an active role in the assessment process and in developing an IEP. After all, they will most likely be the ones held responsible for implementation of the plan.

Developing the educational program requires a multidisciplinary team approach. This is to present a comprehensive view of elements that are related to the child's entry-level skills and behaviors, and to formulate an overview that would give perspective and yet prevent focusing on any single aspect of a student's need. The premise is that no one area of assessment should significantly determine educational goals without the consideration of other areas (Rotatori & Mauser, 1980).

The orchestration of the above depends upon the commitment of professionals to the spirit of Public Law 94-142 in ensuring that all handicapped children are entitled to a free and appropriate education. Effective communication among team members appears to be crucial to the assessment, placement, and evaluation process. The lack of communication between teachers, diagnostic and support staff, or parents and administrators can result in failure to implement team recommendations. Identifying the instructional needs of the child involves collaboration across discipline areas, and only cooperation among team members can ensure that the process will be successful.

Educational Suggestions for Assessment Considerations

The following suggestions can assist teachers in making decisions about using tests and measurement procedures. The suggestions provide a basis for recommending a test or measurement procedure to resolve a specific purpose for assessing a student's difficulty.

At times teachers may need to *select* students for a particular program or remediation. Tests chosen for such a purpose have to be able to predict success and failure with a low chance of risk for the student and the school. This selection process can be enhanced when the teacher selects a test that measures skills, abilities, and attitudes required for success in the program.

Teachers should be aware that test instruments can be useful for selection, but they may not be as useful for optimal program placement. In general, program placement involves decisions and options generated by multidisciplinary teams (e.g., teacher, psychologist, social worker, principal).

Diagnostic tests should be used by teachers to further evaluate a student's problem areas and not be used to *select students*.

Teachers should use criterion-referenced devices when interpretations are necessary for determining whether (1) a student has reached a level of proficiency in a curriculum that is progressive and cumulative in nature, (2) a student has reached a level of mastery in areas that demand it, such as licensing of doctors or psychologists, and (3) a student is experiencing difficulty in a specific area of a curriculum.

Teachers should use norm-referenced devices when interpretations are necessary for determining (1) a student's performance while participating in a curriculum that is not cumulative or dependent upon reaching a level of proficiency in order to progress in it; (2) selection of a student for a program based upon his or her reference point in comparison to other students; (3) a student's potential success in a program of study; and (4) a student's attainment of complex objectives that are difficult to measure with criterion-referenced tests.

Study Questions

1. Describe the major advantages of using a time sampling observational data collection procedure.
2. Describe the difference between norm-referenced and criterion-referenced assessment procedures.
3. What is the main difference between teacher-constructed tests and criterion-referenced tests?
4. What is an IEP? How does it relate to instructional planning?
5. What information do a psychologist, a teacher, and a social worker provide at an IEP meeting?
6. What are the essential elements of an IEP for handicapped students?
7. What is the distinction between mainstreaming and "the least restrictive environment?"
8. What is meant by related services?

Suggested Readings

Brooks, R. (1980). Psychoeducational assessment: A broader perspective. *Professional Psychology, 10,* 708–722.

Dickinson, D. J. (1980). The direct assessment: An alternative to psychometric testing. *Journal of Learning Disabilities, 13,* 8–12.

Pugach, M. C. (1982). Regular classroom teacher involvement in the development and utilization of IEPs. *Exceptional Children, 48,* 371–374.

Tymitz-Wolf, B. L. (1982). Guidelines for assessing IEP goals and objectives. *Teaching Exceptional Children, 14,* 198–201.

References

Beare, P. (1981). Mainstreaming approach for behaviorally disordered secondary students in a rural school district. *Behavioral Disorders, 6,* 209–218.

Bersoff, D. W. (1973). Silk purses into sow's ears: The decline of psychological testing and a suggestion for its redemption. *American Psychologist, 28,* 892–899.

Cullinan, D., & Epstein, M. H. (1982). Behavior disorders. In N. G. Haring (Ed.), *Exceptional Children and Youth* (3rd ed.). Columbus, OH: Charles E. Merrill.

Donder, D., & Nietupski, J. (1981). Nonhandicapped adolescents teaching playground skills to their mentally retarded peers: Toward a less restrictive middle school environment. *Education and Training of the Mentally Retarded, 16,* 270–276.

Federal Register. (1977, January 19). 42479–42480. Washington, DC: U.S. Government Printing Office.

Forness, S. R. (1981). Concepts of learning and behavior disorders: Implications for research and practice. *Exceptional Children, 48,* 56–64.

Holcomb, R. K., & Corbett, E. E. (1975). *Mainstream—The Delaware approach.* Newark, DE: The Margaret S. Sterck Elementary School.

Larry P. v. Riles. No. C-71-2270 RFF, U. S. District Court, Northern District of California. (June 1979).

Maher, C. A. (1981). Learning disabled adolescents in the regular classroom: Evaluation of a mainstreaming procedure. *Learning Disabilities Quarterly, 5,* 82–84.

McHale, S., Olley, G., Marcus, L. M., & Simeonson, R. J. (1981). Nonhandicapped peers as tutors for autistic children. *Exceptional Children, 48,* 263–265.

Rotatori, A. F., Galloway, E. A., & Rotatori, K. M. (1980). Necessary data assessment components for establishing an individual education plan for mildly retarded children. *Journal for Special Educators, 16,* 108–112.

Rotatori, A. F., & Mauser, A. J. (1980). IEP assessment for learning disabled students. *Academic Therapy, 16,* 141–153.

Seigel, E., & Gold, R. (1982). *Educating the learning disabled.* New York: Macmillan.

Stainback, W., Stainback, S., & Jaben, T. (1981). Providing opportunities for interaction between severely handicapped and nonhandicapped students. *Teaching Exceptional Children, 13,* 72–75.

Sternberg, L., & Adams, G. L. (1982). *Educating severely and profoundly handicapped students*. Rockville, MD: Aspen.

Torres, S. (1977). *Special education administrative policies manual*. Reston, VA: Council for Exceptional Children.

Trailor, C. B. (1982). Role clarification and participation in child study teams. *Exceptional Children*, *48*, 529–530.

Turnbull, A. P., Strickland, B. B., & Brantly, J. C. (1982). *Developing and implementing individualized education programs* (2nd ed.). Columbus, OH: Charles E. Merrill.

Williams, R. (1971). Danger: Testing and dehumanizing black children. *School Psychology*, *25*, 11–13.

Wood, F. H., & Lakin, K. C. (Eds.). (1979). *Disturbing, disordered or disturbed?* Minneapolis: Advanced Training Institute (Department of Psychoeducational Studies).

2

Consideration of Bias in the Assessment and Placement Process of Exceptional Children

Stephen J. LaGrow
Jane E. Prochnow-LaGrow

OBJECTIVES

After completing this chapter the teacher should be able to:

1. Identify bias in testing.
2. Define the impact of bias in testing.
3. Define the impact of bias in placement decisions.
4. Discuss the legal requirements mandating nondiscriminatory testing.
5. Identify the effects that bias has had on minority students.

Bias in Testing

Jensen (1980) states that "no theory or practice in modern psychology has been more attacked than mental testing, and that the main target has been 'IQ tests' and similar measures of mental abilities and aptitudes" (p. 1). One of the major issues in the controversy over testing has been the fairness of such tests to minority groups (Brim, 1965). Standardized tests are suspected agents of discrimination. This charge stems from the disproportionately high number of minority and low-income children labeled mentally retarded and the subsequent placement of these children in special education programs (Bailey & Harbin, 1980).

The standardized IQ test has been attacked on the grounds that most standardized tests are biased against children who are culturally or linguistically diverse from the mainstream of American culture or, more specifically, from test producers (Jensen, 1980). IQ tests and other standardized tests are charged with being (1) highly loaded with items based on white, middle-class values and experiences (Williams, 1974); (2) composed of items that sample cognitive styles directly opposed to those found in many children from low-income families (Cohen, 1969) or culturally diverse groups (Kleinfeld, 1973); (3) administered in an atmosphere that may penalize culturally diverse children (Bailey & Harbin, 1980); and (4) scored on norms derived from white, middle-class standardized groups (Bailey & Harbin, 1980). Such tests may also penalize children with linguistic styles differing from that of the dominant culture (Bailey & Harbin, 1980).

Laosa (1977, pp. 10–11) has identified the following principal criticisms of standardized assessment practices:

1. Standardized tests are biased and unfair to persons from cultural and low socioeconomic minorities since most tests reflect largely white, middle-class values and attitudes, and they do not reflect the experiences and the linguistic, cognitive, and other cultural styles and values of minority group persons.
2. Standardized measurement procedures have fostered undemocratic attitudes by their use to form homogeneous classroom groups which severely limit educational, vocational, economic, and other opportunities.
3. Sometimes assessments are conducted incompetently by persons who do not understand the culture and language of minority group children and who thus are unable to elicit a level of performance which accurately reflects the child's underlying competence.
4. Testing practices foster expectations that may be damaging by contributing to the self-fulfilling prophecy which ensures low-level achievement for persons who score low on tests.

5. Standardized testing practices foster a view of human beings as having only innate and fixed abilities and characteristics.
6. Certain uses of tests represent an invasion of privacy.

Definitions of Bias

There seems to be little agreement on what specifically constitutes biased or nonbiased assessment (Duffey, Salvia, Tucker, & Ysseldyke, 1981). The concept of bias in assessment may best be defined by examining the absence of bias, or nonbiased assessment. A number of nonbiased assessment models have been described by Cole (1973) and by Peterson and Novick (1976). These models include the Quota Model, the Equal Risk Model, the Constant Ratio Model, and the Conditional Probability Model.

A test is considered unbiased by the Quota Model if the criterion score predicted for subgroups based on that subgroup's cumulative performance is relatively close to the criterion scores predicted by the common regression line for that test. If, however, the criterion score predicted from the common regression line is consistently too high for a particular subgroup, one would conclude that the test is negatively biased for that group. It can be inferred from the premise of the Quota Model that bias exists in a test or assessment procedure if a particular subgroup consistently scores lower than would be predicted by the performance of the majority of the population. In this model bias would appear to exist within the normative sample, which presumably does not include the subgroup.

The Equal Risk Model assumes that a test is unbiased when groups sharing the same likelihood of success on the criterion task have equal chances of selection. The underlying assumption of this model is best explained through illustration. Match a group of girls and boys on IQ and grade point average. Now assume that they would receive roughly equal scores on the same achievement test and be selected as low, medium, or high achievers with equal frequency. If, however, 70% of the males are selected as low achievers and only 33% of the females are so selected, it would be assumed that the selection criterion (i.e., the test) is in some way biased against males. It can then be inferred from the premise of the Equal Risk Model that bias exists in a test or assessment procedure if a particular subgroup is consistently selected as successful less often than their likelihood of success on the criterion task would predict. In this model, the bias appears to relate to the validity of the test as a selection measure.

If the proportion of cultural groups selected by a test is equal to the proportion that should be selected by scores on the criteria alone, this test meets the assumptions of the Constant Ratio Model for fairness. In other words, if the test purports to select those candidates who would make fine teachers, the test should select those who would actually make fine teachers, regardless of cultural background. If the test fails to select the proportion of candidates who would be successful in meeting the criteria for success due to cultural difference, the test would be considered biased. The bias in this model is also related to the validity of the test in question.

The Conditional Probability Model focuses upon the selection process rather than the test itself. The assumption of this model is that a test is nonbiased if there is an equal probability of selection for both minority and majority groups whose members achieve a satisfactory criterion. Therefore, a test is considered biased if a particular group reaching the criterion for selection is selected proportionately less often than other groups. The bias in this model exists with those making the selection, rather than with the test itself.

Drawing inferences from the four models of nonbiased (fair) tests, we may conclude that bias for that subgroup exists in tests or assessment procedures under the following conditions: (1) consistent test scores much lower than would be predicted from the norms of the test; (2) consistent selection for success less often than their likelihood of success on the criterion task would predict; (3) consistent selection in smaller proportions than the proportion of candidates who would actually be successful in meeting the criterion for success due to cultural differences; and (4) members who reach the criteria for selection are selected proportionately less often than members of other groups.

CASE STUDY

Part I

Name: Susan
Date of Birth: September 16,
   1974
Date of Evaluation: November 16,
   1983

Age: 9 years, 2 months

Grade: 4

Background Information

Susan, a 9-year-old black child, was referred for evaluation by her fourth-grade teacher. School reports revealed that Susan was achieving academically below grade level and that her interactions with peers tended to be quite immature. Susan lives with her grandmother and two younger brothers. Her parents died in an automobile accident four years ago. Presently, her family is living in a small apartment in a city-owned housing project. Susan's grandmother is unemployed and receives financial support from the state and federal government.

Observation

Susan was comfortable and relaxed during the testing situation. She used nonstandard English throughout the testing situation. Her attention to tasks was adequate the majority of the time. Susan's response patterns at times were somewhat hurried and impulsive. A number of times she verbalized the difficulty level of particular items. At other times she talked to herself while working on a task.

Past Testing

Test	Date	Results
Gates MacGinite Reading Test	6/16/82	Reading Recognition: Grade 1.5 Reading Comprehension: Grade 1.4
Slosson Intelligence Test	6/16/82	IQ: 65, Mental Age: 5-0 years

Differential Selection

Black Children

Shuey (1966) reviewed 32 studies that compared the scores of black children on 81 different tests of intellectual ability. This review suggests that, on the average, blacks test about one standard deviation (σ) below the mean of the white population. Jensen (1976) points out that "this finding is fairly uniform across the 81 tests used in the studies reviewed" (p. 373). One can conclude from the above that the majority of tests of intellectual ability in use are biased against black children. Black children as a subgroup do score lower than would be expected from the normative sample; therefore, by definition, these tests can be considered biased. This conclusion, however, is not uniformly held. Jensen (1976, 1980), for one, does not agree with this conclusion. He argues that the differences in scores observed between black and white children primarily, although not totally, reflect actual differences in intellectual ability and that tests of intellectual ability actually measure intellectual ability.

The majority of research investigating differences between subgroups and normative samples on tests of intelligence typically compare the scores of black children to the norm for the test under investigation. The fact that blacks form one of the largest minority groups in the United States has focused attention on comparative studies concerning IQ tests. Studies available for other minority groups indicate that similar differences exist between their expected scores and the scores actually obtained on standardized tests of intelligence (Altus, 1953; Killian, 1971; Talerico & Brown, 1963; Turner & Penfold, 1952).

Other Minority Groups

Killian (1971) found that the Mexican-American children scored an average of 6 to 10 IQ points lower on the WISC than their Anglo-American peers. Altus (1953) reported similar results in which the Anglo-American children scored significantly higher on the full scale IQ score than their Mexican-American peers. Crudnick (1970) investigated the IQ scores that Southwestern American Indian children received on the *Peabody Picture Vocabulary Test* (PPVT). He reported that the IQ scores ranged from 31 to 47 IQ points below the normative mean.

Investigation of these particular studies indicates a systematic discrepancy between the performance IQ and the verbal IQ. A discrepancy also exists between the normative population and minority populations on tests that are highly verbal in nature for minority groups who do not use English as their primary language (Altus, 1953; Crudnick, 1970; Killian, 1971; Turner & Penfold, 1952). The discrepancy existing between the performance IQ and the verbal IQ may be a product of bias. However, to argue that the tests are biased, one must assume that the tests are measuring traits other than intelligence, such as language ability. In other words, the argument for bias would assume that these subgroups are consistently selected for success less often than their likelihood of success of the criterion would predict.

The criterion in this case is intelligence. However, the argument that these tests may actually be evaluating an individual's skill in the use of the English language rather than intelligence is popularly accepted (Gradson & Hall, 1972). The credence of this argument may be evaluated by examining the differences that may exist between the verbal and performance IQ scores obtained on some tests, or by comparing the performance on nonverbal tests.

Killian (1971) investigated the performance of three groups of kindergarten and first-grade students who were matched on school achievement on the *Wechsler Intelligence Scale for Children* (WISC). The three groups investigated were (1) Anglo-American children, (2) Mexican-American monolingual children, and (3) Mexican-American bilingual children. The Anglo-American children scored significantly higher on the full scale (mean IQ = 98) than the Mexican-American bilingual children (mean IQ = 88), who scored lower than both the Anglo-American and the Mexican-American monolingual children (mean IQ = 92). The greatest differences in scores existed on the verbal scale of the IQ test. The Anglo-American children scored an average of 12 points higher on the verbal scale (mean IQ = 100) than the Mexican-American bilingual children (mean IQ = 88), and 8 points higher than the Mexican-American monolingual children (mean IQ = 92). The discrepancy in scores was less obvious on the performance scale, where the Anglo-Americans (mean IQ = 97) outscored the bilingual children (mean IQ = 90) by an average of 7 points, and the monolingual children (mean IQ = 93) by an average of 4 points.

Altus (1953) compared WISC scores of two groups of children who had been referred for special class screening for the educable mentally retarded (EMR). These two groups were monolingual Anglo-American children and bilingual Mexican-American children. He found that the Anglo-American children obtained significantly higher scores on the full scale and the verbal scale, yet there was no significant difference in their performance scale IQ scores. Similarly, Talerico and Brown (1963) reported that Puerto Rican children scored from 6 to 12 points higher on the performance scale than on the verbal scale of the WISC. Also, Turner and Penfold (1952) reported that American Indian children scored an average of 11 points higher on the performance scale than the verbal scale of the WISC. Crundick (1970) reported that Southwestern American Indian children scored well below the expected average on the highly verbal *Peabody Picture Vocabulary Test*. Their IQ scores ranged from 53 to 69, while the same group of children scored near the expected mean of 100 on the *Harris Draw-A-Man Test*, a nonverbal test of intelligence. These findings suggest that the verbal subscales of standardized IQ tests may well be evaluating the child's ability in "good standard English" as well as other traits that purportedly relate to an intelligence quotient.

The Impact of Bias in Testing

If tests for placement are biased, one would expect that "a higher proportion of minority children would be placed into special educable mentally retarded (EMR) classes than one would expect based upon their proportions in the larger society. This has, in fact, been the case" (MacMillan, 1977, p. 188). Tucker (1980) found that 3.0% of all black children enrolled in public schools in 1977 attended classes for the educable mentally retarded, and 1.4% of all Mexican-American children were enrolled in the EMR classrooms, while only 0.7% of all Anglo-American children were so enrolled. Although the proportion of black and other minority children in special classes is greater than that of white children, there is a larger number of whites enrolled in these classes due to the greater absolute number of white children in this society (Cleary, Humphrays, Kendrick, & Wesman, 1975).

Reactions to the Use of Standardized Tests for Placement Purposes

Proponents of standardized tests argue that the tests are not biased; that the items pointed out by critics as biased are not typically the items that minority children have difficulty with, and that critics of tests are often indiscriminant in their criticisms. Jensen (1980) claims that "all the criticisms seem to come from a common grab bag, are dispensed in a shotgun broadside, and convey attitudes and sentiments instead of information that would be needed to evaluate the arguments" (p. 18). Justified or unjustified, criticism of standardized tests as biased measures along with a lack of supporting sound measures of adaptive behavior have led to public stands by professional groups, litigation, and the passage of public laws setting stringent requirements designed to eliminate bias and subjectivity in the assessment and placement process of minority children (Alley & Foster, 1978).

Testing Moratoriums

An extreme reaction to the issue of abuse in the process of using data to make placement decisions is to discontinue the use of all tests. This moratorium on testing was advocated by the Association of Black Psychologists at its annual meeting in 1969, when it claimed that psychological testing of black individuals is being used to (1) label black people as uneducable; (2) place black children in "special" classes and schools; (3) perpetuate inferior education in blacks; (4) assign black children to educational tracks; (5) deny black students higher educational opportunities; and (6) destroy positive growth and development of black people (Williams, 1971).

The National Education Association's Center for Human Relations held a conference in 1972 on the theme "Tests and the Use of Tests—Violations of Human Civil Rights." The result of this conference was a call for an immediate moratorium on all standardized testing, which may be biased toward certain groups. Similarly, the NAACP, at its 1974 meeting, proposed a moratorium on all tests not specifically corrected to eliminate cultural bias (Duffey, Salvia, Tucker, & Ysseldyke, 1981). The Council for Exceptional Children (CEC) issued a resolution in May of 1978, calling for a moratorium on group intelligence testing when that testing plays a role in any placement considerations.

Litigation

Similar positions concerning the use of standardized tests have triggered a number of court cases challenging the use of standardized tests for placement of minority students. The courts have generally ruled in favor of these positions. The court ruled against group tests that it considered biased in the case of *Hobson* v. *Hansen* (1967), against group testing as a basis for pupil placement in the California case of *Spangler* v. *State Board of Education* (1970), and against individually administered tests in the case of *Larry P.* v. *Riles* (1974). In the case of Larry P., a black child, the target of criticism was not the test itself but the examiner's unfamiliarity with the child's cultural background. In a similar case involving individual testing and a Spanish-surname child, the court ruled that the middle-class bias of standardized tests and their reliance on standard English made them inappropriate for labeling and placement decisions for culturally different children (*Diana* v. *State Board of Education*, 1970).

Legal Requirements Mandating Nondiscriminatory Testing

A clear mandate on how nondiscriminatory testing and placement procedures were to be defined and implemented came with the passage of Public Law 94-142, the Education of All Handicapped Children Act of 1975. Compliance with PL 94-142 requires these evaluation procedures:

1. Tests and other evaluation materials (a) are provided and administered in the child's native language or other mode of communication, unless it is clearly not feasible to do so; (b) have been validated for the specific purpose for which they are used; and (c) are

administered by trained personnel in conformance with the instructions provided by their producer.

2. Tests and other evaluation materials include those tailored to assess specific areas of educational need and not merely those which are designed to provide a single general intelligence quotient.
3. Tests are selected and administered so as to best insure that when a test is administered to a child with impaired sensory, manual, or speaking skills, the test results accurately reflect the child's aptitude or achievement level or whatever other factors the test purports to measure, rather than reflecting the child's impaired sensory, manual, or speaking skills (except where those skills are the factors which the test purports to measure).
4. No single procedure is used as the sole criterion for determining an appropriate program for a child.
5. The evaluation is made by a multidisciplinary team or group of persons, including at least one teacher or other specialist with knowledge in the area of suspected disability.
6. The child is assessed in all areas related to the suspected disability, including where appropriate, health, vision, hearing, social and emotional status, general intelligence, academic performance, communicative status and motor abilities. (*Federal Register*, August 23, 1977, pp. 42496–42497)

Strategies to Prevent Discriminatory Testing

Native Language

A test or evaluation procedure may be culturally fair yet still discriminate against the child if the test is not administered in the child's native language (*Diana* v. *Board of Education*, 1973; *Hernandez* v. *Porter*, 1975). The statutes require state education agencies and local education agencies to provide and administer evaluation materials or procedures in the child's native language or mode of communication unless it is clearly not feasible to do so (Sec. 612 [5] [c]; 614 [a] [7]; and Sec. 121a. 532).

If the primary languages of the child and parents are different, the child must be tested in his or her primary language. This provision also includes the phrase "or other mode of communications," which refers to children who are deaf, blind, or have no oral or written communication and whose typical mode of communication must be identified and used for testing (Sec. 121a.9).

Turnbull and Turnbull (1978) point out that feasibility must be defined in the student's interest rather than in the school's interest.

The federal statutes require that when "tests are selected and administered to a child with impaired sensory, manual, or speaking skills, the test results accurately reflect the child's aptitude or achievement level or whatever other factor the test purports to measure, rather than reflecting the child's impaired sensory, manual, or speaking skills (except when those skills are the factors which the test purports to measure)" (Sec. 121a.532). Therefore, it is not sufficient to present the test or materials in the child's primary language or mode of communication if the presenter's level of ability in that language is such that the child is penalized. The school must provide a competent communicator for the child (Bogatz, 1978).

Multifactorial Tests

Federal statutes require that the child be assessed in all areas related to the suspected disability, including, where appropriate, health, vision, hearing, social and emotional status, general intelligence, academic performance, communication status, and motor abilities (Sec. 121a.532). Turnbull and Turnbull (1978) point out that evaluation measures must assess educational need rather than general intelligence or achievement levels and that information from sources other than tests must be used. Gearheart (1980) suggests that common components of assessment include the evaluation of (1) visual and auditory levels of functioning, (2) educational achievement level, (3) adaptive behavior level, (4) speech and language development, (5) level of intellectual functioning, (6) general developmental level, (7) physical examination, (8) health history, (9) psychological testing, and (10) related data from other sources (i.e., social service agencies, mental health agencies, summer sports, or camp programs). In addition to these components of assessment, Turnbull and Turnbull (1978) suggest that the evaluators must give proper consideration to (1) social adjustment with peers, (2) cultural background, (3) language dominance, (4) parental interviews, and (5) direct observation to better understand the child's social, cultural, and personal adjustment and adaptive level.

Multidisciplinary Team

In order to assure that the multifactored evaluation process is carried out in a nondiscriminatory manner, all tests must be administered by trained personnel in conformance with instruction from the producer (Sec. 121a.532) and the evaluation must be made by a multidisciplinary team or group of persons, including at least one teacher or other specialist with knowledge in the area of the suspected disability (Sec.

121a.532). PL 94-142 and Sec. 504 require that the multidisciplinary team include the child's regular teacher, a person qualified to conduct individual diagnostic examinations, and at least one teacher or specialist in the area of the suspected disability (Turnbull & Turnbull, 1978). If the child does not have a regular teacher, a regular teacher qualified to teach the pupil must be included in the team. In addition to these three people, the team should include personnel familiar with the child's cultural, ethnic, racial, or linguistic background.

Validity of Tests Used

The courts have ruled that due process is violated when a child is misclassified on the basis of invalid criteria (*Larry P.* v. *Riles*, 1974). The use of intelligence testing through standardized IQ tests is in violation of the Fourteenth Amendment if the IQ tests are to determine the intelligence of children unfamiliar with the language or the middle-class culture that underlies the test question (*Larry P.* v. *Riles*, 1974; *Mattie T.* v. *Holliday*, 1975; *Hobson* v. *Hansen*, 1967; *Smuch* v. *Hobson*, 1969). Therefore, the courts forbid the use of bias (unvalidated) tests that do not properly account for cultural differences and the experiences of children being tested (*Larry P.* v. *Riles*, 1974; *Diana* v. *Board of Education*, 1973; *Mattie T.* v. *Holliday*, 1975). The law assumes that valid, adequate tests are available or may be made available to adequately and fairly test minority children. However, this assumption may not be totally accurate, for Thurlow and Ysseldyke (1979) reported that of the 30 instruments used by three or more child service learning disability demonstration centers, only 5 (16.7%) had technically adequate norms, 10 (33.3%) had reliability adequate for use in decision making, and 9 (30.0%) had technically adequate validity. Of the 30 tests evaluated, only 7 (23.3%) were judged to be technically adequate in all three criteria used for judging their adequacy.

Tests and other evaluation tools must include materials tailored to assess specific areas of education need, not merely those designed to provide a single general intelligence quotient (Sec. 121a.532). General achievement and intelligence tests do provide general comparative information. However, tests of a different nature should be used in addition to general IQ and achievement tests. Culture-fair tests, the use of pluralistic norms with existing tests, and the use of the *Learning Potential Assessment Device* (Feuerstein, 1979) have all been identified as tests or procedures that may be used with general IQ and achievement tests to better ensure validity and therefore fairness in the assessment of exceptional children (Duffey, Salvia, Tucker, & Ysseldyke, 1981).

Culture-Fair Tests

Culture-fair tests are designed to measure intelligence without measuring language, formal education, or experience. Cattell's *Culture-Fair Intelligence Tests* (1973) are excellent examples of this type. The *Culture-Fair Intelligence Tests* were originally constructed to "meet the need for a test which would fairly measure the intelligence of persons having different languages and cultures, or influenced by very different social status and education" (Cattell, 1962, p. 5). The *Culture-Fair Intelligence Tests* are primarily designed to test intelligence through the use of figural analogies and figural reasoning items. This test is made up of eight subtests, four of which are judged to be fully culture-fair, namely, (1) Substitution, (2) Classification, (3) Mazes, and (4) Similarities (Cattell, 1973).

Use of Pluralistic Norms for Existing Tests

This strategy develops separate norms for existing tests that account for individual social and cultural factors. Mercer's (1977) *System of Multicultural Pluralistic Assessment* (SOMPA) is an example of such a system. The SOMPA is designed for children 5 to 11 years of age. It utilizes two primary sources of information: (1) an interview with the child's principal caregiver and (2) scores from various physical and intellectual measurements. The interview includes questions concerning the child's sociocultural experiences, the administration of the *Adaptive Behavior Inventory for Children*, and specific health inventories. Test scores come from the WISC–R, the Bender-Gestalt, a physical dexterity test, and measures of height, weight, vision, and hearing (Kozel & Rotatori, 1979).

Scores obtained from the administration of tests are weighted by a statistical formula to account for various social and cultural factors on an individualized basis. The weighted scores from the tests produce an estimate of the child's level of performance, which is known as their Latent Scholastic Potential (LSP). The LSP converts WISC–R full scale, verbal, and performance IQ scores so that they may be compared to the national norm while still considering the child's individual sociocultural background. Duffey, Salvia, Tucker and Ysseldyke (1981) identified two possible problems in this model: (1) it may be difficult to account for the extremely heterogeneous nature of any one cultural or ethnic group, and (2) there may be difficulty with this instrument's predictive validity for success in the majority culture.

CASE STUDY

Part II

Present Testing

Medical

Information was collected to assess Susan's medical characteristics in the areas suggested by the *System of Multicultural Pluralistic Assessment* (SOMPA). The results are all within the normal range. A summary of that data is listed below:

Test	Results
Physical Dexterity Tasks (Scaled Score)	
Ambulation	55
Equilibrium	60
Placement	55
Fine-Motor Sequencing	50
Finger-Tongue Dexterity	53
Involuntary Movement	57
Physical Dexterity Average Score	55
Bender Visual Motor Gestalt Test (Scaled Score)	58
Weight by Height (Scaled Score)	50
Visual Activity	Right Eye: 20/20
	Left Eye: 20/20
Auditory Activity	Normal

Health History Inventories	DK Score	Raw Score
Prenatal/Postnatal	0	4
Training	0	4
Disease and Illness	1	3
Vision	0	0
Hearing	0	0

Adaptive

The *Adaptive Behavior Inventory for Children* (ABIC) reveals that Susan scored best in areas concerned with caring for herself and earner/consumer. In contrast, her weak area was in peer relations. A summary of her performance follows:

Area	Scaled Score
Family	63
Community	64
Peer Relations	45
Nonacademic School Roles	50
Earner/Consumer	75
Self-Maintenance	75
ABIC Average Scaled Score	62

School Functioning Level

Susan was administered the *Wechsler Intelligence Scale for Children*—Revised (WISC–R). She attained a Verbal IQ of 68, a Performance IQ of 68, and a Full Scale IQ of 66. A summary of her subtest scaled scores follows:

Verbal		Performance	
Information	4	Picture Completion	6
Similarities	5	Picture Arrangement	6
Arithmetic	6	Block Design	5
Vocabulary	4	Object Assembly	5
Comprehension	5	Coding	6
(Digit Span)	(7)		

Sociocultural Scales

Information was collected on family size, family structure, socioeconomic status, and urban acculturation. Susan's scores reveal a child from a socioeconomically deprived environment. Her grandmother has very little formal education and has not worked since Susan's parents died. Lastly, her grandmother lived in a rural farming area. A summary of Susan's sociocultural scaled scores appear below:

Area	Black Ethnic Group	School Culture
Family Size	57	54
Family Structure	18	10
Socioeconomic States	29	10
Urban Acculturation	17	10

Estimated Learning Potential (ELP)

A calculation of Susan's ELP based upon her scores on the WISC–R and data from her sociocultural scales resulted in a Verbal ELP of 87, a Performance ELP of 87, and a Full Scale ELP of 86.

Summary and Recommendations

Susan's medical assessment data reveals normal functioning with no at-risk indications. Intellectual functioning is depressed and similar to a mildly retarded child. However, when her IQ scores are analyzed with regard to her own sociocultural group she is less than one standard deviation below the mean for her normative group, which is 77. This is not a significant deviation, and Susan's ELP of 86 would be contrary information to placing Susan in a special education class for the mildly retarded. It would be recommended that Susan receive some counseling regarding her immature behavior and peer relationships. Possibly Susan could be encouraged to participate in social recreational organizations such as Girl Scouts or school clubs that would allow for constructive feedback regarding her social interactional behaviors. Lastly, Susan's teachers should meet to discuss educational intervention approaches to increase her academic skills.

Learning Potential Assessment Device

The *Learning Potential Assessment Device* (LPAD; Feuerstein, 1979) departs radically from the traditional psychometric evaluation procedure through a reevaluation of the goals of intelligence testing. LPAD goals may be defined as follows:

1. To assess the modifiability of the student when he or she is confronted with conditions aiming to produce a change in the student.
2. To assess the extent of the student's modifiability in terms of levels of functioning made accessible to the student by this process of modification, and the significance of the levels attained by the student in the hierarchy of cognitive operations.
3. To determine the amount of teaching investment necessary to bring about a given amount or type of modification.
4. To determine the significance of the modification achieved in a given area for other general areas of functioning.
5. To search for preferential modalities of the student, which represent areas of relative strengths and weaknesses both in terms of the student's existent inventory of responses and in terms of preferential strategies for affecting the desired modification in the most efficient and economical way (Feuerstein, 1979, p. 91).

The LPAD was constructed by Feuerstein (1979) as a fairer, less culturally dependent means of assessing children. However, Duffey, Salvia, Tucker, and Ysseldyke (1981) state: "There is no reason to believe that potential for modification is any less subject to cultural influences than other constructs we typically attempt to measure. If learning potential assessment devices were to be used as we currently use traditional assessment devices to label, provide placement, and finance programs, they would have the same potential for bias" (p. 430).

SUMMARY

This chapter addresses the concerns of bias in assessment and the effects that inappropriate or unfair procedures may have on placement decisions There have been many attempts to eliminate or reduce bias in the assessment procedure. These attempts have been directed toward either the instruments used or the evaluation and placement procedure itself. To reduce bias in the instrument, "the most common strategy employed by test developers has been an attempt to minimize cultural and verbal components of testing" (Bailey & Harbin, 1980, p. 590). Examples of these efforts have been reviewed under the rubric of culture-fair testing. However, research indicates that low-income or minority children continue to score lower on these tests than do white, middle-class children (Costello & Dickie, 1970).

Assessment procedures and subsequent placement decisions must be viewed in light of their fairness to children with diverse cultural backgrounds, modes of communication, and learning styles. Section 121a.532 of PL 94-142 provides a minimum standard to be met while attempting to ensure fairness in testing. In order to carry out the mandates of the law and to meet the requirement of nonbiased assessment procedures, technically adequate tests must be designed and used to identify operationalized and agreed-upon criteria that effectively and proportionately identify children's needs regardless of their cultural, racial, or linguistic heritage.

Educational Suggestions for Preventing Bias in the Assessment Process

Certainly teachers do not want to use assessment procedures that discriminate against minority or handicapped students. The following suggestions are guidelines to help ensure nonbiased assessment:

Tests that are used with minority and handicapped students must be interpreted with respect to the student's ethnic and social backgrounds.

Teachers should rule out all medical, visual, auditory, and emotional variables as factors to test performance levels of minority and handicapped students.

Prior to assessing minority students, teachers should determine the student's language dominance.

Teachers must be cognizant of the fact that test results are samples of current behavior and may predict how a student will perform without remedial intervention; however, the test results do not imply that a student cannot learn.

Students from low socioeconomic levels traditionally attain lower test scores than students from the middle and upper socioeconomic levels; however, this does not mean that such differences are unchangeable.

Teachers should rule out poor motivation as a possible deterrent to test success when assessing minority and handicapped students.

Teachers must rule out potential tester bias, which may result from (1) lack of training and experience in assessing minority or handicapped students or (2) a biased attitude toward minority or handicapped students. Tester bias may act as a deterrent to test scores.

Teachers must rule out problematic interaction between the tester and student resulting from (1) lack of rapport, (2) failure to obtain and maintain attending behavior, (3) failure to maintain student's maximum effort, and (4) poor language communication that may have a negative effect on test scores.

Study Questions

1. Define and discuss the definition of bias in assessment in relation to the four models of nonbiased assessment presented in this chapter.
2. The definition of bias in assessment as presented in this chapter is dependent upon the effects of differential selection. Define and illustrate differential selection as the product of biased assessment procedures.
3. PL 94-142 mandates that assessment and placement procedures be conducted in a nondiscriminatory manner. Identify the major requirements of the law that are to be implemented as a means of ensuring that nondiscriminatory assessment procedures are followed.
4. PL 94-142 dictates that "tests and other evaluation materials are provided and administered in the child's native language or other mode of communication, unless it is clearly not feasible to do so." Define the terms (1) *native language*, (2) *other mode of communication*, and (3) identify the parameters defining the term *clearly feasible to do so*.
5. PL 94-142 mandates that "no single procedure be used as the sole criterion for determining an appropriate program for a child." This mandate requires the use of multifactorial testing and the use of more than one valid test. Define the terms (1) *multifactorial testing* and (2) *valid tests*.
6. PL 94-142 further dictates that "the evaluation is made by a multidisciplinary team or group of persons." (1) identify those persons whose membership on this team is mandated by law, (2) identify those persons who may also be included in this team as the circumstances require.

Suggested Readings

Jensen, A. R. (1969). How much can we boost IQ and scholastic achievement? *Harvard Educational Review, 39,* 1–123.

McClung, M. S. (1978). Are competency testing programs fair? Legal? *Phi Delta Kappan, 59,* 397–400.

Mercer, J. R. (1974). A policy statement on assessment procedures and rights of children. *Harvard Educational Review, 44,* 125–141.

Oakland, T., & Matuszek, P. (1977). Using tests in nondiscriminatory assessment. In T. Oakland (Ed.), *Psychological and educational assessment of minority children.* New York: Brunner/Mazel.

Smith, J. D., & Jenkins, D. S. (1980). Minimum competency testing and handicapped students. *Exceptional Children, 46,* 440–442.

References

Alley, G., & Foster, C. (1978). Non-discriminatory testing of minority and exceptional children. *Focus on Exceptional Children, 9,* 1–14.

Altus, G. T. (1953). WISC patterns of a selective sample of bilingual school children. *Journal of Genetic Psychology, 83,* 241–248.

Bailey, D. B., & Harbin, G. L. (1980). Non-discriminatory evaluation. *Exceptional Children, 46*(8), 590–596.

Bogatz, B. E. (1978). *With bias toward none: A national survey of assessment programs and procedures.* Lexington, KY: Coordinating Office for Regional Resource Centers.

Brim, O. G., Jr. (1965). American attitudes towards intelligence tests. *American Psychologist, 20,* 125–130.

Bureau for Education for the Handicapped. (1974). State plan amendment for fiscal year 1975, under part B, Education-of-the-Handicapped Act, as amended by Section 614 of PL 93-380: Basic content areas required by the Act and suggested guidelines and principles for inclusion under each area. Washington, DC: U. S. Department of Health, Education, and Welfare, Office of Education.

Cattell, R. B. (1962). *Handbook for culture-fair intelligence test: Scale I.* Champaign, IL: Institute for Personality and Ability Testing.

Cattell, R. B. (1973). *Measuring intelligence with culture-fair tests: Manual for scales 2 and 3.* Champaign, IL: Institute for Personality and Ability Testing.

Cleary, T. A., Humphrays, L. G., Kendrick, S. A., & Wesman, A. (1975). Educational uses of tests with disadvantaged students. *American Psychologist, 30,* 15–41.

Cohen, R. (1969). Conceptual styles, culture conflict, and nonverbal tests of intelligence. *American Anthropologists, 71,* 828–856.

Cole, N. S. (1973). Bias in selection. *Journal of Educational Measurement, 10,* 237–255.

Costello, J., & Dickie, J. (1970). Leiter and Stanford-Binet IQs of preschool disadvantaged children. *Developmental Psychology, 2,* 314.

Crudnick, B. P. (1970). Measures of intelligence on southwestern Indian students. *Journal of Social Psychology, 81,* 51–56.

Diana v. State Board of Education. CA NO. 70-37 REP (N. D. Cal. January 7, 1970 and June 18, 1973).

Duffey, J. B., Salvia, J., Tucker, J., & Ysseldyke, J. (1981). Non-biased assessment: A need for operationalism. *Exceptional Children, 47*(6), 427–434.

Federal Register. (1977, August 23). 42494.

Feuerstein, R. (1979). *The dynamic assessment of retarded performers: The learning potential assessment device, theory, instrument and techniques.* Baltimore: University Park Press.

Gradson, E. V., & Hall, L. P. (1972). The tenth annual conference of the N.E.H. Center for Human Relations. *The School Psychologist, 21*, 11–13.

Gearheart, B. (1980). *Special education for the 80's.* St. Louis: C. V. Mosby.

Hernandez v. Porter. NO. 57132 (E.D. Mich. filed August 13, 1975).

Hobson v. Hansen, 269 F. Supp. 401, 514 (D.D.C. 1967) aff'd sub. nom.

Jensen, A. R. (1976). Race difference. In. W. Barnette, Jr. (Ed.), *Readings in psychological test and measurements.* Baltimore: Williams & Wilkins.

Jensen, A. R. (1980). *Bias in mental testing.* New York: The Free Press, Macmillan.

Killian, L. R. (1971). WISC, Illinois Test of Psycholinguistic Abilities, and Bender Visual-Motor Gestalt test performance of Spanish-American, kindergarten and first-grade school children. *Journal of Consulting and Clinical Psychology, 37*, 38–43.

Kleinfeld, J. S. (1973). Intellectual strengths in culturally different groups: An Eskimo illustration. *Review of Educational Research, 43*, 341–359.

Kozel, B., & Rotatori, A. F. (1979). Assessment implications of 94-142. *The Journal of Special Educators, 15*, 213–215.

Laosa, L. M. (1977). Non-biased assessment of children's abilities: Historical antecedents and current issues. In T. Oakland (Ed.), *Psychological and educational assessment of minority children.* New York: Brunner/Mazel.

Larry P. v. Riles. (1972). *Federal supplement, 343*, 1306 aff'd 502f.2dl 963.

MacMillan, D. L. (1977). *Mental retardation in school and society.* Boston: Little, Brown.

Mattie T. v. Holliday. CA NO. 753-31-5 (N.D. Miss. July 29, 1975).

Mercer, J. (1977). *System of Multicultural Pluralistic Assessment.* New York: The Psychological Corporation.

Peterson, N. S., & Novick, M. R. (1976). An evaluation of some models for culture-fair selection. *Journal of Educational Measurement, 13*(1), 3–29.

Shuey, A. M. (1966). *The testing of Negro intelligence* (2nd ed.). New York: Social Science Press.

Smuch v. Hobson. 408 F. ad 1975 (D.C. Cir. 1969).

Spangler v. State Board of Education. (1970). *Federal Supplement, 311*, 501 (CA).

Talerico, M., & Brown, F. (1963). Intelligence test patterns of Puerto Rican children seen in child psychiatry. *Journal of Social Psychology, 61*, 57–66.

Thurlow, M. J., & Ysseldyke, J. E. (1979). Current assessment and decision-making practices in model LD programs. *Learning Disability Quarterly, 2*, 15–24.

Tucker, J. A. (1980). Ethnic proportions in classes for the learning disabled issuing on non-biased assessment. *Journal of Special Education, 14*(1), 93–105.

Turnbull, H., & Turnbull, A. (1978). *Free and appropriate public education: Law and implementation.* Denver: Love Publishing.

Turner, G. H., & Penfold, D. V. (1952). The scholastic aptitude of the Indian children on Carodoc Reserve. *Canadian Journal of Psychology, 6*, 31–44.

U. S. Senate Report No. 94-168. Education for all Handicapped Children Act, June 2, 1975, 26–29.

Williams, R. L. (1971). Abuses and misuses in testing black children. *Counseling Psychologist, 2*, 62–77.

Williams, R. L. (1974). Black pride, academic relevance, and individual achievement. In R. W. Tyler & R. M. Wolf (Eds.), *Crucial issues in testing* (pp. 13–20). Berkeley, CA: McCutchan Publishing.

3

Measurement Concepts in Assessment

Anthony F. Rotatori
Faye Macklin
Robert Fox

OBJECTIVES

After completing this chapter the teacher should be able to:

1. Discriminate and describe four scales of measurement.
2. Identify three measures of central tendency and their characteristics.
3. Discuss two measures of variability.
4. Describe what correlation is in regard to direction and strength.
5. List four types of reliability that are used in test construction.
6. Discuss at least three types of validity that are typically reported in test manuals.
7. List seven factors that can have an effect on reliability.
8. Discuss three common considerations that affect the practicality of a test.

Classroom teachers periodically collect data on their students that
represent something (grade level, adaptive skill level). The teacher's
main objective is to reduce the data to some meaningful measure (Ary,
Jacobs, & Razavich, 1979; Badia & Runyon, 1982). However, before
this can be accomplished, the teacher must assign a specific measurement scale. There are four scales of measurement. Each of these scales
allows the teacher to manipulate the data with varying levels of
precision.

Types of Measurement Scales

Nominal Scale

The most limited and simplest type of measurement uses the nominal
scale (Bartz, 1976). Each separate data event in a nominal scale is
assigned a number to distinguish it from another data event. This
identification or labeling process is relatively arbitrary since there is
no inherent relationship between the events. For example, Sue is
assigned a workbook labeled 20, Jack is in a homeroom designated as
201, and Bill plays on a piano numbered 15 during music practice.
Since the nominal scale is for the sole purpose of labeling, differentiating, and distinguishing data events, one cannot add, subtract,
multiply, divide, or average the assigned numbers (Borg, 1981;
Christensen, 1977).

Ordinal Scale

When an ordinal scale is used, a teacher can order, or rank, data events
along a dimension. An ordinal scale not only has the property of
ordering but can also differentiate one data event from another
(Couch, 1982). By using this scale a teacher can describe a data event
as being more than or less than another data event. Typically, ordinal
scales describe data events from lowest to highest with regard to some
measurable characteristic (grade level scores on a reading test).
However, the ordering or ranking of the data events does not allow the
teacher to determine the magnitude of difference between data events.
For example, Joe, Bill, and Sue were ranked 1, 2, and 3 respectively,
based on their performance on an informal first-grade reading test.
We know that Joe performed better in reading than Bill and Bill
performed better than Sue. However, the ordinal scale ranking does
not specify the magnitude of difference between the students' raw
scores (Williamson, Karp, Dalphin, & Gray, 1982).

Interval Scale

The distinguishing feature of the interval scale is the property of equality of units (Cronback, 1970; Guilford, 1965). This means that there are equal quantitative distances between the data events in the scale. Consequently, an interval scale is able to indicate the magnitude and direction of the difference between data events. In the reading example of first graders used above, an interval scale would reveal that Joe had 30 out of 30 items correct, Bill had 20 out of 30 items correct and Sue had 10 out of 30 items correct. The magnitude of difference between Joe and Sue is 20 items and the difference between Bill and Sue is 10 items. This allows the teacher to observe that between Joe and Sue there is twice as much difference in reading performance on this test as there is between Bill and Sue.

Ratio

The ratio scale has all the properties of the interval scale in addition to having an absolute zero (Mook, 1982; Sax, 1980). The characteristic of an absolute zero point is that a data event of zero implies exactly nothing of the quantity being measured. Common ratio scales are weight, time, and length (Keppel & Saufley, 1980).

Summary of the Four Scales

Table 3.1 summarizes the properties of the four scales and lists typical examples. The ratio scale has the most desirable characteristics. However, most data events that teachers deal with do not have an absolute zero point. Thus interval and ordinal scales are the most widely used measurement scales by teachers (Kirk, 1968; Larson, 1975).

Descriptive Statistics

Even though data events are made meaningful through the use of a scale of measurement, the final listing of the data events may not be convenient in describing or summarizing the data events. For example, if a teacher lists the final exam math scores of students in her third-grade class, the listing would not indicate where the concentration of scores is, or how many students had a perfect score, or how many students scored below a passing grade of 70. A means of summarizing and describing data events is to use descriptive statistics, such as (1)

TABLE 3.1 Properties of Measurement Scales

Scale	Characteristics	Examples
Nominal	Labeling, identification	Assignments of numbers to baseball players or highways; categorization by attribute
Ordinal	Ordering, ranking indicates direction of difference (more than/less than)	Ranking of students in a spelling quiz or ordering of students by who is taller; ranking students by polling their preference or proficiency in an area
Interval	Equality of units indicates direction and magnitude of difference	Fahrenheit temperature scale, ranking by test items correct (in general, most behavioral measures)
Ratio	Equality of units and absolute zero point	Time, length, or width

frequency distributions, (2) graphic displays, (3) measures of central tendency, (4) measures of variability, and (5) transformed scores. Each of these procedures is discussed in the following sections.

Regular Frequency Distributions

A regular frequency distribution is constructed by listing every data event in the first column and then listing in the column to the right of the score the number of times that score occurred (Runyon & Haber, 1980). The scores in the first column are listed in descending order with the highest score at the top. Table 3.2 illustrates a regular frequency distribution of reading grade levels achieved by students in an elementary special education program. The number of students who achieved a specific grade score is easily discernible from the table; for example, three students received a grade score of 3.4, whereas only one student received a grade of 4.1. The table allows the teacher to make inferences quickly about the academic skill levels of the students (e.g., that a grade of 3.1 was the most frequently achieved score and that more students tended to achieve below a grade of 3.1 than above that grade).

Grouped Frequency Distributions

At times the number of data events to be listed in a regular frequency distribution is excessively large. One way of describing large data events is by a group frequency distribution (Yaremko, Harari, Harrison, & Lynn, 1982).

TABLE 3.2 Reading Grade-Level Scores of 68 Mildly Retarded Students on the *Peabody Individual Achievement Test*

Grade level score	Frequency
4.1	1
4.0	1
3.9	1
3.8	1
3.7	1
3.6	3
3.5	2
3.4	3
3.3	3
3.2	8
3.1	10
3.0	9
2.9	8
2.8	7
2.7	4
2.6	3
2.5	2
2.4	1

Graphic Displays
Frequency distribution data can be displayed graphically to summarize information. Two common graphic displays are (1) histograms and (2) regular frequency polygons.

Histograms
A histogram (bar graph) is constructed by drawing a graph and marking off the X axis (horizontal) in terms of score values and marking off the Y axis (vertical) in terms of frequencies. Figure 3.1 reveals a histogram of the following math test scores of second-grade students:

Math Score	Frequencies
10	2
9	3
8	4
7	5
6	3
5	2

In Figure 3.1 the height of the bar represents the frequency of any score. Thus, since a test score of 8 occurred four times, a bar 4 units in height is drawn above this math test score. When group frequency distribution data is being made into a histogram, the midpoint of each class interval is used as the score value for that interval that is marked on the X axis.

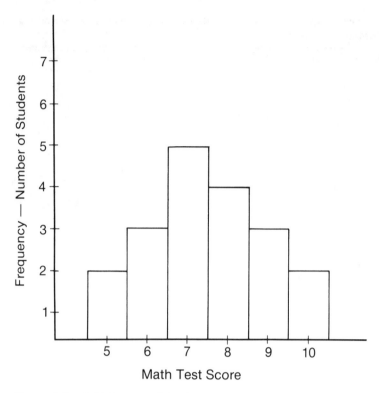

Figure 3.1. A histogram of math test scores.

    The following guidelines can be used when constructing a histo-
gram: (1) the height of the graph should be about three-fourths of the
width; (2) the X axis should include all of the scores plus some unused
space at each end; (3) the X-axis scores should be labeled; (4) the Y
axis should be slightly taller than is needed for the labeling of the
frequency height of each score; and (5) bars should be drawn to mark
off the lower and upper limits of the score value.

Regular Frequency Polygon
The regular frequency polygon is a line graph of a frequency distribution of scores. The height of the line graph represents the frequency of
each score. Figure 3.2 is a regular frequency polygon of the frequency
data in Table 3.2. Points are used to represent the frequency of a score;
for example, the frequency of the grade level score 2.7 is shown by a
dot 4 units up on the Y axis above this score.
    The following guidelines are for constructing frequency polygons:
(1) label the X axis with the representative scores; (2) label the Y axis
with representative frequencies; (3) place a dot at the midpoint of a
score or score interval; and (4) connect the dots by straight lines.

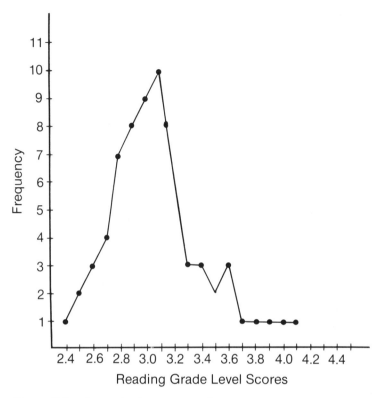

Figure 3.2. A regular frequency polygon.

Typical and Nontypical Shapes of Distributions

The Normal Distribution

The normal distribution is defined by a specific mathematical equation, but to most teachers it is defined approximately by its pictorial characteristics. It is a distribution that forms a symmetrical curve that has a bell-like shape. Figure 3.3 is an illustration of a normal curve. Notice that most of the score values of the distribution are in the middle of the curve. As one goes to the right or left of the midpoint, the frequency of a specific score decreases slowly and then more rapidly toward the ends of the curve. A normal curve has the same number of score values at specified distances below the mean as above the mean. The mean is the midpoint below which exactly one-half of the score values fall and above which the other one-half of the score values fall. In a normal curve the mean, median, and mode are identical score values. A normal curve has 68.26% of all score values between minus

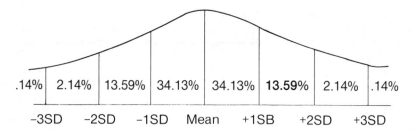

| .14% | 2.14% | 13.59% | 34.13% | 34.13% | 13.59% | 2.14% | .14% |

| -3SD | -2SD | -1SD | Mean | +1SB | +2SD | +3SD |

Figure 3.3. An illustration of a normal curve.

one standard deviation and plus one standard deviation. The area from minus two standard deviations to plus two standard deviations has 95.44% of the score values of the distribution. The area from minus three standard deviations to plus three standard deviations has 99.72% of the score values.

Most score values that teachers work with are not exactly normally distributed. However, the normal curve has mathematical properties upon which a number of statistical techniques are based. These techniques can be used to assist teachers in estimating means as well as solving problems involving percentage distributions.

Skewed Distributions

A skewed distribution is an asymmetrical curve in which most of the score values are at one end of the curve. If most score values are at the right end of the distribution so that the tail of the curve skews to the left, the curve is said to be negatively skewed. A negatively skewed distribution has a greater concentration of score values at the higher end and progressively fewer score values at the low end. When most score values are at the left end of the distribution so that the tail of the curve skews to the right, the curve is said to be positively skewed. In such a distribution, a greater concentration of score values are at the lower end while progressively fewer score values are at the higher end.

Three Common Measures of Central Tendency

Measures of central tendency are often used to highlight important features of a group of data. A measure of central tendency (mean, median, or mode) is a score value that describes the general location of a distribution of scores. In the following sections the computation of the mean, median, and mode will be delineated.

Mean

The mean is calculated by adding all the scores in a distribution and dividing the total by the number of scores. The following formula is used for the mean:

$$\bar{X} = \frac{\Sigma X}{N}$$

where $\bar{X}$ = mean, ΣX = sum of all X scores in the distribution, and N = total number of scores. When like score values have been combined into a regular frequency distribution by a teacher, the following formula can be used to compute the mean:

$$\bar{X} = \frac{\Sigma fX}{N}$$

where $\bar{X}$ = mean, fX = X score multiplied by the number of times that score appears, ΣfX = sum of fX values, and N = total number of scores. The mean indicates a score that is the best single value that describes a distribution of scores. The mean score represents the average performance of the distribution. The teacher can also use the mean score value to compare other scores in the distribution in regard to being below, at, or above the average performance.

Median

The median is the score value at the 50th percentile. In a distribution of scores, 50% are greater than the median and 50% are less than the median. The median is the exact *center* of a distribution of scores when the scores are put in order of size. When there is an odd number of untied scores, the median is the exact middle or central score when the scores are ranked in order of size. When there is an even number of untied scores, the median is exactly halfway between the two center-most scores. The computation of the median is somewhat different when there are a number of tied scores. The procedure involves interpolation among the scores to arrive at the point that exactly divides the distribution.

Mode

The score in a distribution that occurs most frequently is called the mode. The mode is determined by inspection rather than by computation. It is the crudest measure of central tendency because it uses only a small part of scores. Inspection of the scores 20, 25, 30, 35, 40, 45, 50, 55, 55, 55 reveals that the mode for this distribution is 55 because it occurs the most often. At times a distribution may have two modes.

This is evident in the following scores: 20, 25, 30, 30, 30, 40, 55, 55, 55, in which the most frequently appearing scores are 30 and 55. A distribution is said to be bimodal when it has two modes.

Summary of Mean, Median, and Mode

The mean is the most stable and precise measure of central tendency. It is extremely useful as a datum in inferential statistics where there is an analysis of distribution data. However, the mean is affected by extreme scores and by the skewness of a distribution. When a distribution is positively skewed, the mean is the highest value of the three measures of central tendency. In contrast, when a distribution is negatively skewed, the mean is the lowest value of the three measures of central tendency. Because of the effect of skewness on the mean, the median is the preferred measure of central tendency in either extremely positively or negatively skewed distributions.

Measures of Score Variability

An important feature of a distribution is its variability. Variability describes how scattered, dispersed, or spread out the scores in a distribution are. Scores tend to deviate around a measure of central tendency. The precise deviation above, at, or below a central tendency measure is helpful to teachers when comparing scores of different students. Two measures of variability are the range and the standard deviation.

Range

Range is the crudest and simplest measure of variability. When data are arranged in an interval scale or above, the range is calculated by subtracting the lowest score from the highest score in a distribution. The range as a measure of variability can be misleading when the distribution has values that tend to be atypical.

Standard Deviation

A more precise measure of variability than the range is the standard deviation. This widely used measure of variability is a square root average of all the deviations about the mean of a distribution. A distribution in which most scores are closely packed near the mean will have a relatively small standard deviation, which indicates less variability in the scores. In contrast, a distribution that has many scores at a distance from the mean would have a relatively large standard deviation, which reveals much variability in the scores.

Transformed Scores

At times a teacher may want to make a comparison of a student's score with other students' scores or with the student's other test scores. A way of doing this is to transform the original score into a new score. The following sections describe two typical transformed scores— standard scores and percentiles.

Standard Scores

Standard scores transform raw scores into a new score that always has the same mean and the same standard deviation. For example, many educational tests have set the mean of the standard score distribution as 100 and the standard deviation of that distribution as 15. If a student's raw score on an achievement test is transformed to a standard score of 85, then the teacher can see that the student's raw score is one standard deviation below the mean of the norm group for the student's grade. Frequently standard scores are established when determining whether a significant discrepancy exists between a student's actual cognitive ability and his or her achievement level.

Percentile Scores

Percentiles are probably the most common transformed score used by teachers. A percentile is a transformed score that expresses the location of a particular score value in a distribution. For example, a score value of 15 has a percentile rank of 53, revealing that the score is as good as or better than 53% of the scores in the distribution from which it is derived. The percentile rank of 53 also reveals that 47% of the score values in the distribution are greater than the score of 15. The percentile describes the score at or below which a given percent of the scores are ranked in a distribution. However, to properly give meaning to a percentile, the teacher must realize the reference or normed group from which it came. For example, a percentile score of 21 on a math achievement test may seem low for a mildly retarded high school student, but if the reference group included only normal high school seniors, the mildly retarded student did relatively well.

CASE STUDY

Part I

Name: Dan
Date of Birth: September 6, 1974
Date of Evaluation: October 24, 1982

Age: 8 years, 2 months

Grade: 3

Background Information

Dan is a third-grade student who was referred for evaluation by his teacher. The teacher's report indicated that Dan is achieving below his grade in reading and is having difficulty in keeping up with his classmates. The teacher's reports stressed that Dan can be inattentive and refuses at times to complete classroom assignments. Dan's father is a dentist, and his mother a nurse. He has two older sisters. Presently the family is living in an upper-middle-class neighborhood.

Observations

Dan entered the interview and testing situation easily. He conversed easily and readily answered questions about his behavior and school work. Dan enjoyed being praised for his efforts. His attention to task was adequate; however, his concentration was not optimal at all times. A number of times he needed directions repeated. Dan easily admitted he did not know an answer on the more abstract items. Frequently noted were his verbal comments regarding the difficulty of some of the items. The present test scores are an accurate reflection of his skill levels.

Past Testing

Test	Date	Results
Wechsler Intelligence Scale for Children—Revised	9/24/82	Verbal IQ: 109 Performance IQ: 109 Full Scale IQ: 110

Verbal		Performance	
Information	11	Picture Completion	12
Similarities	12	Picture Arrangement	10
Arithmetic	14	Block Design	12
Vocabulary	11	Object Assembly	10
Comprehension	10	Coding	13
(Digit Span)	(10)		

Peabody Individual Achievement Test   9/24/82

Subtest	Age Equivalent	Percentile Rank	Standard Scores	IQ–Standard Score Discrepancy
Mathematics	8-5	60	104	6
Reading Recognition	6-6	6	77	33
Reading Comprehension	6-9	11	82	28
Spelling	7-11	45	98	12
General Information	8-6	59	103	7
Total Test	7-7	32	93	17

An IQ–Standard Score discrepancy analysis revealed that Dan is underachieving in the reading areas, as he falls about two standard deviations below his capacity as shown by his highest IQ. Because of the above test scores, it was decided to comprehensively assess his reading skills.

Correlation

At times a teacher may want to examine the relationship between two sets of data scores. For example, a teacher may want to determine the extent to which those students who scored low on a science exam also scored low on a social studies exam. A statistic that can express the degree of relationship between sets of data is the correlation coefficient. A correlation coefficient can range from −1 through zero to +1. A correlation of +1 reveals that the student who had the highest score on the social studies exam also had the highest score on the science exam; the next highest on the social studies was the next highest on the science, and so on, exactly in agreement through the entire class of students. In contrast, a −1 correlation specifies that the scores on the two exams are exactly in the reverse order, such that the student with the highest score on the social studies exam had the lowest score on the science exam; the next highest on the social studies exam had the next lowest on the science exam, and so on. A correlation coefficient of zero reflects an absence of relationship. Correlation coefficients around zero represent beginning tendencies for a relationship to exist, but with many discrepancies. As correlation coefficients approach −1 or +1, definite relationships exist with fewer discrepancies. A complete lack of relationship would be represented by a zero correlation.

Figure 3.4 illustrates nine different scattergrams of selected correlation values. The scattergrams allow the teacher to view both the *direction* and the *strength* of a relationship. Direction refers to whether the correlation is a positive or negative relationship. Scattergrams A, B, C, and D in Figure 3.4 reveal a positive trend going from the lower

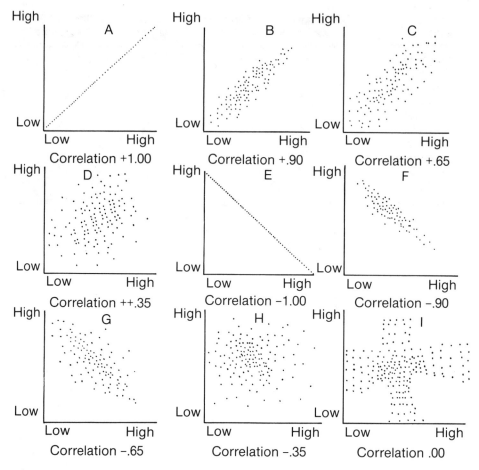

Figure 3.4. Examples of correlation trends.

left to the upper right as low scores in one variable (math quiz scores) are associated with low scores in the other variable (spelling quiz scores), and high scores in one variable are associated with high scores in the other. In contrast, scattergrams E, F, G, and H in Figure 3.4 reveal a negative trend going from the upper left to the lower right, as high scores in one variable are associated with low scores in the other variable. The strength of a relationship is determined by the scatter formed by the dots if a straight line is drawn through the band. When the dots form a very narrow band, the strength of the relationship is strong (scattergrams A, B, E, and F). In contrast, when the dots scatter widely the strength of the relationship is weak (scattergrams D and H). Scattergrams C and G of Figure 3.4 represent a relationship of moderate strength, whereas scattergram I with a correlation of .00 represents a relationship with no direction and no strength.

Criteria for Selecting Tests

The following sections delineate the most important criteria for selecting tests by teachers, namely, reliability, validity, and practicality.

Reliability

Reliability is generally concerned with the fluctuation or variability of a student's score values. The consistency of a test in producing an accurate and precise measure of a student's skills is important to a teacher because many program, placement, and classification decisions are related to the scores students attain on a variety of tests. Statistical indices of reliability can be used to measure the extent to which a test measure is reproducible. There are four methods for assessing the reproducibility or consistency of a score: (1) test-retest, (2) parallel-forms, (3) split-half, and (4) Kuder-Richardson reliability.

Methods of Measuring Reliability

The *test-retest* method of measuring reliability involves administering the same test at least twice to students in the class. The scores from each test are then used to calculate intercorrelations among the scores. This intercorrelation analysis results in a reliability coefficient. Retesting of the students can be the same day or after a short interval of time (a few days to a couple of weeks). However, the time interval is related to the effects of learning that may have occurred between tests, practice, memory, changes in the students resulting from everyday experiences, and changes in the students' speed of work. If a test has a high test-retest reliability coefficient, a student's relative position on the second administration of the test is similar to his or her position on the first administration of the test. The more reliable the test, the closer the coefficient is to +1.00. A change in relative position from one test to the next reflects error in the test.

The *parallel-forms* technique of measuring reliability is most practical when a teacher feels that students may recall test questions and tasks as well as their responses. The parallel-forms method involves calculating the correlation of equivalent forms of the test administered to the same students. When the two forms of the test are given at about the same time (i.e., on the same day), the coefficient that results is called the coefficient of equivalence. When the second testing occurs after an interval of time (e.g., two weeks), the coefficient that results is called the coefficient of equivalence and stability. In this latter situation the reliability coefficient is subject to the effects of learning and changes in the student from everyday living. Parallel-forms reliability eliminates the effect present with test-retest, namely, a sensitization factor of responding to the same test items.

The *split-half* method of reliability, which is sometimes referred to as internal consistency, involves dividing a test into two equivalent halves and then comparing the two halves. A typical procedure for dividing the test in half is by even-numbered and odd-numbered items after the teacher has ranked the items according to difficulty. The level of difficulty can be determined by calculating the percentage failing each item. Once the two halves have been developed, a correlation coefficient is calculated between the two halves to provide a reliability coefficient for the whole test.

Kuder-Richardson reliability is another method of estimating a test's internal consistency and involves only one test administration. The Kuder-Richardson procedure examines each student's performance on each item in the test. The most common statistical formula to estimate the above reliability is the Kuder-Richardson K-R20:

$$\gamma = \left(\frac{N}{N-1}\right)\left(\frac{\sigma_t^2 - \Sigma PQ}{\sigma_t^2}\right)$$

where:

N = number of items in the test
P = percent of students passing a particular item
Q = percent of students failing the same item
σ_t^2 = variance of the total test scores
ΣPQ = sum of the percent of students who pass (P) and percent of students who fail (Q) each item

What Affects Reliability

A teacher must be aware of factors that affect a reliability coefficient. In general they are: (1) range of the group, (2) level of ability in the group, (3) length of test, (4) guessing, (5) variations within the testing situation, and (6) judgment of the examiner.

Range of group is an important factor. A sample of students from a homogeneous group yields lower reliabilities than a heterogeneous sample. When there is a greater range of students in regard to certain variables (age, grade placement, or socioeconomic levels), the resulting reliability coefficient tends to be higher. In fact, reliabilities for age groups tend to be slightly higher than for grade groups because an age group usually has students with a greater spread of talent than a single grade group.

When the *level of ability in the group* is high, many students may find the test easy. This may result in the students having more time to complete the test. In contrast, if the ability of the group is low, the test may seem very hard, which may result in a number of students not having enough time to complete the test.

Length of test is another factor. The longer a test is, the more reliable it becomes as long as negative effects of fatigue are not problematic. This is so because the chance errors of measurement cancel out as the score value is more dependent upon the skills of the student taking the test. However, for certain exceptional populations, the longer tests cause the students to become fatigued, which may decrease the reliability of the test.

Guessing, even if it is random, introduces error into a test score. Guessing may increase depending upon the ability level of the group. When the students are from a low ability level, they may find the test hard and engage in more guessing, which results in low accuracy.

Variations within the testing can also lower reliability. All test sessions, no matter how well controlled, produce situational variables that can result in error. Examples of situational variables include low energy due to recent illness as well as distractions like lightning and thunder.

The *judgment of the examiner* may lower reliability. The ability of teachers to administer a test varies, depending upon their technical training, practice, and experience giving the test. Additionally, a teacher's knowledge in a test area and hands-on experience may be a factor in the scoring of the test responses, which usually involves some subjective judgment. Both of the above can result in error that may lower reliability.

Standard Error of Measurement

As the previous section pointed out, a student's score on a test may or may not be his or her true score due to the presence of error within the test and/or test results. A statistical procedure that can be used to determine the range in which the student's true score lies is the standard error of measurement. The standard error of measurement is defined as the standard deviation of the distribution of score values multiplied by the square root of 1 minus the reliability coefficient. The formula for the standard error of measurement (SEM) is:

$$SEM = \sigma_t \sqrt{1 - \gamma_{tt}}$$

where:

σ_t = standard deviation of the original test scores
γ_{tt} = reliability coefficient of the test

The teacher can conclude from the formula that the SEM is related to the size of both the standard deviation and the reliability coefficient. As the standard deviation increases, the SEM increases; but when the reliability coefficient increases, the SEM decreases. The higher the reliability coefficient, the smaller the standard error of measurement and the greater the accuracy of the score.

The teacher can use the SEM to report the range within which the true score of a student probably lies. Construction of a range involves specifying the number of SEMs above and below the student's score. Typically the range is between 1, 2, or 3 SEMs. The more SEMs used to construct the range, the more certain or confident the teacher can be that the student's true score falls within that range.

Standard Error of Difference

A teacher at times may want to determine whether the difference between a student's spelling test score and a reading test score is a true difference. The standard error of difference statistic can be calculated to assess whether the observed difference between the scores is due to error or to a true difference. The formula for the standard error of difference (SEM_{diff}) is:

$$SEM_{diff} = \sqrt{(SEM_1)^2 + (SEM_2)^2}$$

where:

SEM_1 = standard error of measurement of the first score
SEM_2 = standard error of measurement of the second score

A probability figure can be established to ascertain whether the difference in scores is a true difference. Table 3.3 illustrates the above point for a number of spelling and reading test scores.

Validity

Validity is the extent to which a test measures what it is designed to measure. If a test is designed to measure expressive language skills, then the test results of the students taking the test should reveal the student's expressive ability if the test is valid. There are four specific types of validity that can be considered in most tests: (1) content validity, (2) concurrent criterion validity, (3) predictive criterion validity, and (4) construct validity. A description of these types of validity follows.

Content Validity

Content validity describes the degree to which the content of the test covers an adequate sample of behavior to be measured. The tests must have a sufficient number of representative items to measure tasks that the teacher considers to be learner outcomes in an instructional area. Content validity is established by specialists in the area by visually examining the items for appropriateness and by comparisons with other tests.

Concurrent Criterion Validity

Concurrent criterion validity examines the extent to which a test measures what it purports to measure at the *time* the test is given. A test that has high concurrent criterion validity is able to accurately

TABLE 3.3 Calculation of Probability of a True Difference for Various Scores and SEM Differences

Test score		Observed difference	SEM difference	Probability of a true difference
Spelling	Reading			
100	90	10	5	Equal to or greater than 1 SEM difference? YES
				Equal to or greater than 2 SEM difference? YES
				Equal to or greater than 3 SEM difference? NO
				95%
120	105	15	5	Equal to or greater than 1 SEM difference? YES
				Equal to or greater than 2 SEM difference? YES
				Equal to or greater than 3 SEM difference? YES
				Equal to or greater than 4 SEM difference? NO
				99%
130	125	5	5	Equal to or greater than 1 SEM difference? YES
				Equal to or greater than 2 SEM difference? NO
				68%

assess the student's current status or skill level. For example, if a student is reading at a high third-grade level in a well-standardized reading series, then a reading achievement test should be able to assess that the student is reading at a high third-grade level. If the achievement test indicates the student is only at a high second-grade level, the test has poor concurrent criterion validity. The procedure to determine concurrent criterion validity is to establish a correlation coefficient between scores on the test of interest and another well-established criterion test or measure in that area. For example, a teacher may compare math scores on a standardized achievement test with scores the student has been attaining on the math textbook tests as well as on teacher quizzes.

Predictive Criterion Validity

Predictive criterion validity determines the extent to which the test can *predict* future performance. In other words, predictive criterion validity allows the teacher to estimate what the performance level of a student will be at a future time (6 months, 1 year, or 2 years later) based upon the student's present test score. The establishment of this validity is accomplished by administering the test and then following the student's performance over a period of time and correlating the student's performances with the original test scores. For example, a school readiness test is administered by a school district to all preschool children who will be entering kindergarten in the next three months. The purpose of the readiness test is to identify and predict those students who will have to be retained in first grade due to academic failure. Then all students are given achievement tests at the end of first grade and these scores are then correlated with the school readiness test scores. The school readiness test is said to have good predictive criterion validity if it accurately predicted the majority of the students who were failing first grade as determined by the achievement test scores.

Construct Validity

Construct validity is concerned with determining the extent to which a test measures the concept, model, or theory upon which the test was developed. In other words, how valid is the procedure the test author has established to measure a particular construct, concept, or idea about how specific behaviors go together. Construct validity is measured by comparing a student's score on a test against an outside criterion. For example, a test author believes that high school students who are able to accurately draw three-dimensional geometric designs after viewing them in a mirror will predict artistic skills necessary for specialized drafting programs in vocational trade school. The test is said to have good construct validity if the test scores are highly correlated with the students' success in the specialized drafting program as determined by the students' instructors.

Practicality

Practicality of a test is concerned with basic common-sense considerations for the use of a test by a teacher. Three common considerations follow.

Economy

Each school system must be cognizant of the cost of testing. Tests in which the test booklets can be reused are highly desirable. It is also more economical to use separate answer sheets rather than answer on the individual test booklet. Scoring the test can be quite economical if clerical personnel can score the test using an overlay stencil. Tests that require interpretation to score are more costly due to the time required to score each test as well as the professional staff needed to score the test.

Convenience
A test that is easy to administer because of clear and full instructions is highly desirable because it requires only a small amount of practice for effective administration. In general, tests that have only a few timed sections and those that have fewer items requiring close timing tend to be easy to give. Lastly, the layout of a test can be a factor in convenience. The test will be easier to give if (1) the print is large and clear, (2) response options are well separated, (3) all parts of an item are on the same page, and (4) item and related figure are on the same page.

Interpretation
Interpretation can be made easy for the teacher if a number of facets are present. First, the manual should state clearly what the test is designed to measure and what procedures were used in the development of the test. Second, the test should have clear directions for computing the score from the test. Third, norms should be from appropriate reference groups with a description of how the norms were developed. Fourth, the manual should indicate reliability and validity information that has been gathered on the test. Fifth, the manual should direct the teacher in interpretations regarding the test score and factors that may affect the obtained score (age, sex, race, culture, geographic region, socioeconomic level, educational background of parents). Last, the manual should be able to assist the teacher in describing a student with regard to strengths, weaknesses, relationship or standing to other students, diagnosing, placing, grouping, organizing remedial treatment plans, classifying, or screening for further testing.

CASE STUDY

Part II

Present Testing

Dan was administered the word lists and the oral graded passages of the *Analytical Reading Inventory* (ARI) by Woods and Moe. His performance revealed an independent level at the primer–first grade, an instructional level at the second grade, and a frustration level at the third grade.

Word Identification

Dan's word identification strategy showed an overemphasis on the use of phonics. In addition, Dan tended to substitute words, sometimes without retaining meaning. At times Dan would simply stop reading, not knowing what to do next.

Fluency/Automaticity

Dan read quite slowly and the above problem, that of not having a usable word identification strategy, further hindered his reading. Dan did recognize punctuation cues and sometimes used the technique of repeating words or sentences in order to retain meaning. This led to a lack of automaticity and ability to see a unity of ideas within the story.

Sight Vocabulary

Dan would, at times, substitute words that looked similar, such as *though* and *through*. When the words were seen in context and their difference in meaning was pointed out, Dan did not appear to have further difficulty. Also, sometimes Dan would substitute certain common words or fail to identify a word.

Reading for Meaning

Dan had the ability to read for meaning, but needed a specific purpose—determined beforehand and during the reading—to guide and direct him.

Attitude

Dan seemed to be a little timid in terms of his own abilities. Rather than take a chance, for example, when reading a new word, Dan would ask the tester how a word sounded. He did not seem to be aware of his actual skills in this area. This could be due to the fact that clear and usable methods had not been taught.

Summary and Recommendations

Dan is a disabled reader who is functioning about one and a half years below his age group. It is suggested that Dan participate in the university tutoring program at the reading clinic. The tutoring program should emphasize the following:

1. Reinforcement of further reading will aid Dan toward improving his reading. Books should be chosen that are not frustrating to him. A visible means of recording his progress is a good idea. A period of silent reading each day should be encouraged.
2. Dan should be encouraged to use a total word identification strategy. Emphasis on only one aspect, such as phonics, will not help Dan's total reading growth.

3. Activities that encourage reading for meaning should be emphasized, and individual work miscues should not be concentrated on. Activities that encourage Dan to read on his own, find information, raise his own questions, evaluate, infer, set purposes, and make some decisions are recommended.
4. Activities such as tape recording and repeated readings may be beneficial for his automaticity.
5. Dan benefits from being read to in terms of fluency. In addition, Dan's listening level is about third grade, meaning that he can benefit from materials read to him at those levels. Dan's interest level goes beyond material found at only the first or second grade.
6. Dan should be taught functional word identification strategies such as: (a) Skip the word and read the rest of the sentence; (b) Can you think of a word that makes sense? (c) Substitute "blank" for the unknown word.
7. Dan's sight vocabulary within context needs to be expanded by making a word bank. The word bank can be developed from books of interest and words associated with holidays. Also, Dan can play games such as Sight Word Checkers and Sight Word Roulette.
8. Reading for meaning should be emphasized through setting purposes, predicting, and verifying. Techniques and materials that can be used to reinforce Dan's ability to set a purpose in his reading are Directed Reading-Thinking Activities and the Request Method. The Directed Reading-Thinking Activity involves the reader in (a) setting purposes for reading, (b) adjusting the rate for these purposes and the material, (c) reading to verify purposes, (d) pausing to evaluate understanding, and (e) proceeding to read with same or different purposes. The Request Method involves both the child and tutor silently reading sections of a selection. The tutor serves as a model for appropriate questioning and makes sure the student is formulating correct purposes for reading the remainder of the passage.

Summary

The topic of measurement often engenders negative feelings in teachers. Many teachers recall struggling through a tests and measurements course at some point in their teacher training program. However, much of this information is forgotten soon after the course is over. The purpose of this chapter was to acquaint potential users of tests with information crucial to test selection, test administration, and test interpretation practices. While this material is admittedly difficult, it comprises an essential framework for the development and use of assessment instruments.

How can a teacher make any meaningful sense out of a person's test performance unless that teacher knows something about the norming sample's characteristics? How can a student's individual performance on a test of reading achievement be compared with the norming group's performance unless the test user has familiarity with common statistics such as medians, modes, means, standard deviations, and percentiles? How can a teacher select an appropriate reading test from a host of available reading instruments without knowledge of reliability and validity constructs? These questions and numerous others dictate that teachers be familiar with the basic measurement concepts presented in this chapter if ethical and competent tester behavior is to emerge. Repeated exposure to these concepts combined with exploring their extensive application potential should lead to subject mastery of the measurement area.

Educational Suggestions Based on Measurement Concepts in Assessment

Teachers should be aware of the measurement concepts in assessment procedures. Manuals, test sheets, and test items should be reviewed thoroughly before selecting a test. The following suggestions should aid in test selection and interpretation.

Teachers must ensure that the test selected is designed to measure the functions or skills with which the teacher is concerned. This can be determined by reviewing the test manual's validity.

Tests with detailed instructions present fewer problems in their administration than do tests with limited details.

Test manuals that describe comprehensive procedures for scoring eliminate errors in computation and point out how teachers should treat errors or part scores.

Teachers should select tests with norms that are representative of the students to be assessed. If the norms are not representative of the students' characteristics, the interpretation of the scores may be inaccurate or unfair.

It is important to select tests that have good test-retest reliability if teachers retest their students with the same test a number of times during the academic year. This will ensure consistent ordering or ranking of the students.

If test scores are used for grouping students, it is crucial that teachers take into consideration the standard error of measurement. This information assists the teacher in grouping more wisely because it indicates to the teacher the range of scores for which the test maintains its accuracy.

Most of the time, student's performance on subtests of an assessment device differ. The meaning in differences between the subscores can be determined by the intercorrelations of the subtests. Thus, if the subtests correlate to a high degree, the differences between them will be largely meaningless and uninterpretable.

At times teachers use tests as a predictive device. To ensure the usefulness of the test for such a purpose, teachers should analyze the manual's information regarding the test's correlations with criterion measures. If the correlations are low, then the test will be a poor predictor and should not be used.

Many times teachers use group tests to measure skills of their students. When selecting group tests teachers should review the test manual to determine how well that test correlates with other measures of the same function as evidence of the validity of the test. For example, it is better to select a group achievement test that correlates well with an accepted individually administered test than one that correlates only moderately.

Teachers must select tests that have well-established relationships to the age, sex, socioeconomic level, geographic region, and similar facets of the students being assessed. A review of the manual regarding these relationships will assist teachers in judging the sensitivity of the test to the demographic characteristics of the students. If the test describes relationships unlike those of the students, then the teachers must be very cautious in interpreting the test findings.

Teachers should select tests that delineate the use of the test for such purposes as grouping, organizing remedial instruction, or selecting students for placement or remedial experiences. If the test authors do not provide this information, teachers should be wary of the usefulness of the test.

When teachers are describing test results, it is important that they select the best descriptive statistic for the characteristics that they want to emphasize. As such, teachers must be aware of the strengths and weaknesses of specific descriptive statistics.

Study Questions

1. Discuss the educational uses of the four scales of measurement. Give a practical example of each.
2. Compute measures of central tendency, standard deviation, and standard error for the following raw reading test scores: 18, 26, 35, 4, 8, 10, 22, 16, 11, 12, 27, 4, 8, 7, 15, 13, 12, 21. How would you interpret these data? (That is, what does the distribution of scores tell you?)
3. Define the term *correlation* and discuss its practical usefulness for a classroom teacher. Are there any dangers in using correlations for making instructional decisions for a particular individual?
4. Distinguish between reliability and validity.
5. Which form of validity is most often used in education with standardized tests?
6. Draw a histogram for the following reading test scores: 10, 10, 10, 9,

9, 9, 9, 8, 8, 8, 8, 7, 7, 7, 7, 7, 6, 6, 6, 5, 5, 4, 3, 2, 1. What can you say about the distribution of the children's scores?

7. Why do grouped frequency distributions lose information?

Suggested Readings

Cook, T. D., & Campbell, D. T. (1979). *Quasi-experimentation: Design and analysis issues for field settings.* Chicago: Rand McNally.

Hartnett, D. L. (1975). *Introduction to statistical methods.* Reading, MA: Addison-Wesley.

Hays, W. (1981). *Statistics.* New York: Holt, Rinehart and Winston.

Tukey, J. W. (1977). *Exploratory data analysis.* Reading, MA: Addison-Wesley.

References

Ary, D., Jacobs, L. C., & Razavich, A. (1979). *Introduction to research in education.* New York: Holt, Rinehart & Winston.

Badia, P., & Runyon, R. P. (1982). *Fundamentals of behavioral research.* Reading, MA: Addison-Wesley.

Bartz, A. E. (1976). *Basic statistical concepts in education and the behavioral sciences.* Minneapolis: Burgess.

Borg, W. R. (1981). *Applying educational research: A practical guide for teachers.* New York: Longman.

Christensen, H. B. (1977). *Statistics.* Geneva, IL: Houghton Mifflin.

Couch, J. V. (1982). *Fundamentals of statistics for the behavioral sciences.* New York: St. Martin's Press.

Cronback, L. (1970). *Essentials of psychological testing.* New York: Harper & Row.

Guilford, J. P. (1965). *Fundamental statistics in psychology and education.* New York: McGraw-Hill.

Hays, W. L. (1973). *Statistics for the social sciences.* New York: Holt, Rinehart, & Winston.

Keppel, G., & Saufley, W. H. (1980). *Introduction to design and analysis: A student's handbook.* San Francisco: W. F. Freeman.

Kirk, R. E. (1968). *Experimental design: Procedures for the behavioral sciences.* Belmont, CA: Brooks/Cole.

Larson, H. J. (1975). *Statistics: An introduction.* New York: John Wiley & Sons.

Mook, D. G. (1982). *Psychological research: Strategy and tactics.* New York: Harper & Row.

Runyon, R. P., & Haber, A. (1980). *Fundamentals of behavioral statistics.* Reading, MA: Addison-Wesley.

Sax, G. (1980). *Principles of educational and psychological measurement and evaluation.* Belmont, CA: Wadsworth.

Williamson, J. B., Karp, D. A., Dalphin, J. R., & Gray, P. S. (1982). *The research craft: An introduction to social research methods.* Boston: Little, Brown.

Yaremko, R. M., Harari, H., Harrison, R. C., & Lynn, E. (1982). *Reference handbook of research and statistical methods in psychology*. New York: Harper & Row.

4

Assessment of Cognition and Intelligence

Ellen Weinhouse
Robert Fox
Anthony F. Rotatori

OBJECTIVES

After completing this chapter the teacher should be able to:

1. Provide a brief description of the current field of intelligence testing including its pros and cons.
2. Distinguish between intelligence and cognition.
3. Describe the problems associated with testing children in the sensorimotor period of development; list cognitive behaviors expected in children during this period and available formal and informal assessment instruments; and summarize research findings in this area.
4. Compare Piagetian-based instruments with standardized intelligence tests.
5. Describe cognitive functioning within and between each major stage of development.
6. Compare the Stanford-Binet and the Wechsler scales.
7. Discuss the field of testing as it might look in 20 years.

The history of formal efforts to assess individual differences in mental abilities dates back to the work of Alfred Binet in France. His original Binet-Simon intelligence scale was published in 1905. Intelligence tests, as they presently exist, have not kept pace with our expanding research knowledge and related theorizing efforts. Kaufman (1979) provides a cogent discussion of where intelligence tests fall short. Included in this discussion are several revealing points concerning the current content and structure of intelligence tests. First, the content of the most frequently used tests has not changed significantly since their inception in Binet's laboratory at the turn of the century; even the popular Wechsler scales are heavily laden with test data available 50 years ago. Second, tests do not reflect the growing literature that points to the fact that children learn differently—that is, have different cognitive styles. Similarly, research findings pertinent to how a child learns (memory, discrimination learning, concept formation research) have not been extended to the testing field. Third, current intelligence tests focus on performance. We can certainly tell which items a child passes and fails, but we fall short of explaining *why* a child passed or failed a particular item and/or identifying what cognitive processes underlie test performance. Fourth, the whole area of the unique influences of the child's central nervous system on his or her functioning has largely been left to neurologists or neuropsychologists. Yet the assessment devices used to evaluate neuropsychological functioning (e.g., the Halstead-Reitan battery) have important implications for the appropriate education of children. Fifth, current intelligence tests are based largely on empirical and psychometric theoretical principles. Developmental theory (such as Piaget's), which could potentially help us understand the qualitative aspects of children's test performance, has not been seriously integrated into current test practices.

Despite their limitations, intelligence tests have a profound impact on the lives of countless numbers of people. As a result, a variety of concerns have been raised including test bias, racial/cultural fairness of intelligence testing, hereditary and environmental influences on intelligence, and the use of standardized tests with nonstandardized populations (e.g., the handicapped). It seems difficult for many in this present atmosphere of extremism—ranging from blind acceptance of the IQ as an adequate construct for intelligence and as a necessary and sufficient condition for making major life decisions about individuals, to declarations of the illegality of intellectual testing and the need for their immediate demise—to remember that the intelligence tests used today represent only limited *samples of behavior*. From an empirical perspective the "good" intelligence tests currently available (e.g., Wechsler scales) are psychometrically sound given the limited samples of behavior and the circumscribed population upon which they are based. It is the lack of sufficient knowledge regarding each individual intelligence test's development, content, psychometric properties, interpretive limitations, and uses that has created the problems we are currently experiencing. Rather than throwing away the tests as a solution to these problems, efforts have to be made to curb the abuses and misuses of the tests that result from an inadequate information base concerning intelligence and its measurement. As Kaufman (1979) asserts, "*intelligent* testing is the key" (p. 1).

Although the burden for intelligent testing falls on the tester (or indirectly on the program where the tester was trained), it quickly extends beyond the examiner-examinee relationship to those involved in the uses of the information gathered in the testing situation. For example, a school psychologist may conscientiously administer, score, and interpret an intelligence test for a given child. The resulting psychological report may reflect a deemphasis of global scores obtained on the scale (e.g., IQ), concentrate on the child's strengths and weaknesses, include descriptions of how the child approaches and solves learning tasks, and include helpful insights and recommendations pertaining to the child's specific programming needs. Yet at a staffing concerning the child, the members may focus on the IQ score found for the child and decide on placement based largely on this one piece of data. The literature supports the fact that the preceding scenario is not an uncommon occurrence in our educational system (Junkala, 1977). While realizing that abuses of intelligence tests are and will continue to be of concern, few would disagree that measures of intelligence comprise a significant component of our assessment of children.

Traditional discussions of test instruments generally focus on the psychometric properties and subtests of available standardized intelligence tests. Within this chapter, a slightly different approach will be followed. First, the overall chapter framework corresponds to the Piagetian periods of cognitive development—that is, the infant or sensorimotor period, the preschool or preoperational period, and the school age or concrete and formal operations period. Each section begins with a description of the cognitive development within that period. Second, assessment instruments appropriate for each age period are grouped as to whether they are Piagetian-based, formal, or informal instruments. The instruments are in turn analyzed in terms of the cognitive processes they assess, and research concerning these processes is discussed where available. A logical starting point would be to define what we mean by cognition.

CASE STUDY

Part I

Name: Jill
Date of Birth: January 25, 1979
Date of Evaluation: October 30, 1982

Age: 3 years, 9 months
Schooling: Preschool, two times each week

Background Information

Jill was referred for a psychological evaluation by her parents. Her parents reported that Jill's preschool teacher was concerned about the quality of Jill's speech and her difficulty in following directions in the classroom. The mother reported that Jill's birth had been very difficult. During the delivery, Jill was without oxygen for an undetermined amount of time, as she was born with the umbilical cord wrapped around her neck. She also had seizures as an infant for which she received medication. Both parents reported being very careful with Jill during the first several months of her life as she was "so fragile looking." While the parents were becoming increasingly aware of Jill's speech problems, they felt it was probably due to her stubbornness and would be something that she would just grow out of. When asked if Jill's hearing had ever been evaluated, the father quickly reported that she could hear fine. In fact, he mentioned that she often heard fire whistles and police sirens before he did.

While both parents were not convinced of the necessity of a psychological evaluation, they were worried about the preschool teacher's concerns and wanted to make sure everything was okay with their daughter.

Past Test Results

Jill had no previous formal evaluations other than periodic pediatric assessments. Jill's mother reported that her pediatrician was not concerned over Jill's development.

Definition of Cognition

From the Piagetian perspective, cognition is the development of intelligent functioning and ultimately of logical thought. Cognitive development arises from the interaction between maturation of the central nervous system and environmental input or experience. As a result of the maturational factor, an invariant developmental sequence is thought to exist, whereas the environmental factor influences the rate at which cognition develops.

For growth to occur, a balance of equilibrium needs to be achieved between what is already known and what is new. For example, if what you read in this chapter is not at all new, you are likely to feel bored and wish you did not have to read the chapter. If, on the other hand, what you read is entirely new, you may respond by rejecting the viewpoint presented here and cling instead to your previous framework. The ideal would be for this chapter to contain a balance of old and new material that could allow you, as reader, to accept immediately what is old while thinking over what is new.

Cognitive functioning proceeds through four general periods of development, each of which comprises several substages. The earliest is the *sensorimotor period*, roughly corresponding to the infant period of birth to two years. Within the sensorimotor period, true thought or internalized representation emerges. This mental representation takes the forms of mental images, language, symbolic play, symbols, and dreams. The second period of cognitive development, termed the *preoperational period*, corresponds to the preschool age range of two to six years. During this period, the child's thought processes are perceptually bound, that is, tied to what he or she perceives. Movement into the third or *concrete operations period* of cognitive development, occurring at about six to seven years of age, signals the ability to operate on and understand the properties of objects independent of their physical appearance. Development of this ability continues throughout the elementary school years. Concurrent with entrance into adolescence, the child enters the first phase of the fourth period, the *formal operations period*. During the formal operations period, the adolescent's thinking becomes hypothetical and is no longer tied to operations that can be performed only on objects.

Infant: Sensorimotor Period

Cognitive Development within the Sensorimotor Period

Within the sensorimotor period, cognition develops through actions on the environment. These actions are organized sets of behaviors termed *schemas* and represent the infant's cognitive framework through action. Throughout the sensorimotor period, objects become incorporated in existing schemes, and schemes become increasingly differentiated as a result of adapting to the properties of objects. For example, an infant who bangs objects exhibits the schema that objects are bangable. The infant, in turn, incorporates all objects encountered into this schema by banging them. The infant subsequently discovers that objects are shakeable also. In adapting to the shakeable property of objects, the infant generates a new schema, that is, all objects are shakeable and bangable.

The sensorimotor period of development comprises six stages, each of which involves increasing adaptation to the properties of objects. These stages of development are defined as representing qualitatively different processes, although movement from one stage to the next is continuous. In stage I, *reflexive schemes* comprise the infant's exercise of innate reflex behaviors. Here reflex behaviors (e.g., sucking) are applied to a variety of objects and are modified by these experiences. Stage II, termed *primary circular reactions*, involves repetition (circular) of actions centered around the infant's own body (primary). Such behaviors as bringing thumb to mouth, looking at spectacles, and babbling are accidently encountered and then immediately repeated. By stage III, *secondary circular reactions*, the infant begins to act on objects (secondary) as well as his body, but these actions continue to be repetitious (circular). The onset of stage III is the emergence of visually directed reach—that is, intentionally reaching toward and grasping a seen object. Simple actions with objects, such as shaking and tapping, are repeated as well as motor movements that seem to cause spectacles to occur in the environment. At this stage the infant repeats accidentally encountered movements to keep interesting things happening, but does not know how to create new procedures. During stage IV, or *coordination of secondary schemata*, the infant can intentionally combine two of the behaviors engaged in during stage III in order to accomplish some goal. Although actions on objects become increasingly differentiated (e.g., pulling, pushing, stretching, crumpling), functional use of objects is not yet developed. The hallmark of stage V, *tertiary circular reactions*, is experimentation with the properties of objects independent of the infant's earlier schemes (tertiary) and by continued repetition of actions (circular) involving trial and error. Stage V is distinguished from stage VI by the infant's inability to use purely mental means to solve problems. Instead, problems are solved through hindsight—that is, by using trial and error sequences and observing their effect. Stage VI is termed *invention of new means by mental combination* and involves the beginning use of all forms of mental representation in order to solve problems.

Piagetian-Based Assessment Instruments

Sensorimotor cognitive functioning is assessed by Piagetian-based instruments in up to seven subareas of functioning: object permanence, means-end, causality, object schemes, spatial relations, verbal imitation, and motor-gestural imitation. Table 4.1 contains examples of behaviors assessed within stages II through VI for each of the seven subareas.

The *Uzgiris-Hunt Ordinal Scales of Psychological Development* (1975) contain all seven subscales but do not subdivide items into the six sensorimotor stages. The items included were derived from

TABLE 4.1 Sensorimotor Assessment Items

Subareas	Stage II	Stage III	Stage IV	Stage V	Stage VI
Object permanence	Look at point where object disappeared	Retrieve partially covered object	Find objects visibly hidden under one or more screens	Find objects invisibly hidden under one of multiple screens	Reverse sequence of hiding to find object
Means-end	Repeat accidental movements	Visually directed reach	Move barrier, pull string, crawl to obtain object, pull supports	Accidentally discover use of unattached tools	Solve problems by foresight (mental reflection)
Causality	Same as means-end	Movements as procedures	Manually activate objects	Give object for assistance, attempt to activate with demonstration	Mechanically activate objects
Spatial relations	Visually/auditorally localize objects	Look for objects dropped from view	Put objects in and take out of containers	Recognize gravity, detour around barriers	Indicate absence of familiar persons
Object schemes	Simple schemes (hit, pat)	Examine, beginning differentiation	Complex schemes (push, roll, crumple, swing, etc.) Drop, throw	Functional use singly and in combination by trial and error Point, show, name	Pretend play
Imitation	Movement/sound to familiar schemes	Imitate visible and gradually approximate invisible actions in repertoire	Gradual approximation of similar new movements	Direct imitation of new movements, movement combinations, and words	Deferred imitation–free of object, place, and person

Piaget's writings and were researched with normal infants utilizing carefully developed situations and instructions for each item. Within the test, instructions are given for each item separately, including the appropriate location for administering the item, materials to be used, directions for presenting item trials, and infant actions likely to be elicited. For example, to test "Finding an Object Which is Completely Covered," the infant is presented with a highly desired object. The object is placed in front of the infant and within reach, and is then covered with an opaque white scarf. To receive credit for understanding the continued existence of the object, the infant must remove the cover and obtain the object. Behaviors such as playing with the scarf or losing interest with the object as soon as it is covered indicate a lack of understanding that objects can continue to exist even when they are no longer in view.

Utilized primarily as a research instrument, the Corman-Escalona scales contain both object permanence and spatial relations subscales, while the Casati-Lezine scales comprise four scales (exploration of objects, visual pursuit, search for hidden objects, and combination of objects). Assessments for use with developmentally delayed infants and children have also been derived from the above assessment instruments. The sensorimotor assessment developed by Robinson (Robinson & Robinson, 1978) and used by the Infant and Deaf-Blind Program at Meyer Children's Rehabilitation Institute is based on the Uzgiris-Hunt scales and the Corman-Escalona scales, whereas Dunst (1980) provides alternative instructions and procedures for administering, scoring, and interpreting the Uzgiris-Hunt.

Interpretation of performance on the sensorimotor assessments need not be confined to reporting a global functioning level. Rather, strengths and weaknesses can be identified based on the individual profiles or patterns of subscales. In addition, the individual's approach to each item is a direct reflection of cognitive functioning level and provides a richer source of information than the "correctness" of the responses per se.

Standardized Instruments

A number of important factors must be considered prior to using standardized measures of intellectual development with infants and young children. Administration procedures for test instruments are complex and difficult to standardize with this young population. They have not learned to sit and respond to standardized situations as might be expected of school-age children. Consequently, the examiner must, as naturally as possible, enter into the infant's "nonstandardized world" and carefully observe the child's responses to various test items. These responses may require a subjective appraisal by the examiner (e.g., determining whether or not a child responds to a ringing bell).

In addition to the practical problems imposed in testing young children, intelligence in infants and toddlers is qualitatively different from cognitive abilities developed or acquired as the child matures. Early infant cognition develops primarily around the child's maturing motoric-perceptual systems; later cognition emphasized the emergence and elaboration of the verbal system. Consequently, tests given in infancy cannot be expected to be accurate predictors of later intellectual performance because they are measuring two different phenomena. In fact, studies that have tested infants and young children and correlated these results with tests given when the children were school age have consistently found poor relationships between the measures. For example, McCall, Hogarty, and Hurlburt (1972) reported that infant intelligence tests given between 1 and 6 months of age did not correlate with the test results obtained when the children were between 5 and 7 years of age ($r = .01$). Even when the initial testing is done at a later age (13–18 months) the results correlate poorly ($r = .21$) with intelligence scores obtained when the children were older (8–18 years old).

The problems of predictive validity in testing this age range are not only academic. Parents who bring their young children in for early assessments are often interested in knowing what they can expect in the future from their child, who is already exhibiting some noticeable delays. Given the predictive data available on these infant tests, the only accurate response to this important question has to be a modest "we don't know." Making such predictions is further complicated by research findings which indicate that an individual's IQ may change drastically from one testing session to another (Anastasi, 1976). Such factors as early intervention programs, recovery from illness, improved nutritional or living conditions, and others may strongly influence a child's improvement or regression in intellectual performance over time. With the multitude of issues relevant to testing infants and young children, including IQ instability, poor predictive validity, and testing difficulties, it is not surprising that relatively few standardized assessment instruments are available. In fact, many professionals are more comfortable using informal measures with this population (e.g., the *Denver Developmental Screening Test* or *Developmental Programming for Infants and Young Children*). However, if used with caution, the more formal measures can be beneficial for providing a contemporary picture of the child's developmental level.

Bayley Scales of Infant Development
The *Bayley Scales of Infant Development* (Bayley, 1969) were designed to provide a comprehensive evaluation of children's developmental status between 2 and 30 months of age. The scale includes three major

components: the Mental Scale, the Motor Scale, and the Infant
Behavior Record. The Mental Scale includes 163 items designed to
assess memory, object constancy, problem-solving ability, sensory-
perceptual activities, vocalizations, and other factors. For example, at
approximately 2½ months of age a child would receive credit for
attending briefly to a 1-inch cube placed on the table in front of her; at
4½ months of age the child would have to reach out and pick up the
cube to receive credit; and finally at around 6½ months the child
would receive credit for retaining two cubes in one hand. Clearly this
series of test items corresponds to the child's maturing visual-motor
abilities. Although not divided into subscales, many of the items are
similar to those included in Piagetian-based assessments. The Motor
Scale, comprising 81 separate test items, assesses the child's body
control and gross- and fine-motor coordination. At approximately the
level of 2–2½ months, the child receives credit for sitting with support;
and at the 7-month level, the child will receive credit for sitting alone
with good stability. In the final component of the Bayley scales, the
Infant Behavior Record, the examiner rates the child's social and
objective orientation toward the environment (e.g., cooperativeness,
responsiveness to examiner, activity level) using a scale of 1 (none) to
9 (much).

Based on the test results from the Mental and the Motor scales, the
examiner may derive a Mental Development Index (MDI) and a
Psychomotor Development Index (PDI), each with a mean of 100 and a
standard deviation of 16. The MDI score should not be interpreted as
analogous to the child's IQ. In fact, reporting age equivalency scores
for the two Bayley scales will provide a valid indicator of the child's
cognitive and motor abilities at the time without implying future
developmental expectations. Naturally these age equivalency scores
must be considered within the perspective of the child's test behavior
and general environmental orientation as measured by the Infant
Behavior Record. In terms of using the Bayley scales in clinical
practice, Bayley (1969) clearly states:

> The indexes derived from the Mental and Motor Scales have limited value
> as predictors of later abilities, since rates of development for any given
> child in the first two years of life may be highly variable over the course
> of a few months. The *primary* value of the development indexes is that
> they provide the bases for establishing a child's current status, and thus
> the extent of any deviation from normal expectancy. Also together with
> the mental and motor age equivalents, they provide a basis for instituting
> early corrective measures . . . (p. 4).

The technical quality of the Bayley scales is excellent when
compared with other scales available for infants (Anastasi, 1976).
Norms were carefully established on 1,262 children. Split-half reliability coefficients have a median value of .88 for scores on the Mental

Scale by age and of .84 for the Motor Scale; and tester-observer percent agreement averaged 89.4 percent for the Mental Scale and 93.4 percent for the Motor Scale (Werner & Bayley, 1966).

Other Formal Infant Measures
After years of studying normal development in infants and young children, Gesell and his associates developed the *Gesell Developmental Examination Schedule* (Gesell, Halverson, Thompson, Ilg, Castner, Ames, & Amatruda, 1940), which was recently updated by Knobloch and Pasamanick (1974). The schedules were developed for children between 4 weeks and 6 years of age to assist physicians in identifying neurological problems in early life to facilitate early intervention. Descriptions of a child's expected behavior at specific age intervals are provided in four general categories: motor, adaptive, personal-social, and language. Anastasi (1982) reports that examiner reliability with the Gesell scales of over .95 can be attained with adequate training.

Another rather specialized instrument for assessing the neonate's behavioral capacities was developed by Brazelton (1973). The *Brazelton Neonatal Behavioral Assessment Scale* consists of 27 items that measure, on a nine-point scale, the infant's responses to various environmental stimulation (visual and auditory). Infant response areas scored include alertness, consolability, cuddliness, activity level, motor maturity, and others. Interobserver reliability for this scale ranges from 85% to 100%. Available evidence supports the Brazelton scale's ability to differentiate high-risk and normal pregnancies. Current researchers are investigating the use of neonatal examinations as a predictor of later development.

Preschool: Preoperational Period

Cognitive Development

With entry into the preoperational period, intelligent functioning through action is replaced by internalized representation or symbolic thought. Symbolic thought takes the form of universal word usage (words or formal signs mean the same thing to the child as they do to other people), beginning classification (objects are grouped according to similar physical characteristics), graphic depiction (drawing), and symbolic play (pretend play). Although representing a qualitative change from sensorimotor functioning, the preoperational child's thinking is illogical; hence the term preoperational or prelogical.

The preoperational period is generally divided into two substages: the preconceptual substage, covering from 2 to 4 years, and the intuitive substage, extending from 4 to 6 or 7 years. Whereas

sensorimotor speech (a limited number of single words during stage V
and increased vocabulary and beginning word combinations at stage
VI) fluctuates according to the child's immediate actions, the preconceptual child gradually is able to use words to discuss the past and
future as well as the present. However, the child's reasoning is colored
or distorted to correspond to the child's desires (e.g., "I want to go
outside; therefore, it is *not* raining."). The child also believes that
things that have been observed together will always occur together
(e.g., a loud, frightening noise occurred when the child entered a
particular room; therefore, a loud noise will always occur when
entering the same room). And causal relations are misconstrued as
involving physical proximity (e.g., the child will put the toy iron on the
ironing board and expect the iron to become hot). However, with
increasing development, the child begins to abandon these more
primitive ways of thinking.

Similarly, the child's thinking is perceptually bound, that is, tied
to the physical characteristics he or she happens to notice. Symbolic
play also develops within the first substage from making toys portray
the child's own actions (making the teddy bear sleep or cry) and using
inadequate objects to represent real ones (using blocks to represent
food) to much more complex symbolic representation. By the end of
the preconceptual period, the child uses play to recreate both pleasant
and unpleasant events, to change unpleasant real occurrences into
more desired ones, to cope with fearful situations by causing others
(e.g., dolls) to experience them, and to deal with anticipated fears by
playing out their anticipated consequences. During the second or
intuitive substage, the child's play becomes orderly, following the
sequence in which events actually occur. The details of these events
more closely mirror reality; and actual roles are assigned, adopted,
and maintained.

Piagetian-Based Assessment Instruments

Instruments available for assessment of preoperational thought are
less well developed than those for either the sensorimotor or concrete
operations periods. A series of research tasks used with middle-class
and disadvantaged children are available through Educational Testing
Service (Melton, Charlesworth, Tanaka, Rothenberg, Pike, Bussis, &
Gollin, 1968). However, application of Piagetian theory to the preschool years has primarily involved curriculum development. These
include Lavatelli's (1970) *Teacher's Guide, Early Childhood Curriculum*,
which focuses more on late preoperational and beginning concrete
operations concepts; and Weikert, Rogers, Adocock, and McClelland's
(1971) *Cognitive Oriented Curriculum*. A critical review of these and
other programs can be found in Lawton and Hooper (1978).

Standardized Assessment Instruments

The majority of intelligence tests available contain subtests beginning at approximately the 2-year level and continue up through the adolescent years. The most popular tests of intelligence currently available are described below.

The Stanford-Binet Intelligence Scales (Form L-M)

The Stanford-Binet scales were originally devised in 1905 to discriminate between mentally retarded children and those with normal intelligence. A major revision of the Stanford-Binet scales occurred in 1937. At that time two equivalent forms of the scales were available, Form L and Form M. In 1960, the best items of these two forms were combined to produce one scale. Finally in 1972 the scales were standardized on a representative sample of approximately 2,100 individuals. The content of this 1972 edition was essentially unchanged from the 1960 revision of the test.

The current 1972 edition of the *Stanford-Binet Intelligence Scales* (Form L-M) encompasses items ranging in difficulty from the 2-year level through a superior-adult level III. These items are arranged at year levels based on the percentage of individuals in the standardization population passing the items at each age level. The test in general is highly verbal in nature, although items at the early age levels do assess some motor responses. Following administration of the scales, a mental age is derived from the number of subtests passed by the child at each age level and a deviation IQ (mean = 100, SD = 16) is obtained from conversion tables.

The Stanford-Binet views intelligence as reflecting acquired skills and is not specifically designed to differentiate among differing abilities that individual children exhibit. However, various methods have been developed for interpreting clusters of subtests. For example, Valett (1965) groups the subtest items into six categories, including general comprehension, visual-motor ability, arithmetic reasoning, memory concentration, vocabulary and verbal fluency, and judgment and reasoning. From a diagnostic perspective, "It is important to recognize that the categories should not be used to determine special abilities, since research has generally shown that special groupings of tests are not reliable" (Sattler, 1974, p. 134).

In her review of the 1972 restandardization sample, Waddell (1980) reported that one cannot determine the adequacy of the standardization sample used (i.e., its representativeness) from the information currently available on the Stanford-Binet. Thus caution must be taken when using the normative tables (e.g., deviation IQ) for interpretation. Further, although some construct and content validity data have been reported for the 1972 Stanford-Binet, both reliability and predictive validity data are missing.

The current limitations regarding the technical data available on the 1972 Stanford-Binet are not stated to suggest that it is a bad test nor that its use should necessarily be discouraged. In fact, the Stanford-Binet is especially useful for testing very young children (Evans & Richmond, 1976) and those functioning within the lower mental age range. However, in the absence of sound technical data, greater caution must be exercised by examiners in their interpretation of the test results.

McCarthy Scales of Children's Abilities

The *McCarthy Scales of Children's Abilities* (MSCA) is an instrument used with children between 2½ and 8½ years of age and, as such, covers concepts at the preoperational and beginning concrete operations levels (McCarthy, 1972). The purpose of this instrument is to provide a measure of general intellectual levels as well as strengths and weaknesses in important abilities for young children. The MSCA consists of 18 separate tests which are grouped into six scales. The first three of these scales are mutually exclusive in that they do not share any common tests. These include the Verbal Scale (V), the Perceptual-Performance Scale (P) and the Quantitative Scale (Q). The V Scale assesses level of verbal concept maturity and verbal expression (e.g., Word Knowledge); the P scale includes performance subtests that measure the child's reasoning and ability to manipulate the test materials (Block Building, Draw-A-Design), and the Q Scale measures number concepts (e.g., Counting and Sorting). The fourth scale, the Memory Scale (Mem), utilizes both verbal and nonverbal responses to assess the child's short-term memory and overlaps with the three previously described scales. The fifth scale, the Motor Scale (Mot), which assesses the child's coordination in the fine- and gross-motor areas, contains three noncognitive tests (e.g., Leg/Arm Coordination) as well as two Mot Scale subtests that overlap with the P Scale subtests (e.g., Draw-A-Design). The sixth and final scale is called the General Cognitive Scale (GC) and is composed of all the V, P, and Q scale tests. This scale provides an overall picture of the child's cognitive functioning.

The GC Scale when scored yields a general Cognitive Index (GCI) with a mean of 100 and an SD of 16. McCarthy (1972) favors the term GCI over IQ because of the "many misinterpretations of that concept [IQ] and the unfortunate connotations that have become associated with it" (p. 5). The GCI is best understood within the context of the child's performance on the five scales that comprise it. The scores on these five scales are converted for interpretation purposes to standard scores with a mean of 50 and SD of 10.

Both standardization and reliability data for the MSCA are excellent. The standardization sample for the MSCA included 1,032 children representative of the U.S. population of children between 2½ and 8½ years of age (using 1970 U.S. Census data).

Split-half reliability data obtained for the MSCA ranged by age level from .90 to .96 for the GCI and averaged between .79 to .88 for the other five scales; test-retest reliability coefficients averaged .90 for the GCI.

Validity data for the MSCA are currently limited. Correlations of .71 between the GCI and WPPSI full scale IQ, and .81 between the GCI and Stanford-Binet IQ have been obtained on a sample of 35 first-grade children. Other concurrent validity studies reviewed by Waddell (1980) led her to conclude that the MSCA correlates better with the Stanford-Binet at lower levels of intellectual functioning than at average levels. One of the strengths of the McCarthy is its interest and appeal for young children due to the alternation of verbal, fine-motor, and gross-motor items. For individuals planning to administer and interpret this relatively complex instrument, Kaufman and Kaufman (1977) have provided a useful resource.

Other Multiple Ability Tests

The *Wechsler Preschool and Primary Scale of Intelligence* is a downward extension of the *Wechsler Intelligence Scale for Children* and as such generates a profile of abilities within both the verbal and performance areas. This test will be discussed in detail in a later section along with its sister tests, the *Wechsler Scale for Children—Revised* and the *Wechsler Adult Intelligence Scale—Revised*.

The *Hiskey-Nebraska Test of Learning Aptitude* provides separate norms in the form of learning ages and learning quotients for deaf and hearing-impaired children. Similarly, instructions can be presented in pantomime or verbally. Unfortunately, no other multiple ability tests are available for young handicapped children. Although test authors may recommend that individual subtests from other tests be administered as appropriate, there is no evidence that items developed for normal children are equivalent when administered to special populations.

Performance Tests

Although nonverbal tests all share the characteristics of being performance tests, they by no means tap the same abilities. For example, the *Merrill-Palmer Test* is primarily a perceptual motor test rather than a concept test. The *Leiter International Performance Test* includes a variety of concepts such as matching simple colors and shapes, social concepts, and matching by one or more stimulus attributes. The major advantages of the Leiter are its appeal to young children and its adaptability to various special populations including the deaf, the language delayed or disordered, and the physically handicapped; a disadvantage has been the inadequate research on the instrument. The Leiter is also based on the assumption that ability to learn within the testing situation is a measure of intelligence. However, no evidence exists concerning the extent to which allowing multiple trials actually affects obtained performance levels.

The *Columbia Mental Maturity Scale* (CMMS), designed as a screening test for use with physically handicapped children, can be used at 4 years of age. The CMMS includes 92 large cards, each with a series of three to five drawings on the card (e.g., one large drawing in an array of four smaller drawings). The CMMS yields a standard score with a mean of 100 and an SD of 16.

The *Slosson Intelligence Test* (SIT) was devised to measure intellectual functioning in young children and adults (Slosson, 1963). It is used extensively by teachers to estimate the cognitive level of students. The test was recently renormed and deviation IQs were established (Slosson, 1981). The manual indicates a high correlation ($r = .979$) between mental ages for the 1972 Stanford-Binet Intelligence Scale and the Slosson. The average difference between IQs generated by the Stanford-Binet and the Slosson has been reduced from 4.09 IQ points to four hundredths (.04) of an IQ point. Research indicated that teachers can reliably administer this brief test (Rotatori & Epstein, 1978; Rotatori, Sedlak, & Freagon, 1979).

Vocabulary Tests

The use of vocabulary tests to determine intelligence levels is based on their high correlation with scores on intelligence tests. As tests of receptive vocabulary, requiring only pointing to the picture of the named word, these can be used with both normal and physically handicapped children. For example, the *Peabody Picture Vocabulary Test—Revised* (Dunn & Dunn, 1981) is an adequate standardized screening test that requires the child to point to the correct picture among an array of four pictures. Mental age equivalents are based on the number of pictures correctly identified, and the corresponding intelligence quotient is obtained from the conversion table. As with most standardized tests usable with preschool children, the PPVT–R actually extends throughout the school age years. The PPVT–R has adequate reliability for screening purposes.

CASE STUDY

Part II

Present Assessment Instruments

Stanford-Binet Intelligence Scale, Form L-M
Peabody Picture Vocabulary Test—Revised (PPVT–R)
Beery Development Test of Visual Motor Integration

Test Behavior

During the first 30–40 minutes of the 1-hour testing session, Jill remained in her seat and maintained a good level of concentration. After that time she became easily distracted and more difficult to keep in her seat. It was hard to tell whether this off-task behavior was the result of the task difficulty or simply the length of time she had already been consistently working, and was most likely a combination of the two factors. However, it is felt that Jill's current test performance reflects a valid measure of her present level of intellectual functioning. Throughout the testing session Jill's speech was very difficult to understand. She also appeared to watch closely the examiner for additional cues to verbal instructions (e.g., gestures).

Test Findings

On the Stanford-Binet, Jill obtained a basal score at the 3-year, 6-month level and a ceiling score of 5 years. She passed five of the six subtests at the 4-year level, failing only the Comprehension II subtest (i.e., "Why do we have houses?"), and passed two subtests at the 4-year, 6-month level. On the Stanford-Binet, Jill obtained a mental age score of 4 years, 1 month and a corresponding intelligence quotient of 96 ± 5. On the PPVT–R, Jill obtained a raw score of 15 and an age equivalent score of 2 years, 6 months.

On the Beery test, Jill obtained a visual-motor age equivalent score of 4 years, 0 months.

Interpretation

Overall, Jill's performance on the Stanford-Binet indicates functioning in the normal range of general intellectual functioning. Jill's test behavior was good. She responded very well to social praise and pats on the back. Although no obvious strengths or weaknesses emerged from this test, Jill did appear to have more difficulty with items that included only verbal instructions. Also, on several subtests requiring a verbal response from Jill, the examiner frequently needed to repeat the item to ensure accurate understanding of Jill's speech. Jill occasionally used gestures to aid her communication. Jill's performance on the PPVT–R was lower than expected, given her performance on the Stanford-Binet. Her PPVT–R score, which assesses only receptive vocabulary, may be consistent with the teacher's concern about her having difficulty following instructions.

Jill's 4-year level performance on the Beery test indicates that her visual-motor skills are commensurate with her age and probably represent a relative strength area for her. It is difficult given the limits of this present assessment to determine whether Jill's expressive speech problems (particularly articulation) are related to her difficulty in comprehending the speech of others (e.g., a processing problem) and/or to other factors (e.g., a hearing problem).

Recommendations

It is recommended that Jill be evaluated by an audiologist to rule out the possibility of hearing problems. If Jill is found to have hearing in the normal range, it is further recommended that she be seen by a speech/language therapist who can specifically address the basis of her communication difficulties.

Follow-up

Jill was evaluated on two separate occasions by an audiologist. The audiologist found a high-frequency hearing loss in both ears, which he felt had significantly impeded Jill's understanding of others' speech. An independent audiological evaluation requested by the parents by a second agency confirmed these findings. Jill was subsequently fitted with a hearing aid for one ear, with a second hearing aid scheduled for fitting after an initial adjustment period. The prognosis for Jill's future receptive and expressive speech development, given her normal intellectual functioning and the continuous wearing of the hearing aids, was for normal communication development.

School Age: Concrete and Formal Operations Periods

Cognitive Development

The concrete operations period, covering approximately 6 to 11 years of age, involves logical reasoning applied to the concrete attributes of materials as opposed to reliance on perceptual features. Development within this period is understood most easily in relation to the concepts often assessed (e.g., classification, conservation, seriation, and spatial relations). Classification abilities are reported by Lowery (1974) to emerge in the following order: sorting by multiple attributes (6–8 years), understanding that objects can belong to more than one class simultaneously (8–10 years), and class inclusion or recognition that a whole equals the sum of its parts (10–12 years).

Conservation concepts involve understanding that the quantity of a substance remains constant regardless of its physical appearance. At the onset of the concrete operations period, the child knows that the number of objects remains constant regardless of perceptual configuration only by recounting the objects. As development progresses, the child knows without counting that the number remains the same. This understanding of one-to-one correspondence is considered the necessary condition for learning beginning math. Next, the concrete operations child realizes that the amount of a substance remains constant regardless of its appearance. This understanding is rapidly generalized from liquids to solids to weight.

Seriating objects can be accomplished without trial and error using more than one attribute simultaneously with a large number of objects (e.g., ten). Furthermore, when a sequence of objects is reversed, the child can imagine what the new or reversed order will be. A later development in spatial relations involves the ability to mentally determine the placement of objects moved in space.

The formal operations period, beginning in adolescence and continuing into adulthood, is the last, as well as the least developed, of the cognitive periods formulated by Piaget. During the first substage, spanning from about 11 to 15 years of age, the adolescent begins to develop the ability to think hypothetically. With attainment of formal thought, an individual can consider what might be possible as opposed to what actually is, can generate hypotheses or hypothetical questions, and can solve problems without actually observing effects of solutions. The latter is accomplished by systematically imagining all the combinations possible (combinatorial logic).

In considering the probable existence of additional substages within the formal operations period, Stephens, Smith, Fitzgerald, Grube, Hitt, and Daly (1977) observed:

> To date no one has determined whether substages exist at the formal level just as they do at the sensori-motor and pre-operational levels. Yet it seems rather obvious that they must. Einstein probably functioned at a few substages above the general population. Not only did he operate on operations, he went beyond that to abstract from the abstract. When Inhelder, Piaget's collaborator, was asked why the Geneva group had not explored upper levels of formal thought . . . she replied, "Have you ever tried to devise an assessment that would measure the higher levels of Einstein's thought, and if you did where would you find someone to check on the accuracy of his answers?" (p. 57)

Piagetian-Based Assessment Instruments

Instruments currently used to assess concrete and formal operations thought are derived from measures developed by Piaget and his colleagues. As compared to most standardized tests, which request and score right or wrong answers, these Piagetian tasks employ a clinical method. This method involves specific procedures to investigate the child's thought processes relative to each task and to determine the extent to which the child will maintain his or her original answer given alternate suggestions by the examiner. As a result, it is possible to score each child's response along a continuum from concept absent (illogical response) to concept achieved (logical response).

Batteries of assessments have been developed by Pinard and Laurendeau (1964) and translated from Genevan measures by Stephens (1972). Stephens' Piagetian reasoning assessments have been used with normal, retarded, and visually handicapped children. Testing with this instrument begins with establishing that the child understands the terms "same" versus "different" and "more" versus "less." Testing then proceeds in three areas: classification, conservation, and spatial relations/mental imagery.

Example subtests for assessing conservation include term-to-term correspondence (recognizing that two sets of poker chips and checkers contain the same number of objects regardless of how they are arranged on the table), conservation of substance (knowing that two identical balls of clay contain the same amount regardless of how they are shaped—that is, as a hot dog, a pancake, or several small pieces), and conservation of volume (acknowledging that regardless of how they are shaped these balls of clay will displace the same amount of water in a glass). Mental imagery of spatial relations is assessed by rotation of beads (turning a sequence of three different beads in various directions and predicting the resultant order) and rotation of a square (predicting the position of a square on a board from the end point of one corner of the square).

Individual tasks that reflect various concepts at the concrete operations level are also included in numerous tests summarizing Piaget's theory of cognitive development, such as Phillips' (1969) *The Origins of Intellect* and Wadsworth's (1978) *Piaget for the Classroom Teacher*.

Standardized Assessment Instruments

Standardized assessment of infants and preschoolers generally is undertaken only in special instances. However, virtually all children are tested before or soon after entrance into formal school programs, and children with learning problems or other handicapping conditions may be tested periodically thereafter. Given this widespread usage, what information can we expect to obtain from a standardized assessment of intellectual functioning? The answer to this question depends on several factors, including the level of training, experience, and sophistication of the examiner and the ultimate users of the testing information (e.g., school administrator, judge). One might expect the minimally trained and unsophisticated users of test data to perceive the IQ score as the paramount piece of information obtained from the testing situation. We have seen the dangers of maintaining this limited perspective in terms of the potential it poses for misuse of testing information. In fact, this continuing presence of abuse of test data has led some test developers to abandon the use of the IQ score (for example, McCarthy's GCI).

The standardized testing situation provides an excellent opportunity to study a child's behavior when confronted with a difficult and potentially frustrating situation. As Anastasi (1976) points out, standardized tests allow the examiner to observe how a child approaches problems, works through them, and deals with frustration. Other child characteristics such as activity level, response to task-oriented social praise, and ability to concentrate and stay with a task may be assessed by a skilled examiner. In fact, in the authors' experience with young children, these observations of qualitative aspects of performance may yield the most important data from the assessment session. In several cases we have seen, our manner of test administration (which was forced to become nonstandardized by the child's test behavior) or the child's minimal responses to test items led to our reports emphasizing clinical aspects of the child's test behavior in preference to actual performance on the particular test instrument.

Combined with a clear conceptualization of the child's test behavior should be a logical integration of the child's test performance within and between tests administered. Sound interpretation of most standardized assessment instruments requires a firm foundation in psychological and measurement theory. The goal of a good standardized assessment would include: (1) a clear picture of the child's test behavior; (2) estimates of the child's strengths and weaknesses in particular abilities, described within the context of the individual's global capacity; and (3) a data-based interpretation of the child's test performance (see Kaufman, 1979). This last component should be holistic in nature and bring together relevant data necessary to provide a comprehensive and useful picture of the child's present status. Obviously, additional information gathered by the examiner such as personality or achievement measures, ancillary information (e.g., medical records), and classroom observational data would be appropriately interpreted here. The final outcome of the testing situation should be (4) logical suggestions or recommendations for facilitating children's success in their environments. In the final analysis, the ultimate test for determining the success of a standardized assessment would be its degree of usefulness for those working with the children in the natural environment.

The standardized test most commonly used with school-age children is the *Wechsler Intelligence Scale for Children* (WISC). Because the *Wechsler Preschool and Primary Scale of Intelligence* (WPPSI), the WISC, and the *Wechsler Adult Intelligence Scale* (WAIS) reflect the same theoretical viewpoint and are constructed similarly, they are discussed jointly.

The three tests of intellectual functioning developed by David Wechsler are designed around his concept of intelligence, which he described as " . . . multifaceted as well as multidetermined. What it [intelligence] calls for is not a particular ability but an overall competency or global capacity, which in one way or another enables a sentient individual to comprehend the world and to deal effectively with its challenges'' (Wechsler, 1981, p. 8).

The *Wechsler Preschool and Primary Scale of Intelligence* (WPPSI) (Wechsler, 1967) was tailored to meet the needs of 4- to 6½-year-old children; the *Wechsler Intelligence Scale for Children—Revised* (WISC–R) (Wechsler, 1974) of 6- to 16-year, 11-month-old children; and the *Wechsler Adult Intelligence Scale—Revised* (WAIS–R) (Wechsler, 1981) of 16- to 74-year-old individuals. All three Wechsler scales are divided into verbal and performance scales comprising 11 subtests. Some verbal subtests are Comprehension, Arithmetic, and Vocabulary; performance subtests include Block Design, Object Assembly, and others. All Wechsler scales are individually administered by an experienced examiner and usually require between 50 and 90 minutes to complete. From the Wechsler scales one can determine a Verbal Scale IQ, a Performance Scale IQ, and a combined or Full Scale IQ (all means = 100; SD = 15).

The actual administration and scoring of the Wechsler scales can be efficiently accomplished by a well-trained examiner. However, interpretation of the results is a complex task and requires further training and experience. The various IQs obtained on the scale are useful only within the context of a careful analysis of the person's subtest performance (or in some cases, specific subtest item analysis) and general test behavior. The outcome of interpretation should be a careful and integrated delineation of the individual's unique assets and weaknesses (based on current research findings) as well as logical recommendations that facilitate the person's success in dealing with the environment. Kaufman (1979) has provided an excellent resource for interpreting the WISC–R. Other sources are available for interpreting the WPPSI (Sattler, 1974) and the original WAIS (Zimmerman & Woo-Sam, 1973).

The Wechsler scales are popular instruments in the testing field. Their standardization samples have been carefully selected, and the reliability data is good. A review of the instruments (Anastasi, 1982) suggests that more empirical data regarding the validity of the instruments are needed. A strength of these instruments is their multifaceted design, which allows a clear delineation of an individual's unique strengths and limitations. Ultimately their value must be assessed in terms of the contribution they make toward our understanding of persons we choose to assess.

Future of Testing

What should we expect in the future from the intelligence testing field? Obviously, in the near future, the IQ score will continue to be used to make special education placement decisions for children. This practice is likely to continue even in the face of mitigating evidence that such special class placement may not be in the best interests of the individual child.

However, over time, the focus of intelligence tests is likely to shift from the present concentration on global abilities to one of measuring multiple aspects of intelligence. Turnbull (1979) states, "The multiple-test scores will be used for short-term predictions and decisions, related especially to schooling, and the idea of making 'life' predictions or sorting children according to long-term tracks will fade" (p. 237). However, before we can move beyond the most current useful function of intelligence tests, that is, predicting academic success or failure (Brown & French, 1979), we must first more fully understand the phenomenon of intelligence itself. For example, what underlying cognitive processes (e.g., perception, thinking, learning) are common to intelligence tests and school performance? How should we assess individuals' differences in these specific cognitive processes or learning styles? These questions and related issues must be addressed before we can move the field of intelligence testing from a science of *prediction* to a science of *prescription*.

This is not to say that current efforts designed to match learner characteristics with specific instructional efforts (Cronbach & Snow, 1977) to enable a more prescriptive approach should be discouraged. Realistically, the day when our educational programs and related intervention efforts are ideally tailored to meet each child's unique array of characteristics and abilities in order to foster maximal individual growth is many years away. However, if users of testing information can be made acutely cognizant of the limitations and strengths of our present testing efforts, and if our examiners will make full use of the clinical data present in the testing situation as well as the empirical data available in the expanding research literature, the individual child can be expected to benefit from these combined efforts.

Summary

Assessment of cognition and intelligence historically and presently plays a major role within our educational system. Almost from its inception, testing in this area has been fraught with controversies regarding the meanings, implications, and ultimate use of our intelligence test findings. In this chapter we have attempted to distinguish between definitions of cognition and intelligence. The former area, cognition, demands attending to a developmental phenomena of extremely complex proportions. Our study of this area continues to remain largely at the basic research level. We are only beginning to ask the question, "What are the educational implications of this body of knowledge?" Assessment measures designed to tap the cognitive processes are still in their infancy.

The latter area, intelligence, has received a disproportionate share of attention from educators relative to the study of cognition. This current situation is understandable given how closely our definitions of intelligence are aligned with the tests used to measure it. The often heard phrase, "Intelligence is what intelligence tests measure," although inaccurate, does describe the usual status that intelligence is relegated to in education.

Within this chapter, we have attempted to sample the array of formal and informal measures currently available to assess cognitive and intellectual functioning. Despite the many instruments available, concerns continue to exist regarding our limited ability to derive intervention strategies from assessment findings.

This contemporary atmosphere of discontent is a healthy one. Researchers, psychologists, teachers, and administrators should never feel satisfied with current methods of assessing cognitive and intellectual performance. Working toward developing better linkages between our assessment findings and what happens to a given child in the classroom should continue to be a common goal for all individuals interested in education.

Educational Suggestions for the Assessment of Cognition and Intelligence

The assessment of cognition and intelligence of students has become quite a controversial issue in the past 15 years. The issues raised against the use of such testing with regular and special education students is at times based upon misconceptions and a lack of understanding of the process. The following suggestions should make teachers more cognizant of the nature of intelligence testing and more knowledgeable about the results (Sattler, 1974).

The stability of students' assessed IQs is affected by errors of measurement, environmental influences, and inherited developmental trends.

Teachers should understand that intelligence tests differ from achievement tests in the measurement of learning in that intelligence tests assess learning that results from a greater variety of settings and experiences.

Teachers must recognize that intelligence tests do not measure innate intelligence and that IQs are only estimates of ability.

Teachers should understand that IQs from different tests may not be interchangeable.

Teachers must recognize that IQ tests measure a restricted small sample of behaviors and, as such, cannot inform teachers about everything that needs to be known about a student.

Teachers should be aware that IQs of children change due to developmental and environmental factors, especially from birth through 6 years of age.

Teachers must be aware that there is no procedure to separate the influence of environmental and genetic factors on the IQ test.

Study Questions

1. Distinguish between cognition and intelligence in terms of definition and implications for educational assessment and intervention.
2. Why have intelligence tests created so much controversy in the field of education?
3. Describe the cognitions expected for normal development within each stage of cognitive growth.
4. Summarize the available informal and formal instruments used to assess infants and toddlers. What are their uses and limitations?
5. Compare the Stanford-Binet and the McCarthy scales, especially in terms of their relative value to the classroom teacher.
6. In what cases will performance tests be preferred over the more verbally loaded tests of intelligence?
7. What are the advantages and disadvantages of standardized measures over informal measures? Do they each have unique users? If so, what are they?
8. Provide a futuristic perspective on what IQ testing might look like 20 years from now.

Suggested Readings

Anastasi, A. (1982). *Psychological testing* (5th ed.) New York: Macmillan.

Kaufman, A. S. (1979). *Intelligence testing with the WISC–R*. New York: John Wiley & Sons.

Sattler, J. M. (1982). *Assessment of children's intelligence and special abilities* (2nd ed.). Boston: Allyn and Bacon.

References

Anastasi, A. (1982). *Psychological testing* (5th ed.). New York: Macmillan.

Bayley, N. (1969). *Bayley scales of infant development manual*. New York: The Psychological Corporation.

Brazelton, T. B. (1973). *Neonatal behavioral assessment scale*. (Clinics in Developmental Medicine, No. 50.) Philadelphia: Lippincott.

Brown, A. L., & French, L. A. (1979). The zone of potential development: Implications for intelligence testing in the year 2000. In R. J. Sternberg & D. K. Detterman (Eds.), *Human intelligence: Perspectives on its theory and measurement*. Norwood, NJ: Ablex Publishing.

Cronbach, L. J., & Snow, R. E. (1977). *Aptitudes and instructional methods: A handbook for research on interactions*. New York: Irvington.

Dunn, L. M., & Dunn, L. M. (1981). *Peabody Picture Vocabulary Test—Revised*. Circle Pines, MN: American Guidance Service.

Dunst, C. J. (1980). *A clinical and educational manual for use with the Uzgiris and Hunt scales of infant psychological development*. Austin, TX: PRO-ED.

Evans, P. L., & Richmond, B. O. (1976). A practitioner's comparison: The 1972 Stanford Binet and the WISC–R. *Psychology in the Schools, 13*, 9–14.

Gesell, A., Halverson, H. M., Thompson, H., Ilg, F. L., Castner, B. M., Ames, L. B., & Amatruda, C. S. (1940). *The first five years of life*. New York: Harper & Brothers.

Junkala, J. (1977). Teachers' assessments and team decisions. *Exceptional Children, 44*, 31–32.

Kaufman, A. S. (1979). *Intelligent testing with the WISC–R*. New York: John Wiley & Sons.

Kaufman, A. S., & Kaufman, N. L. (1977). *Clinical evaluation of young children with the McCarthy Scales*. New York: Grune & Stratton.

Knobloch, H., & Pasamanick, B. (Eds.). (1974). *Gesell and Amatruda's developmental diagnosis: The evaluation and management of normal and abnormal neuropsychologic development in infancy and early childhood* (3rd ed.). Hagerstown, MD: Harper & Row.

Lavatelli, C. S. (1970). *Teacher's guide, early childhood curriculum*. Boston: American Science and Engineering, Inc.

Lawton, J. T., & Hooper, F. H. (1978). Piagetian theory and early childhood education: A critical analysis. In L. S. Siegel & C. J. Brainerd (Eds.), *Alternatives to Piaget: Critical essays on the theory*. New York: Academic Press.

Lowery, L. F. (1974). *Learning about learning: Classification abilities*. Berkeley: University of California.

McCall, R. B., Hogarty, P. S., & Hurlburt, N. (1972). Transitions in infant sensorimotor development and the production of childhood IQ. *American Psychologist, 27*, 728–748.

McCarthy, D. (1972). *Manual for the McCarthy scales of children's abilities*. New York: Psychological Corporation.

Melton, R. S., Charlesworth, R., Tanaka, M. N., Rothenberg, B. B., Pike, L. W., Bussis, A. M., & Gollin, E. S. (1968). *Cognitive growth in preschool children*. Princeton, NJ: Educational Testing Service.

Phillips, J. L. (1969). *The origins of the intellect*. San Francisco: W. H. Freeman.

Pinard, A., & Laurendeau, M. (1964). A scale of mental development based on the theory of Piaget. *Journal of Research in Science Teaching, 2*, 253–260.

Robinson, C. C., & Robinson, J. H. (1978). Sensorimotor functions and cognitive development. In M. E. Snell (Ed.), *Systematic instruction of the severely handicapped*. Columbus, OH: Charles E. Merrill.

Rotatori, A. F., & Epstein, M. (1978). The Slosson intelligence test as a quick screening test of mental ability with profoundly and severely retarded children. *Psychological Reports, 42*, 1117–1118.

Rotatori, A. F., Sedlak, B., & Freagon, S. (1979). Usability of the Slosson intelligence test with severely and profoundly retarded children. *Perceptual and Motor Skills, 48*, 334.

Sattler, J. M. (1974). *Assessment of children's intelligence*. Philadelphia: W. B. Saunders.

Slosson, R. L. (1963). *Slosson Intelligence Test (SIT) for Children and Adults*. East Aurora, NY: Slosson Educational Publications.

Slosson, R. L. (1981). *Slosson Intelligence Test (SIT) for Children and Adults* (2nd ed.). East Aurora, NY: Slosson Educational Publications.

Stephens, B., Smith, R. E., Fitzgerald, J. R., Grube, C., Hitt, J., & Daly, M. (1977). *Training manual for teachers of the visually handicapped: A Piagetian perspective*. Richardson, TX: University of Texas at Dallas.

Stephens, W. B. (1972). The development of reasoning, moral judgement and moral conduct in retardates and normals. Phase II (Final Report Project #15-P-5512/3-02). Philadelphia: Temple University.

Turnbull, W. W. (1979). Intelligence testing in the year 2000. In R. J. Sternberg, & D. K. Detterman (Eds.), *Human intelligence: Perspectives on its theory and measurement*. Norwood, NJ: Ablex Publishing.

Uzgiris, I. C., & Hunt, J. M. (1975). *Assessment in infancy: Ordinal scales of psychological development*. Urbana, IL: University of Illinois Press.

Valett, R. E. (1965). *A profile for the Stanford-Binet (L-M)*. Palo Alto, CA: Consulting Psychologists Press.

Waddell, D. O. (1980). The Stanford-Binet: An evaluation of the technical data available since the 1972 restandardization. *Journal of School Psychology, 18*, 203–209.

Wadsworth, B. J. (1978). *Piaget for the classroom teacher*. New York: Longman.

Wechsler, D. (1974). *Manual for the Wechsler intelligence scale for children—revised*. New York: Psychological Corporation.

Wechsler, D. (1981). *Manual for the Wechsler adult intelligence scale—revised*. New York: Psychological Corporation.

Weikert, D. P., Rogers, L., Adocock, C., & McClelland, D. (1971). *The cognitive oriented curriculum*. Washington, DC: Publications Department, National Association for the Education of Young Children.

Werner, E. E., & Bayley, N. (1966). The reliability of Bayley's revised scale of mental and motor development during the first year of life. *Child Development, 37*, 39–50.

Zimmerman, I. L., & Woo-Sam, J. M. (1973). *Clinical interpretation of the Wechsler adult intelligence scale*. New York: Grune & Stratton.

5

Assessment of Reading Skills

John Wills Lloyd
Norma A. Cameron
Patricia A. Lloyd

OBJECTIVES

After completing this chapter the teacher should be able to:

1. Describe skill problems related to poor reading performance.
2. State and explain the purposes of reading assessment.
3. Compare and contrast screening, diagnostic, and progress monitoring assessments.
4. Describe several achievement tests, diagnostic tests, and progress monitoring systems.
5. Describe appropriate assessment strategies for specific problems in decoding and comprehension.
6. Discuss the use of reading achievement tests to measure reading progress.
7. Develop several informal reading assessments, including teacher-constructed informal reading inventories; graded word lists; and progress monitoring systems.
8. Discuss instructional implications of reading assessment.

Acquisition of reading skills is an important aspect of schooling in the United States. Ask any group of preschool children why they will be going to school, and they are likely to answer that they are going so that they can learn to read. Ask secondary school teachers whether learning to read is important in later academic areas, such as social studies, and they are likely to answer that reading skills are *essential*. In fact, despite arguments that rapid development of other communication media such as audiotape recordings may lead to a "bookless curriculum" there is little reason to believe that teachers will not continue to teach and require reading skills in the foreseeable future.

Additionally, reading skills are important in other areas of school performance and even outside the school setting. For example, most students who are identified as having behavior problems are likely to have deficits in reading achievement (Cullinan, Epstein, & Lloyd, 1983). Inadequate reading has also been implicated in social, economic, and political problems. For example, reading problems are uncommonly frequent in school histories of delinquents and law-breaking adults (Robins, 1979).

Because the acquisition of reading skills is important, it is clear that successful reading instruction must be provided. This is particularly true for students identified as atypical learners who (regardless of their categorical labels) are not likely to learn reading skills without special instruction. Providing reading instruction for exceptional learners involves many actions (e.g., planning carefully and using effective methods), not the least of which is assessing reading performance. Without adequate assessment, it is not possible to know which students require special reading instruction, in what specific area students need instruction, and whether the instruction provided is working.

The purposes of assessing reading are discussed and methods and tests for attaining these purposes are described in this chapter. Before presenting this information, however, it is necessary to discuss the task of reading in order to have a general background of information that will allow judgments about the appropriateness of assessment procedures.

The Task of Reading

Reading is one of the most sophisticated of human behaviors. Readers take in information presented in a code by using their visual systems, perform some transformations of that information so that it is recoded into information that is understandable on the basis of previous learning, and then may alter their behavior or opinions on the basis of what they have read. To illustrate, people who look at an odd set of squiggles such as STOP first perceive the information with their visual systems. They perform some operations on the odd set of squiggles and transform it into something meaningful. As a result of this transformation, they may cease whatever they were doing when they encountered the squiggles.

Viewed in this simplistic light, reading does not seem so sophisticated. However, its complexity becomes more obvious under closer scrutiny. Some factors that illustrate the sophistication of reading are (1) the amount of time that elapses after taking in the visual information and before moving to the next word is incredibly brief (only a fraction of a second); (2) people's actions may or may not change as a result of reading, depending on the situation in which the squiggles are encountered (e.g., one does not actually stop when one encounters the word *stop* in this sentence: "The robbers' car did not stop for red lights"); (3) printed information contains many highly confusing parts (e.g., *b*, *d*, *p*, and *q*; *left* and *loft*); and (4) unfamiliarity with the language in which the squiggles are printed may render the information meaningless (e.g., we would hardly expect our first visitors from another planet to halt their spaceship at a red, octagonal sign with the squiggles STOP on it).

Reading Difficulties

Children who have had difficulty learning reading skills have frequently been studied to assess where their difficulties lie. Many studies have indicated that poor readers make more errors on vowels in words, omit sounds from words, substitute words, and so forth (e.g., Sheperd, 1967). Results such as these provide valuable information about reading performance. Other studies describe difficulties with the task. For example, several researchers have reported that poor readers have unusual difficulty in handling automatic or rote aspects of language (Kass, 1966; Sheperd, 1967). That is, students with reading problems are not facile with some of the skills that are required by reading. They do not blend orally presented sounds into words, do not accurately recall series of items, and do not fill in missing words for sentences that they have heard as well as normal readers do.

Some of these skill problems are closely related to reading performance. For example, skills in taking words heard at a normal speech rate and segmenting them into their parts distinguishes between good and poor readers (Wallach, Wallach, Dozier, & Kaplan, 1977). When shown pictures depicting familiar things (e.g., a picture of a rake and a picture of a lake), students have no difficulty with the instruction "Point to the rake." However, some students—those likely to have difficulty in learning to read—have great difficulty in pointing to the picture for a word that begins with the sound "rrr," even when they can reliably name the objects in the pictures and the choices are as different as *rake* and *pot*. Skill in taking words apart, or phonemic segmentation, is important for understanding the alphabetic nature of English.

The opposite task—taking parts of words and blending them into wholes—has also been implicated in reading failure. A widely known test, the *Roswell-Chall Auditory Blending Test* (1963), assesses blending skills and has been repeatedly shown to be a good predictor of reading success. Students who are not skilled in taking the orally presented sounds *sss—aaa—t* and responding "sat," are less likely to learn beginning reading skills well.

Previously, it was often assumed that one of the essential skills in reading was visual discrimination of letters. Because many of the symbols encountered in reading (e.g., *b,d*; *saw, was*) are visually confusing to students who have difficulty with decoding, it was widely assumed that a prerequisite skill for reading was the ability to make these discriminations in isolation. However, more recently, it has been convincingly argued that problems with such easily confused symbols are not a product of simple visual discrimination but rather a problem in establishing *verbal labels* for the symbols (Calfee, 1977). This is illustrated in the following example. One of the ways that visual acuity is tested is to show students the letter *E* printed in different rotations (E, Ǝ , ᗰ , Ш) and ask them to point in the direction that the letter is pointing. Even students with reading problems do not have any difficulty with this task. Their difficulties arise when they have to attach a label (e.g., the sound "buh" for *b*) to the symbol. Other evidence (e.g., Gibson & Levin, 1975) also indicates that it is easier for children to make discriminations between graphemes (letters) than between phonemes (sounds).

In the preceding paragraphs the difficulties encountered by students who are poor readers have included the problems involved in converting printed material into oral language representations. Of course, not all of the problems students encounter have to do with the decoding aspect of reading. Some students manifest difficulties in understanding what they have read—comprehension. Interestingly, many poor comprehenders differ from good comprehenders in decoding skills (Kavale, 1980). While normal readers apparently overcome problems in comprehension associated with word-reading and vocabulary deficits, poor readers are adversely affected by them and, consequently, employ unsuccessful reasoning strategies to comprehend what was read (Kavale, 1980). Additionally, when students who would be expected to have reading difficulties have been taught efficient decoding skills and strategies for logical analysis, then impoverished vocabulary appears to be the major factor inhibiting their adequate comprehension of written material (Becker, 1977).

Taken together, these factors illustrate the breadth of difficulties that students encounter in learning to read. Furthermore, they indicate that reading assessment must address these areas if students with reading difficulties are to be identified and their difficulties are to be diagnosed and remediated.

Assessment Implications

Information gained from analyses of the task of reading and the study of difficulties in reading provides direction about reading skills assessment. Calfee (1977) and Calfee, Fisk, and Piontkowski (1975) described a methodology for constructing "clean" tests of reading skills: "A clean test is constructed so as to measure a selected skill as precisely as possible. The task demands are kept minimal, and the context and materials are chosen such that children should make very few errors" (Calfee et al., 1975, p. 141). When clean tests have been constructed, factors that might influence performance can be systematically introduced. When students' performance changes after a new factor has been introduced, one can be fairly certain that the newly introduced factor is responsible for the decrement in performance. For example, if students perform inaccurately on a word matching task when told to mark any alternative that looks exactly like a standard, they may fail items because they have not understood the instructions or because they do not have the skill. If we wish to know whether they have actual skill deficits, then we must be certain they understand the instructions—that they know that letter order is important in making the correct alternatives "look exactly like" the standard. Several recommendations are as follows:

1. Assess skills appropriate to the competence of readers. If students are beginning or remedial readers, expect to assess skills involved in phonological aspects of reading while expecting to assess more comprehensive skills for more competent readers.
2. Use tests that cleanly discriminate between students who are and are not competent in a skill area. Beware of tests that may be failed for more than one reason because it is not possible to know for which reason students fail them.
3. Assess skills that have been shown to be related directly to reading competence, not skills that are tangentially related. That is, do not expect a test of grapheme (letter) discrimination to provide useful information. Instead, assess skills in forming grapheme-phoneme (letter-sound) relationships.

CASE STUDY

Part I

Name: Don Jones   Age: 7 years, 9 months
Date of Birth: October 18, 1973   Grade: 3
Date of Evaluation: 7-22-81

Background Information

Don is a 7-year, 9-month-old student who was referred by his parents because of
poor progress in reading. He will be in third grade in the fall at Best School. He is
one of the youngest children in the class.

When talking briefly with the examiner, Mrs. Jones expressed concern about
Don's reading development and felt that some suggestions for the home would be
beneficial. She also expressed concern as to where Don is actually functioning
and what plans could be implemented at school.

Don's second-grade teacher reported that Don's comprehension skills were
improving and that phonics continues to be a weak area. Don's present reading
level was determined to be at the first part of grade two. He had completed Ginn
360 *Seven is Magic*, Unit 3.

Observations

Don reacted positively to the testing situation. He was very cooperative and
initiated much social interaction. He appeared to be genuinely interested in doing
a good job. The results of this testing are considered a valid estimate of Don's
present developmental level.

Past Test Results

Test	Date	Results
Wechsler Intelligence Scale for Children—Revised (WISC-R)	7-6-81	*Verbal IQ: 127* *Performance IQ: 117* *Full Scale IQ: 125*
Peabody Individual Achievement Test (PIAT)	7-6-81	Grade Level Mathematics 3.3 Reading Recognition 1.6 Reading Comprehension 1.6 Spelling 2.5 General Information 3.7

Purposes of Reading Assessment

Assessment of reading performance serves at least five purposes: (1) maintaining administrative records; (2) identifying students in need of special reading instruction, (3) identifying a student's specific instructional needs; (4) monitoring a student's progress toward attainment of reading goals; and (5) evaluating the effectiveness of instructional procedures and programs. Proper maintenance of administrative records is a basic requirement for virtually all school systems and is important because, among other reasons, educational administrators must justify classification decisions in order to obtain funding for providing special education. Identifying students in need of special reading instruction serves the dual purposes of providing administrative justification for special programs and gaining admittance to those programs for students who need them. Identifying an individual student's instructional needs amounts to determining what reading skills a learner must be taught and is the initial step in designing an individualized educational program. Progress monitoring allows teachers, students, parents, and administrators to determine whether learners are moving toward attaining educational goals and objectives. Evaluating the effectiveness of procedures allows teachers and others to go beyond monitoring of an individual's progress and to assess the effectiveness of instructional procedures across many students.

To be of optimal value, an assessment system should serve all of the purposes described above, but of course there is no one instrument that does so reliably and efficiently. Consequently, it is necessary to use a battery of reading assessment procedures. A variety of formal achievement tests, criterion-referenced instruments, and informal assessment techniques are required. Maintenance of administrative records may require use of formal, commercially available reading assessment instruments and criterion-referenced tests. Identification of students in need of special services or screening may also be accomplished by administering formal tests. While there are commercially available diagnostic tests of reading performance, identification of a student's specific instructional needs or making a diagnosis is most likely to require criterion-referenced and informal assessments. Monitoring students' progress almost invariably is accomplished by repeated use of carefully planned informal assessments, although achievement tests and criterion-referenced instruments often are used on a pretest-posttest basis in order to assess changes in performance. Evaluation of instructional programs and procedures, although usually a research endeavor, can be important to teachers who wish to determine what programs and procedures to use in the future. As a research activity, such evaluation usually involves use of formal achievement tests and criterion-referenced instruments. However, for teachers seeking to improve their instruction, such evaluation can be accomplished by use of carefully developed, informal, criterion-referenced measures.

By conducting screening, diagnostic, and progress monitoring assessments, all of the major purposes of reading assessment can be accomplished. The information gained from these analyses can also be used to maintain administrative records and to evaluate program effectiveness. Means for accomplishing the various purposes of reading assessment are described and evaluated in the following sections.

Achievement Tests

Published reading achievement tests are probably the most common means for assessing reading performance. These norm-referenced tests indicate how an individual compares to other students in reading achievement and may help a teacher screen students with reading difficulties. These tests are useful, however, only if they meet certain criteria. In addition to meeting high psychometric standards, there are other characteristics to be considered before using published instruments. One concern is the usefulness of grade level scores. Grade equivalent scores are global scores derived from the raw scores (total correct) obtained on most reading tests. Grade equivalents may be used for (1) assigning children to various levels of a reading curriculum, (2) evaluating the effectiveness of a particular reading program, or (3) comparing different reading programs. However, such scores may be misleading in each of these areas, and they do not provide information about specific skills that are deficient or how to plan for instruction.

A final concern when using standardized reading tests, especially tests designed for upper grade levels, is that the resulting scores tend to overestimate reading abilities (Durkin, 1978). Norms on these tests extend down only to a particular grade level. If 2.8 is the floor of the norms for a test, that score could be assigned to a learner despite the fact that he or she cannot decode even first-grade words. By just recognizing and matching certain letters, for example, a learner can score grade 1.3 in reading on the *Wide Range Achievement Test*. Circumstances such as these are of particular concern when assessing atypical students. In these situations, the reading skills that are known are much more important to ascertain than general grade-equivalent scores (Lloyd, 1979).

Group Achievement Tests

Many widely used reading achievement tests are designed so that they can be administered to students in groups. A major advantage of group testing is savings in time. Group achievement tests may be used for the purposes of screening and large-scale program evaluation. Several important tests of this type are described below.

The *California Achievement Tests* (CAT; CTB/McGraw-Hill Staff, 1977–1978) assess reading skills from kindergarten through grade 12 using 10 separate test levels. The levels include: Level 10 for pre-reading in kindergarten; Level 11 for grades K.6 to 1.9; Level 12 for grades 1.6 to 2.9; Level 13 for grades 2.6 to 3.9; Level 14 for grades 3.6 to 4.9; Level 15 for grades 4.6 to 5.9; Level 16 for grades 5.6 to 6.9; Level 17 for grades 6.6 to 7.9; Level 18 for grades 7.6 to 9.9; and Level 19 for grades 9.6 to 12.9. Administration takes 63 to 75 minutes for Levels 10 to 13 and 82 minutes for the upper levels. Grade equivalents, percentile ranks, stanines, and other scores may be derived. The four main subtests are: Phonic Analysis, Structural Analysis, Vocabulary, and Comprehension. The Phonic Analysis subtest, composed of 20 to 25 items to assess phonics skills, is included at only Levels 11, 12, and 13. In the Structural Analysis subtest, found only at Levels 12 and 13, the teacher reads the directions orally for the 11 test items. The Reading Vocabulary subtest is included at all levels. Students indicate vocabulary knowledge by identifying synonyms and antonyms for test items. The Comprehension subtest is also found at all levels. Literal and interpretive comprehension is measured by having students read a passage and then answer multiple choice questions. Critical comprehension skills are also measured at Levels 13 to 19. An accompanying guidebook is available with teaching activities related to the reading skills that are assessed.

The *Gates-MacGinite Reading Tests* (MacGinite, 1978) have been completely revised to assess reading in grades 1 through 12 with seven levels of tests, each level requiring 1 hour to administer. Two or three forms of each level are available. Level R surveys skills taught in the first grade and can be viewed as a readiness test. Levels A through F each have two subtests: Vocabulary and Comprehension. The Vocabulary subtests in Level A and Level B measure the decoding skills used in selecting the word that corresponds to a picture from four choices. The test words were chosen from high-frequency word lists and common basal series. In the Comprehension subtest at these levels, a picture is chosen that best describes the meaning of a short passage.

The subtest formats in Levels C through F differ from those in the lower levels. The Vocabulary subtest requires the student to select synonyms for test words. The Comprehension subtest consists of a series of short passages with two to five multiple-choice questions per passage. The questions are primarily literal and inferential.

In addition to typical derived scores, the Gates-MacGinite supplies two additional scores. The Normal Curve Equivalent Score is an equal-interval percentile scaled score. The Extended Scale Scores are available for measuring reading performance over long periods of time (i.e., several years).

The *Metropolitan Achievement Tests* (MAT; Durost, Bixler, Wright-stone, Prescott, & Balow, 1970) include a reading section and are currently available for use with learners in kindergarten through grade nine. Administration time is 40 to 60 minutes. The levels and corresponding grades are: Primer for K.7 to grade 1.4; Primary I for grades 1.5 to 2.4; Primary II for grades 2.5 to 3.4; Elementary for grades 3.5 to 4.9; Intermediate for grades 5.0 to 6.9; and Advanced for grades 7.0 to 9.5. All three subtests (Word Knowledge, Word Analysis, and Reading Comprehension) are available at only some of the levels. The Word Knowledge subtest measures reading vocabulary, while the Word Analysis subtest concentrates on decoding skills. The general battery may be used as a survey or screening instrument. The 1978 edition of the MAT includes a Reading Instructional Battery designed to provide guidance in instructional planning. This latest edition also yields an estimated reading level at which 70% of the comprehension questions are answered correctly.

The *Stanford Achievement Tests* (SAT; Madden, Gardner, Rud-man, Karlson, & Merwin, 1973) include a separate reading battery. There are six levels: Primary I for grades 1.5 to 2.4; Primary II for grades 2.5 to 3.4; Primary III for grades 3.5 to 4.4; Intermediate I for grades 4.5 to 5.4; Intermediate II for grades 5.5 to 6.9; Advanced for grades 7.0 to 9.5. Each level is available in two forms. Vocabulary and reading are assessed at all levels; Primary I and Primary II measure word meaning and paragraph comprehension separately. A Word Study Skills subtest measures decoding skills except at the Advanced level. The tests that assess reading skills require from 55 to 90 minutes to administer, depending on the levels used. Special editions are also available that have been standardized on deaf and visually impaired populations. The SAT has been recognized as an excellent psycho-metric instrument and recommended as one of the most useful tests for classroom teachers (Traxler, 1972).

Individual Achievement Tests

Individually administered reading achievement tests are used widely by teachers to ascertain approximate reading levels. Because they are norm-referenced, the reading levels obtained may be discrepant from the reading program being currently used. Jenkins and Pany (1978) compared the words taught in the Macmillan reading series to those tested in the *Wide Range Achievement Test* (WRAT) and the *Stanford*

Achievement Test (SAT). Their results indicated that even if every word presented in the reading series was learned, a child could still expect to obtain an SAT score as low as 1.1 or a WRAT score as high as 2.3. Clearly caution is warranted in making major placement decisions based on these tests. Nevertheless, one of the advantages of individual achievement tests is that many of them require students to decode aloud rather than make multiple choices. Thus, the results may provide additional information about actual reading performance.

The *Diagnostic Achievement Battery* (DAB; Newcomer & Curtis, 1984) assesses eight areas of achievement, including reading. Scores on two subtests, Alphabet/Word Knowledge and Reading Comprehension, are combined to determine the level of reading performance. On the Alphabet/Word Knowledge subtest of the DAB, students read words in isolation; low-achieving pupils may also be administered items requiring identification of written letters and selection of spoken words based on letters identified by the examiner. On the Reading Comprehension subtest, the student reads increasingly more difficult passages and orally answers questions asked by the examiner about the passages' content. The DAB yields a wide variety of scores including standard scores, percentiles, and quotients.

The *Gilmore Oral Reading Test* (Gilmore & Gilmore, 1968) is composed of 10 paragraphs arranged in order of increasing difficulty. Each reading selection is read aloud and is followed by five comprehension questions. The test is timed and yields a reading rate score as well as grade equivalents for reading accuracy and comprehension. Performance ratings (ranging from superior to poor) for accuracy and comprehension are determined from stanine scores. Test administration requires approximately 20 minutes. Salvia and Ysseldyke (1981) criticized the lack of reliability and validity data on the revised forms (Forms C and D) of the test; technical characteristics found in the manual are only for the earlier edition. Spache (1976) has suggested that readibility levels for each reading passage be determined.

The *Gray Oral Reading Test* (Gray & Robinson, 1967) is available in four different forms, each of which is composed of 13 reading selections ranging in difficulty from first grade to college reading level. Like the Gilmore, the Gray is a timed test that can be administered within 20 minutes. Both the number of errors and the reading rate are reflected in the resulting grade score. Percentages correct on four comprehension questions for each passage are also tabulated. Salvia and Ysseldyke (1981) caution against relying on the Gray for other than global estimates of reading levels because of the absence of data on norming, reliability, and validity. Perhaps, as Wallace and Larsen suggest (1978), the Gray should be relied on more for analyzing types of errors in oral reading.

The *Peabody Individual Achievement Test* (PIAT; Dunn & Markwardt, 1970) includes two subtests that assess reading recognition and comprehension. The test is appropriate for learners in kindergarten through grade 12. Demonstration items are provided for each subtest to assure that students understand what is required, thus increasing how "clean" the tests are. The first 18 items on the reading recognition subtest require students to match and name letters. The rest of the items are words in isolation to be read aloud. The reading comprehension subtest uses a multiple-choice format. The first page for each item contains one sentence that is read silently by the student. On the second page, the student selects from four pictures the one that best describes what has just been read. These two subtests can be administered within 20 minutes. Age equivalents, grade equivalents, percentile ranks, and standard scores can all be computed for each subtest. The standardization of the PIAT is adequate in comparison to many other individual achievement tests, but low test-retest reliability (e.g., .61 for comprehension at eighth grade) suggests caution in use of the PIAT for purposes other than screening.

The *Wide Range Achievement Test* (WRAT; Jastak & Jastak, 1978) assesses achievement in reading, spelling, and arithmetic. The reading subtest is divided into two levels to cover reading skills from prekindergarten to college. The skills assessed range from letter recognition and matching to increasingly more difficult words to be read aloud. As the student reads the items aloud, the teacher records whether words are read correctly and may note the types of errors made. Grade equivalent scores, standard scores, and percentile scores may be derived from the manual; users should be certain to determine scores from the 1978 manual. Salvia and Ysseldyke (1981) raised serious questions about the norming, reliability, and face validity of the WRAT. One of the major advantages of the WRAT is that it can be administered in its entirety (including spelling and arithmetic) in a very brief period of time.

Diagnostic Tests

Major achievement tests such as those just described primarily serve the purposes of screening but provide little help in planning educational programs. It is, of course, important to identify students in need of special services, but once they have been identified, it is necessary to specify the instructional needs of individual students. Diagnostic tests are designed to provide information about deficits in student performance and, as such, should lead to remedial prescriptions.

Group Diagnostic Tests

The purpose of group diagnostic tests is to gather more information than is available from a group achievement test in reading. One of the major constraints of group diagnostic reading tests is failure to assess oral reading. Typically, the subtests assess common reading skills (e.g., syllabication, rhyming sounds), but they do so neither as precisely as an individually administered diagnostic test nor as "cleanly."

The *Stanford Diagnostic Reading Test* (SDRT; Karlsen, Madden, & Gardner, 1976) is available in two forms for assessing reading skills in grades 1.5 to 13.0. Colors are used to indicate the various grade levels: Red Level for grades 1.5 to 3.5; Green Level for grades 2.5 to 5.5; Brown Level for grades 4.5 to 9.5; Blue Level for grades 9.0 to 13.0. The SDRT is designed to measure comprehension, decoding, and vocabulary at the elementary level. The Brown Level and the Blue Level also assess the ability to scan and skim easy reading material. In addition to the more typical norms of percentile ranks, stanines, grade equivalent scores, and scaled scores, Progress Indicators are provided. Progress Indicators are criterion-referenced scores that determine competency on various reading skills. Administration requires 90 minutes to 145 minutes, depending on the level used.

The *Silent Reading Diagnostic Tests* (Bond, Balow, & Hoyt, 1970) are a series of eight subtests for students in grades 2 through 6 and take 90 to 135 minutes to administer. The subtests focus solely on word-recognition and word attack skills: word recognition, recognition of words in context, root words, syllabication, sound blending, distinguishing beginning and ending sounds, and vowel and consonant sounds. A pupil profile can be graphed so that the student can be evaluated in comparison to his or her own average reading score. Bond, Tinker, and Wasson (1979) viewed the pupil profile as an aid for planning individual instruction. Salvia and Ysseldyke (1981), however, caution against sampling across various reading skills and then using an average of the subtest scores as a standard for comparisons. A reading score that is a mean of other scores may not accurately represent any one of the skill areas sampled.

The *Doren Diagnostic Reading Test of Word Recognition Skills* (Doren, 1973), appropriate for students in grades 1 through 4, assesses word-attack skills. Twelve subtests include the evaluation of spelling phonetic and nonphonetic words and the ability to identify the phonetic spelling of sight words. Comprehension ability is not evaluated. Spache (1976) has criticized the Doren for not supplying subtest norms in the test manual. One to three hours should be allowed to administer the Doren.

The value of information gained from administering a group diagnostic reading test will depend, of course, on why it was given in the first place. It is certainly a quick and easy way to gain survey-level information on more than one student. However, if a guide is needed for dividing a class into high, middle, or low reading groups, having children read from the basal text would certainly be less costly and would provide a means of grouping students that is based on performance closer to what will be required of them. The lack of rigorous psychometric qualities of the majority of these tests will probably make whatever information is gathered questionable.

Individual Diagnostic Tests

Individual diagnostic tests are probably the most popular means for assessing reading skills of children with suspected reading problems. These tests tend to be very comprehensive since diagnosing a reading problem requires a survey of a wide variety of skills. Most of the tests considered in this category assess oral reading. Typically, the number and kinds of errors made on an individually administered diagnostic reading test are determined and then used for planning remedial instruction. Test manuals should be studied carefully before attempting to use the following individual diagnostic tests because the test instructions are more detailed and particularly crucial to the validity of the testing session.

The *Durrell Analysis of Reading Difficulty* (Durrell, 1975) is designed for assessing skills of students who are nonreaders up through the sixth grade. Subtests evaluate silent and oral reading, listening comprehension, word analysis, phonetics, faulty pronunciation, and handwriting and spelling. Accompanying checklists allow the teacher to record specific difficulties and strengths in reading. Testing takes 30 to 45 minutes per student. The Durrell is most useful for its qualitative information rather than the grade scores, since technical information (e.g., norms, validity, reliability) is not provided by the authors (Bond, Tinker, & Wasson, 1979). The *Durrell Analysis of Reading Difficulty: Revised* (Durrell & Catterson, 1980) is also available.

The *Gates-McKillop Reading Diagnostic Tests* (Gates & McKillop, 1962) are available in two forms for assessing reading skills in grades 2 through 6. The Gates-McKillop surveys a wide range of reading behaviors: oral reading, timed and untimed flash presentation of words, flash presentation of phrases, word attack knowledge (sound blending, letter sounds, vowels), auditory blending, spelling, oral vocabulary, syllabication, and auditory discrimination. The survey of skills is very complete except for ommission of a comprehension section. Surprisingly, despite questionable validity and reliability (Salvia & Ysseldyke, 1985), the Gates-McKillop has been recommended as a complete reading diagnostic test for students with severe reading problems (Wallace & Larsen, 1978).

The *Diagnostic Reading Scales* (Spache, 1972) are composed of three main subtests to assess word recognition, passage reading, and phonics skills. Learners in kindergarten through high school are required to read words orally from graded word lists to estimate their reading level. A checklist allows the teacher to classify reading errors. Reading passages are also presented to assess oral and silent reading as well as listening comprehension. Depending on the need for detailed information on specific phonics skills, any of the eight supplementary phonic subtests can be selected for administration. These subtests identify weaknesses in sound-symbol relationships, blending, and syllabication. As has been reported with the previous diagnostic tests discussed, standardization procedures, validity, and reliability are questionable.

The *Test of Reading Comprehension* (TORC; Brown, Hammill, & Wiederholt, 1978), although not expressly a diagnostic instrument, may be used in this way. The TORC is composed of three core subtests, four supplementary subtests, and one optional subtest. The three core subtests are designed to measure general vocabulary, syntactic similarities, and paragraph reading. Three of the supplementary subtests are designed to measure content area vocabulary in mathematics, social studies, and science; the fourth is designed to measure pupils' skill in reading the directions of schoolwork. The optional subtest assesses sentence sequencing. The TORC requires students to read silently materials for each item and mark answers on their answer sheets. Although it was designed to be administered individually, the TORC may be given to groups of students. The TORC yields scaled scores for each subtest and a reading comprehension quotient.

The *Woodcock Reading Mastery Tests* (WRMT; Woodcock, 1973) are a series of five reading tests for students in kindergarten through grade 12. The five subtests include letter identification, word identification, word attack (using nonsense words), word meaning, and passage comprehension. The WRMT, which is available in two forms, is contained in an easel-type notebook for ease of administration. All of the subtests can be given within 20 to 30 minutes. WRMT scores that can be derived include grade equivalent, percentile rank, age, and mastery scores. The mastery scores indicate reading proficiency at various levels of reading and are analogous to more traditional ratings of independent, instructional, and frustration levels in reading. Since reliability for the different subtests vary, the WRMT manual should be consulted along with more detailed reviews of the test (Laffey & Kelly, 1979).

The purpose of using individually administered reading diagnostic tests is to assess specific reading skills (e.g., word recognition, word analysis, reading rate, comprehension, and oral or silent reading). Unfortunately, the skills assessed are often not associated with the particular reading program used by the teacher. Additionally, many diagnostic tests have weak psychometric characteristics. Further screening will be necessary, even after administering a diagnostic reading test, before placing a child appropriately in a reading program.

Informal Reading Inventories

Informal reading inventories (IRI) are often recommended as diagnostic devices (e.g., Ekwall, 1976). An IRI is a series of graded passages administered to individual students for assessing skill levels and for diagnosing specific problems in reading. Students read passages orally and then answer comprehension questions asked by the teacher. Some proponents of IRIs also recommend including a check of silent reading comprehension (Ekwall, 1976).

An IRI indicates three reading levels for each student. The first is an independent reading level. At the independent level, material should be read with no more than two decoding errors in a 100-word passage and comprehension should be 100% (i.e., no errors on questions). The instructional reading level indicates the level at which a 100-word passage can be read with 95% accuracy in decoding and at least 75% accuracy in comprehension. When decoding accuracy drops to 90% or less and comprehension drops to 50% or less, the reading material is too difficult for the student. The last is called the frustration level.

In addition to indicating three different reading levels, IRIs allow the teacher to record various types of reading errors, word attack strategies, and other reading behaviors (e.g., finger pointing, restlessness, loss of place while reading). Informal reading inventories can be teacher-constructed or selected from those available commercially.

Teacher-Constructed IRIs

Ideally, IRIs should be constructed using passages from the basal readers that will be used for reading instruction. Because of this feature "IRIs have far greater face validity than do other means of reading placement" (Jenkins, 1979, p. 75). An IRI can be constructed from any basal series. Even though the initial investment in time is considerable compared to that of administering a published standardized reading test, the IRI can be used for as long as the particular series is used.

Zintz (1980) recommended selecting two reading passages from the end of the first third of each book—one to be read silently and one to be read orally. By avoiding using the first third of the book, chances of selecting vocabulary that merely reviews the previous level are reduced. The length of the passage should vary with reading levels. Kaluger and Kolson (1978, p. 142) suggested the following passage lengths: levels 1.0 to 2.0: 35–40 words; levels 3.0 to 4.0: 50–76 words; levels 5.0 to 6.0: 75–100 words; upper levels: 100–200 words. Next, five to seven comprehension questions are written for each passage to assess recall of facts, understanding of main ideas and vocabulary, and skill in making inference. Guidelines for formulating comprehension questions are available (Valmont, 1972). Duplicate copies of the IRI are made so that one copy can be read by the student while errors are recorded on the second copy. Teachers interested in secondary-age students should consult Vaughan and Gaus (1978).

To administer an IRI, a student is given a selection to read that is estimated to be below the student's independent reading level. As the passage is read, the teacher marks a copy of the passage, noting the types of decoding errors that are made (see Table 5.1). When the learner has completed the passage, comprehension questions are answered and scored. Harris and Sipay (1979) also recommended having students retell what they have read in a "free response comprehension check" (p. 188). If a pupil is confused or hesitant, supplementary questions can then be asked as guides.

The next higher reading passage is presented in the same manner. This procedure continues until the teacher is certain that decoding accuracy is below 90%. The teacher can read higher passages orally to the student and ask comprehension questions if a measure of listening comprehension is desired. Silent reading is started "one reader level below the highest level at which oral reading criteria were met" (Harris & Sipay, 1979, p. 193). Additionally, if oral and silent reading are timed, reading rate can be measured.

Reading levels are determined by calculating the percentage of correct decoding and responses for each passage. The percentages are then compared to those set as the criteria for independent, instructional, and frustration levels. For example, if a learner reads a passage at the 2.4 reading level with 93% accuracy in decoding and answers comprehension question with 80% accuracy, then the passage is probably at the student's instructional level. Decoding rate can be calculated by dividing total reading time by the number of words read correctly in the passage. A more detailed analysis of errors can be made by consulting specific reading texts (e.g., Durkin, 1978; Ekwall, 1976; Harris & Sipay, 1979).

Despite their popularity, IRIs have been debated on several issues: how to count errors (Ekwall, 1976), how to determine reading levels (Jenkins, 1979), what types of questions to include, and whether IRIs are really valid and reliable (Pikulski, 1974). These are all important concerns that restrict the interpretation of IRI results. A final concern relates to the clinical skill of the teacher. The quality of construction, administration, and evaluation of IRIs depends on the expertise of the teacher. These skills improve with practice, but initially the chances of inappropriate decisions are higher. Perhaps combining IRIs with results from other forms of assessment will increase the probability of assigning learners to the correct reading level (Lloyd, 1979).

Lovitt and Hansen (1976a) provided an excellent example of how IRI techniques can be used carefully to make placement decisions. Five passages from each of the reading books in the Lippincott program were selected, and comprehension questions for each pas-

TABLE 5.1 Some Conventions for Marking Errors in Oral Reading

Type of error	Description	Marking
Assistance	Teacher had to supply word after 5 seconds.	<u>Underline words added.</u>
Hesitations	Learner hesitated at word but teacher did not have to supply assistance.	$\sqrt{}$ check above hesitated word.
Insertions	Learner inserts word not on page.	extra Put in ∧ word or word parts with caret.
Mispronunciation	Learner does not accurately pronounce word.	Write in learner's pro-noun-shun pronunciation above the missed word.
Omissions	Learner leaves out a word or words and reads on.	Circle the ⟨omitted⟩ word(s) or punctuation.
Order Reversals	Learner inverts word order.	Mark ⌐reversals⌐ ‿with this symbol.
Regressions	Learner reads word(s) and then rereads them.	Put a wavy line under word(s) repeated.
Self-Corrections	Learner makes a mistake but corrects it spontaneously.	When the learner sc errors errs, note the mistake and write sc above it.
Substitutions	Learner reads one word as another	Then <u>When</u> the learner substitutes a word, underline the omitted word and write in the given one.

Sample Passage:

These people   They had been
The person had been waiting all afternoon for a call. She was   anxious to

the   fifteen
know whether her poem would win the contest and the fifty-dollar prize. If it

              would make
did then she could take her friend Jack, out to a fine dinner. But little did she
know that the phone

Adapted from Lloyd, J. (1979). Ascertaining the reading skills of school-age learners. In D. Sabatino & T. Miller (Eds.), *Describing learner characteristics for special education instruction.* New York: Grune & Stratton.

sage were prepared. Students read from passages at each level on several occasions and were placed in the highest reader in which they averaged 45–60 correctly read words per minute, 4–8 incorrectly read words per minute, and 50–75% correctly answered comprehension questions. The procedure resulted in reliable and accurate placements. Although time-consuming, this method of placing students using IRI techniques overcomes some of the problems associated with IRI.

Commercial IRIs

Commercially produced IRIs have become more widely available in recent years, even though their time-saving advantages are countered by many disadvantages. Commercial IRIs place emphasis on the diagnosis of reading skills rather than the determination of reading placement, since content is not related to a particular reading series. Consequently, there is an increased likelihood that the match between the reading level obtained on a commercial IRI and classroom instructional materials will not be accurate (Gerke, 1980).

Jongsma and Jongsma (1981) compared 11 commercial IRIs on content, procedures for administering and scoring, and recommendations for explaining the results. Their review highlighted the wide variability among the instruments on these features. For example, some inventories disregard age and reading ability by requiring all students to begin at the lowest level for testing. This procedure would usually make test administration more lengthy. Commercial IRIs also vary on the types of comprehension questions asked. The *Informal Reading Assessment* (Burns & Roe, 1980) surveys six areas of comprehension in its questions (i.e., main idea, literal, sequence, vocabulary, inferential, and factual). Silvaroli's (1979) *Classroom Reading Inventory* and Ekwall's (1979) *Ekwall Reading Inventory*, however, only ask the basic literal, inferential, and vocabulary comprehension questions. In conclusion, one should "shop" for commercial IRIs cautiously. Passage contents, types of questions, scoring criteria, and correspondence to the materials used for reading instruction should be critically examined.

Graded Word Lists

Teachers often administer a word recognition list to determine an approximate grade level at which to begin passage reading on an IRI. Commercially produced word lists are available with tables to convert the number of recognized words to grade levels. Graded word lists can also be teacher-constructed. Harris and Sipay (1979) suggested selecting a list of 10 to 20 words from the vocabulary taught in each book in a reading series. The student reads word lists until the "highest level at which the child scores 80% or more on the word list" (p. 188) is obtained. The starting IRI level should be one book below this point. Zintz (1980) recommended taking the total vocabulary words taught in a reader and dividing that number by 20. The quotient would then be used to determine the intervals for selecting words to include in a word recognition test: "For example, if there are 200 words in the list, $200 \div 20 = 10$; the teacher will thus select every tenth word in the list" (p. 455). If a student can recognize 80% of the list that has been constructed, it can be assumed that the material represents the student's instructional reading level.

CASE STUDY

Part II

Present Testing

Capacity to Read

The Bond Reading Expectancy Formula was used to calculate Don's expected reading grade level:

$$\text{R.E.} = \text{years in school} \times \frac{IQ}{100} + 1.0$$

According to this formula, a child completing the second grade with a CA of 7-9 and an IQ of 125 would normally be expected to read at a 3.5 grade level (middle part of third grade) with little difficulty.

Comparison of Reading Achievement with Potential to Read

Don was administered both the word lists and the oral graded passages of the *Analytical Reading Inventory* (ARI), an informal inventory by Woods and Moe. Below is a summary of the results in regard to independent (IND), instructional (INS), and frustration (FRUS) levels:

Grade	Word Lists (% Correct)	Graded Passages WR	Comp.	Listening
Primer	95% IND	INS 2	IND	
First	85% IND	FRUS 13	IND	
Second	90% IND	FRUS 12	INS	
Third	75% INS		FRUS	
Fourth	FRUS			INST

   Donald's independent reading level is about primer, instructional about first grade, and frustration about second. His listening level is about third grade or higher.

   The independent level is the level at which the child can read with no more than 1 uncorrected miscue in each 100 words (99%) and with at least 90% comprehension. The reading is fluent and expressive, and the student can read with confidence.

The instructional level is the level at which the child can read with no more than five uncorrelated miscues in 100 words (95%) and with at least 75% comprehension. The student's reading is generally expressive, although this level is slower than the previous.

The frustration level is the level beyond which reading has little meaning. Miscues exceed 10% (less than 90% correct) with comprehension at about 50%. The child is obviously frustrated due to the material's difficulty.

Summary

Don does not appear to have a problem with sentence structure. His knowledge of terms in the ARI was a strength. Also, Don's verbal skills are good. His good vocabulary knowledge with the use of context appears to be an aid that can be used for unlocking unknown words.

There is a significant discrepancy between Don's reading level (first grade) and his expected reading level of middle path of third grade. Although Don is a disabled reader, it may be more appropriate to consider him as a reader who is still at a beginning reader stage.

Don began to consistently repeat, substitute, and omit words and sentences at the first grade level. Many substitutions and omissions did not affect the meaning or subsequent comprehension. The repetitions served mainly to clarify word meanings. These problems were also evident in the second-grade passage.

Don can use phonics, but it is a laborious process that interferes with his fluency, and overall comprehension is difficult. If phonics fails, he is able to use context clues with some guidance. Don is comprehending some words that he apparently omits. Also, he does not have a large sight vocabulary, which would help him to read more fluently.

Donald was able to recall most of the stories of the ARI graded passages at the primer level and first grade level. He answered all types of questions, ranging from main idea to inferential. Don's word-analysis difficulties began to interfere with comprehension and fluency at the first grade level; although he did try various techniques, such as repetition, to acquire meaning, Don's comprehension remained good at the second grade level. The third-grade passage was then administered to assess listening comprehension, which was instructional.

Recommendation to the Parents

Don's good vocabulary, general knowledge, and interest can all be capitalized on when instructing him to read. He indicated an interest in fishing, biking, and reading comic strips. He may enjoy saving comic strips and making booklets from different ones. Also, games involving words such as Go Fish, using sets of word cards, would be good. Don may want to choose which words to use. Games like Concentration can also be played with the sets of cards. Since his vocabulary is good, Don should be able to understand stories you read to him of up to about the fourth grade level. (Some are listed in the following section). Don might want to make up stories about special events (such as a trip to the zoo). These can be put in a special folder and illustrated with Don's art work.

Donald might like to record the books he reads and be reinforced in some way for this. Your praise for his attempts to read even portions of a book will encourage his further efforts. You may want to set up a system where Don can receive points for each book read (or a part of the book) which can be exchanged for a favorite activity. After he reads the book, you might want to discuss it with him—maybe his favorite part or something he knows about that can be related to the story. Certain subjects he reads about may be of particular interest, which might provide for further reading or writing. Also, movies or television shows may be a basis for an original story.

It is recommended that Donald receive tutoring at the University Reading Clinic.

Recommendations to the Teacher

Donald is a bright boy and has many skills that can be used to help with his reading development. He is interested in a number of activities and subjects. These interests (e.g., biking, fishing, science) can be used as a source for reading materials. Also, Don's vocabulary and conceptual knowledge are strengths. He can be encouraged to write stories and to read independently, and can benefit from listening to stories read to him.

Don's good speaking vocabulary should be a basis for increasing his limited sight vocabulary. As revealed by the test, Don is able to make excellent use of context clues with guidance. This skill should be emphasized for Don in the work analysis procedure, along with the initial sound of the word.

Don appears to be reading for meaning, although at times he skips words. When this is the case, the oral reading miscue should be ignored. Increasing Don's sight vocabulary should aid his fluency. His repetitions are a way of attempting to derive meanings from unknown concepts. It may help to set a purpose for Don's reading so that he has some concept of the overall story line; then questions to set specific purposes can be used as guidelines along the way. Since Don is comprehending most of the material, and even a good portion of what he omits, it may be beneficial to tell him to go on if a certain phrase or word is apparently not familiar, rather than losing the continuity and meaning of the entire passage by dwelling on it. For example, in the case of the unknown phrase "Kill the ball," the next sentence provides a clue: "I would hit it right out of the park." If the word is essential to the sentence meaning, then he may have to regress to find meaning in context.

Progress Monitoring Systems

Reading achievement tests provide some information about how much students have learned and, thus, whether they need special educational services. Diagnostic tests provide some additional information about in what specific areas students need assistance and, perhaps, in what ways teaching should be arranged for them. However, another crucial purpose of assessment is to determine whether students are making progress in a particular instructional system. This purpose is served, at best, only partially by traditional forms of reading assessment.

Indeed, readministering standardized achievement tests provides some insight as to whether students are making progress. For example, if students progress from a third-grade to a fourth-grade score in the time of one school year, then we might say that they have made "normal" progress. But there are several limitations to the assessment information obtained through repeated administration of standardized instruments. One problem is that there are very serious drawbacks inherent in using "gain" or "change" scores (i.e., subtracting a score on an instrument at Time 1 from a score on the same instrument at Time 2 and considering the difference to represent change, gain, or growth). Test scores are representations of performance at a given time under given conditions; consequently, they are most appropriately represented as scores within a range (e.g., the score was 94 ± 8 or within the range 86–102), meaning that a "true" score lies somewhere within a given range. An obtained score at time 1 may actually overlap with a score obtained at Time 2; for example, a 94 ± 8 (86–102) in the fall may not really be very different from a 98 ± 8 in the spring, even though the simple score of 94 looks lower than 98. Other statistical reasons for not using retesting as an index of progress are particularly relevant to the use of grade equivalent scores. Grade equivalents are not arithmetic scores that can be added, subtracted, and so forth. Thus, it makes no sense to say that a student "gained 8 months in reading," even though this kind of use of achievement scores is very common. Unless reading "gain" scores are handled very carefully (e.g., corrected for regression), they do not provide appropriate information about progress.

Another problem with using change scores to assess reading progress is that there may be only a limited relationship between the skills tested by an achievement instrument and the skills in which instruction was provided during the time between testings. That is, an instructional program may focus on teaching reading skills A, B, C, and D during the first year while a test used to evaluate progress may assess performance on reading skills B, R, F, M, and X. For example, some beginning reading programs place very little emphasis on the skill of saying letter names (emphasizing instead mastery of letter sounds), but some achievement tests (e.g., the WRAT) require students to name letters as a part of the reading achievement subtest. Clearly, students may have learned very valuable decoding skills (i.e., association of symbols with sounds), but their skills may not be assessed by an instrument used to measure progress.

Perhaps the most important drawback to using achievement tests to measure progress is that, in most common applications of reading achievement testing, performance is measured in the fall and in the spring. For teachers who work with individual students for only one year, obtaining information about student progress after they have done their teaching does not allow them to alter instruction in a way that benefits individual students. When end-of-the-year test results are obtained, it is already too late to change what they are doing so that low-performing students can be helped to master what they are not mastering.

In the past, monitoring student progress in reading was mostly a subjective process in which teachers simply said that they thought individuals were or were not improving in skills. However, recent developments have made it possible and necessary to assess progress more objectively. Individualized educational programs require that evaluations of progress have been described, and some have been made available commercially.

Commercial Systems

Most commercially available progress monitoring systems have been developed to accompany particular reading instructional programs. Thus, they are criterion-referenced instruments in the sense that they are designed to provide information with reference to specific curricula-related criteria. Additionally, they should—and some do—provide information about instruction because identification of skill areas that have not been mastered can be translated directly into recommendations about remedial activities. For example, mastery tests designed to accompany *Corrective Reading* (Zintz, 1972) identify specific parts of lessons to be presented again when students fail certain items on the mastery tests. Detailed discussions of all the commercial systems designed to accompany instructional programs is beyond the scope of this chapter, but several will be presented so that readers can be familiar with their structure and use.

The *Tests of Basic Reading Skills* (Brzeinski & Schoephoerster, 1976) are a part of the assessment component of the Houghton Mifflin Reading Series. Test items for the skills in Levels B, C, and D are contained in one booklet, with each of the upper levels (E through M) having its own test booklet. Tests are administered at the end of each of the major selections within each level of the reading program. The purpose of these criterion-referenced tests is: "(1) to give periodic indication of mastery and provide information the teacher must have in order to determine the need for remedial instruction, or (2) to supplement and confirm the information obtained from the lesson-by-lesson assessment tests, or (3) to establish a permanent record of reading progress" (Brzeinski & Schoephoerster, 1976, p. 3). Criterion level is 80%; scores below this level indicate that students may need more skill practice.

Excellent examples of progress monitoring systems accompanying instructional programs are provided in the *DISTAR Mastery Tests* and *Corrective Reading*. The *DISTAR Mastery Tests* are criterion-referenced tests for assessing skills presented in the DISTAR Reading I and II programs. Three test items are used for measuring mastery on each program objective. Test results help pinpoint objectives not yet mastered so that particular lessons pertaining to a skill can be retaught. Similar tests accompanying the *Corrective Reading* program provide both remedial and acceleration information. For example, mastery checks written into the teacher's presentation materials provide the items to be presented, directions for review of items that have not been mastered, and directions for skipping lessons for students who display high levels of mastery.

Another form of commercially available progress monitoring systems is not directly tied to specific reading programs. Instead, these systems are composed of tests of areas of reading skill that are presumed to be appropriate for various different instructional programs. Consequently, these assessment systems cannot provide specific remedial recommendations. Science Research Associates publishes an instrument of this sort. *Diagnosis: An Instructional Aid—Reading* consists of two kits (Level A: grades 1 to 4; Level B: grades 3 to 6). The kits contain a Survey Test that is administered to identify the approximate starting point for skill development in the following areas: phonetic analysis, structural analysis, comprehension, and vocabulary. Level B also surveys study skills. To narrow these broad areas to more specific skills, a series of probes or objective-based skills tests is administered. Accompanying Prescription Guides provide numerous references to other reading texts and kits for instructional materials related to skill areas.

School-Developed Systems

Noncommercial systems for progress monitoring have been developed by staffs from different school systems and special projects. Similar to the commercial systems, these methods for monitoring progress may be referenced to specific instructional programs or may be designed to assess skills considered essential regardless of the instructional program used.

It is not terribly difficult to construct a progress monitoring system. The skills to be assessed must be identified; items that provide clean and accurate tests of the skills must be selected; a suitable format presenting the items must be devised; the resulting tests must be tried out to determine whether they are reasonable and to establish some criteria for passing or failing them.

One feature common to many monitoring systems is the adoption of evaluation recommendations presented by behaviorally oriented educators. Lovitt (1975), for example, recommended that measurement of academic (and other) behaviors have several characteristics. First, it should be direct; that is, instead of measuring performance on tasks that are related to the task, actual performance on the task of concern should be assessed. Second, measurement should be conducted daily. This implies that tests be constructed that allow teachers to observe small changes in performance often and, thus, make instructional decisions as soon as it is clear that they are needed. Third, the conditions under which performance is measured should be carefully specified to determine how these features affect performance. Direct, daily measurement under known conditions allows teachers to become more scientific in making decisions about placements in instructional programs and to have more than just an intuitive idea of what instructional practices are effective.

In practice, these guidelines have resulted in progress monitoring systems that are composed of loosely sequential series of tests that are often called *probes* and are given daily with the results plotted on a graph. For example, the Regional Resource Center at the University of Oregon provided a series of probes based on Starlin's (1971) analysis of reading; the Exceptional Education Unit at the University of Washington provided similar probes, and Project SIMS in Minnesota developed a monitoring system that can be used in several different ways (e.g., first assess all short vowel sounds or first assess all sound variants for one vowel). Additionally, some similar systems have been developed that correspond to particular instructional programs; for example, School District 4-J in Eugene, Oregon, developed several systems, one of which followed the sequence of skills and the content of the Merrill Linguistic Reading Series.

Refinements of behaviorally based progress monitoring systems have made it possible to judge whether handicapped students attain levels of competence commensurate with the performance of students in regular education classrooms (e.g., Epstein & Cullinan, 1979). For example, when a student performs on a probe at a level that is at or above the level displayed by many students in regular classrooms at his or her grade level, then teachers may reasonably assume that his or her skill on that probe is appropriate and may move on to another skill. Additionally, frequent collection of data about progress and careful manipulation of instructional variables can allow teachers to ascertain whether those particular instructional procedures are effective (see Repp & Lloyd, 1980, for a discussion of methods for conducting such analyses of effectiveness). For example, Lovitt and Hansen (1976b) described how an instructional procedure called ''contingent skipping and drilling'' was evaluated by using direct, daily assessment of performance.

Summary

Reading represents one of the most difficult challenges students will encounter in their early school years. Failure to meet this challenge successfully may result in an individual having continued problems throughout formal schooling. One could also argue that reading problems that remain in adolescence and adulthood restrict the number of potential career options available to an individual. Given the importance attached to attaining sound reading skills, it is critical that significant efforts be expended toward students who demonstrate difficulties in learning to read early in their school experiences. An initial step in this direction demands that children with potential reading problems be identified early. Assessment of prerequisite skills necessary for reading acquisition as well as the specific skills comprising successful reading is necessary to some degree for all children.

Assessing reading performance is not simply accomplished by giving standardized achievement tests in the fall or spring of each school year. Far more extensive assessment is needed if teachers are to make educational decisions about handicapped and nonhandicapped students. Assessment data appropriate for determining whether students are in need of special services must be obtained. Data about what specific areas of reading skills require remediation must be gathered and used carefully. Information about students' progress during the remedial process must be obtained and judiciously considered in order to make instructional decisions that promote remediation.

To accomplish these ends, assessment instruments must be selected that provide appropriate and trustworthy information. Although they serve admirably as *screening* instruments, most achievement tests do not provide teachers with direction about what instructional services are needed and how they should be provided. Most progress monitoring systems may provide instructional direction, but they cannot legitimately be used to determine which students are in need of special instructional services. Consequently, it is necessary that a battery of reading assessment instruments be used. Careful consideration of the purposes of assessment, the psychometric adequacy of reading assessment instruments, and the value of the information gained from an instrument must guide selection of assessment tools that make up a battery.

Educational Suggestions for Students with Reading Difficulties

There are numerous procedures for remediating severe reading difficulties. However, the following suggestions can be used by teachers for students who have less severe problems (Cohen & Plaskon, 1980).

When assessment data reveal that students are unable to follow a line of print on a page, teachers can give the students markers to accent a word, a phrase, or a line at one time.

At times students are assessed as having difficulty with comprehension questions about a reading assignment. Such students can be given a study guide that has focus questions prior to the reading assignment. Additionally, the students could be encouraged to read the assignment twice, once for decoding and then once for content comprehension.

Some students are assessed as having difficulty mastering new sight vocabulary. These students often benefit from a multisensory strategy to master the words. Another strategy would be to encourage the students to attend to configuration cues.

Certain students are identified as having difficulty transferring words mastered in isolation to context reading. Many times these students can benefit from accenting newly mastered words in an assignment by underlining them. However, this cue would have to be gradually faded out.

When a student's reading difficulty is assessed as resulting from substitutions that result in total loss of meaning, encourage the student to correct such reading errors if they do not sound alright in the phrase.

When a teacher identifies a student that is frustrated by oral reading and thus supplies his or her own meaning and language structure, a change of reading materials to an easier level can be helpful.

At times assessment may indicate that students are not reading for meaning. Many students with this difficulty benefit from reading language experience stories into a tape recorder and then playing them back to determine whether they sound alright.

When reading assessment reveals that students use phonic cues consistently but unsuccessfully, teach the students to use language and other cues.

Study Questions

1. Discuss the relationship of reading difficulties with behavior problems in school.
2. List potential areas of difficulty in learning to read.
3. Define what is meant by a "clean" reading test.
4. What are the purposes of reading assessment? What is its primary goal in terms of the learner?
5. List and critique achievement tests used in reading assessment.

6. Distinguish between diagnostic and achievement tests used in reading assessment.
7. What is an IRI and what are its advantages and limitations?
8. How do we monitor a student's reading progress once the initial reading assessment is complete?

Suggested Readings

Gillespie-Silver, P. (1979). *Teaching reading to children with special needs.* Columbus, OH: Charles E. Merrill.

Otto, W., & Smith, R. J. (1980). *Corrective and remedial teaching* (3rd ed.). Boston: Houghton Mifflin.

Silberberg, N. E., & Silberberg, M. C. (1977). A note on reading tests and their role in defining difficulties. *Journal of Learning Disabilities, 10,* 100–103.

Spache, G., & Spache, E. 1977. *Reading in the elementary school* (4th ed.). Boston: Allyn and Bacon.

Williams, J. (1979). Reading instruction today. *American Psychologist, 34,* 917–922.

References

Becker, W. C. (1977). Teaching reading and language to the disadvantaged—What we have learned from field research. *Harvard Educational Review, 47,* 518–543.

Bond, G. L., Balow, B., & Hoyt, C. (1970). *Silent Reading Diagnostic Tests.* Chicago: Lyons & Carnahan.

Bond, G. L., Tinker, M. A., & Wasson, B. B. (1979). *Reading difficulties* (4th ed.). Englewood Cliffs, NJ: Prentice-Hall.

Brown, V. L., Hammill, D. D., & Wiederholt, J. L. (1978). *Test of Reading Comprehension.* Austin, TX: PRO-ED.

Brzeinski, J., & Schoephoerster, H. (1976). *Tests of Basic Reading Skills (manual).* Boston: Houghton Mifflin.

Burns, P. C., & Roe, B. D. (1980). *Informal Reading Assessment.* Chicago: Rand McNally.

Calfee, R. C. (1977). Assessment of independent reading skills: Basic research and practical applications. In A. S. Reber & D. L. Scarborough (Eds.), *Toward a psychology of reading.* Hillsdale, NJ: Erlbaum.

Calfee, R. C., Fisk, L. W., & Piontkowski, D. (1975). "On-off" tests of cognitive skills in reading acquisition. In M. P. Douglass (Ed.), *Claremont reading conference: 39th yearbook.* Claremont, CA: Claremont Graduate School.

Cohen, S. B., & Plaskon, S. P. (1980). *Language arts for the mildly handicapped.* Columbus, OH: Charles E. Merrill.

CTB/McGraw-Hill Staff. (1977–1978). *California Achievement Test.* Monterey, CA: Author.

Cullinan, D., Epstein, M. H., & Lloyd, J. (1983). *Introduction to behavior disorders.* Englewood Cliffs, NJ: Prentice-Hall.

Dunn, L., & Markwardt, F. (1970). *Peabody Individual Achievement Test.* Circle Pines, MN: American Guidance Service.

Doren, M. (1973). *Doren Diagnostic Reading Test of Word Recognition Skills*. Circle Pines, MN: American Guidance Service.

Durkin, D. (1978). *Teaching them to read* (3rd ed.). Boston: Allyn & Bacon.

Durost, W., Bixler, H., Wrightstone, J., Prescott, G., & Balow, I. (1970). *Metropolitan Achievement Tests* (1970 ed.). New York: Harcourt, Brace, Jovanovich.

Durrell, D. D. (1975). *Durrell Analysis of Reading Difficulty* (Rev. ed.). New York: Harcourt, Brace, & World.

Durrell, D. D., & Catterson, J. (1980). *Durrell Analysis of Reading Difficulty* (Rev.). New York: Harcourt Brace Jovanovich.

Ekwall, E. E. (1976). *Diagnosis and remediation of the disabled reader*. Boston: Allyn & Bacon.

Epstein, M. H. & Cullinan, D. (1979). Social validation: Use of normative peer data to evaluate LD interventions. *Learning Disability Quarterly, 2*, 93–98.

Gates, A. I., & McKillip, A. S. (1962). *Gates-McKillop Reading Diagnostic tests*. New York: Teachers College Press.

Gerke, R. (1980). Critique of informal reading inventories: Can a valid instructional level be obtained? *Journal of Reading Behavior, 12*, 155–158.

Gibson, E., & Levin, H. (1975). *The psychology of reading*. Cambridge, MA: MIT Press.

Gilmore, J. V., & Gilmore, E. C. (1968). *Gilmore Oral Reading Test*. New York: Harcourt Brace Jovanovich.

Gray, W. S., & Robinson, H. M. (1967). *Gray Oral Reading Test*. Austin, TX: PRO-ED.

Harris, A. J., & Sipay, E. R. (1979). *How to teach reading*. New York: Longman.

Jastak, J., & Jastak, S. (1978). *Wide Range Achievement Test*. Wilmington, DE: Jastak Associates.

Jenkins, J. R. (1979). Oral reading: Considerations for special and remedial education teachers. In J. E. Button, T. C. Lovitt, & T. D. Rowland (Eds.), *Communication research in learning disabilities and mental retardation*. Baltimore: University Park Press.

Jenkins, J. R., & Pany, D. (1978). Curriculum biases in reading achievement tests. *Journal of Reading Behavior, 10*, 345–357.

Jongsma, E. A. (1980). Test review: Gates-MacGinite Reading Tests (2nd ed.). *Journal of Reading, 23*, 340–345.

Jongsma, K. S., & Jongsma, E. A. (1981). Test review: Commercial informal reading inventories. *Reading Teacher, 34*, 697–705.

Kaluger, G., & Kolson, C. J. (1978). Reading and learning disabilities. *Reading Teacher, 34*, 697–705.

Karlsen, B., Madden, R., Gardner, E. F. (1976). *Stanford Diagnostic Reading Test*. New York: Harcourt Brace Jovanovich.

Kass, C. E. (1966). Psycholinguistic disabilities of children with reading problems. *Exceptional Children, 32*, 533–539.

Kavale, K. (1980). The reasoning abilities of normal and learning disabled readers on measures of reading comprehension. *Learning Disability Quarterly, 3*, 34–35.

Laffey, J., & Kelly, D. (1979). Test review: Woodcock Reading Mastery Tests. *Reading Teacher, 33*, 335–339.

Lloyd, J. (1979). Ascertaining the reading skills of atypical learners. In D. Sabatino & T. Miller (Eds.), *Describing learner characteristics for special education*. New York: Grune & Stratton.

Lovitt, T. C. (1975). Applied behavior analysis and learning disabilities: Part I. *Journal of Learning Disabilities, 8*, 432–443.

Lovitt, T., & Hansen, C. L. (1976a). Round one—Placing the child in the right reader. *Journal of Learning Disabilities, 9*, 347–353.

Lovitt, T., & Hansen, C. L. (1976b). The use of contingent skipping and drilling to improve oral reading and comprehension. *Journal of Learning Disabilities, 9*, 481–487.

Madden, R. Gardner, E. R., Rudman, H. C., Karlsen, B., & Merwin, J. C. (1973). *Stanford Achievement Test*. New York: Harcourt Brace Jovanovich.

MacGinite, W. H. (1978). *Gates-MacGinite Reading Tests* (2nd ed.). Boston: Houghton Mifflin.

Newcomer, P. L., & Curtis, D. (1984). *Diagnostic Achievement Battery*. Austin, TX: PRO-ED.

Pikulski, J. (1974). A critical review: Informal reading inventories. *The Reading Teacher, 28*, 141–151.

Repp, A. C., & Lloyd, J. (1980). Evaluating educational changes with single-subject designs. In J. Gottleib (Ed.), *Educating mentally retarded persons in the mainstream*. Austin, TX: PRO-ED.

Robins, L. N. (1979). Follow-up studies. In H. C. Quay & J. S. Werry (Eds.), *Psychopathological disorders of childhood* (2nd ed.). New York: John Wiley & Sons.

Roswell, F. G., & Chall, J. S. (1963). *Roswell-Chall Auditory Blending Test*. New York: Essay Press.

Salvia, J., & Ysseldyke, J. E. (1985). *Assessment in special and remedial education* (3rd ed.). Boston: Houghton Mifflin.

Sheperd, G. (1967). Selected factors in the reading ability of educable mentally retarded boys. *American Journal of Mental Deficiency, 71*, 563–570.

Silvaroli, N. J. (1979). *Classroom Reading Inventory* (3rd ed.). Dubuque, IA: William C. Brown.

Spache, G. D. (1972). *Diagnostic Reading Scales*. Monterey, CA: California Test Bureau.

Spache, G. D. (1976). *Diagnosing and correcting reading disabilities*. Boston: Allyn & Bacon.

Starlin, C. (1971). Evaluating progress toward reading proficiency. In B. Bateman (Ed.), *Learning disorders* (Vol. 4), Seattle: Special Child Publications.

Traxler, A. (1972). Review of the Stanford Reading Tests. In O. K. Buros (Ed.), *Seventh mental measurements yearbook*. Highland Park, NJ: Gryphon Press.

Valmont, W. (1972). Creating questions for informal reading inventories. *The Reading Teacher, 25*, 509–512.

Vaughan, J. L., & Gaus, P. (1978). Secondary reading inventory: A modest proposal. *Journal of Reading, 21*, 716–720.

Wallace, G., & Larsen, S. (1978). *Educational assessment of learning problems: Testing for teaching*. Boston: Allyn & Bacon.

Wallach, L., Wallach, M. A., Dozier, M. G., & Kaplan, N. E. (1977). Poor children learning to read do not have trouble with auditory discrimination but do have trouble with phoneme recognition. *Journal of Educational Psychology, 69,* 36–39.

Woodcock, R. W. (1973). *Woodcock Reading Mastery Tests.* Circle Pines, MN: American Guidance Service.

Zintz, M. V. (1972). *Corrective reading.* Dubuque, IA: William C. Brown.

Zintz, M. V. (1980). *The reading process: The teacher and the learner* (3rd ed.). Dubuque, IA: William C. Brown.

6

Assessment of Oral Language Skills

Blanche Podhajski

OBJECTIVES

Upon completion of this chapter the teacher should be able to:

1. Outline the major stages of language acquisition.
2. Identify those formal assessment instruments currently employed to measure oral language skills in structured language situations along the dimensions of receptive/expressive processes observed in communicative behaviors.
3. Identify tests that assess a student's articulation, vocabulary, sentence structure, and overall language use.
4. Identify informal techniques of assessment that can be enlisted from spontaneous speech samples in order to investigate oral language abilities in students. Such informal techniques can be used in conjunction with formal procedures to assess receptive/expressive functions of communicative behavior.
5. Elucidate the complexities of language impairments and the implications of formal and informal language measurement for suitable remedial intervention.

Oral language skills are generally examined through formal and informal procedures. Formal approaches entail administration and interpretation of standardized test instruments in structured language situations. Informal techniques analyze language spontaneously generated in unstructured settings. A multitude of measures of both kinds are currently available and in use.

In all cases, it must be cautioned that most methods used to evaluate oral language skills originated from normal language acquisition models. Predictions made for children with language problems based upon knowledge gleaned from normal populations may be unsuitable since sequences of language behaviors may not be the same for the two groups (Dale, 1976). This precaution should be taken into account before the adoption of any approach to language assessment. General guidelines of normal speech and language development in children should nonetheless be considered and compared with developmental history information obtained from parents before assessment of oral language deficits begins.

Table 6.1 by Bartel (1982) offers a detailed outline of the major stages in receptive and expressive language acquisition. If further information is desired, the teacher is referred to deVilliers and deVilliers (1978) for a detailed discussion.

Formal Assessment of Oral Language Skills

Oral language skills in students can be formally evaluated using standardized testing instruments. In essence, such measurement tools assess small samples of language behavior from students during structured testing situations. Representative verbal responses are then subjected to standardized interpretation. Standardized tests provide (1) a common set of specific directions for administration and scoring; (2) an established format of specific test items designed to sample particular language behaviors; and (3) norms to allow comparison of an individual's score with groups of others who have been given the same test.

Criticism of standardized language tests has proliferated in recent years (Lyon, 1982). Variables such as examiner training, experience, and expectations (Anastasi, 1976) have been found to significantly influence test administration and interpretation, particularly in situations where cultural and ethnic backgrounds differ from the prototypic, middle-class white child (Oakland, 1974). Other factors affecting standardized tests include lack of reliability, validity, and normative data. However, the most distressing fact about standardized test results is that they do not consistently provide meaningful information to guide remedial instruction (Lyon, 1982). Despite the proliferation of oral language tests with coordinated teaching programs, such as the *Boehm Test of Basic Concepts*/Concept Understanding Program; the *Lindamood Auditory Conceptualization Test* (LAC)/ Auditory Discrimination in Depth (ADD); and the *Illinois Test of Psycholinguistic Abilities* (ITPA)/ Minskoff, Wiseman, Minskoff Program (MWM), complaints persist that language knowledge is not generalized but rather taught to the test through these programs.

Standardized tests have been reviewed in the literature along a variety of theoretical linguistic constructs. Wiig and Semel (1980) outline assessment procedures according to those behaviors that characterize the component language functions of morphology, syntax, semantics, and memory (retention and retrieval). Specifically, they describe test instruments that assess a student's skill at forming words and sentences, understanding words and word relationships, and remembering spoken messages.

Other distinctions among assessment measures are made on the basis of the nature and comprehensiveness of language abilities examined. Wallace and Larsen (1978) consider three types of standardized language tests: (1) those that analyze overall language functioning; (2) those that measure the specific component systems of linguistic performance—phonology, linguistic structure of semantics; and (3) those that assess language "correlates" (i.e., such factors as perception and related cognitive skills).

Phonology

Most children acquire the sounds of language (phonemes) in a developmentally regular fashion. It is not unusual to observe differing levels of speech intelligibility among preschool children. Many children master all English sounds by the age of 3 (Roskam & Podhajski, 1980), while others demonstrate articulatory differences beyond the age of 6.

Assessment of a student's articulation skills is regarded as a complicated process because of the complex perceptual and physiological processes involved. Auditory receptive skills implicit to satisfactory articulation have long been believed to include auditory discrimination. Tests assessing student's abilities to detect minimal differences among auditory stimuli are regularly included in speech test batteries. Recently, researchers (Weiss, Lillywhite, & Gordon, 1980) have been critical of the traditional way in which auditory discrimination is measured, that is, by listening to another speaker. Self-discrimination is espoused as a more sensitive means of obtaining useful information about a student's aritculation abilities, particularly when discrimination tasks include those phonemes that the student misarticulates.

TABLE 6.1 Stages in Receptive and Expressive Language Acquisition

Age	General Characteristics	Purpose of Vocalization	Vocabulary
1–4 weeks	Undifferentiated crying		
4–6 weeks	Crying becomes differentiated	Show pleasure, distress	
6 weeks to 6 months	Babbling—vocal play, calling, gurgling	Show pleasure, distress	
6–9 months	Lalling—intonation present, syllables are present	Getting attention, socialization	
9–12 months	Echolalia—repetition of sounds made by self and others	Responds to adult stimulation—self-satisfaction	Sometimes first word appears
12–18 months	Intentional use of speech, beginning of true speech	Generalized use of vocabulary, e.g., "dada" might mean "daddy is coming," "where's daddy," "I want my daddy"	1–20 words, nouns, verbs, adjectives, adverbs
18–24 months	Intentional, meaningful speech	Satisfaction of needs, exploration of environment, egocentric speech	Up to 300 words

TABLE 6.1 *(continued)*

Sentence Length	Phonology	Syntax	Comprehension
			Responds to human voice by attending
	Mostly front vowels, /g/, /k/, /l/		
	Mostly front vowels, some syllables, /m/, /n/, /p/, /b/		Responds to human speech by smiling & vocalizing, may understand some words or intonations, verbal syncretism
	Consonants begin to exceed vowels		Inner language (Myklebust), some receptive ability—will do patta-cake or wave "bye-bye"
1 word	Monosyllabic or disyllabic		Responds to simple commands, understands words, phrases, e.g., "No," "Come"
2-word sentences appear, beginnings of form-class differentiation, begins use of nouns	Consonants: mostly initial and medial; final pronunciation rarely inconsistent	Uses simple rule, Sentence (pivot or modifier) + open or lexical item	Uses input from adults for inducing own grammatical rules. Comprehends more than he produces

(continued)

Age	General Characteristics	Purpose of Vocalization	Vocabulary
2–3 years	Speech becoming more intelligible & diffentiated, sometimes beginning of stuttering	Satisfaction of needs, exploration of environment, egocentric speech. Words still general in content	Up to 900 words

From "Assessing and remediating problems in language development" by N. Bartel, 1982, in D. D. Hammill and N. Bartel (Eds.), *Teaching children with behavior problems*, (pp. 242–245). Boston: Allyn & Bacon.

CASE STUDY

Part I

Name: Timothy Maker   Age: 8 years, 3 months
Date of Birth: January 15, 1975   Grade: 2
Date of Evaluation: April 15, 1983

Background Information

Timothy is an 8-year, 3-month-old second-grade student referred for speech and language assessment to help determine whether he should be retained in second grade. His teacher's concerns include poor phonics skills, inability to learn to read, inattention, difficulty following directions, inconsistent task learning, and problems acquiring math concepts.

Past Test Findings

Results of a psychoeducational evaluation revealed average intellectual functioning with a significant verbal-performance discrepancy on the *Wechsler Intelligence Scale for Children—Revised* (WISC–R). IQ scores obtained were as follows: Verbal Scale IQ of 89, Performance Scale IQ of 110, and Full Scale IQ of 100.

Verbal		Performance	
Information	6	Picture Completion	12
Similarities	9	Picture Arrangement	8
Arithmetic	5	Block Design	13
Comprehension	11	Object Assembly	14

Sentence Length	Phonology	Syntax	Comprehension
3–4 words	Masters 2/3 of adults speech sounds	Simple & compound sentences; differentiation of pivot class to demonstratives, adjectives, determiners, expanded noun phrase, conjunctions such as "and" appear; begins to use auxiliary verb	Understands tense, basic numberical concepts, e.g., "many," "few," but doesn't produce these. Can understand rudimentary causality

Vocabulary	8	Coding	9
Digit Span	(6)	Mazes	(10)

Examples of Timothy's responses to two questions on the Information subtest are provided below:

Examiner: What must you do to make water boil?
Timothy: Hot water.
Examiner: Name the month that comes next after March.
Timothy: Fall.

On the Arithmetic subtest, when asked "If we were to add one tree at each end of the line, how many trees would there be altogether?" as part of this subtest, Timothy replied, "Where's 'each'?"

Academic complaints regarding Timothy's problems in associating sounds with letters were confirmed. Those sight words he was able to decode in his basal reader could not be decoded when presented individually on index cards. Reading comprehension was low, barely approximating first grade level. Spelling skills were limited to three sight words: /cat/, /boy/, and /the/.

Tests of Auditory Discrimination

The *Goldman-Fristoe-Woodcock Test of Auditory Discrimination* (Goldman, Fristoe, & Woodcock, 1970) is an attractive, popularly employed package designed to assess whether a student can distinguish sound differences within words. It is appropriate for students age 3 years, 8 months to adult. The test, comprised of a booklet of stimulus test pictures and a test tape, is divided into three parts: (1) a training procedure; (2) a quiet subtest, and (3) a noise subtest. The pictures within the test booklet are black-and-white line drawings, presented four on a plate. There are 16 training plates and 60 test plates (30 for the quiet subtest, 30 for the noise subtest). The training procedure is designed to ensure that the student associates the stimulus vocabulary with the test pictures. The teacher reads each word and the student points to his or her choice from the four pictures on each plate; a second word is then read and responded to on the same plate. When all 16 plates are completed, they are presented again to elicit word-picture associations for the remaining two items per plate. Training is repeated for any errors until either all pictures are correctly identified or three attempts to match words with pictures are made.

The quiet subtest is then presented using a test tape. The teacher turns the test plates to coincide with the recording while marking the student's response to one of four pictures on each plate. The noise subtest is presented in identical fashion except that background noise 9 decibels less intense than the signal is superimposed on the tape to simulate cafeteria noise.

Validity and reliability of this auditory discrimination measure are adequate, although it has been pointed out that the strongest normative data are for children 3 through 12 years old (Vetter, 1979). Ease of administration and control of the prerecorded teacher's voice are appreciable strengths of this instrument. However, each strength is offset by potential detractors. For example, the teacher must take care to assure familiarity with the administration sequence of looking at the student's pointing response, turning the plate, and then recording the response. Transposition of the last two activities can seriously interfere with fluent pacing, and since presentation of stimuli can be considered rapid by some students, steady manipulation of frames is critical. The tape can be stopped momentarily if students seem in need of extra time; however, items cannot be repeated. Use of a tape-recorded female voice, while important in controlling for pronunciation and loudness level, has the disadvantage of being detached from the student interpersonally. Some students find it hard to relate to taped stimuli. The regional speech pattern of the speaker may also influence some students' auditory adaptability. As on other tests that employ nonverbal responses to pictures, picture interpretation problems should not be overlooked. Regardless of pretraining, when more abstract linguistic representations are depicted (e.g., a picture of a girl pointing to herself as ''me''), confusions in meaning between stimulus word and picture can result.

The *Auditory Discrimination Test* (ADT; Wepman, 1973) is a brief, easy-to-administer measure that assesses a student's abilities to discriminate the difference between auditorily presented word pairs for students 5-0 years to 8-0 years of age. Forty pairs of monosyllabic English words are read (lips covered) to the student, 30 of which differ by one sound (e.g., cat/cap; moon/noon). The remaining 10 pairs do not differ and are included to aid judging test validity. The student is instructed to indicate whether the word pairs are the same or different by verbalizing a "yes" or "no" response. It is appropriate for the teacher to modify instructions to ensure that the student knows what he or she is expected to do. Comprehension of directions is often a major impediment to effective administration of this measure. Many of the students to whom this test is most frequently given may be those experiencing receptive language confusions with such abstract concepts as same/different. Blank (1968) indeed found that results on the ADT often reflect this conceptual deficit rather than auditory discrimination problems.

It has been cautioned that the ADT be used only as an informal measure of auditory skills. Although test-retest reliability is high, there is limited description of the normative population (Wallace & Larsen, 1978). Furthermore, questionable cause-effect relationships between perception and production given different phonetic contexts and the limited number of sound pairs sampled (Locke, 1979) raise issues open to serious deliberation when interpreting this clinical tool. That is, sound contrasts considered relevant to articulation (e.g., b/v, w/r, th/s) are not included and, even if they were, would not provide conclusive information regarding auditory discrimination ability on the basis of one presentation.

Tests of Auditory Conceptualization

Some auditory receptive skill measures extend beyond discrimination of speech sounds to incorporate higher-level cognitive functioning of the auditory system. This area is called auditory conceptualization. The *Lindamood Auditory Conceptualization Test* (LAC; Lindamood & Lindamood, 1971) is administered individually to assess auditory discrimination and the ability to perceive the number and order of sounds in sequence. The test can be used with preschoolers to adults. Test administration is divided into three parts: (1) precheck, during which time the teacher ascertains that the student is familiar with the concepts same/different and first/last, left to right order, and numbers one to four; (2) Category I (Parts A and B), in which the student must determine the number and order of sounds heard while discriminating whether they are the same or different; and (3) Category II, in which the student must detect the number of sounds in a syllable and determine where changes occur when sounds are added, omitted, substituted, shifted, or repeated. All responses are obtained through student manipulation of colored blocks to represent sound, number, order, and differences.

The LAC is a novel approach to assessing auditory perception, which attempts to meaningfully extend interpretation beyond auditory discrimination to auditory analysis skills important not only for listening and speaking but also for reading and spelling. Remedial implications for teachers follow easily. For example, students beginning to read who do well on this measure and do not demonstrate difficulty acquiring sound/symbol relationships appear as suitable candidates for phonics training. Less can be inferred when students do not do well on the LAC. Very young children and those less intellectually capable often have difficulty understanding the nature of the task, particularly in Category II. In fact, differences of opinion exist among reviewers as to ease of examiner administration of tasks (see Burke, 1979; Compton, 1984).

Raw scores on the LAC are converted to grade level scores, the usefulness of which is controversial (Burke, 1979; Compton, 1984). Standardization procedures have also been questioned with regard to test/retest reliability (Burke, 1979). When further insights regarding auditory perceptual abilities are sought, teachers may find subjective observations and objective results of performance on this measure useful for instruction.

Auditory memory skills should also routinely be assessed to aid in analyzing the student's articulation. Inability to recall numbers of sounds and their sequential order, for example, can have serious consequences on speech intelligibility. The LAC includes tasks that evaluate these abilities.

Tests of Articulation

Expressively, articulation tests traditionally elicited samples of student's sound production by presentation of picture stimuli of words or contexts in which target sounds were embedded. The following section discusses a number of such tests.

The *Goldman-Fristoe Test of Articulation* (Goldman & Fristoe, 1972) has three component subtests—Sounds in Words, Sounds in Sentences, and Stimulation—to provide assessment of sounds both in words and context for students 3 to 16 years of age. Colorful pictures are used to elicit production of sounds in words while equally interesting picture stories are presented to evaluate sounds in sentences. Phonemes misarticulated during the Sounds in Words subtest are presented again by the teacher in the context of syllables, words, and sentences during the Stimulation subtest. An easy-to-manipulate easel kit facilitates administration.

Most valuable as a descriptive measure, the Goldman-Fristoe does have normative data for the Sounds in Words subtest and the syllabic portion of the Stimulation subtest. Test-retest and interjudge reliabilities are available for the Sounds in Words and Sounds in Sentences subtests, while only interjudge reliabilities have been established for the Stimulation subtest. While these are adequate, the absence of reliability estimates for age levels despite the use of age levels as the basis for the presentation of norms has been criticized (Mecham, 1979).

One of the most common criticisms of the Goldman-Fristoe is its neglect of distinctive feature theory (Compton, 1984; Mecham, 1979). Not unlike other standardized articulation measures, the Goldman-Fristoe concentrates on the analysis of a student's motor production of speech sounds rather than on the evaluation of a student's use of those rules which determine effective articulation of certain phonemes. While lauded for its attempt to include assessment of articulation of language in context, concerns persist regarding the weakness of standardization of the Sounds in Sentences subtest and its subsequent interpretation (Mecham, 1979). Difficulties with easy recording of results on the complicated recording form have also been reported by clinicians (Compton, 1984).

The *Templin-Darley Tests* (Templin & Darley, 1969) are comprised of a 50-item Screening Test, a 141-item Diagnostic Test, and a 43-item Iowa Pressure Articulation Test. The Screening Test is intended for use as a measure of general articulation adequacy while the Diagnostic Test provides a more detailed analysis of articulation abilities. The Iowa Pressure Articulation Test assesses the adequacy of velopharyngeal closure.

The Templin-Darley elicits production of vowels; diphthongs; single consonants in initial, medial, and final positions of words; and consonant blends in varying combinations in response to colored picture stimuli. Error sounds are stimulable through imitation. Norms are available for students 3 to 8 years of age.

Criticisms of the Templin-Darley generally stem from linguistic concerns that the limited sound-in-word approach may not accurately reflect speech in context and the importance of phonological rule learning and distinctive feature analysis. It continues to be regarded as a practical, versatile set of instruments and is often employed in public school settings.

The *Fisher-Logemann Test of Articulation Competence* (Fisher & Logemann, 1971) uses an approach to articulation assessment that is inspired by Jakobson's (1968) theory of phonological development, which is based upon distinctive-feature analysis. Distinctive features are phonemic characteristics that are specified in terms of articulatory patterns and acoustic properties. For example, the distinctive feature of voicing distinguishes the consonant sounds /b/ from /p/ despite their identical articulatory positions. The Fisher-Logemann is designed to test production of all English phonemes in systematic occurrence according to syllabic function (prevocalic, intervocalic, postvocalic). Two test forms are available: one uses colored pictures to elicit articulation of target phonemes, while the other permits articulation evaluation as students read sentences within which target phonemes are included. A short form using pictures is also available for screening. Errors are summarized and analyzed according to the distinctive features that are violated. Voicing, place of articulation, and manner of articulation are those distinctive features of tongue height, place of articulation, degree of tension, and lip-rounding.

Both the picture version and the sentence version of the Fisher-Logemann are presented attractively and conveniently for administration. Excellent content validity is demonstrated by the thorough inclusion of all consonant and vowel sounds in the English language as well as by the well-chosen familiar and frequently occurring children's vocabulary stimuli. However, information about reliability is not available. The Fisher-Logemann deserves recognition for its uniquely comprehensive approach to articulation assessment. Recommendations for therapy are greatly assisted by the useful linguistic considerations given to both phonological commonalities and the nature of articulatory inadequacies. Differences in dialect are also taken into account.

The *Test of Articulation Performance—Screen* (TAP–S) was developed to identify children who have significant articulation difficulties and who need more intense articulation evaluation (Bryant & Bryant, 1983a). It is composed of 31 word items, each of which represents a key English phoneme. A word is elicited from the student by using a stimulus picture and sentence. If a student has difficulty with the standard format, he or she is requested to repeat the word spoken by the examiner. The child's response is then compared to Standard English production and scored accordingly. Raw scores from the test are converted to articulation quotients, percentile ranks, and age equivalents.

The TAP–S standardization sample included 1,014 children from 18 states. The characteristics of the sample were similar in regard to sex, residence, race, geographic areas, and occupation of parents as reported in the *Statistical Abstract of the United States* (1980). Age equivalents are available for raw scores from 3-0 to 9-0 years. The manual reports the following reliability coefficients: internal, .92 to .97; test-retest, .93 to .94; alternate form, .95 to .98. A number of validity studies were also performed and are reported in the test manual. These studies reveal adequate concurrent validity coefficients. An advantage of the TAP–S is that the articulation quotients (i.e., mean 100, SD 15) allow teachers to compare the test scores to other frequently used educational instruments (e.g., WISC–R, K–ABC, VSMS) that use a similar distribution.

A more comprehensive system to measure articulation difficulties is the *Test of Articulation Performance—Diagnostic* (TAP–D) (Bryant & Bryant, 1983b). Detailed information on a student's strengths and weaknesses results from the administration of the following procedures (1) Isolated Words evaluates phonemic errors in terms of substitutions, omissions, and distortions; (2) Distinctive Features assesses speech performance in terms of place, manner, and voicing characteristics; (3) Selective Deep Testing examines phonemic errors in conjunction with other speech sounds; (4) Continuous Speech; (5) Stimulability evaluates phonemes produced in syllables, words, and sentences during modeling situations; and (6) Verbal Communication Scales measures the student's overall speech adequacy at home and school (Bryant & Bryant, 1983c).

A number of studies were carried out to assess the reliability of the TAP–D. The reliability coefficients resulting from these studies exceeded .80 with a few above .90. Additionally, the test manual describes a number of validity studies that demonstrate the components of the TAP–D as highly valid measures. The value of this 160-item instrument is the remedial intervention information that results from the analysis of the student's articulation difficulties.

Semantics

Children's meaningful use of words and sentences comprises another area of investigation in oral language assessment. By 5 years of age most youngsters use about 1,500 words, approximately one-half of the average adult's active vocabulary (Walechinsky & Wallace, 1981). The child's first 50 words typically include names of salient objects or events in his or her immediate environment (e.g., Mommy, Daddy, cookie, juice). Soon the names of animals and the associated sounds they make are added to the child's verbal repertoire (deVilliers & deVilliers, 1978). Overextensions, or the use of words for objects to which these words are not normally applied (e.g., "horsie" for all four-legged large animals), are frequent during emerging language years. Children's learning of categorization skills facilitates the use of word forms when they begin to classify word meanings (e.g., apples, bananas, and pears are considered as fruits). Similarly, children's increasingly adept social interaction skills help them learn more about the appropriate functions of language (e.g., correct association of referring forms with their respective objects in a way that takes the previous knowledge of the listener into account).

Tests of Receptive Vocabulary
While context is recognized as critical in the study of semantics, most assessment tools restrict diagnostic concerns to the evaluation of words. Understanding words in isolation and within connected language is a routine procedure in oral language assessment. Tests of receptive vocabulary are reviewed below.

A multidimensional instrument that assesses expressive and receptive skills of young children is the *Test of Early Language Development* (TELD). It is an untimed test that is administered individually to children from 3-0 to 7-11 years of age (Hresko, Reid, &

Hammill, 1981). Raw scores from the TELD are transformed to language quotients, percentile scores, and age equivalents.

The TELD was standardized on 1,184 children who lived in 11 states and one Canadian province. The characteristics of the children in the standardized sample very closely paralleled the United States population as reported in the *Statistical Abstract of the United States* (1980) relative to sex, place of residence, geographic area, race, occupation of parents, and age. Studies on the reliability of the TELD revealed internal consistency reliability coefficients around .90 and test-retest stability coefficients in the mid-range of the .80s. A construct validity study reported in the manual indicated a .80 correlation coefficient between test scores and ages of the children in the standardized sample.

The TELD's response format is convenient for the evaluator to plot a student's performance in the receptive and expressive channels with regard to content and form. This feature allows for quick profiling of the student's language strengths and weaknesses. Since the test has good reliability and validity, it can be useful in identifying children who are not keeping pace with peers in the language domain. Lastly, because it can be administered in about 15 minutes, this test would be useful for monitoring the language progress of a student when routine documentation is required.

The *Peabody Picture Vocabulary Test—Revised* (PPVT–R; Dunn & Dunn, 1981) is a classically popular measure in speech/language assessment that assesses a student's single-word vocabulary understanding within a 10- to 20-minute administration period. Easy to give, score, and interpret, the PPVT–R consists of a book of black-and-white line drawings, four on a page. The teacher asks the student to select the one picture from the four that best represents the stimulus word, using the instruction "Put your finger on the picture of the word I have just said." (Older students are permitted to call out the number of the picture.)

Well standardized and recently revised, the PPVT–R is generally considered well-designed and reliable. The question of validity, however, has become much more controversial primarily because of its employment as a measure of verbal intelligence rather than as a test of auditory receptive vocabulary (Weiner, 1979). Since revision, however, the PPVT no longer yields an "intelligence quotient." Mental ages (age equivalents) and percentile equivalents are still obtained.

In most cases, administrative care can be taken to help students maintain attention and monitor for impulsive responses on the PPVT. Inattention and impulsivity are commonly evidenced, however, as in perseveration to a picture position, e.g., lower right-hand corner. Interfering problems with picture interpretation may also be observed, such as a "spatula" being depicted by a long, narrow server as opposed to a more rectangular instrument, while an alternative easily confused picture choice of a rectangular "scoop" demands visual interpretation of shading representing depth. It cannot be assumed that all students share the ability to attach meaning to two-dimensional visual representation which often includes symbolic images.

The *Test of Auditory Comprehension of Language* (TACL; Carrow, 1973) assesses receptive language skills for selected vocabulary and linguistic structures. English and Spanish versions are available. Four subscales of language categories are measured: (1) form class and function words, (2) morphological constructions, (3) grammatical categories, and (4) syntactic structures. All test items are presented to the student auditorily; he or she must point to one of the three drawings on each plate of the test book that best represents the stimulus. Because items are sequenced by grammatical levels and not by item difficulty, the entire test of 101 items must be administered. While this procedure minimizes feelings of mounting frustration for some students, order effects may occur (Miller, 1979). In addition, criticisms have been made in reference to the limited size and geographic distribution of the standardization sample, the inability of the teacher to repeat stimulus items, and the failure of test results to discriminate students with less than serious language problems. However, high test-retest reliability has been demonstrated, and the developmental progression in language comprehension is valuable to diagnosis and remediation.

A screening version of the TACL, STACL, designed for group administration, is also available. Cautions regarding picture interpretation problems similar to those that may be encountered on the PPVT and that may detract from an assessment of pure language processing should also be extended.

The *Boehm Test of Basic Concepts* (BTBC; Boehm, 1971) combines cognitive and linguistic principles in an instrument that measures understanding of verbal concepts of space, quantity, and time for students in kindergarten through second grade. The BTBC has two equivalent forms and may be administered as a group or individual test in Spanish as well as English. Fifty items of increasing difficulty are presented via black line drawings within two test booklets. The teacher provides the directions orally, and the student marks an X on his or her selected pictorial choice. Results can be compared intra-individually or by class groups as record forms are available which aid in determination of appropriate individual or group remedial programming.

Attractive in presentation and simple to administer and interpret, the BTBC makes an adequate attempt to identify students with cognitive and/or linguistic deficiencies that may disrupt early academic learning. While teachers appreciate the bridge the BTBC provides between diagnostic and remedial information, there is a lack of documentation to show that those items selected do in fact correlate with early academic success, thus raising questions about test validity (Compton, 1984). Ascertaining whether errors reflect deficits in conceptual or linguistic competence also becomes crucial when making diagnostic interpretations. Reliability is generally agreed to be adequate (Hannah, 1979), and large standardization samples representative of different socioeconomic classes and geographic regions within the United States provide impressive normative data.

Similar concerns to those raised with other tests that utilize picture stimuli for response measurement must be addressed. The numbers of stimulus pictures within an item (four) and the number of items on a page (four) may prove overwhelming to easily distracted children. Picture interpretation problems may also be contaminating. Generally, however, teachers report enthusiasm for the relevance and straightforwardness of this tool and express interest in an advanced form that might assist assessment of those cognitive-linguistic skills that affect academic performance in such areas as math and social skills.

Tests of Expressive Vocabulary

Tests for measuring expressive vocabulary are not numerous, and many of those available are often criticized by speech/language pathologists for failing to accurately identify children whose expressive vocabulary problems appear to significantly affect classroom performance when observed subjectively. Selected items from intelligence test measures are often employed informally to supplement standardized instruments (e.g., Picture Completion on the WISC–R). Word-finding deficits are also often explored through rapid naming drills (Rutherford, 1977) such as those found in the Verbal Expression and the Auditory Association subtests of the *Illinois Test of Psycholinguistic Abilities* as well as the Producing Names on Confrontation and the Producing Word Associations subtests of the *Clinical Evaluation of Language Functions* (CELF; Semel & Wiig, 1980).

The Producing Names on Confrontation subtest of the CELF evaluates the student's accuracy, fluency, and speed in naming colors, forms, and color-form combinations in response to a picture card showing 36 randomly sequenced colored shapes. The limited nonverbal visual stimuli elicit limited vocabulary options (red, blue, yellow, black, circle, square, triangle), resulting in a task that differs from more open-ended naming functions demanded by tasks such as those involved in picture/object identification or spontaneous thinking and speaking.

The Producing Word Associations subtest of the CELF provides another measure of word retrieval. It evaluates the quantity and quality of verbalizing semantically related word series from long-term memory. Students are asked to name as many "foods" and "animals" as they can within periods of 60 seconds each. Responses are scored for quantity (number of different items mentioned) and quality (numbers of shifts within subclasses, such as pets, wild animals, farm animals).

All standardized tests of expressive vocabulary should be augmented by language samples that can reflect word retrieval abilities in natural speaking environments.

Syntax

Appraisal of a student's arrangement of words into phrases and sentences is popularly performed receptively and expressively. The student's assimilation of those roles of language that permit him or her to grammatically express ideas and relationships between them is an exciting accomplishment. The child developing language learns meanings of words in their isolated forms as well as relationships held between them that are demonstrated by his or her word order. Comprehension and application of certain linguistic structures in connected language are thus important areas to examine when assessing a student's communicative abilities. The following section reviews tests that are frequently employed to evaluate student's comprehension of use of syntactic structures.

The *Northwestern Syntax Screening Test* (NSST; Lee, 1971) is an instrument for the assessment of children's comprehension and use of syntactic structures. It consists of 40 items, 20 intended to measure receptive syntax and 20 to examine expressive syntax. Stimulus items are presented using black-and-white line-drawn pictures, 10 four-choice plates for the receptive section and 10 two-choice plates for the expressive section. The same linguistic structures are tested receptively and expressively: personal pronouns, possessives, question words beginning with *wh*, demonstratives, verb tenses, plural inflections, negation, yes/no questions, active/passive voice, and double-object constructions. On the receptive portion, the teacher verbalizes a pair of stimulus sentences and then repeats one, the representation of which the student is to point to from among four alternative pictures. On the expressive section, the teacher again says two stimulus sentences as the student views the two stimulus pictures on the plate. The teacher then points to one of the two pictures, requesting the student to verbalize the correct sentence match from the two choices provided by the teacher.

The NSST is respected as a pioneer among oral language assessment tools. It has been shown to differentiate among normal language development, severely delayed expressive language, and retarded language development (Ratusnik & Koenigsknecht, 1975). Perhaps the test's greatest criticisms resulted from the zeal with which it was applied. Lee (1977) emphasized that the NSST is only a screening test and does not include all syntactic structures in need of evaluation nor other facets of language development important to study, i.e., semantics. She advises establishment of local norms, recognizing that the standardization sample was limited in size as well as socioeconomically and geographically. Beyond the level of 6-0 years to 6-11 years, norms are doubtful. The NSST is quick and easy to give. The format of oral sentence presentation and repetition to measure receptive abilities, followed by the expressive syntax subtest, can prove tedious to some students. In spite of the latter, the NSST remains an adequate guide for further diagnosis and/or remediation.

The *Token Test* (DeRenzi & Vignolo, 1962) was designed to assess auditory disturbances in aphasia. It consists of five parts that measure the ability to retain, recall, and execute a series of oral directions of increasing length and complexity with minimal redundancy. The student performs the auditorily presented commands by manipulating tokens that vary along three dimensions—color, shape, and size. The *Token Test* is commonly employed to evaluate a student's auditory comprehension skills in receptive syntax.

Numerous forms of the Token test are currently in use (e.g., Spellacy & Spreen, 1969; McNeil & Prescott, 1978). While all forms are considered valid (Wertz, 1979), the test's limited standardization information and the absence of measures of test-retest reliability must be recognized. Knowledgeable researchers generally agree that the strengths of the *Token Test* include its quick and easy administration, its simple materials, its wide range of linguistic forms and concepts tapped, its control of redundancy, and its independence of intelligence. Wiig and Semel (1980) distinguish Parts I–IV from Part V for clinical use, suggesting that Part V has particularly valuable application with learning disabled adolescents in whom subtle, high-level language processing deficits are suspected.

Pragmatics

Concerns regarding children's pragmatics, or language in use, have burgeoned. However, tests for the assessment of pragmatic skills in children are just beginning to be developed. Parts of the *Preschool Language Assessment Instrument* (Blank, Rose & Berlin, 1978) help provide information about the "language of learning in practice" but do not supply normative data since the test is still an experimental version. Informal procedures can be devised to elicit information about this important component of communicative functioning. These will be discussed later in this chapter.

Tests of General Language Abilities

The following tests attempt to examine language abilities by including a number of subtests that tap different components of communicative functioning.

An instrument that evaluates a child's strengths and weaknesses in language is the *Test of Language Development—Primary* (TOLD–P). More specifically, the TOLD–P is useful in identifying children who function below their peers in language usage and in profiling children's skill development in language as a result of remedial instruction (Newcomer & Hammill, 1982). According to the manual, the test can be used with children from the age of 4 through 8 years. Its eight subtests include: Picture Vocabulary; Oral Vocabulary; Grammatic Understanding; Grammatic Completion; Sentence Imitation; Word Discrimination; and Word Articulation. The subtests are grouped to construct five composites: semantics, syntax, receptive, expressive, and total. Raw scores for the subtests are converted into language age, percentiles, and standard scores. Quotients are used for the composites. The quotients have a mean of 100 and a standard deviation of 15, whereas the standard scores have a mean of 10 and a standard deviation of 3.

The TOLD–P was standardized on 1,836 children who lived in 19 states and one Canadian province. The sample's distribution with regard to sex, place of residence, race, geographic areas, and occupation of parents is very similar to the United States population that was reported in the *Statistical Abstract of the United States* (1980). Information in the test manual indicated internal consistency reliability coefficients ranging from .57 to .96 and test-retest reliability coefficients ranging from .86 to .99. Extensive studies were carried out to measure content, criterion-related, and construct validity. Factor analysis studies revealed strengths of the test in measuring language areas of phonology and semantics and a weakness in the area of syntax. Overall, the TOLD–P has adequate reliability and validity to be used as a multicomponent language instrument.

A test that is useful in the assessment of language skills of students 8 through 12 years of age is the *Test of Language Development—Intermediate* (TOLD–I). Two subtests measure understanding and meaningful use of spoken words and three subtests assess aspects of grammar usage (Hammill & Newcomer, 1982). Scores are reported as in the TOLD–P.

The standardization sample for the TOLD–I consisted of 871 children from 13 states. Characteristics of the sample approximate those reported in the *Statistical Abstract of the United States* (1980) for sex, place of residence, race, geographic area, and occupation of parents. Internal consistency reliability coefficients reported in the manual are adequate except for Word Ordering. Test-retest stability reliability is acceptable for all scores at all ages. The manual describes a variety of validity studies. Information from these studies support the use of the test to discriminate children who have language difficulties and those who do not.

Another test that provides data about general language ability is the *Detroit Tests of Learning Aptitude—Revised Edition* (DTLA-2). This is a completely revised version of an earlier popular battery first normed in the 1930s. The DTLA-2 (Hammill, 1985) now has 11 subtests that are grouped in such a manner as to yield important information about four domains (i.e., linguistic, cognitive, attentional, and motoric) within the psychological constitution.

Of interest here are the two groups of subtests that comprise the linguistic domain: the Verbal Composite and the Nonverbal Composite. The Verbal Composite is made up of measures of vocabulary, grammar, following commands, repeating words, story telling, and closure function. A child's performance on the Verbal Composite is contrasted with performance on the Nonverbal Composite to identify the presence of general verbal (language) problems.

The DTLA-2 was normed on more than 1,500 students from 31 states. Standard scores and percentiles are provided. Characteristics of the normative group are the same as those for the 1980 census relative to sex, geographic region, ethnicity, race, and urban/rural residence. Internal consistency reliability of subtests and composite scores approximate .80 at all age levels. Criterion-related validity is evidenced by a large (.60–.80) correlative relationship with other tests of aptitude (WISC–R, PPVT). Construct validity is evidenced by moderately large significant correlations with the SRA Achievement Series and by five additional analyses.

The *Illinois Test of Psycholinguistic Abilities* (ITPA; Kirk, McCarthy, & Kirk, 1968) is one of the best known tests designed to evaluate oral language skills in children from 2 to 10 years of age. Devised according to Osgood's (1957) model of communication as a diagnostic instrument that would help prescribe remediation needs, the ITPA is composed of 12 subtests that tap different aspects of the model. Subtests are intended to isolate specific psycholinguistic strengths and weaknesses along three dimensions of cognitive abilities: (1) processes; (2) channels referring to modalities of communication (auditory-vocal, auditory-motor, visual-motor, visual-vocal); and (3) levels relating to presumed forms of language organization, automatic and representational. Scores within and among these dimensions can be compared. Raw scores can be converted into scaled scores or age scores for individual subtests, and the total of the 10 subtests considered basic can yield an overall "psycholinguistic age." Individual subtests are presented in Table 6.2.

Innumerable studies have been conducted to evaluate the ade-

TABLE 6.2 Subtests of the Illinois Test of Psycholinguistic Abilities

Representational level	Automatic level
Auditory Reception	Visual Memory
Visual Reception	Auditory Memory
Auditory Association	Visual Closure
Visual Association	Grammatic Closure
Verbal Expression	Auditory Closure[a]
Manual Expression	Sound Blending[a]

[a]Supplementary

quacy of the ITPA as a language test (Carroll, 1972). While it is a carefully constructed diagnostic instrument with exhaustive statistical data suggesting adequate reliability, standardization procedures are questionable. Norms were derived from a limited sample of middle-class children who were not experiencing difficulties in school. The validity of the ITPA has also become widely debated. Whether this test does indeed test what it purports to is questioned (Carroll, 1972). In addition to the limited evidence that psycholinguistic abilities can be isolated and measured, the individual subtests of the ITPA have been criticized for their content (Prutting, 1979). For example, a picture analogy task on the Visual Association subtest depicts a cat and bird; the student is to match a dog in an analogous relationship to either a horse, a pair of shoes, a rabbit, or a fish. The correct answer is rabbit, operating on the assumption that the act of "chasing" is what links both pairs of animals together. Were the student to identify "attacking" as the critical attribute, the pair of shoes would be equally logical (i.e., cats attack birds and dogs attack shoes).

The questionable developmental ordering of items in the subtests, as in Grammatic Closure (Prutting, 1979), and the combined language/nonlanguage demands of tasks supposedly designed to measure one of the two, as in the nonlanguage subtest Visual Memory, which can be influenced by verbal mediation (Compton, 1984), have also been viewed skeptically. Most of all, ITPA items have been criticized because of their failure to meaningfully relate to academic tasks. Making associations between pictures (Visual Association) or finding objects embedded among many pictures on a paper strip (Visual Closure) does not necessarily help identify students who display problems making sound/letter associations or who have problems keeping their place on a page of print or selecting out relevant visual differences within words. Johnson (1975) has stressed the importance of differentiating such verbal from nonverbal task demands when making predictions about reading performance.

Despite the recent onset of concerns regarding the limitations of the ITPA, it remains a potential tool for the teacher when included within a comprehensive test battery. Increased understanding of its ability to assess cognitive skills, nonverbally and verbally with and without linguistic accompaniment through visual and auditory modalities, can add important information to the diagnostic prescriptive process.

The *Clinical Evaluation of Language Functions* (CELF; Semel & Wiig, 1980) exemplifies recent trends to investigate language *functions* as well as *forms*. It addresses the interests of teachers and special educators in examining interactions of cognition and language in school-age children. The areas of syntax, semantics, memory, and word finding and retrieval are evaluated in the Diagnostic Battery through six processing subtests and five production subtests. Individual subtests are presented in Table 6.3.

Two supplementary subtests (Processing Speech Sounds and Producing Speech Sounds) are also included to examine phonology. The authors indicate that the CELF is not designed to provide in-depth assessment at the levels of phonology or pragmatics and should be complemented by other standardized language/learning tests and behavior observations. The CELF has been welcomed as a measurement tool that assists the subsequent development of language objectives for student's individualized educational programs (IEPs). Many of the items provide information similar to that available on other formal subtests (e.g., Processing Spoken Paragraphs/Durrell Analysis of Reading Difficulty Listening Comprehension subtest); however, their inclusion on one standardized instrument is facilitating.

Information provided regarding the CELF's standardization, reliability, and concurrent validity is adequate. Following numerous

TABLE 6.3 Subtests of the Clinical Evaluation of Language Functions

Processing subtests
Processing Word and Sentence Structure
Processing Word Classes
Processing Linguistic Concepts
Processing Relationship and Ambiguities
Processing Oral Directions
Processing Spoken Paragraphs

Production subtests
Producing Word Series
Producing Names on Confrontation
Producing Word Associations
Producing Model Sentences
Producing Formulated Sentences

expressions of concern that the original grade-level criteria supplied in lieu of norms were too "low" and thus failed to identify children whose language disabilities seemed apparent clinically, traditional normative data were made available in 1982.

CASE STUDY

Part II

Present Test Findings

Oral language assessment included administration of the following formal standardized tests, listed along with the scores Timothy obtained on each.

Peabody Picture Vocabulary Test
On the PPVT Timothy scored a Mental Age of 7-8 years (46th percentile).

Boehm Test of Basic Concepts
Timothy's score on the BTBC was at the 35th percentile. He had difficulties comprehending the following concepts: separately, pair, equal, least, some/not many, in order, skip.

Wepman Auditory Discrimination Test
Timothy's performance on the Wepman showed average ability.

Goldman-Fristoe Test of Articulation
Timothy obtained a perfect score on the Goldman-Fristoe.

Illinois Test of Psycholinguistic Abilities
Timothy's scores on the various subtests of the ITPA were as follows:

Subtest	Scaled Score	Psycholinguistic Age Score
Auditory Reception	27	6-2 years
Auditory Association	26	6-2 years
Grammatic Closure	20	5-10 years
Visual Reception	39	9-4 years
Visual Association	41	8-11 years
Verbal Expression	25	5-6 years
Manual Expression	29	7-3 years

Informal language assessment included the following excerpt from a language sample obtained in response to a picture stimulus:

He holded the kite real tight. The other kid pulled more, morest. But I . . . me—that's me [pointing to third boy in picture] pulled most. Nobody got this kite. It gots one down in the back, down bottom or up top.

Summary

Timothy demonstrates a receptive language problem that is particularly manifest when he is confronted by abstract vocabulary concepts and connected language. Problems with auditory memory skills were also evidenced. Expressive language skills are thus affected.

Results of formal oral language assessment were significant in identifying difficulties with abstract vocabulary concepts (BTBC). Single-word understanding of more concrete nouns and verbs, as measured by the PPVT, was noticeably better, distinguishing selected areas of receptive vocabulary as problematic. Comprehension of corrected language was also poor as evidenced by comparison between the Auditory Reception and Visual Reception subtests of the ITPA. Auditory discrimination skills were not affected.

Supplementary informal data (e.g., responses on the Information and Arithmetic subtests of the WISC–R) further collaborated teacher reports of difficulties understanding language heard and problems with math reasoning. The language involved in directions and math was implicated as an interferent to academic learning.

Analysis of expressive language findings revealed verbal deficits in semantics and syntax. Note the contrast between Auditory Reception and Visual Association on the ITPA and the depressed Grammatic Closure score. Similarly, the difference between Verbal Expression and Manual Expression is worth noting. Although the latter subtest does not approach age expectations or visual subtest results, it does compare favorably with tasks that demand verbal formulation. How much verbal mediation may influence manual expression has likewise not been explored.

Auditory memory skills, which were tested by obtaining verbal responses to orally presented stimuli, were also found to be disproportionately low. Interrelationships between linguistic rule learning, as needed in the acquisition of morphology and auditory memory skills, should be recognized. Limited auditory memory skills may also be implicated in restricting phonics learning.

Timothy's expressive phonology skills, as reflected in his perfect GFT articulation score were not a problem area. It could be posited that his good auditory discrimination abilities positively influenced the acquisition of well-developed aritculation.

Informal language assessment via the language sample excerpt quoted suggests that language in use, or pragmatics skills, are also underdeveloped. Failure to demonstrate a sense of audience or awareness of the listener's lack of knowledge about topics addressed is apparent in Timothy's reliance upon pronouns to introduce referents (e.g., *"He* holded the kite . . . " Further examination in this area would be advised).

Recommendations

Whether Timothy is retained in second grade is secondary to whether or not his academic curriculum will address his receptive/expressive language needs. Modification of oral direction giving in the classroom as well as within instructions related to math concepts and basic reading skills will be important. Timothy was referred for a period of diagnostic teaching to help determine those educational strategies that would best interface with the learner characteristics described above.

Informal Assessment of Oral Language Skills

While standardized test instruments are often the measures of choice when documenting a student's oral language disorder, much can also be learned from thoughtful informal assessment. In fact, professionals in speech/language research have strongly stated that competent informal assessment must accompany formal testing if language disorders are to be examined effectively (Danwitz, 1981).

Informal assessment provides teachers opportunities to observe speech and language behaviors in unstructured contexts. Greater opportunities exist to evaluate a student's oral language skills in spontaneous communicative environments such as the student's language in the classroom. Informal assessment permits the teacher to gather information about self-generated articulation and semantic, syntactic, and pragmatic skills, and allows for contrasts between structured linguistic test performance and generalization of linguistic structures for functional communicative purposes. It is felt that the use of informal assessment instruments in combination with formal assessment results provides the teacher with a total perspective concerning a youngster's oral language abilities. A review of commonly used informal assessment techniques is presented below.

The Language Sample

The most commonly used procedure for the informal assessment of oral language skills is the language sample. The language sample can be obtained through questioning formats, informal conversation, storytelling, and use of picture stimuli. The student's spontaneous speech in response to these stimulus situations is tape recorded and transcribed for analysis.

The way in which a language sample is structured can significantly influence the language obtained. An adequate sample of language must be gathered in order to make any meaningful judgments. Generally, language that is collected in 30 minutes and that contains 50–100 utterances is considered adequate. However, this general rule remains open to question (Dale, 1976). Care must also be taken in stimulating discourse through inquiry since question formats determine the nature of the response as in yes/no or one-word utterances.

Open-ended requests to "tell me" about an object or events, and questions such as "What's happening in this picture?" or "How did it happen?" generally yield increased output.

Techniques such as using picture sequencing cards to encourage verbal storytelling should also be carefully monitored. Pictures that are clear and lend themselves well to the narration of cause-effect relationships are preferable to stimuli that are ambiguous. Storytelling to pictures can reveal differences in metalinguistic functioning or a student's knowledge about the language he or she uses. The "language of narration" (Podhajski, 1980) is a particularly interesting area to explore as part of an oral language assessment. Table 6.4 notes the differences between narrations by a 7-year-old learning disabled student and a 7-year-old nonlearning disabled student when asked to tell a story about a series of pictures each child had just sequenced. For the learning disabled child, picture sequences did not serve a facilitating function for eliciting a language sample. However, the sequences did reveal useful clinical data regarding a possible lack of metalinguistic awareness of the language of storytelling. This learning disabled student, who was known to have a history of oral language problems, chose to refer to the process of picture placement rather than the pictured events. The nonlearning disabled child, on the other hand, offered a representative sample of his oral language abilities when asked to tell a story to pictures.

Language samples also afford opportunities for teachers to evaluate students' speech intelligibility, level of vocabulary usage, sentence type and syntactic structures employed, and overall ability to formulate ideas. Numerous researchers (e.g., Crystal, Fletcher, & Garman, 1976) have developed detailed methods of analyzing students' language samples according to syntactic patterns. The reader is

TABLE 6.4 Samples Obtained from Two Seven-Year-Old Children in Response to a Five-Part Picture Sequence

Learning disabled student	Nonlearning disabled student
This one	A little boy went fishing
And this one	He got a worm, put it on the hook
And this one	And he put it in the water
And this one	Sat down
And this one	And he got a teddy-bear
(Learning disabled student verbally referring to process of picture placement)	(Nonlearning disabled student describing story pictures)

From "Picture Arrangement and Selected Narrative Language Skills in Learning Disabled and Normal Seven-Year-Old Children" by B. R. Podhajski, unpublished doctoral dissertation, 1980, Northwestern University, Evanston, Illinois.

directed to these sources if further information regarding syntactic analyses of spontaneous language is desired.

Mean Length of Utterance (MLU) and Developmental Sentence Analysis (DSA)

Two other frequently used procedures for informally assessing spontaneous language are the *Mean Length of Utterance* (MLU) procedure (Brown, 1973) and *Developmental Sentence Analysis* (DSA; Lee, 1974). The MLU procedure is one by which utterance length provides a simple measure of grammatical development. MLU is considered the best single indicator of language development for youngsters under 5 years of age (Dale, 1976). Validity has been demonstrated through correlation studies with psychological scaling judgments of development by adults as well as with specific aspects of syntactic development (Dale, 1976).

Perhaps the most powerful informal diagnostic assessment device is the *Developmental Sentence Analysis* (DSA), which incorporates a sentence scoring system. Comprehensive in nature, the DSA procedure is time-consuming but provides helpful information for educational intervention. Constructed upon developmental stages of language acquisition, DSA is a method whereby a student's use of grammatical rules in spontaneous language can be quantified and scored. Grammatical structure within sentences is analyzed by means of the *Developmental Sentence Scoring* (DSS) technique. Table 6.5 presents the developmental sequence of grammatical forms in each of the following eight categories: indefinite pronouns, personal pronouns, main verbs, secondary verbs, negatives, conjunctions, interrogatives, and questions beginning with *wh*. The DSA's highly structured format and its provision of goals for future lesson planning is very valuable. Its complementary program—Interactive Language Development Teaching (Lee, Koenigsknecht, & Mulhern, 1974)—offers suggestions to teachers for beginning remedial intervention with students found to demonstrate oral language problems.

Two other informal tests that can be helpful to teachers of students who have difficulties with morphological rule application are the *Berry-Talbott Language Tests* (Berry & Talbott, 1966) and the *Berko Experimental Test of Morphology* (Berko, 1961). Both use nonsense words to elicit knowledge about rules for formulating such morphological constructs as noun plurals, past and future tense, comparative adjectives, and singular and plural possessives. Test presentation involves having the teacher read the stimulus frame, which is accompanied by pictures so that the student can supply the appropriate morphological form. For example, "This is a nad. Now there is another one. There are two of them. There are two _____."

TABLE 6.5 Developmental Sentence Scoring Sequence of grammatical forms for scoring analysis

Score	Indefinite Pronouns or Noun Modifiers	Personal Pronouns	Main Verbs	Secondary Verbs
1	it, this, that	1st and 2nd person: I, me, my, mine, you, your(s)	A. Uninflected verb: I *see* you. B. copula, is or 's: *It's* red. C. is + verb + ing: He *is coming*.	
2		3rd person: he, him, his, she, her, hers	A. -s and -ed: *plays, played* B. irregular past: *are, saw* C. Copula: *am, are, was, were* D. Auxiliary *am, are, was, were*	Five early-developing infinitives: I *wanna see* (want to *see*) I'm *gonna see* (going to *see*) I *gotta see* (got to *see*) Lemme [to] see (let me [to] *see*) Let's [to] play (let [us to] *play*)
3	A. no, some, more, all, lot(s), one(s), two (etc.), other(s), another B. something, somebody, someone	A. Plurals: we, us, our(s), they, them, their B. these, those		Non-complementing infinitives: I stopped *to play*. I'm afraid *to look*. It's hard *to do* that.

Negatives	Conjunctions	Interrogative Reversals	Wh-Questions
it, this, that + copula or, auxiliary is, 's, + not. It's *not* mine. This is *not* a dog. That is *not* moving.		Reversal of copula: *Isn't it* red? *Were they* there?	
			A. who, what, what + noun: *Who* am I? *What* is he eating? *What book* are you reading? B. where, how many, how much, what . . . do, what . . . for *Where* did it go? *How much* do you want? *What* is he *doing*? *What* is a hammer *for*?
	and		

TABLE 6.5 *(continued)*

Score	Indefinite Pronouns or Noun Modifiers	Personal Pronouns	Main Verbs	Secondary Verbs
4	nothing, nobody, none, no one		A. can, will, may + verb: *may go* B. Obligatory do + verb: *don't go* C. Emphatic do + verb: I *do see*.	Participle, present or past: I see a boy *running*. I found the toy *broken*.
5		Reflexives: myself, yourself, himself, herself, itself, themselves		A. Early infinitival complements with differing subjects in kernels: I want you *to come*. Let him [*to*] *see*. B. Later infinitival complements: I had *to go*. I told him *to go*. I tried *to go*. C. Obligatory deletions: Make it [*to*] *go*. I'd better [*to*] *go*. D. Infinitive with wh-word: I know what *to get*.

Negatives	Conjunctions	Interrogative Reversals	Wh-Questions
can't, don't		Reversal of auxiliary be: *Is he* coming? *Isn't he* coming? *Was he* going? Wasn't *he* going?	
isn't, won't	A. but B. so, and so, so that C. or, if		when, how, how + adjective *When* shall I come? *How* do you do it? *How big* is it?

(continued)

TABLE 6.5 (continued)

Score	Indefinite Pronouns or Noun Modifiers	Personal Pronouns	Main Verbs	Secondary Verbs
				I know how *to do* it.
6		A. Wh-pronouns: who, which, whose, whom, what, that, how many, how much I know *who* came. That's *what* I said. B. Wh-word + infinitive: I know *what* to do. I know *who(m)* to take.	A. could, would, should, might + verb: *might come, could be* B. Obligatory does, did + verb C. Emphatic does, did + verb	
7	A. any, anything, anybody, anyone B. every, everything, everybody, everyone C. both, few, many, each, several, most, least, much, next, first, last, second (etc.)	(his) own, one, oneself, whichever, whoever, whatever Take *whatever* you like.	A. Passive with *get*, any tense Passive with *be*, any tense B. must, shall + verb: *must come* C. have + verb + en: *I've eaten* D. have got: *I've got* it.	Passive infinitival complement: With *get*: I have to *get dressed*. I don't want to *get hurt*. With *be*: I want *to be pulled*. It's going *to be locked*.

Negatives	Conjunctions	Interrogative Reversals	Wh-Questions
	because	A. Obligatory do, does, did: *Do they* run? *Does it* bite? *Didn't it* hurt? B. Reversal of modal: *Can you* play? *Won't it* hurt? *Shall I* sit down? C. Tag question: It's fun, *isn't it?* It isn't fun, *is it?*	
All other negatives: A. Uncontracted negatives: I can *not* go. He has *not* gone. B. Pronoun-auxiliary or pronoun-copula contraction: I'm *not* coming. He's *not* here. C. Auxiliary-negative or copula-			why, what if, how come how about + gerund *Why* are you crying? *What if* I won't do it? *How come* he is crying? *How about* coming with me?

(continued)

TABLE 6.5 *(continued)*

Score	Indefinite Pronouns or Noun Modifiers	Personal Pronouns	Main Verbs	Secondary Verbs
8			A. have been + verb + ing had been + verb + ing B. modal + have + verb + en: *may have eaten* C. modal + be + verb + ing: *could be playing* D. Other auxiliary combinations: *should have been sleeping*	Gerund: *Swinging* is fun. I like *fishing*. He started *laughing*.

From Lee, L. (1974). *Developmental Sentence Analysis*. Evanston, IL: Northwestern University Press.

Negatives	Conjunctions	Interrogative Reversals	Wh-Questions
negative contraction: He *wasn't* going. He *hasn't* Been seen. It couldn't be mine. They *aren't* big.			
	A. where, when, how, while, whether (or not), till, until, unless, since, before, after, for, as, as + adjective + as, as if, like, that, than I know *where* you are. Don't come *till* I call. B. Obligatory deletions: I run faster *than* you [run]. I'm *as big as* a man [is big]. It looks *like* a dog [looks] C. Elliptical deletions (score 0): That's *why* [I took it]. I know *how* [I can do it]. D. Wh-words + infinitive: I know *how* to do it. I know *where* to go.	A. Reversal of auxiliary have: *Has he seen you?* B. Reversal with two or three auxiliaries: *Has he been* eating? *Couldn't he have* waited? *Could he have been* crying? *Wouldn't he have been* going?	*whose, which, which + noun* *Whose* car is that? *Which book* do you want?

Information obtained from such tests can be compared with performances on formal tests such as the Grammatic Closure subtest of the ITPA to determine whether morphological rule application skills are consistent across nonsense and meaningful contexts. Inability to apply such rules in novel situations may have further implications for rule learning in other language tasks such as reading, as well as with regard to pragmatics.

Informal Pragmatics Assessment

Since formal test instruments available to investigate students' pragmatics of their application of "rules governing the use of language in context" (Bates, 1976) are limited, several parts of tests originally designed for other purposes have been utilized to assess pragmatics informally. These include the Comprehension and Picture Arrangement subtests of the *Wechsler Intelligence Scale for Children—Revised.* Mercer (1979) suggests informal assessment of pragmatics through situation-specific stimuli. For example, the use of picture cards or picture sequences that depict cause-effect relationships and subsequent interpersonal reactions (e.g., Why is the boy crying?) can be helpful. The *Preschool Language Assessment Instrument* (Blank, Rose, & Berlin, 1978) also taps skills important for classroom discourse.

Students' social perception skills are often linked to their knowledge of pragmatics. There is a paucity of information related to the assessment of social perception abilities in children despite the fact that such skills directly influence total communicative effectiveness and academic learning. It has been suggested that nonverbal skills, including social perception, are affected by linguistic variables (Podhajski, 1980). Because language is regarded as a primary tool for thinking (Bruner, 1973), it has been recognized as important in children's academic problem solving. More recently, "meta" skills such as "metamemory"—knowledge about how we remember for purposes of facilitating recall—are often linked with linguistic competence. For example, the use of verbal mediation, or talking through a task, often serves to enhance problem solutions and retention. Metalinguistics—knowledge about one's own language use—has also become a popular focus of recent research. Some children's inability to appreciate how to use language has been shown to affect oral as well as written language (Hook, 1976). Further study in the areas of pragmatics, social perception, and metalinguistics should be forthcoming.

Summary

Language is a complex process whereby thoughts and ideas are communicated verbally through the interacting systems of phonology, semantics, morphology, syntax, and pragmatics. The assessment of oral language skills in students is important because of the impact dysfunctioning language abilities can have upon a student's academic and social life.

Oral language skills significantly influence children's learning. Effective listening and speaking are precursors not only to successful reading and writing, but also to other school-related activities such as mathematics and the learning of social skills. When children demonstrate oral language deficits, their participation in school activities may be noticeably altered. The nature of language deficits may be blatant or subtle. Thus, a careful subjective and objective analysis of the difficulty is imperative.

Teachers are often among the first to detect the presence of an oral language disorder. Parents frequently become so accustomed to their children's communicative style that they neglect to consider it atypical and usually lack sufficient comparative information to notice how it varies. Similarly, pediatricians, while versed in child development, many times apply too general a criterion to children's language use or obtain such limited samples of verbal behavior from their patients that they draw inappropriate and incomplete conclusions. Because teachers are in the best position to identify the kinds of language disorders that may manifest themselves in classroom situations, it is important for them to be aware of the types of evaluative means available for diagnosis and subsequent remediation.

This chapter has addressed each of the component systems of language and has discussed how changes in the study of language development have influenced their assessment. Formal standardized test instruments and informal evaluation techniques were described to assist teachers in the selection and interpretation of those measures best suited to the assessment and subsequent remediation of students with oral language problems.

Educational Suggestions for Students with Language Difficulties

Students with assessed language difficulties can benefit from instruction that stresses remediation of these difficulties. For teachers concerned with a discussion of specific language training models, a good reference is Bloom and Lahey (1978). The following suggestions can be used with students who have mild language difficulties (Mercer & Mercer, 1981).

Students who have been assessed as having difficulty with the classification of associated words can benefit from instruction that involves the student in sorting various association pictures.

Some students have assessed difficulty with prepositions (in, out, front, back, side, up, down). These students can be taught the prepositions by using hula hoops and physical activity. For example, the teacher can give the directions to students to move in relation to the hoops: "Stand *in* the hula hoops."

If students have identified difficulties with the use of linguistic forms to other environments, they can benefit from sessions in which the teacher describes an object to the students such that the students can select a similar object from several objects placed in front of them.

Students who have assessed difficulty with conjunctions (and, but, because, so) can benefit from instruction that emphasizes the Cloze procedure with multiple choice items. For example: He goes to school _____ [and, but, or] he plays football.

Some students are identified as having difficulty with vocabulary likeness. They can benefit from activities that ask students how to pair action words and objects. For example, write the following verbs and objects on the chalkboard:

hitting	swing
pushing	ball
sewing	barn
building	pants

and ask how hitting the ball is like pushing a swing (idea: verb actions result in objects moving away from student).

Study Questions

1. Define the component systems of language—phonology, semantics, syntax, and pragmatics—and cite examples of behavior for each system defined.
2. Name two tests that measure receptive syntax and describe examples of classroom behaviors that might suggest problems in this area.
3. Name three criticisms that have been leveled against standardized instruments that measure oral language skills. How might each influence test results?
4. Name two tests that measure expressive phonology. Cite sound

production errors that may occur on these that would not be considered significant for a 7-year-old.
5. Describe how you would obtain a language sample from a 9-year-old child. What other informal oral language assessment techniques could be used?
6. Prepare a battery of formal and informal test procedures to be used to assess the oral language skills of an 8-year-old child referred because of delayed speech development.

Suggested Readings

Bloom, L., & Lahey, M. (1978). *Language development and language disorders*. New York: John Wiley & Sons.
Darley, F. L. (Ed.). (1979). *Evaluation of appraisal techniques in speech and language pathology*. Reading, MA: Addison-Wesley.
Newcomer, P. L., & Hammill, D. D. (1976). *Psycholinguistics in the schools*. Columbus, OH: Charles E. Merrill.
Vygotsky, L. S. (1962). *Thought and language*. Cambridge, MA: MIT Press.
Wallach, G. P., & Butler, K. G. (1984). *Language learning disabilities in school-age children*. Baltimore, MD: Williams & Wilkins.

References

Anastasi, A. (1976). *Psychological testing*. New York: Macmillan.
Baker, H. J., & Leland, B. (1976). *Detroit Tests of Learning Aptitude*. Austin, TX: PRO-ED.
Bartel, N. (1982). Assessing and remediating problems in language development. In D. D. Hammill & N. Bartel (Eds.), *Teaching children with language and behavior problems*. Boston: Allyn & Bacon.
Bates, E. (1976). Pragmatics and sociolinguistics in child language. In D. M. Morehead & A. E. Morehead (Eds.), *Normal and deficient child language* (pp. 411–463). Baltimore: University Park Press.
Berko, J. (1961).The child's learning of English morphology. In S. Saporta (Ed.), *Psycholinguistics*. New York: Holt, Rinehart & Winston.
Berry, M. F., & Talbott, R. (1966). *Berry-Talbott Language Tests: Comprehension of Grammar*. Rockford, IL: Berry Language Tests.
Blank, M. (1968). Cognitive process in auditory discrimination in normal and retarded readers. *Child Development, 39*, 1091–1101.
Blank, M., Rose, S. A., & Berlin, L. J. (1978). *Preschool Language Assessment Instrument: The Language of Learning in Practice*. New York: Grune & Stratton.
Bloom, L., & Lahey, M. (1978). *Language development and language disorders*. New York: John Wiley & Sons.
Boehm, A. E. (1971). *The Boehm Test of Basic Concepts*. New York: The Psychological Corporation.
Brown, R. (1973). *A first language: The early stages*. Cambridge, MA: Harvard University Press.
Bruner, J. S. (1973). *Beyond the information given*. New York: W. W. Norton.

Bryant, B. R., & Bryant, D. L. (1983a). *Test of Articulation Performance— Screen.* Austin, TX: PRO-ED.

Bryant, B. R., & Bryant, D. L. (1983b). *Test of Articulation Performance— Diagnostic.* Austin, TX: PRO-ED.

Bryant, B. R., & Bryant, D. L. (1983c). *Verbal Communication Scales.* Austin, TX: PRO-ED.

Burke, J. B. (1979). Lindamood auditory conceptualization test. In F. L. Darley (Ed.), *Evaluation of appraisal techniques in speech and language pathology.* Reading, MA: Addison-Wesley.

Carroll, J. B. (1972). A review of the Illinois test of psycholinguist abilities. In O. K. Buros (Ed.), *Seventh mental measurements yearbook.* Highland Park, NJ: Gryphon.

Carrow, E. (1973). *Test of Auditory Comprehension of Language.* Austin, TX: Learning Concepts.

Compton, C. (1984). *A guide to 75 tests for special education.* Belmont, CA: Pitman Learning, Inc.

Crystal, D., Fletcher, P., & Garman, M. (1976). *The grammatical analysis of language disability.* London: Edward Arnold.

Dale, P. S. (1976). *Language development.* New York: Holt, Rinehart & Winston.

Danwitz, M. W. (1981). Formal versus informal assessment: Fragmentation versus holism. *Topics of Language Disorders, 1,* 95–106.

Darley, F. L. (Ed.) (1979). *Evaluation of appraisal techniques in speech and language pathology.* Reading, MA: Addison-Wesley.

DeRenzi, E., & Vignolo, L. A. (1962). The token test: A sensitive test to detect receptive disturbances in aphasics. *Brain, 85,* 665–678.

deVilliers, J. G., & deVilliers, P. A. (1978). *Language acquisition.* Cambridge, MA: Harvard University Press.

Dunn, L, & Dunn, L. (1981). *Peabody Picture Vocabulary Test—Revised.* Circle Pines, MN: American Guidance Service.

Fisher, H. B., & Logemann, J. A. (1971). *The Fisher-Logemann Test of Articulation Competence.* Boston: Houghton Mifflin.

Goldman, R., & Fristoe, M. (1972). *Goldman-Fristoe Test of Articulation.* Circle Pines, MN: American Guidance Service.

Goldman, R., Fristoe, M., & Woodcock, R. W. (1970). *Goldman-Fristoe-Woodcock Test of Auditory Discrimination.* Circle Pines, MN: American Guidance Service.

Hammill, D. D., & Newcomer, P. L. (1982). *Test of Language Development— Intermediate.* Austin, TX: PRO-ED.

Hammill, D. D. (1985). *Detroit Tests of Learning Aptitude—2.* Austin, TX: PRO-ED.

Hannah, E. P. (1979). Boehm test of basic concepts. In F. L. Darley (Ed.), *Evaluation of appraisal techniques in speech and language pathology.* Reading, MA: Addison-Wesley.

Hook, P. (1976). *A study of metalinguistic awareness and reading strategies in proficient and learning disabled readers.* Unpublished doctoral dissertation, Northwestern University, Evanston, IL.

Hresko, W. P., Reid, D. K., & Hammill, D. D. (1981). *Test of Early Language Development.* Austin, TX: PRO-ED.

Jakobson, R. (1968). *Child language aphasia and phonological universals*. The Hague: Mouton.

Johnson, D. J. (1975). Clinical teaching of children with learning disabilities. In S. Kirk & J. McCarthy (Eds.), *Learning disabilities: Selected ACLD papers*. Boston: Houghton Mifflin.

Kirk, S. A., McCarthy, J. J., & Kirk, W. D. (1968). *Illinois Test of Psycholinguistic Abilities*. Urbana, IL: University of Illinois Press.

Lee, L. L. (1971). *Northwestern Syntax Screening Test*. Evanston, IL: Northwestern University Press.

Lee, L. L. (1974). *Development sentence analysis*. Evanston, IL: Northwestern University Press.

Lee, L. L. (1977). Reply to Arndt and Byrne. *Journal of Speech and Hearing Disorders, 42*, 323–327.

Lee, L. L., Koenigsknecht, R., & Mulhern, S. (1974). *Interactive language development teaching*. Evanston, IL: Northwestern University Press.

Lindamood, C. H., & Lindamood, P. C. (1971). *Lindamood Auditory Conceptualization Test*. Boston: Teaching Resources Corporation.

Locke, J. L. (1979). Auditory discrimination test. In F. L. Darley (Ed.), *Evaluation of appraisal techniques in speech and language pathology*. Reading, MA: Addison-Wesley.

Lyon, R. (1982). Social and legal issues in testing. In L. Swanson & B. Watson (Eds.), *Educational and psychological assessment of exceptional children*. St. Louis: C. V. Mosby.

McNeil, M. R., & Prescott, T. E. (1978). *Revised Token Test*. Austin, TX: PRO-ED.

Mecham, M. J. (1979). Goldman-Fristoe test of articulation. In F. L. Darley (Ed.), *Evaluation of appraisal techniques in speech and language pathology*. Reading, MA: Addison-Wesley.

Mercer, C. D. (1979). *Children and adolescents with learning disabilities*. Columbus, OH: Charles E. Merrill.

Mercer, C. D., & Mercer, A. R. (1981). *Teaching students with learning problems*. Columbus, OH: Charles E. Merrill.

Miller, J. (1979). Test for auditory comprehension of language, English/ Spanish and screening test for auditory comprehension in language. In F. L. Darley (Ed.), *Evaluation of appraisal techniques in speech and language pathology*. Reading, MA: Addison-Wesley.

Newcomer, P. L., & Hammill, D. D. (1976). *Psycholinguistics in the schools*. Columbus, OH: Charles E. Merrill.

Newcomer, P. L., & Hammill, D. D. (1982). *Test of language development— Primary*. Austin, TX: PRO-ED.

Oakland, T. (1974). Assessment, education, and minority group children. *Academic Therapy, 10*, 133–140.

Osgood, C. E. (1957). A behavioristic analysis. In C. E. Osgood (Ed.), *Contemporary approaches to cognition*. Cambridge, MA: Harvard University Press.

Podhajski, B. R. (1980). Useful diagnostic tests. In A. J. Gomez & B. R. Podhajski (Eds.), *Common neurologic and language disorders: Selected readings for school personnel*. Middlebury, VT: Addison Press.

Prutting, C. A. (1979). The Illinois test of psycholinguistic abilities, revised edition. In F. L. Darley (Ed.), *Evaluation and appraisal techniques in speech and language pathology*. Reading, MA: Addison-Wesley.

Ratusnik, D. L., & Koenigsknecht, R. A. (1975). Internal consistency of the Northwestern syntax screening test. *Journal of Speech and Hearing Disorders, 40*, 59–68.

Roskam, W. C., & Podhajski, B. (1980). Useful diagnostic tests. In A. J. Gomez & B. R. Podhajski (Eds.), *Common neurologic and language disorders: Selected readings for school personnel*. Middlebury, VT: Addison Press.

Rutherford, D. (1977). Speech and language disorders and MBD. In J. G. Milichap (Ed.), *Learning disabilities and related disorders* (pp. 45–50). Chicago: Year Book Medical Publishers.

Sander, E. K. (1972). When are speech sounds learned? *Journal of Speech and Hearing Research, 37*, 55–63.

Semel, E. M., & Wiig, E. H. (1980). *Clinical evaluation of language functions*. Columbus, OH: Charles E. Merrill.

Spellacy, F. J., & Spreen, O. (1969). A short form of the token test. *Cortex, 5*, 390–397.

Statistical abstract of the United States. (1980). Washington, DC: US Department of Commerce, Bureau of the Census.

Templin, M., & Darley, F. (1969). *Templin-Darley Test of Articulation*. Iowa City: Bureau of Education Research and Service, University of Iowa.

Vetter, D. K. (1979). Goldman-Fristoe-Woodcock test of auditory discrimination. In F. L. Darley (Ed.), *Evaluation of appraisal techniques in speech and language pathology*. Reading, MA: Addison-Wesley.

Vygotsky, L. S. (1962). *Thought and language*. Cambridge, MA: MIT Press.

Walechinsky, D., & Wallace, I. (Eds.). (1981). *The people's almanac #2*. New York: Morrow.

Wallace, G., & Larsen, S. C. (1978). *Educational assessment of learning problems: Testing for teaching*. Boston: Allyn & Bacon.

Weiner, P. S. (1979). Peabody picture vocabulary test. In F. L. Darley (Ed.), *Evaluation of appraisal techniques in speech and language pathology*. Reading, MA: Addison-Wesley.

Weiss, C. E., Lillywhite, H. S., & Gordon, M. E. (1980). *Clinical management of articulation disorders*. St. Louis: C. V. Mosby.

Wepman, J. (1973). *Auditory Discrimination Test*. Chicago: Language Research Association.

Wertz, R. T. (1979). The token test. In F. L. Darley (Ed.), *Evaluation of appraisal techniques in speech and language pathology*. Reading, MA: Addison-Wesley.

Wiig, E. H., & Semel, E. M. (1980). *Language assessment and intervention for the learning disabled*. Columbus, OH: Charles E. Merrill.

7

Assessment of Arithmetic Performance

Terry Rose

OBJECTIVES

After completing this chapter the teacher should be able to:

1. Describe possible reasons for a student's failure in arithmetic.
2. State the primary purpose of arithmetic assessment.
3. Distinguish between the following three learning levels as they apply to arithmetic: the acquisition stage, the proficiency stage, and the generalization stage.
4. Identify four basic assessment areas in arithmetic.
5. Explain the difference between curriculum and task analysis.
6. List three types of error analysis procedures used in math assessment.
7. List five standardized tests used in arithmetic assessment.

Arithmetic skills and the underlying concepts that constitute mathematics are generally considered part of a basic educational curriculum. Few teachers would argue for any comprehensive educational plan that did not include reading, writing, and arithmetic. And yet teachers working in the area of arithmetic find that there is relatively little information available regarding the types of arithmetic difficulties that students encounter and that there are few diagnostic instruments designed to identify these difficulties. Explanations of this paradoxical situation have ranged from the general overriding educational concern with literacy (Hammill & Bartel, 1982) to a lack of interest in arithmetic instruction by many parents and teachers (Otto & Smith, 1980). Regardless of the reasons for this situation, the indisputable fact remains that many students experience difficulty in acquiring basic and higher-level arithmetic skills. Young students may fail to learn the basic skills or may learn them at a much slower rate than their classmates. Older students, whose teachers may assume they have already acquired basic skills, may be unable to solve higher-level problems that are predicated on those basic skills. This cycle of cumulative deficits may leave the student with few problem-solving skills for use in his or her adult life.

The key to interrupting the accumulating spiral of arithmetic deficits is the use of assessment devices that are designed to identify specific strengths and weaknesses. Information gained in this manner will allow the teacher to answer the question of where to begin instruction. Thus, the major assumption of arithmetic assessment must be to accumulate the types of specific information that can be used primarily for instructional purposes.

When to Assess

Certainly, the presence of arithmetic-specific difficulties indicates a need for some assessment of the student's performance, not only for the specific skill in question, but also for the skills that are prerequisites for the troublesome skill. Arithmetic skills are clearly hierarchical in nature, so that performance on higher-level skills is dependent on the acquisition of lower-level or basic skills. In assessing a particular skill and those that "surround" it in a skill sequence, one should also be aware of the student's demonstrated learning level for each of the assessed skills. The notion of distinct learning levels has recently begun to receive attention, and three learning levels have been tentatively identified: (1) the acquisition stage, in which a student's percentage of correct responses is near zero; (2) the proficiency stage, in which the skill has been acquired but the student cannot perform the skill fast enough to be proficient with its use; and (3) the generalization stage, in which the student has acquired proficiency with the skill and can use it in new situations or circumstances (Rose, Epstein, Cullinan, & Lloyd, 1981; Smith & Lovitt, 1976). Quite often students who are having difficulty with a particular arithmetic skill have been advanced to higher-level skills before they have become proficient with the more basic skills. Thus, the arithmetic-specific performance problems are an accurate answer to the "when to assess" question, but the assessment of any specific skill may yield incomplete information. (The reader who is interested in learning levels will find more complete discussions in Lovitt [1978] and Smith [1981].)

The presence of nonarithmetic-specific difficulties may also indicate a need for assessing the student's arithmetic performance. Problems such as tardiness to math class, excessive absences, and resistive behaviors (including temper tantrums or daydreaming) during the period of arithmetic instruction may indicate difficulties with the subject matter rather than behavior problems. Students who experience difficulty with arithmetic are often able to either "mask" their difficulties or compensate for their lack of knowledge in a variety of ways, including rote learning in the absence of any conceptual knowledge (Hammill & Bartel, 1982). Consequently, overt inappropriate behaviors, even though apparently unrelated to arithmetic, may be evidence of content-specific difficulties.

CASE STUDY

Part I

Name: Willie M.   Age: 7 years, 10 months
Date of Birth: January 6, 1976   Grade: 2
Date of Evaluation: November 16,
  1983

Background Information

Willie is a 7-year old student in a regular second-grade class who was referred for assessment by his second-grade teacher. Willie is being considered for placement in a remedial or special education program because he is doing poorly in arithmetic and displays a great deal of inappropriate behavior during the arithmetic instructional period. These problems were evident in his first-grade class, but were attributed to a lack of readiness skills because his kindergarten placement was only for half days. At the present time, Willie is falling farther behind his peers, and his behavior is becoming progressively more disruptive in class.

Observations

While Willie was cooperative during testing and appeared to be trying to do his best, he would frequently get off task and try to initiate conversation about irrelevant topics. Willie displayed a great deal of distractibility during the testing periods and took much longer than normal to complete the untimed instruments. His performance during timed assessment periods was much more task-oriented until the material became too difficult. Then many of the off-task behaviors noted during the untimed sessions began to be observed. Willie's behavior prompted the examiner to allow frequent breaks and extend the assessment period to 2 days.

Past Test Results

Test	Date	Results
Peabody Picture Vocabulary Test	9-23-81	Receptive Vocabulary Age: 7–10
Peabody Individual Achievement Test (PIAT)	9-23-81	Percentile Scores: Math: 2 Reading Recognition: 52 Reading Comprehension: Not given Spelling: 41 General Information: 46.

Math Assessment Areas

Two broad areas require attention in a thorough arithmetic assessment: content variables and environmental variables. Often content variables are sufficient for assessment purposes, but environmental variables are also important and should be considered, even if only informally.

Content Variables

Factors related to arithmetic content are the focus of most assessment procedures. These factors may be separated into three categories: skill areas, curriculum and task analysis, and error analysis. Although interrelated, these categories view a student's performance from differing perspectives.

Skill Areas

The broadest level of categorization within the content area delineates arithmetic performance by the uses of general arithmetic skills.

Assessment at this level will indicate whether the student is having difficulty at the readiness, computation, problem-solving, or application level.

Readiness for learning arithmetic skills should be considered in most assessment procedures, regardless of the level of arithmetic achievement. Skills such as spatial discrimination, classification, and one-to-one correspondence appear to be related to subsequent success in higher-level skills, such as counting and computation. Table 7.1 lists several skills that may be considered representative of the readiness level.

Computation skills allow a student to accurately calculate answers to addition, subtraction, multiplication, and division problems. Computation problems require the student to attend to the critical stimuli presented by the problem (e.g., the operations symbols +, −, ×, ÷, or $\overline{)}$), retrieve the appropriate basic math fact, and apply the correct algorithm, or strategy, to the problem. While computation skills are usually assessed by paper-and-pencil tests, basic computation facts (e.g., addition facts with sums less than 18) may be also assessed with flashcards. Table 7.1 lists several representative computation skills.

A higher-level skill requires that the student use computation skills to solve problems that are representative of those likely to be encountered in daily life. *Problem-solving* skills require that the student first identify the correct operation (e.g., addition) or sequence of operations (e.g., addition, then subtraction, then multiplication). Subsequently, the student must also identify the correct numbers for each specific operation and then calculate the answer(s). Examples of problem-solving skills are found in Table 7.1.

Application skills require that the student generalize previously learned arithmetic skills to problems that are actually encountered in daily life. As such, application skills are viewed as the highest skill level. In addition to generalization of previously learned computational and problem-solving skills, the student must also learn new terminology (e.g., penny, triangle), symbols (e.g., $), and facts (e.g., a triangle has three sides). Examples of application skills are found in Table 7.1.

Curriculum and Task Analysis

In order to assess arithmetic performance adequately, it is necessary to delineate the types of responses a student must make and then to specify the skills that must be learned in order to make those responses. This procedure requires a specification of the terminal goals and the components leading to that goal. The product of this procedure is a sequence of tasks that may be used to assess the

TABLE 7.1. Arithmetic Skill Areas and Selected Skills

Readiness	Computation	Problem Solving	Application
Sequencing	Addition	Identify operation(s)	Measurement
Quantitative terms (e.g., more, less)	Compute sums to 18	Identify sequence of operations	Read and interpret thermometer
One-to-one correspondence	Compute multi-digit without regrouping	Solve story problem with single instance of one operation	Interpret clothing size
Count by rote	Compute multi-digit with regrouping	Solve story problem with multiple instances of one operation	Convert metric to nonmetric
Count objects in a set	Select commutative property	Solve story problem with multiple instances of multiple operations	Identify comparable volume in differing containers
Order objects, events, etc.	Subtraction		
Recognize numerals	Compute minuends to 18		Time
Write numerals	Compute multi-digit without regrouping		Read time in clockface
Sort by size, shape, etc.	Compute multi-digit with regrouping		Read time on digital clock
	Use identity property		Estimate time
	Multiplication		State equivalent measures of time
	Compute products to 81		Money
	Compute multi-digit without regrouping		Name bills and coins
	Compute multi-digit with regrouping		State equivalent values of differing coins and bills
	Select associate property		Make change
	Division		Estimate cost of variety of items
	Compute with dividends to 81		
	Compute with no remainder		
	Compute with remainder		
	Use distributive property		

student's skill levels for the particular goals. Subsequently, each task may be further analyzed in order to identify any necessary subskills.

The analysis of curriculum goals is known as *curriculum analysis*. To illustrate curriculum anaylsis, consider the skill area of multiplication computation. The goal for this skill area may be stated as follows: "The student will solve computation problems requiring multiplication." The first step in the curriculum analysis might be to delineate the types of numbers to be used in the computation problems—for example, whole numbers, fractions, and mixed (whole and fractional) numbers. As seen in Figure 7.1, multiplication problems involving whole numbers have been selected for analysis. (However, the process is essentially the same for other computation skills.) Multiplication problems using whole numbers are further analyzed into two subgroups: those requiring regrouping and those not requiring regrouping. Whole-number multiplication computation problems that do not require regrouping may be further subdivided into those problems composed of one-, two-, or multiple-digit multipliers and multiplicands. When considering only whole-number multiplication problems, which do not require regrouping and are composed of single-digit multipliers and multiplicands, the resultant type of problem is commonly referred to as a basic fact.

The outcome of a curriculum analysis is a sequence of tasks arranged hierarchically. Each level provides information that relates directly to adequate assessment of the original skill area. The extent to which formal and informal assessment instruments include items that

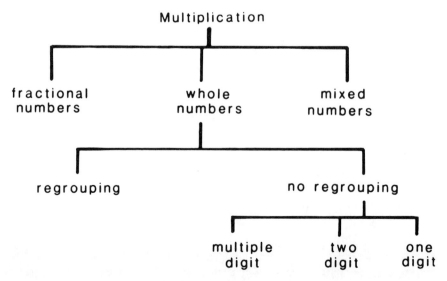

Figure 7.1. Curriculum analysis of multiplication computation.

reflect the various hierarchical levels of a skill area will have a direct bearing on the amount of instructional information that may be obtained from that particular instrument.

Task analysis refers to the identification of the subskills that must be mastered in order for the student to perform a skill previously identified in a curriculum analysis. For example, recognizing the symbol for multiplication (×) and the properties of multiplication of whole numbers can be considered subskills of a basic fact multiplication problem. Few formal instruments adequately assess the subskills that are the result of a task analysis. Thus, accurate information regarding a student's performance on these subskills is usually obtained through informal assessment procedures.

While curriculum and task analyses are usually thought to relate more to instruction than to assessment, it must be remembered that a major goal of arithmetic assessment is to provide instructional information. When selecting any assessment instrument, the degree to which it provides for acquiring information at these various levels must be a primary factor in its selection.

Error Analysis

No assessment of arithmetic performance can be considered complete until attention has been directed to the strategies used by the student to solve a particular type of problem. Students who are having difficulties in arithmetic may use strategies that are logical and consistent but also incorrect. Identification of correct and incorrect responses and resultant test scores based on only this type of information will often overlook these erroneous strategies.

Several types of errors have been categorized (Ashlock, 1976; Cox, 1975; Moran, 1978; Reisman, 1978). The following types of systematic errors have been described by Moran (1978, p. 58) and are representative of many categorization systems:

1. Inadequate facts—the student uses the correct operation, but errors occur because of incomplete knowledge of computation facts.
2. Incorrect operation—the student has a complete knowledge of computation facts but uses an incorrect operation.
3. Ineffective strategy—the student uses the correct operation and accurate facts but applies steps out of sequence, skips steps, or applies problem-solving strategies which, although consistent, do not always yield correct answers.

Many of these types of errors are difficult to analyze because the student will occasionally answer problems correctly even when using an ineffective strategy. Moreover isolated errors do not indicate an error pattern. The interested reader is referred to Ashlock (1976) for a discussion of analyses of ineffective strategies and to Reisman (1978) for a discussion of a variety of arithmetic errors.

Environmental Variables

Even though arithmetic assessment usually focuses on a student's performance, it may be helpful to consider the environmental situation in which those responses occur. The instructional environment may occasionally have a deleterious influence on a student's performance. Hence, it may be important to interpret arithmetic assessment information within an environmental context, especially when the assessment procedures are conducted in a setting different from the one in which the performance problems typically occur (e.g., a counselor's office versus the classroom).

The instructional environment is composed of elements that relate directly to teacher-student interactions, including the curriculum, teaching methods, materials, activities, reinforcement strategies, provisions for corrective feedback, and even grouping arrangements. For example, different curricula may emphasize computational skills, problem solving, or application. Arithmetic difficulties may be related to the specific curricular emphasis, and meaningful remedial suggestions based on assessment information must take these environmental factors into consideration.

Formal Assessment Procedures

Standardized Achievement Tests

Formal arithmetic assessment instruments may be conveniently separated into two relatively distinct categories: (1) standardized achievement tests that include measures of arithmetic performance and (2) diagnostic arithmetic instruments. Within each of these categories are found norm-referenced and criterion-referenced instruments. Several achievement tests that include arithmetic subtests or sections may be found in Table 7.2.

Of the general achievement tests listed in Table 7.2, the Brigance inventories provide the most specific information for instructional

TABLE 7.2. General Achievement Tests with Arithmetic Measures

Name of Test	Grade Level	Characteristics
Brigance Diagnostic Inventory of Basic Skills (Brigance, 1977)	K–7	Individual Criterion-referenced
Brigance Diagnostic Inventory of Essential Skills (Brigance, 1981)	7–12	Individual Criterion-referenced
California Achievement Tests (CTB/McGraw-Hill, 1978)	1–12	Group Norm-referenced
Comprehensive Tests of Basic Skills (CTB/McGraw-Hill, 1977)	K–12	Group Norm-referenced
Iowa Tests of Basic Skills (Hieronymus, Lindquist, & Hoover, 1982)	K–9	Group Norm-referenced
Metropolitan Achievement Tests (Balow, Farr, Hogan, & Prescott, 1978)	K–12	Group Norm-referenced
Peabody Individual Achievement Test (Dunn & Markwardt, 1970)	K–12	Individual Norm-referenced
SRA Achievement Series (Science Research Associates, 1978)	K–12	Group Norm-referenced
Stanford Test of Academic Skills (Gardner, Callis, Merwin, & Rudman, 1983)	8–13	Group Norm-referenced
Wide Range Achievement Test— Revised (Jastak & Jastak, 1985)	Preschool– Adult	Individual Norm-referenced
Woodcock-Johnson Psycho- Educational Battery (Woodcock & Johnson, 1977)	Preschool– Adult	Individual Norm-referenced

purposes. The *Brigance Diagnostic Inventory of Basic Skills* (Brigance, 1977) includes measures of arithmetic readiness as well as measures of the various arithmetic skill areas. A Math Grade Level Test is also included, which yields a grade equivalence score. These grade equivalence scores should be interpreted cautiously, however, because the *Brigance Diagnostic Inventory of Basic Skills* is not normed, nor are the procedures that were used to determine these scores described in the test manual. The *Brigance Diagnostic Inventory of Essential Skills* (Brigance, 1981) includes items that measure higher-level arithmetic skills in the various skill areas and application skills in several other areas of the test, such as Money and Finance, Travel and Transportation, and Vocation.

The Brigance inventories offer several advantages in addition to the specificity of the information they provide. The inventories are easy to administer and require very little special training. In addition, instructional objectives are available for each of the tests, which may greatly facilitate further assessment activities and subsequent remedial efforts.

Diagnostic Arithmetic Instruments

Norm-referenced instruments are discussed before criterion-referenced instruments in order to conform to the assessment sequence that teachers should follow: from a general screening level (general achievement tests) through progressively more specific levels that culminate in enough information to diagnose accurately and remediate efficiently the student's specific arithmetic deficiencies. However, it should be noted that even the norm-referenced tests discussed in this section may also be used as criterion-referenced tests. (See Table 7.3).

The *KeyMath Diagnostic Arithmetic Test* (Connolly, Nachtman, & Pritchett, 1971) is probably the most widely used individual diagnostic arithmetic instrument, especially in special education (Mardell-Czudnowski, 1980; Thurlow & Ysseldyke, 1979). The KeyMath is an individually administered diagnostic instrument designed to assess arithmetic skill development from kindergarten through the eighth grade. The 14 subtests, contained in an easel kit, are organized into three areas: content, operations, and application.

The items within each subtest are sequentially arranged from least to most difficult. Because only the four computation subtests require written responses, students experiencing difficulties with either fine-motor responses on the see-write input-output modalities are minimally penalized by the KeyMath.

The administration of the KeyMath is relatively simple, requires no formal training, and can usually be completed within approximately 30 minutes. Each of the subtests has a basal level of three consecutive correct responses and a ceiling level of three consecutive incorrect responses. The authors feel that familiarity with the KeyMath and a background in teaching arithmetic are two factors that are related to maximum efficiency in administering and interpreting the test.

Four progressively more specific levels of diagnostic information are provided by the KeyMath: (1) total test performance, expressed in grade equivalents; (2) area performance, based on performance in the three areas; (3) subtest performance, expressed in a diagnostic profile that compares relative scores across all subtests; and (4) item performance, based on behavioral descriptions on each item's content. An appendix containing specific behavioral objectives for every test item links the fourth-level diagnostic information to remedial instruc-

TABLE 7.3 Diagnostic Arithmetic Instruments

Name of Test	Grade Level	Characteristics
Basic Educational Skills Inventory—Math (Adamson, Shrago, & Van Etten, 1972)	Preschool–Primary	Group or individual Criterion-referenced
Diagnosis: An Instructional Aid in Mathematics (Guzaitis, Carlin, & Juda, 1972)	K–6	Individual Criterion-referenced
Diagnostic Mathematics Inventory (Gessell, 1977)	1.5–8.5	Individual Criterion-referenced
Diagnostic Test of Arithmetic Strategies (Ginsburg & Mathews, 1984)	1–6	Individual Criterion-referenced
KeyMath Diagnostic Arithmetic Test (Connolly, Nachtman, & Pritchett, 1971)	K–8	Individual Norm- or Criterion-referenced
Stanford Diagnostic Mathematics Test (Beatty, Madden, Gardner, & Karlsen, 1976)	1.5–high school	Group Norm- or criterion-referenced
Test of Early Mathematics Ability (Ginsburg & Baroody, 1983)	Preschool–3	Individual Norm-referenced
Test of Mathematical Abilities (Brown & McEntire, 1984)	3–12	Individual or Group Norm-referenced

tion. Information obtained and analyzed at this fourth level is criterion- rather than norm-referenced. However, it should be noted that, unlike many criterion-referenced tests, there are relatively few test items to sample each specific skill. More detailed information may be required before completing the assessment process.

Standardization of the KeyMath was accomplished by administering it to 1,222 students in kindergarten through grade 7 in 42 school systems. The post hoc description of the normative sample and a lack of attention by the authors to several traditional normative conventions (e.g., descriptions of community size and types of math curricula) raise serious questions regarding the KeyMath's standardization data. However, when used as a criterion-referenced diagnostic instrument, normative comparisons are not required. The KeyMath appears to be technically adequate for use as a criterion-referenced instrument (Thurlow & Ysseldyke, 1979).

Reliability coefficients, using a split-half analysis, range from .94 to .97 for total test performance. Reliability coefficients for individual subtests were lower than those for the total test, ranging from .64 to .84. The absence of any test-retest reliability data is considered to be a drawback because of the heterogeneous nature of the test items. Standard errors of measurement are available in the manual.

Content validity seems assured because the authors carefully selected the items and field tested the scale with over 3,000 students. If the KeyMath is to be used as a criterion-referenced instrument, content validity is all that is required. However, when the KeyMath is viewed as a norm-referenced test, then the lack of information in the test manual regarding concurrent validity is a serious weakness.

The *Test of Early Mathematics Ability* (TEMA; Ginsberg & Baroody, 1983) is an individually administered diagnostic arithmetic instrument designed to assess skill development in preschool and early elementary grade children (ages 4-0 to 8-11 years). The TEMA is based upon the theoretical development of informal mathematical thinking (i.e., those skills and concepts developed prior to formal training) as well as formal mathematical thinking (i.e., the rules, principles, and procedures taught formally in school). Fifty test items were developed to assess these stages of mathematic skill development, with 23 items measuring informal mathematics, including Concepts of Relative Magnitude, Counting, and Calculation; 27 items measure formal mathematics skills, including Knowledge of Convention, Number Facts, Calculation, and Base-Ten Concepts. The authors of the TEMA have identified several important uses for the instrument, including identifying children who are significantly ahead of or behind their peers, identifying special mathematical strengths and weaknesses of each child, suggesting appropriate instructional procedures, documenting instructional effectiveness, and as a reliable dependent measure in applied research activities.

The items are arranged sequentially, beginning with those that measure informal skills. Because the test relies primarily on verbal interactions between the examiner and the child, reading and writing abilities have apparently been eliminated as confounding factors.

Administration of the TEMA is reasonably easy, requiring no formal training for the examiner, and can usually be completed within approximately 20 minutes. A basal of five consecutive correct items and a ceiling of five consecutive incorrect items have been established, although the manual recommends omitting the basal requirement for either very young children or those children who are very poor in math.

Three types of normative scores are reported in the TEMA manual. Math Quotients (MQ) are scaled scores with a mean of 100 and a standard deviation of 15. Math Ages (MA) are age equivalence scores ranging from 4-0 to 9-4 years. Finally, percentiles are also reported. The authors recommend the use of percentiles and MQ rather than MA when communicating test results. Tables in the manual transform raw scores to each of the normative scores.

Prior to standardization, a 96-item version of the TEMA was

subjected to item analyses to determine those items that have the most discriminating power. The findings of these item analyses resulted in the identification of the 50 items contained in the final version of the TEMA.

The TEMA employed a standardization sample of 617 children who lived in 12 regionally diverse states. Characteristics of the children's sex, residence, geographic area, race, parents' occupations, and age are listed in the manual. In many cases, these characteristics are compared to census data in order to document the representativeness of the sample along these variables. The method used to select the standardization sample is not described, however.

Reliability information is clearly and adequately reported. Internal consistency coefficients (identified as content sampling in the manual) range from .86 to .94. Test-retest reliability procedures (identified as time sampling in the manual), implemented with a one-week interval, yielded a coefficient of .94.

Several types of validity are discussed in the TEMA manual. The discussion of content validity is brief and relies on previously discussed procedures (i.e., item selection, sampling procedures, format, item difficulty, and item discrimination power) to establish content validity. The TEMA's criterion-related validity is supported by data correlating it with the Math Calculation subtest of the *Diagnostic Achievement Battery*, which yielded coefficients of .40 and .59 in two studies. Construct validity is discussed in considerable detail, especially focusing on three constructs hypothesized to underlie the TEMA. The first hypothesis is that "abilities measured are developmental in nature"; thus test performance should be related to chronological age. Means and standard deviations of raw scores for groups of varying ages are reported in the manual, along with the results of a "correlational procedure" that indicates a correlation of .94 for chronological age and test performance. Second, "abilities (measured) are influenced by cognitive and thinking processes"; thus test performance should be related to tests of intelligence and language. Correlational data between the TEMA and the *Slosson Intelligence Test* (.66) and the *Test of Early Language Development* (.39) are reported in the manual. Third, "the TEMA measures math abilities"; thus test performance should differentiate between normal and poor achievers in math. The manual describes briefly the results of an unpublished research report that indicated significant differences in performance on the TEMA between groups of "at-risk" and "normal" children.

The TEMA appears to be an adequately designed and developed assessment instrument that may be especially useful for those who work with young children. Considerable attention has been paid to the psychometric characteristics of the TEMA. However, because the TEMA has only recently become available, no studies have been reported regarding its usefulness. Therefore, more thorough analyses of its uses and efficacy await the data that will accrue following its more widespread use.

The *Stanford Diagnostic Mathematics Test* (SDMT; Beatty, Madden, Gardner, & Karlsen, 1976) is a norm-referenced group-administered instrument that is also designed to be used as a criterion-referenced test. The SDMT was developed to identify specific arithmetic difficulty areas by measuring a student's competence in basic mathematical concepts and arithmetic skills. Four levels of the test are available: Red (for grades 1.5 to 4.5), Green (for grades 3.5 to 6.5), Brown (for grades 5.5 to 8.5), and Blue (for grades 7.5 to high school). Each level is composed of three subtests: Number System and Numeration, Computation, and Applications. Two parallel forms are available for each level of the SDMT.

Administration of the SDMT requires no special training and is relatively simple. The time required to administer the SDMT varies depending on the test level, but averages approximately 90 minutes. There are no basal or ceiling levels. All responses are recorded by the student.

The standardization sample for the SDMT was selected using a stratified random-sampling procedure, which resulted in administration of the test to approximately 38,000 students in 37 school districts. Although students' age and sex variables were not controlled, many other student and demographic variables were well controlled through various sampling and weighting procedures.

Reliability information for the SDMT is adequately reported. The internal-consistency coefficients of the raw scores range from .84 to .97 for all levels. Student performance on both forms of the test was correlated to yield alternate-form reliability coefficients that range from .64 to .94. Standard errors of measurement are provided in the examiner's manual.

Little attention is paid to validity data in the examiner's manual. Criterion-related validity data were computed after correlating students' performances on the SDMT and the arithmetic subtest of the *Stanford Achievement Test*, which is a technically adequate instrument. The reported correlations range from .64 to .94.

The SDMT may be considered a criterion-referenced instrument because groups of items have been clustered to represent particular concepts or domains. These groups of items each have "Progress Indicator cutoff scores." These are essentially mastery level scores which, if met or exceeded by the student, indicate competence for the objective. Behavioral objectives for each concept and for each test item correspond to the groupings of test items and should be useful when planning remedial instruction based on the test results.

The *Test of Mathematical Abilities* (TOMA; Brown & McEntire, 1984) is unique among arithmetic assessment instruments because it is designed to assess a student's attitudes toward mathematics, under-standing of mathematical vocabulary, and understanding of the cultural uses of mathematics in addition to the more traditional skills of computation and solving story problems. The TOMA was designed for use in grades 3 through 12 and may be administered individually or to groups. The authors have indicated that the TOMA may be useful for identifying students who are significantly behind or ahead of their peers, identifying specific mathematical strengths and weaknesses within each student, suggesting appropriate instructional procedures, documenting instructional effectiveness, and as a reliable dependent measure in applied research activities.

Five subtests comprise the TOMA: Attitudes toward Math, Vocab-ulary, Computation, General Information, and Story Problems. Atti-tudes toward Math, derived from the *Estes Attitude Scales* (Estes, Estes, Richards, & Roettger, 1981), requires the student to respond to the examiner's verbal statements by marking a Likert-type response format. Vocabulary consists of 20 items for which the student must write an acceptable definition. Computation is composed of 25 items requiring written responses. General Information is the only subtest that must be administered individually. Students are to respond verbally to items requiring convergent thinking regarding mathe-matical concepts or skills. Story Problems requires the student to separate extraneous information from that information relevant to the correct solution. The TOMA relies heavily on language, reading, and prior information acquisition.

The TOMA is relatively easy to administer, requires no formal training for examiners, and can usually be completed within 60 to 90 minutes. Every item in the Attitudes toward Math subtest must be presented, while the basal level for the other subtests is three consecutive items correct and the ceiling is three consecutive items incorrect.

The TOMA was standardized on a sample of 1,560 students in five regionally diverse states. Information regarding the sex, residence, race, and region of the normative sample is provided in the manual. In many cases, these data are compared with census data to demonstrate the representativeness of the sample. Unfortunately, the sampling procedures used to select the students to comprise the sample is not discussed, nor is a delineation of the proportion of the normative sample who responded in either individual or group administrations presented in the manual.

Two types of normative scores are available to users of the TOMA. Two types of standard scores may be obtained. Individual subtest standard scores are scaled scores with a mean of 10 and a standard deviation of 3. A total test Math Quotient (MQ), derived from the individual subtest standard scores, have a mean of 100 with a standard deviation of 15. The reader should note that standard scores are not available for the Vocabulary subtest for students younger than 11 years of age. Percentile scores are also provided.

Information regarding reliability is clearly and thoroughly reported. Internal consistency coefficients are reported for each subtest across 10 age groups. Means of these coefficients across ages within subtests range from .77 to .92. Test-retest reliability (identified as stability reliability in the manual) data were collected twice from two samples: (1) nonhandicapped 11-year-olds yielded reliability coefficients ranging from .71 (Attitude toward Math) to .81 (General Information); (2) learning disabled students ranging in age from 9 to 17 years yielded reliability coefficients ranging from .71 (Story Problems) to .94 (General Information). Standard errors of measurement data are also reported in the manual.

Data regarding the TOMA's criterion-related validity and construct validity are reported in the manual. In order to establish criterion-related validity, the TOMA was compared to several previously published measures of math abilities and skills. The total test reliability coefficients between the TOMA and the following tests were reported: *KeyMath*, .46; *Peabody Individual Achievement Test* (math subtest), .45; *Wide Range Achievement Test* (math subtest), .34. Although correlations between each of the TOMA's subtests and the above tests are also reported in the manual, the process by which these data were compared remains unclear, hence the total test coefficients, which are much less sensitive than subtest coefficients, are reported here. Construct validity is discussed in relation to the hypothesized constructs measured by the TOMA. The first of these is that "the contents of four subtests are developmental," so performance should be related significantly to chronological age. Correlations between test performance and chronological age and grade level yielded coefficients ranging from .60 to .66 and .63 to .72 respectively. Correlation coefficients between these same variables for the Attitude toward Math were reported to be .05 with age and .04 with grade. These discordant findings are discounted by the authors because this subtest is not hypothesized to measure attitudes acquired developmentally. Second, "four of the subtests are cognitive" and therefore should be related to measures of intelligence. Correlation coefficients between four of the TOMA's subtests and the Full Scale WISC–R ranged from .38 to .59; between the TOMA and the *Slosson Intelligence Test* ranged from .50 to .80. Data from the Attitude toward Math subtest were not used to substantiate this hypothesis, because the authors did not view these attitudes as being cognitive in nature. Third, "abilities measured by the subtests are related to each other" because each subtest measures some aspect of math; thus the subtests should be intercorrelated. The results of correlating each subtest yielded a range of .02 to .84. The authors conclude that these data indicate support for the construct validity of every subtest except Attitude toward Math.

Fourth, since the TOMA is supposed to be a test of math attitudes and abilities, it should discriminate between normal and poor achievers in math. The only data reported that relate to this hypothesized construct were obtained by the authors during the test-retest reliability procedures. While generally supportive, these data are too limited to substantiate this construct.

In summary, the TOMA seems to be an adequately developed assessment instrument that may prove especially beneficial when the focus of the assessment process is on language and attitudinal attributes that may be indirectly related to inadequate mathematical performance. As with any newly developed assessment instrument, however, increasing light will be shed on the TOMA's capabilities once the instrument begins to be used more frequently.

CASE STUDY

Part II

Present Testing: Formal Assessment

The *KeyMath Diagnostic Arithmetic Test* was administered as a first step in the diagnostic process. Willie's total test grade equivalent score was 1.1. Several subtest scores were significantly low, including Addition, Subtraction, Multiplication, Division, Mental Computation, and Numerical Reasoning. Willie demonstrated strengths in the following subtests: Numeration, Fractions, Money, and Time. Willie has difficulty with skills involving operations, particularly those problems requiring addition and subtraction. In several instances, Willie demonstrated difficulties with addition and subtraction tasks when these tasks were part of the Content and Application subtests. Willie appears to have difficulty with addition and subtraction at the symbolic level (i.e., requiring operations with numerals) rather than the concrete or representational level (e.g., combining sets of pictured objects).

Selected subtests of the *Stanford Diagnostic Arithmetic Test* were administered. On Level I, Test 1, Part B, Willie had a great deal of difficulty with problems tapping the inverse relationship between addition and subtraction (e.g., $2 + 4 = 6$, then $6 - \_ = 2$). He did not answer any of these problems correctly; however, we cannot tell whether he missed these problems because he lacked an understanding of the inverse relationship or because he lacked basic addition and subtraction skills. Willie performed very poorly on the portion of the test that measured positional systems (e.g., "ones," "tens," "hundreds," "greatest," and "least"). On Level I, Test 2, Part A, Willie worked from left to right on all addition and subtraction problems, regardless of the number of digits involved in the problem. Addition and subtraction of whole numbers proved very difficult for Willie, including basic facts. Other observations include: (1) consistent finger-counting and (2) usually subtracting the smaller number from the larger, regardless of position. It is still questionable at this point whether Willie understands the meaning of addition (and subtraction) or has an incomplete knowledge of basic facts.

The *Basic Educational Skills Inventory—Math* (BESI; Adamson, Shrago, & Van Etten, 1972) is a criterion-referenced instrument composed of two levels: Level A, which generally focuses on readiness skills, and Level B, which assesses higher-level arithmetic skills. Both levels are designed to assess a student's specific arithmetic skill strengths and weaknesses. The BESI is most appropriate for use with students in the lower grades or for older handicapped students whose arithmetic skills are at the primary level.

All or parts of the BESI may be administered to either an individual student or to a small group. The BESI is very easy to administer and requires little specific training. Parents and other volunteers are frequently used to administer the BESI.

Student performance is reported in terms of correct and incorrect answers to specific problems. Items answered incorrectly by the student are to be used to indicate where instruction should begin. Posttests, following instruction, provide an index of the effectiveness of the instructional procedures.

The *Diagnostic Test of Arithmetic Strategies* (DTAS; Ginsburg & Mathews, 1984) is an innovative diagnostic instrument that focuses on the strategies that students, especially in grades 1 through 6, employ to solve computation problems. If we assume that one of the major purposes of assessment is to facilitate effective instruction, then the DTAS appears to address this assessment goal in a thoroughly useful manner because it should allow instructional personnel to perform systematic error analyses, as discussed previously in this chapter. The DTAS is an individually administered diagnostic instrument that may be most accurately described as criterion-referenced, although the particular skills assessed are the strategies employed to solve given problems rather than the result of those strategies (answers). Four sections are included in the DTAS in order to assess a student's strategies over a wide range of calculations: (1) Setting Up the Problem, which involves writing and aligning numerals, (2) Number-Fact Knowledge, (3) Calculational Processes, which assesses the several algorithms available to solve any given problem, and (4) Informal Skill, which requires the student to employ informal or innovative problem-solving procedures. The authors have identified four major uses for the DTAS, including to identify strengths and weaknesses in the student's calculation processes, to suggest appropriate instructional practices, to document a student's progress, and to serve as a measure of problem-solving strategies for research purposes.

Administration of the DTAS is relatively easy and no special training is required for examiners. After reviewing the manual, however, it becomes apparent that many of the items require careful administration and interpretation. Furthermore, a large number of effective and ineffective problem-solving strategies are presented, both as aids to assessment and subsequent instruction. Therefore, examiners should thoroughly familiarize themselves with the contents of the manual. Each section of the test is included in four subtests arranged by operation (i.e., addition, subtraction, multiplication, and division). Each subtest should be presented in its entirety. With the exception of the number-fact items in each subtest, the DTAS is untimed, with each subtest expected to be completed within approximately 20 minutes. The authors suggest that each subtest be given in separate sessions.

Because the DTAS is a criterion-referenced instrument, no normative data are presented in the manual. Nevertheless, two significant factors are not discussed in the manual. First, interrater reliability should be established, especially given the interpretative responsibilities expected of the examiners. Second, as with any criterion-referenced instrument, content validity remains a question. We may find, for example, that particular strategies are not taught in certain schools or districts. Research should be conducted to address the interrater reliability issue, although given the relative newness of the DTAS we may expect that these data will be forthcoming when the DTAS is used more widely. Individual examiners will have to assume responsibility for assuring that suggested strategies are, in fact, being taught in their locales.

Despite its relative newness, the DTAS appears to be a most promising assessment instrument because of its apparent ability to provide useful instructional information. Increasing evidence indicates that students experiencing difficulties in arithmetic operations may actually be using consistent yet inefficient or ineffective strategies. The DTAS appears to be the first test designed specifically to evaluate these strategies. An added benefit for the DTAS user is the inclusion of a large number of inappropriate strategies and error patterns typical of students as well as inclusion of appropriate strategies that are useful for instructional as well as evaluative activities. Users of the DTAS must remember that its intended use is diagnostic/instructional rather than comparative or administrative. As such, it should not be considered part of any placement battery, but should prove most effective when used to increase instructional efficiency regardless of the outcome of any placement decisions.

Diagnosis: An Instructional Aid in Mathematics (Guzaitis, Carlin, & Juda, 1972) is a criterion-referenced instrument designed to assess specific arithmetic skills and to enhance the teacher's efforts to provide systematic, individualized instruction. *Diagnosis* is composed of two levels (K–3 and 3–6) that consist of survey tests, specific probes, and prescriptive guides. In addition, a teacher's handbook and a progress chart for the class are provided.

The administration of *Diagnosis* is a two-step process that requires no special training for the teacher. The initial assessment procedure is the administration of a survey test that measures a student's arithmetic skills for a variety of objectives. The survey test, as the name implies, provides assessment information on a wide variety of skills but presents very few items per skill. Thus, the survey test provides general diagnostic information. Areas in which the student appears to be having difficulty may be assessed further through the use of one or more of the 32 specific probes, which measure in more detail a student's competence in whole-number computation, fractional computation, decimal computation, numeration, operations, geometry, measurement, and problem solving. The probes may be self-scored by the student, which should increase the time available to the teacher for instruction.

Following the administration of the various specific probes, the teacher can identify those skills a student has not yet acquired or mastered. Because *Diagnosis* is cross-referenced to a variety of elementary-level arithmetic curricula, the teacher may use this feature to plan instruction using locally available materials.

The *Diagnostic Mathematics Inventory* (DMI; Gessell, 1977) is a criterion-referenced instrument designed to measure student arithmetic skill levels on 325 objectives. The DMI is composed of seven levels, each of which measures a grade level in half-year increments from grades 1.5 to 8.5. The stated purposes of the DMI are to facilitate the design of educational programs, diagnose strengths and weaknesses in students' arithmetic skills, and provide an ongoing measure of student progress. Other uses of the DMI may include more efficient grouping of students (based on test scores) and the evaluation of instructional materials and procedures.

Administration of the DMI is relatively easy and requires no special training, although a background in teaching arithmetic may prove helpful to the teacher. Three levels of information are reported: (1) Premastery Analysis, which provides information on the student's response prior to his or her demonstration of mastery of a particular objective and is essentially an error analysis; (2) Objective Mastery Report, which is prepared for any or all class members and identifies the specific objectives that each student has or has not mastered; and (3) Individual Diagnostic Report, which is prepared for each student individually and lists the specific objectives that student has or has not mastered.

Several special features make the DMI an attractive diagnostic instrument. Practice exercises are provided for each level so that students may "warm up" before beginning the test. Separate evaluation tests are provided for the specific purpose of providing formative, or ongoing, evaluative data in order to assess student progress throughout the year. A major advantage of the DMI is the inclusion of three guides that should greatly enhance remedial efforts based on the student's test performance: (1) Learning Activity Guides match specific objectives, as measured by specific test items, to learning activities developed to teach each objective; (2) the Guide to Ancillary Materials cross-references the DMI's specific objectives to a large number of arithmetic instructional materials; and (3) Master Reference Guides list specific pages in arithmetic textbooks that address a given objective. Finally, the DMI may be machine-scored or self-scored by the students, which should allow more efficient use of the teacher's time.

CASE STUDY

Part III

Present Testing: Informal Assessment

Further assessment information was obtained by administering teacher-developed probes of specific skills.

    1. *Basic facts*: Willie performed very poorly on the several 1-minute timed samples of the basic addition and subtraction facts. He averaged 8 addition problems correct per minute and 2 subtraction problems correct per minute. Several randomly selected classmates averaged 20 addition problems correct per minute and 16 subtraction problems correct per minute. Willie consistently answered addition problems involving the 1, 2, and 3 facts correctly. However, his answers to basic addition facts that did not contain these numerals were answered in an apparently random manner when Willie was not allowed to finger-count. His answers to subtraction problems were apparently always random, unless finger-counting was allowed. Willie also wrote his numerals very slowly. Assessment of his numeral writing speed indicated that he wrote an average of 16 numerals per minute, while his classmates averaged 47 numerals per minute.

    2. *Assessment of higher-level addition and subtraction facts* indicated very low performance levels. An error analysis indicated that Willie was not making consistent types of errors. Rather, his errors appeared related to a lack of knowledge of basic facts instead of any systematic errors in strategy.

Summary

The sum of the assessment information obtained indicates that Willie needs immediate help in mathematics, especially in addition and subtraction operations. While special class placement is not recommended at this time, immediate remedial activities must be implemented. Specific conclusions are listed below:

1. Basic addition facts have not been mastered so as to be functional. In some cases these facts do not appear to have been acquired at all.

2. Basic subtraction facts have not been acquired.
3. Willie does not understand the relationship between addition and subtraction.
4. Willie writes numerals too slowly. The weakness in this tool skill may have a negative effect on higher-level computation skills.
5. Although Willie's problem-solving strategies (algorithms) do not appear to be a problem at the current time, his reliance on finger-counting and his consistent left-to-right strategy indicate a potential for future problems. Careful attention must be paid to instruction in these areas as they become appropriate (i.e., after Willie has mastered the basic facts).

Recommendations

In general, work should be done on the symbolic (or abstract) level.

1. Basic facts need to be memorized. The following suggestions may be helpful: (a) work with flashcards; (b) use basic fact worksheets, giving Willie a limited amount of time to complete them; (c) use answers from previously solved problems to decipher coded messages or puzzles; use dice to generate addition problems, then solve the problems in a game format or situation.
2. Willie needs frequent practice in numeral writing. The emphasis at this point should be on speed rather than legibility. In other words, Willie needs to be able to write numerals fast enough so the mechanics of numeral writing do not interfere with calculation.
3. Estimation skills should be taught so Willie can better monitor his own performance and make corrections. A calculator may be used most effectively for this purpose.
4. When progressing beyond basic facts, provide problem-solving strategies (algorithms) that can be used independently by Willie. For example, when given a problem involving column addition:

$$
\begin{array}{r}
5 \\
8 \\
3 \\
+\,9 \\
\end{array}
$$

have Willie think "5 + 8 = 13," then "13 + 3 = 16," then "16 + 9 = 25."

Informal Assessment Procedures

Teacher Observation

Accurate observations of a student's math work and work habits may be one of the easiest ways to acquire diagnostic information. Observations may be separated into two distinct operations. When using an *interview* technique, the teacher asks the student to describe orally how a specific math problem was solved. The student is then asked to solve the problem again, describing each step in the process. Interview techniques may be most useful for identifying erroneous problem-solving strategies (e.g., a student who regroups in every subtraction computation, even when it is unnecessary). The use of *direct observation* techniques requires the teacher to observe carefully the student's performance on specific arithmetic problems. Behaviors such as facial grimaces, pencil tapping, and squirming in the seat should also be observed because they may indicate the student's frustration.

Teacher-Developed Probes

Teacher-developed tests, or probes, are one of the most effective ways to gather adequate performance samples because they combine the task-analytic approach of criterion-referenced instruments with a greater number of test items per skill than is typically available in formal instruments. *Probes* are collections of specific examples of a given class of academic tasks, for example, arithmetic tasks. Within each class, specific levels of performance are identified by answers to sequentially arranged problems (Rose et al., 1981).

Two types of probes can be constructed, each serving a different but related purpose. A *mixed probe* is a general assessment instrument that can be used to determine a student's general skill level. Mixed probes are constructed so as to contain problems that tap the various skills in a class of arithmetic curricular goals (see the example in Figure 7.1). For example, a mixed probe of multiplication of whole numbers will include samples of multiple-, two-, and one-digit problems with and without regrouping. After assessment of an untimed mixed probe, the teacher possesses information that indicates the skill level at which more specific assessment should be conducted.

After analyzing the data from the mixed probe, the teacher can then present *specific probes*, which assess a student's performance on a specific skill. For example, a student who, on the mixed probe, frequently made errors when presented multiplication problems of the type "two-digit × one-digit, with regrouping in the tens place" may be given a specific probe similar to the one in Figure 7.2. The data from this probe should provide answers to the major instructional questions about the student's proficiency with the specific skill. Instruction on this particular skill may be indicated if many problems are answered incorrectly, answered correctly but too slowly to be considered functional, or answered in ways that clearly demonstrate an error pattern. However, if the student performs adequately, then further assessment activities should focus on higher-level skills.

Probes can serve two assessment functions. First, they complete the initial assessment and provide detailed information regarding the student's mastery or nonmastery of specific arithmetic skills. Second, they provide a method for collecting ongoing performance data. A teacher may provide daily probes to acquire direct measures of the student's acquisition of the specific skill being taught. By limiting

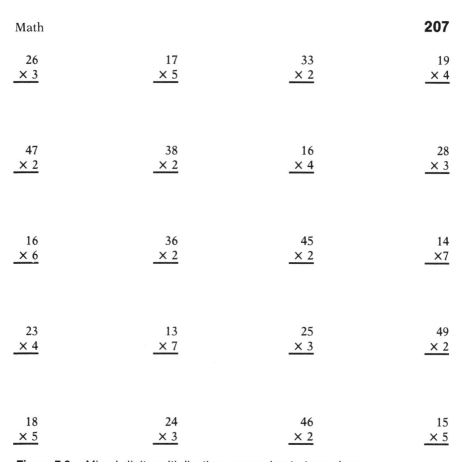

Figure 7.2. Mixed-digit multiplication-regrouping to tens place.

these specific-probe sessions to one minute per day, the teacher will have access to accurate information that has been collected most economically.

Summary

The acquisition of arithmetic skills poses problems for many students. Unfortunately there is relatively little information regarding the types of arithmetic difficulties that students may encounter. Not surprisingly, we currently have few diagnostic instruments available to identify these difficulties. Several major assessment questions related to arithmetic have been discussed in this chapter: when to assess, what to assess, and how to assess. The first two questions require that the teacher be sensitive to both arithmetic-specific performance problems (such as trouble with addition) and nonarithmetic-specific difficulties (such as being tardy for math class). The latter area represents a more subtle indicator of possible arithmetic problems. The teacher should also be knowledgeable of the numerous subcomponents of successful math performance, including readiness skills, computational skills, and environmental variables.

With respect to the latter question, the chapter discussed how to assess several assessment instruments and procedures. The discussion of assessment devices was presented from the perspective that adequate assessment leads to adequate instruction. Formal arithmetic assessment instruments were discussed in the order in which they met this basic assumption, with general achievement tests being least efficient and specific diagnostic instruments (especially criterion-referenced instruments) being most efficient. Informal assessment procedures were also discussed within this assessment-instruction perspective. Likewise, teacher observation strategies were seen to provide less specific instructional information, while probes provide the most specific information for instructional purposes.

Educational Suggestions for Students with Math Difficulties

The teaching of mathematics to students with difficulties in this area is very structured and sequential. The following suggestions can be used as a guide when specific math difficulties have been assessed (Reisman & Kauffman, 1980).

When students have been assessed as having sequencing difficulties, they can benefit from instruction that emphasizes chunking, redundancy, and the control of dimensions that define a linear sequence.

Students who have identified difficulty in one-to-one correspondence respond well to instruction that uses frequency and familiarity to develop number and word-object associations.

Students assessed as having difficulty with duality respond to instruction that restricts complexity and uses familiarity and redundancy while pointing out relevant dimensions.

When students are identified as having difficulty in judging and estimating, they can benefit from instruction that provides sequencing experiences made of a more abstract nature.

Students assessed as having deficits in basic facts can benefit from instruction that stresses the emphasis of patterns, the use of rehearsal strategies, and the restriction of size of sum.

If students have identified difficulties in solving word problems, they can benefit from instruction that presents problems with an unstated problem, uses problems with surplus information, and presents problems with incomplete information.

Study Questions

1. Why are curriculum and task analyses so important to a thorough assessment of arithmetic performance?
2. How does an error analysis provide useful instructional suggestions?
3. When you suspect a student is having difficulty in arithmetic, which type of assessment instrument should be administered first? Why?
4. Given a choice of a formal standardized instrument or a criterion-referenced instrument of equal quality, which would you expect to provide the most relevant information for instructional/remedial purposes? Why?
5. List the types of assessment instruments that are most appropriate for identification purposes or for diagnostic/remedial purposes. Defend your selections.
6. Why is it important to collect and use informal assessment information?

Suggested Readings

Cawley, J. F. (1984). *Developmental teaching of mathematics for the learning disabled.* Rockville, MD: Aspen Systems.

Higgins, J. L., & Sachs, L. A. (1974). *Mathematics laboratories: 150 activities and games for elementary schools.* Columbus, OH: ERIC Center for Science, Mathematics, and Environmental Education.

Howell, K. W., & Kaplan, J. S. (1980). *Diagnosing basic skills: A handbook for deciding what to teach.* Columbus, OH: Charles E. Merrill.

Mercer, C. D., & Mercer, A. R. (1981). *Teaching students with learning problems.* Columbus, OH: Charles E. Merrill.

Silbert, J., Carnine, D., & Stein, M. (1981). *Direct instruction mathematics.* Columbus, OH: Charles E. Merrill.

References

Adamson, G., Shrago, M., & Van Etten, G. (1972). *Basic Educational Skills inventory—math.* Torrace, CT: Brad Winch & Associates.

Ashlock, R. B. (1976). *Error patterns in computation* (2nd ed.). Columbus, OH: Charles E. Merrill.

Balow, I. H., Farr, R., Hogan, T. P., & Prescott, G. A. (1978). *Metropolitan Achievement Test* (1978 ed.). New York: Psychological Corporation.

Beatty, L. S., Madden, R., Gardner, E. F., & Karlsen, B. (1976). *Stanford Diagnostic Mathematics Test.* New York: Harcourt Brace Jovanovich.

Brigance, A. H. (1977). *Brigance Diagnostic Inventory of Basic Skills.* North Billerica, MA: Curriculum Associates.

Brigance, A. H. (1981). *Brigance Diagnostic Inventory of Basic Skills.* North Billerica, MA: Curriculum Associates.

Brown, V. L., & McEntire, E. (1984). *Test of Mathematical Abilities*. Austin, TX: PRO-ED.

California Achievement Tests. (1978). Monterey, CA: CTB/McGraw-Hill.

Comprehensive Tests of Basic Skills. (1977). Monterey, CA: CTB/McGraw-Hill.

Connolly, A. J., Nachtman, W., & Pritchett, E. M. (1971). *KeyMath Diagnostic Arithmetic Test*. Circle Pines, MN: American Guidance Services.

Cox, L. S. (1975). Diagnosing and remediating systematic errors in addition and subtraction computation. *The Arithmetic Teacher, 22,* 151–157.

Dunn, L. M., & Markwardt, F. C. (1970). *Peabody Individual Achievement Test*. Circle Pines, MN: American Guidance Services.

Estes, T. H., Estes, J. J., Richards, H. C., & Roettger, D. (1981). *Estes attitude Scales: Measures of Attitudes Toward School Subjects*. Austin, TX: PRO-ED.

Gardner, E. F., Callis, R., Merwin, J. C., & Rudman, H. (1983). *Stanford Test of Academic Skills*. New York: Psychological Corporation.

Gessell, J. K. (1977). *Diagnostic Mathematics Inventory*. Monterey, CA: CTB/McGraw Hill.

Ginsburg, H. P., & Baroody, A. J. (1983). *Test of Early Mathematics Ability*. Austin, TX: PRO-ED.

Ginsburg, H. P., & Mathews, S. C. (1984). *Diagnostic Test of Arithmetic Strategies*. Austin, TX: PRO-ED.

Guzaitis, J., Carlin, J. A., & Juda, S. (1972). *Diagnosis: An Instructional Aid (Mathematics)*. Chicago: Science Research Associates.

Hammill, D. D., & Bartel, N. R. (1982). *Teaching children with learning and behavior problems* (3rd ed.). Boston: Allyn & Bacon.

Hieronymus, A. N., Lindquist, E. F., & Hoover, H. D. (1982). *Iowa Test of Basic Skills*. Lombard, IL: Riverside.

Jastak, J. F., & Jastak, S. (1985). *Wide Range Achievement Test—Revised*. Wilmington, DE: Jastak Associates.

Lovitt, T. C. (1978). Arithmetic. In N. G. Haring, T. C. Lovitt, M. D. Easton, & C. L. Hansen (Eds.), *The fourth r: Research in the classroom*. Columbus, OH: Charles E. Merrill.

Mardell-Czudnowski, C. (1980). The four w's of current testing practices: Who, what, why, and to whom—An exploratory survey. *Learning Disabilities Quarterly, 3,* 73–83.

Moran, M. (1978). *Assessment of the exceptional learner in the regular classroom*. Denver: Love Publishing.

Otto, W., & Smith, R. J. (1980). *Corrective and remedial teaching* (3rd ed.). Boston: Houghton Mifflin.

Reisman, F. K. (1978). *A guide to the diagnostic teaching of arithmetic* (2nd ed.). Columbus, OH: Charles E. Merrill.

Reisman, F. K., & Kauffman, S. (1980). *Teaching mathematics to children with special needs*. Columbus, OH: Charles E. Merrill.

Rose, T. L., Epstein, M. H., Cullinan, D., & Lloyd, J. (1981). Academic programming for behaviorally disordered adolescents. In G. Brown, R. McDowell, & J. Smith (Eds.), *Educating children with behavior disorders*. Columbus, OH: Charles E. Merrill.

Smith, D. D. (1981). *Teaching the learning disabled*. Englewood Cliffs, NJ: Prentice-Hall.

Smith, D. D., & Lovitt, T. C. (1976). The differential effects of reinforcement contingencies on arithmetic performance. *Journal of Learning Disabilities,* *9,* 21–29.

SRA Achievement Series. (1978). Chicago: Science Research Associates.

Thurlow, M. L., & Ysseldyke, J. E. (1979). Current assessment and decision-making practices in model LD programs. *Learning Disabilities Quarterly, 2,* 15–24.

Woodcock, R. W., & Johnson, M. B. (1977). *Woodcock-Johnson Psycho-Educational Battery.* Boston: Teaching Resources.

8

Assessment of Written Expression and Handwriting Skills

Sandra B. Cohen
Michael M. Gerber

OBJECTIVES

After completing this chapter the teacher should be able to:

1. Relate spoken language ability to written language ability and student motivation.
2. Select appropriate formal and informal assessment strategies based upon specific assessment concerns in written expression.
3. Develop an informal assessment device to gather information concerning written expression abilities.
4. Use both formal and informal asssessment instruments to gain diagnostic information about children's writing samples.
5. Discuss the implications of assessment for developing an instructional program in written expression.

Instruction in written expression is one of the oldest components of formal school programs. The public belief that schools teach each child the basic writing skills is clearly reflected by the concept of "the three R's" and the colloquial phrase "Reading, 'Riting, and 'Rithmetic." In the past, writing instruction centered on the more mechanical aspects of writing, such as penmanship, grammar, and spelling. Children were first instructed to copy recognized masters of literary style. Only after mechanical proficiency was achieved were the students allowed to engage in their own writing endeavors. Today's curricula still include writing mechanics. However, knowledge of the area has broadened sufficiently to include child-generated writings.

Written expression is one of the highest forms of communication and incorporates almost all other language-related skills (Myklebust, 1965). A proficient writer is one who has mastered spoken language, reading, handwriting, spelling, vocabulary, and writing conventions (punctuation, capitalization, and organization). A child experiencing problems in any one or in a combination of these areas may have difficulty communicating effectively in written form. Teachers of the language arts often observe student writings, noting general strengths and weaknesses, without clearly understanding how to evaluate the written product or remediate problem areas. Written expression as an instructional area reflects a final product that is more than the sum of its parts. Although the subskills underlying written expression can be assessed and taught independently, it is the composite of all related skills that produces a level of quality in written language products. A high quality end product is an implicit goal of the educational program.

Spoken Language and Written Expression

The child who has not yet mastered the basic tenets of spoken language will have difficulty transferring language skills to the writing task. The teacher must recognize the relationship between spoken and written language in order to assess written products accurately. The interrelationship between oral and written language is a direct result of the function of writing: to represent language in a lasting and stable form.

Writing, whenever possible, should be preceded by oral language activities. Commonly called "warm-ups," these tasks allow children (1) to become familiar with the appropriate vocabulary; (2) to experience the language "flavor" associated with the situation (e.g., similes and metaphors); and (3) to experiment with ideas that may be included in the written message. Writing can help foster oral language skills by focusing attention upon expression in an alternative form.

The child who speaks in confused, choppy, or irrelevantly worded sentences will most likely write in a similar manner. In contrast, a student who is able to articulate clear and expressive language in most instances will transfer these skills to writing. The writing difficulties of many children are reflected in their oral language skills; therefore, assessment of written language begins with an observational analysis of oral language. Several observations are necessary to gain an accurate picture of language ability. The checklist in Table 8.1 summarizes the speaker's language strengths and weaknesses in areas that may be reflected in writing ability.

Motivation for Written Expression

A child's earliest self-initiated attempts to write are usually represented by pictures and "pretend" letters, words, and sentences. When the young child asks an adult to "look at" or "listen to" a picture

TABLE 8.1 Spoken Language Checklist

	Yes	No
1. Is oral language punctuated by lack of or inappropriate use of		
a. pauses	____	____
b. intonation	____	____
c. gestures	____	____
d. facial expressions	____	____
2. Is the oral communication decreased because of consistent sound or word		
a. omissions	____	____
b. substitutions	____	____
c. repetitions	____	____
3. Is the effectiveness of the oral message decreased by		
a. lack of variety in vocabulary	____	____
b. insufficient descriptive elements	____	____
c. short sentences	____	____
d. incorrect use of pronouns	____	____
e. incorrect use of tenses	____	____
4. Is oral language characterized by		
a. choppy phrases	____	____
b. incomplete thoughts	____	____
c. confused word order	____	____
d. unrelated sentences	____	____
e. poorly sequenced thoughts	____	____

symbol story, the intent is to communicate in a more sophisticated manner than the spoken word. The presence of such motivation should be recognized and expanded upon as a prerequisite to formal instruction. It is indeed unfortunate that, as the majority of students progress through the school curriculum, a natural desire for self-expression is not continuously reinforced. In some instances, students who have experienced academic failure in the past anticipate failure in their writing attempts and are hesitant to apply themselves. In other cases students may desire to write but feel that they lack sufficient experiences or that their writing will not be appreciated.

Assessment of a student's motivation for written expression begins with an evaluation of the environment in which writing is to take place. Teachers must question themselves regarding the experiences they provide and the atmosphere they create for nurturing self-expression. Questions such as those provided in Table 8.2 will guide teachers in developing a supportive environment for written expression.

Writing Assessment Issues

The earliest writings children generate are usually represented by dictated stories that teachers or parents write down for them. Having their own thoughts and ideas translated into visual form is rewarding for young children, and the repetition of this activity eventually leads toward an understanding that what can be thought can be said, what is said can be written down, and what is written can be read and remembered. The goal of writing, therefore, is to communicate a message.

Standards for writing increase as students progress through the grades. At the primary grade level the emphasis is on spoken language and self-expression. The student is expected to write original pieces only after dictating the content to the teacher. Skills such as writing mechanics, spelling, and handwriting are slowly learned, and the student must incorporate these into each composition. As the opportunity to write increases, so does the student's writing facility. Experienced writing is fluent, organized, and expressive, with relatively few conventional errors impeding the communication message.

Unfortunately, not all students progress with equal success through writing instruction. Specific writing difficulties, which reduce the written communication, may occur as a result of skill inadequacy in spoken language, limited experience, poor concept development, ineffectual reasoning and organization skills, and insufficient instruction in fundamental writing conventions.

TABLE 8.2 Assessing the Writing Environment

Environmental Question	Writing Rationale
1. Does the environment promote oral expression?	1. Talking allows students to expand their own experiences, organize their thoughts, and determine ideas they would like to express in a written form.
2. Are the students read to often?	2. The selection of good writing models from a variety of literary forms helps students to experience the impact of writing and increases writing interests.
3. Are a variety of experiences included in the lessons?	3. Students can only write about what they have experienced.
4. Do students feel that what they say and write is positively received?	4. Students must feel that their ideas and feelings are valued. All feedback should be corrective and put into positive terms.
5. Are there effective models who demonstrate good communication skills within the daily routine?	5. Clearly stating a rationale for writing, giving directions, and providing feedback will increase the student's chances for successful writing.
6. Is writing stimulated by "warm-ups" and focusing activities?	6. Students need activities which will help them to focus upon the main elements of the writing assignment.
7. Is written expression an integral part of the instructional curriculum?	7. Writing tasks should be included as part of each curriculum topic giving the child multiple opportunities to practice skills and express ideas.

One of the most often heard debates relating to written expression concerns the goal of and procedures for assessment. "Some educators rail against the practice of writing assessment on 'humanitarian' grounds, assserting that it stifles creativity, disregards individuality, and has assorted other nasty consequences" (Hogan & Mishler, 1979, p. 142). The complexity of the writing task has led others to claim that assessment is unreliable due to a lack of valid standardization. In the end, a great deal of writing assessment remains subjective in nature. A need for fundamental diagnosis as a relevant part of instructional programs has, however, promoted the practice of evaluating student writing. Possible objectives of such written assessment practices are:

1. To provide the student with feedback of an instructive nature that will lead to more growth and writing fluency.
2. To encourage writing by providing motivational feedback based on previous attempts.
3. To assess strengths and weaknesses of the instructional program.
4. To determine grades when necessary (e.g., on report cards).

Assessment of written expression should also be contingent upon the writer's age and achievement level. Primary-level students need time to develop writing fluency. The two most important aspects of writing for this student are enjoyment and a feeling of competence in communication abilities. Exercises aimed at developing writing mechanics should initially be separated from expressive writing tasks so that assessment can be divided for corrective procedures and motivational aspects. Gradually, feedback for mechanical elements can be included in an analysis of spontaneous writings, but caution should be taken against "red marking" a composition when the goal of the writing is the expression of content.

For intermediate and older students for whom expression is more fluent, corrective feedback can be used regularly. Again, it is important to achieve a fine balance when assessing and providing feedback for written expression. A number of studies of teacher evaluations of written expression were reviewed by Braddock, Lloyd-Jones, and Shoer (1963), who concluded that: "It has *not* been proved that the intensive marking of writing samples, with or without revision, is the best procedure to use with upper elementary or junior high schoolers" (p. 36). In other research, Beaver (1977) and Lundsteen (1976) noted positive effects in student writing from positive comments on writing samples. Too great an emphasis on writing standards can destroy the writer's motivation, and over time a sense of "writing apprehension" may result. A way of combatting this is to let the students know ahead of time which writings will be evaluated for content and which for writing mechanics. Allow the writers to edit their work before submitting it for assessment, be consistent in providing feedback to the established evaluation goal, and always include positive as well as any necessary constructive comments.

CASE STUDY

Part I

Name: Kay
Date of Birth: July 20, 1975
Date of Evaluation: December 20, 1983

Age: 8 years, 5 months
Grade: 3

Background Information

Kay was referred for evaluation by her classroom teacher due to Kay's difficulties in completing written classroom and homework assignments. The teacher's reports indicate that Kay is attentive to directions and appears to comprehend complex verbal instructions. She is not considered a behavior problem. Her social interaction with peers is adequate. Kay lives with her parents and a younger brother. Her father works on the assembly line at a local car factory, whereas her mother is a social worker at a large nursing home. The family's home is in a middle-class neighborhood in the older part of the city.

Observations

Kay was at ease and friendly during the testing situations. Her attentiveness to directions and tasks was adequate. Kay displayed a tendency to give up easily on the more difficult tasks. She responded well to praise for her correct responses. Positively, Kay accepted feedback on ways to improve her performance.

Past Testing

Test	Date	Result
Slosson Intelligence Test	12/20/80	Mental Age: 5–8 years IQ: 105
Wide Range Achievement Test	12/20/80	Reading grade 1.0 Math grade 1.0 Spelling grade .8
Developmental Test of Visual Motor Integration	12/20/80	Visual Motor Integration Age 5-0 years

Formal Assessment of Written Expression

Written expression is a complex integration of many skills. Writing, the highest form of verbal achievement, is preceded by listening, speaking, and reading. Difficulty in writing may reflect problems not only in these requisite areas but in emotional, physical, or instructional realms as well (Cohen & Plaskon, 1980). Formal assessment instruments of written expression are usually designed as components of standardized achievement tests or as more specialized diagnostic measures.

Standardized Achievement Tests

The subcomponents of standardized achievement tests pertaining to writing are vocabulary ability, grammatical usage, punctuation, and capitalization knowledge. In addition, some tests measure sentence sequencing and topic-sentence development. The format for writing subtests is usually a *contrived* situation in which the student must select the appropriate word, punctuate or capitalize a sentence, select the topic sentence, or sequence a series of sentences.

Standardized written achievement tests provide grade equivalent or percentile scores and do not offer much diagnostic or useful instructional information. Commonly used achievement tests that have writing subcomponents are summarized in Table 8.3. The teacher should be aware of the limited function of such tests and of the fact that ability to manipulate writing mechanics in a contrived instance does not always result in accurate or high-level spontaneous writing.

Diagnostic Tests of Writing Ability

Diagnostic tests, standardized on normative populations, are designed to assess a student's relative writing strengths and weaknesses. The teacher should be aware that, although diagnostic tests that use writing samples may take time to score and interpret, their usefulness in detecting writing problems is worth the time. The three most currently used diagnostic tests are described below.

The *Test of Written Language* (TOWL; Hammill & Larsen, 1983) is designed to be administered either to individuals or groups of students 7 years through 18 years of age. This highly reliable test yeilds standard scores and percentiles that are helpful in identifying students whose writing is markedly below that of the peer group. Additional student writing samples should be informally diagnosed to gain maximum assessment information.

The TOWL consists of six subtests measured within two formats, contrived and spontaneous. Table 8.4 presents each subtest and describes its general content and test format. The information provided by analysis of individual subtest and general test scores should be helpful in formulating relevant instructional goals for written expression.

The *Picture Story Language Test* (PSLT; Myklebust, 1965) studies the student's spontaneous writing based on a picture stimulus. Evaluation of the written composition includes three scales: Produc-

TABLE 8.3 Achievement Tests with Writing Components

Test and Publisher	Writing Components	Grade Level	Comments
Comprehensive Tests of Basic Skills (CTB/McGraw-Hill, 1977)	Vocabulary, language mechanics (punctuation, capitalization), and language expression	2.5–12	Test objectives systematically measure prerequisite skills for subject courses; emphasis is given to application of concepts and principles in a contrived format.
Metropolitan Achievement Test (Balow, Farr, Hogan, & Prescott, 1978)	Word knowledge (primary through advanced level), language mechanics, and grammar (elementary through advanced level)	1.5–9.5	Provides three forms at each of six levels; forms are comparable in difficulty and content and are appropriate for repeated testing.
Iowa Test of Basic Skills (Hieronymous, Lundquist, & Hoover, 1982)	Vocabulary, capitalization, punctuation, and word usage	1–9	Individualized testing of pupils at different levels in one classroom is a key feature of the multilevel forms.
California Achievement Test (CTB/McGraw-Hill, 1978)	Capitalization, punctuation language usage, and structure	1.5–12	Developed in five levels to assess grade ranges across grades; revised based upon subject area textbooks in reading, mathematics, and language.
ITED/Assessment Survey (Science Research Associates, 1972)	Vocabulary and language usage (punctuation, capitalization, word usage, sentence development, organization)	9–12	A multiform high school test designed to measure general skills of lasting importance in adult life.

TABLE 8.4 Subtest Description of the *Test of Written Language* (TOWL)

Subtest	Description
CONTRIVED FORMAT	
Spelling	A shortened version of the *Test of Written Spelling* (TWS). Student writes the dictated word. The list of 25 words represents phonemically regular and irregular words.
Style	The subtest measures capitalization and punctuation rule mastery. Student rewrites given sentences using correct stylistic form.
Word Usage	The student's ability to form tenses and plurals and to use objective and normative cases is the rationale behind this subtest. Testing is based on a Cloze format.
SPONTANEOUS FORMAT	
Handwriting	Graded rating scales are used as assessment guides for measuring handwriting ability.
Vocabulary	The student receives one point for each seven-letter word used in the story.
Thematic Maturity	The writing sample is examined for clarity and logical sequencing. Twenty criterion statements guide the examiner's judgment.

tivity Scale (length of sentences and of total composition); Syntax Scale (word usage, word endings, and punctuation); and Abstract-Concrete Scale (assessment of content).

Appropriate for students 7 to 17 years of age, the PSLT has often been criticized for its complex scoring procedures and low reliability and validity (Anastasiow, 1972). The PSLT scores, when carefully interpreted, can provide the teacher with diagnostic information, but the difficulty in obtaining the information makes the effort questionable.

The *Diagnostic Evaluation of Writing Skills* (DEWS) is a diagnostic writing instrument recently developed for use with learning disabled children that has direct application for remediation (Weiner, 1980a, 1980b). The DEWS uses 41 writing criteria divided into six categories: graphic, orthographic, phonologic, syntactic, semantic, and self-monitoring. The DEWS criteria, listed in Table 8.5, may be applied to any written composition, regardless of topic. However, the author suggests an autobiography for older students and "My Favorite Day" for younger writers as appropriate and motivating writing topics. DEWS criteria have been successfully used to evaluate the effectiveness of reading and writing objectives (Weiner, 1980b).

TABLE 8.5 Criteria in the *Diagnostic Evaluation of Writing Skills* (DEWS)

Graphic (Visual Features)	Examples of Errors

1. Excessive pencil pressure marks
2. Letter formation ambiguities, erasures
3. Capital and lowercase letter mixture
4. Size or spacing irregularities
5. Off-line writing
6. Margin slant or crowding

Orthographic (Spelling)	Examples of Errors

7. Sequencing of letters, three-consonant clusters
8. Doubling final consonant
9. *-ed* ending with sound of *d* or *t*
10. Prefix or suffix generalizations
11. *ie* becomes *ei* after *c* with the sound of *a*
12. *y* becomes *i*, except before *-ing*
13. *c* or *g*, followed by *e, i,* or *y*
14. *ch* = *k* and *sh, sh* = *si, ti, ci, ce, su*
15. *ph* and *gh* = *f*
16. Silent letters in special spellings
17. Schwa sounds, related words
18. Word division by syllable

Phonologic (Sound Components)	Examples of Errors

19. Nonphonetic spelling (bizarre)
20. Strictly phonetic spelling
21. Letter or syllable omissions
22. Run-together words

Syntactic (Grammatical)	Examples of Errors

23. Subject and predicate agreement
24. Tense, plural, possessive endings
25. Word order, omissions
26. Incomplete sentences (fragments)
27. Run-on sentences
28. Punctuation, paragraphing
29. Variety in sentence structure
30. Coordination (*and/but*)
31. Complex sentences, subordination
32. Amount of information per sentence

Semantic (Meaning)	Examples of Errors

33. Flexible vocabulary; connotative-denotative
34. Coherence, focus, and tense shifts

(continued)

TABLE 8.5 (continued)

Semantic (Meaning) *(continued)*

35. Logical sequencing
36. Transitions
37. Distinction between major and minor points
38. Inferential thinking, cause-effect
39. Idomatic and figurative language

      Self-Monitoring Skills   Examples of Errors

40. Self-correction: spelling and punctuation
41. Improvement through revision

From "The Diagnostic Evaluation of Writing Skills (DEWS) Application of DEWS Criteria to Writing Samples," by E. S. Weiner, 1980, *Learning Disabilities Quarterly*, *3*(2), p. 54.

Informal Assessment of Written Expression

Informal assessment of writing skill can focus on many interlocking elements of the writing task: expressive content, punctuation, vocabulary, capitalization, organization, and handwriting. The rule-governed nature of punctuation and capitalization conventions makes these two components the easiest to assess. Vocabulary usage, sentence and paragraph development, and expressive content demand more subjective judgments. Expressive content is considered to be the most difficult to assess because of a complete absence of normative data.

The difficulty of assessing written content should not cause teachers to avoid giving feedback on writing assignments. Although research studies pertaining to the accuracy of teachers' abilities to evaluate written content have been inconclusive (Breland & Gaynor, 1979; Hogan & Mishler, 1979; Diederich, 1974), evidence suggests that teachers are influenced by both subjective and objective factors in writing assessment. Diederich (1974) found five major factors (i.e., ideas, mechanics, organization, vocabulary, and flavor) that distinctly impacted upon teacher evaluations of written products.

Early in the assessment process, attention should be given to general work habits, language performance, and writing samples. All assessment information should be organized and recorded for interpretation. Checklists, graphs, descriptive statements, and coding sheets are the most common recording forms. A diagnosis of writing difficulties should always be established on the basis of more than one writing sample in order to ensure reliability.

There are two commonly used informal writing assessment formats: *contrived* and *spontaneous*. Contrived statements may be dictated for the student to write for demonstrating correct spelling, punctuation, and capitalization. In a more controlled case the student is given written statements in which errors or omissions are made and is instructed to correct the sentence. An alternate assessment format is spontaneous writing. Most often the writer is provided a stimulus as the focus of the writing task. Different writing stimulus formats are as follows:

1. Writer is given a key word plus a picture.
2. Writer is given a key word.
3. Writer is given a picture.
4. Writer is given a title.
5. Writer is given a general topic.

In each format instance, the writer is asked to demonstrate the highest level of writing achievement possible. Evaluation of writing performance begins with the teacher establishing an assessment goal. Focusing upon the specific assessment question will (1) efficiently guide the development of an appropriate informal assessment device; (2) determine whether to use a contrived writing situation or student-generated writing; and (3) help in the selection of existing materials.

Checklists

Using standards established within the writing curriculum enables teachers to develop criterion-referenced assessment measures. Informal assessment devices can be constructed from listings of capitalization and punctuation rules, analysis of vocabulary and word fluency, evaluation of sentence and paragraph structures, and systematic observation of other writing factors. Specific writing skills such as punctuation rules, capitalization rules, and use of parts of speech can be conveniently recorded in teacher-devised checklists. An assessment checklist of general progress in written expression is illustrated in Figure 8.1. This Progress Profile focuses on both the expressive content and the mechanical aspects of the writing sample, and is intended to be used in the assessment of repeated writing measures.

Assessment Formulas

The vocabulary aspect of written expression is assessed by specific strategies designed to determine the writer's word variety. The nature of vocabulary assessment does not lend itself to a checklist format unless one is examining parts of speech used in the writing. As a result, several assessment formulas have been devised. Three specific strategies of vocabulary analysis are (1) the type-token ratio, (2) the Index of Diversification, and (3) average sentence length. *The type-token ratio*

Writing Sample Date/Description	Content				Mechanics	
	Expression	Sentences	Paragraphs	Vocabulary	Punctuation	Capitalization
	Main idea is clearly stated and logically supported	Express complete thoughts	Adequately developed paragraphs consisting of closely related sentences	Varied and appropriate word choice	All punctuation placed appropriately throughout writing	Appropriate use of capital letters

Scoring: + satisfactory skill
     – unsatisfactory skill
     (+) skill is evident but confusion exists
     NA skill is not attempted

Figure 8.1. Sample of a general Progress Profile for Written Expression. Source: Cohen, S. B. & Plaskon, S. P. (1980). Language arts for the mildly handicapped. Columbus, OH: Charles E. Merrill.

technique (Johnson, 1974) examines vocabulary redundancy. The ratio is formulated by placing the word types (number of different words used) over word tokens (total number of words). In the example "The house on the corner is the largest house on the street," there are 7 word types (*the* is used 4 times, *on* is used 2 times, and *house* is used 2 times) and 12 word tokens.

$$\frac{7 \text{ types}}{12 \text{ tokens}} = .58 \text{ (type-token ratio)}$$

The lower the type-token ratio, the greater the word redundancy. In general, word redundancy signifies a lower level of writing maturity and should alert the teacher to the need for more instruction in self-expression and vocabulary usage. The *Index of Diversification* (Carroll, 1938) was modified by Cartwright (1969) to be calculated more easily. The total number of composition words is divided by the number of occurrences of the word "the," or the most common word in the composition. Vocabulary variety is designated by a high index value. *Average sentence length* is another means of assessing vocabulary fluency. Average sentence length can be derived by dividing the total number of words in a composition by the number of sentences. Sentence length increases with vocabulary growth and writing maturity.

Rating Scales

Analyzing writing skills according to mastery levels suggests the use of a rating scale. Poteet (1980) combines ratings and a comprehensive checklist to assess written expression and to guide the teacher's decision-making in program development. In developing a rating scale it is necessary to specify sequential growth by assigning a point value, for example, from 0 (no apparent use of skill or concept) through 3 (mastery level) to objective statements of skill acquisition or performance. Writing rating scales can be developed from portions of curriculum guides or scope and sequence charts. Hammill and Bartel (1982, pp. 98–105) provide a curriculum sequence for written expression for grades 1 through 8, and Poteet (1980) offers one that extends through grade 12. A sample written expression rating scale is provided in Figure 8.2.

Peer Evaluation/Self-Evaluation

Many writing skills workshops are currently promoting peer evaluation and self-evaluation techniques in which students learn to assess writing samples. Guidance is provided by a checklist, rating scale, or question analysis that helps the evaluators in offering suggestions.

Student Name _____   Grade/Age _____
Writing sample format: expressive _____ date _____
                        transactional _____ date _____
                        poetic _____ date _____

Directions:

Review one or more writing samples and rate each element below according
to:

   0 - no apparent use of skill/concept
   1 - limited evidence of skill/concept
   2 - emerging use of skill/concept
   3 - mastery of skill/concept

I.   *Writing Content*:

   1. ideas and details are focused on a specific writing
      purpose   0   1   2   3
   2. events and ideas are clearly stated   0   1   2   3
   3. expresses original ideas using descriptive details   0   1   2   3
   4. age-appropriate perception of a writing stimulus or
      task   0   1   2   3

Comments:

II. *Organization*:

   1. ideas and events are logically sequences   0   1   2   3
   2. completely develops topic using both details and
      generalizations   0   1   2   3
   3. writes in complete sentences using:
          a. simple sentences   0   1   2   3
          b. compound sentences   0   1   2   3
          c. complex sentences   0   1   2   3
          d. varied sentence types (declarative, interrogative, 0   1   2   3
              etc.)
   4. paragraphs accurately structured, including:
          a. topical focus   0   1   2   3
          b. appropriate introductions   0   1   2   3
          c. supported facts and opinions   0   1   2   3
          d. paragraph transitions   0   1   2   3

Comments:

III. *Vocabulary*:

   1. writing shows deliberate word choice   0   1   2   3
   2. appropriately uses various parts of speech:
          a. noun   0   1   2   3

	0 1 2 3
b. verb	0 1 2 3
c. pronoun	0 1 2 3
d. adjective	0 1 2 3
e. adverb	0 1 2 3
f. preposition	0 1 2 3
g. conjunction	0 1 2 3

3. number of words is appropriate to:
  a. age of writer   0 1 2 3
  b. topic   0 1 2 3

Comments:

IV. *Writing Mechanics*:

1. uses correct capitalization elements   0 1 2 3
   Specify errors: _____
2. punctuation is used correctly   0 1 2 3
   Specify errors: _____

Comments:

V. *Handwriting*:

1. handwriting is readable   0 1 2 3
2. spacing is appropriate
   a. between letters   0 1 2 3
   b. between words   0 1 2 3
   c. between sentences   0 1 2 3
   d. paragraphs indented   0 1 2 3
3. margins are correctly used   0 1 2 3

Comments:

Figure 8.2. Sample of a Written Expression Rating Scale.

Peer evaluation is often done by a small group who have had the composition read to them (Hall, 1981). Although self-evaluation basically follows the same procedures, teachers should realize the student's personal involvement with the material and provide guidance in accurate self-assessment.

Handwriting

Good handwriting is ultimately valued because it facilitates written expressiveness and communication with the reader. For skilled writers, well-formed letters of consistent shape and slant should be effortless and automatic. The mechanics of the handwriting process should not interfere with the writer's larger purpose—that of communicating in clear, logical, and precise language.

Figure 8.3 shows a handwriting sample from a 10-year-old learning disabled boy. The student was unable to read what he had written, even though the first part or stem of the sentences was copied from the teacher's example.

Judgments are often made about the writer based upon the legibility of the work sample. For example, Chase (1979) found that when handwriting was poor, scores given on essays were based more on reader expectations than on content. When handwriting was legible, however, grades reflected content quality. The consequences of unskilled handwriting may be more severe than failing to communicate with readers or creating a poor impression. Some degree of legibility and motor control may be necessary for the writer to monitor written expression efficiently. For example, several researchers have proposed a proofreading step in the spelling process that cannot be separated from the handwriting and spelling act itself (Farnham-Diggory & Simon, 1975; Personke & Yee, 1966).

In part, what is "proofread" may not only be the letter patterns but also the *motor* pattern that produces them. Self-monitoring during writing and self-correction may rely on the availability of redundant kinesthetic and visual "feedback" information. The writer both examines what has been written and modifies what will be written on the basis of what has been seen.

Self-correction in writing often appears in younger and learning handicapped students at much higher rates than in writings of older,

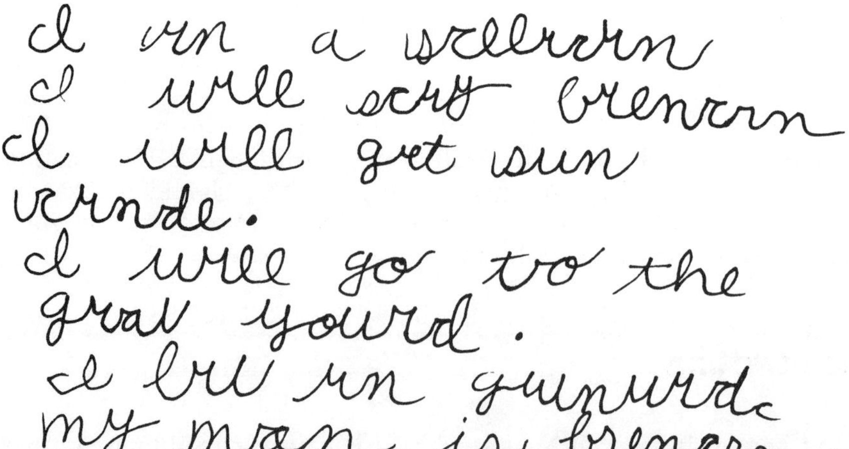

Figure 8.3.   Writing example from a 10-year-old learning disabled boy.

more skilled individuals. Some self-correction occurs almost on a letter-by-letter basis. In very young pupils who are just learning to form letters as part of writing words, self-correction may be observed while the component strokes of letters are being produced. Figure 8.4 shows some examples resulting from this closely coordinated self-monitoring (handwriting/spelling) process. The writers are learning disabled children between 8 and 11 years of age.

Task Analysis of the Handwriting Process

A number of entry-level or preskill behaviors are required before instruction and assessment of handwriting can proceed. Students should be able to:

1. Grasp the pencil so that its weight is balanced (i.e., the pencil does not "drag" on its point or require excessive finger pressure to resist the weight of the blunt end).
2. Control angle and pressure at the point without constantly "squeezing" the pencil.
3. Draw letter strokes (e.g., vertical and horizontal lines, circles, and

Figure 8.4. Spontaneous spelling self-corrections made by learning disabled students. (Ordinal numbers refer to sequence of self-correction.)

diagonals) so that most of the motion is controlled by shoulder and wrist rather than finger joints.
4. Adjust paper, body, arm, and head positions to permit easy maintenance of slant and visual guidance (i.e., paper and head are vertical for manuscript, tilted for cursive).
5. Write the alphabet from memory, spontaneously and on command.
6. Draw a direct and even pencil line to target points without hesitations or breaks in motion (e.g., lifting point).

The first four preskills are required to make writing comfortable. Imbalance and "overgrip" make writing fatiguing and fingers cramped. Improper posture and paper position interfere with visual and motor functioning. The fifth preskill, writing the alphabet, is necessary so that interruptions in the writing rhythm will not occur from an inability to recall what the letters look (or "write") like. The final prerequisite is necessary to assure that learning standard letter form and slant will not be impeded by poor hand-eye coordination. Since most strokes originate or terminate at the horizontal guidelines, it is believed that students who can draw a line to a target will also be able to make a stroke or sequence of strokes in a uniform manner.

It is important to note that very young children, who eventually will develop increasing motoric and cognitive control of writing as they mature and receive instruction, may not exhibit such control when they enter school. Relative immaturity in the skills enumerated above may falsely suggest handwriting errors to the person attempting to assess writing skills. For example, problems observed in the writing of young students that are assessed in terms of slant, form, size, spacing, and so forth may actually reflect immature control of the pencil and difficulty in making it obey cognitive commands. Assessment should begin at these fundamental levels and then proceed to more specific handwriting elements.

Another example of insufficient maturity, rather than insufficient skill, knowledge, or effort, is the naturally occurring tendency for young students to reverse, invert, or rotate letters. In terms of assessment, these behaviors would be of interest only if they persisted over time when the writing of normally achieving students no longer showed similar signs.

When deficiencies in preskills are suspected, direct reteaching of lagging abilities should precede further handwriting instruction. Once preskills are mastered, the following represent the next steps to becoming a skilled writer:

1. Make letters of uniform and consistent size, shape, slant, line quality, spacing, and alignment (Cohen & Plaskon, 1980).
2. Write letters in words rhythmically at a fairly uniform and high rate of speed.

3. Maintain a neat and organized appearance in terms of line length, margins, cleanliness of paper, and visual consistency (i.e., letters across words and lines appear the same).

Considerations in Handwriting Assessment

Determination of the best handwriting product is purely subjective. However, once certain characteristics or elements of "good" handwriting are identified and defined, they may be assessed objectively within a range of personal writing styles. It is important for teachers to tolerate such variance and fix their attention on the ultimate goals of expressive fluency and communicability.

The developmental level of the student and the objectives of the writing program must be taken into account when judging handwriting skills. It may be insufficient, and perhaps uninformative, to regard a student's product simply as "wrong," "sloppy," "bad," or "disturbed." An even less defensible approach would be to evaluate students by the characteristics observed in their handwriting. Though it is generally true that the persistence of immature writing behaviors is suggestive of underlying learning difficulties, it is more useful for teachers to attend to well-defined writing skills and related deficits rather than to infer global "learning problems" when conducting handwriting assessments.

Teachers must also be aware of the special difficulty writing presents for left-handed students, especially when taught by right-handed teachers (Cohen & Plaskon, 1980). English handwriting, like most mechanical skills in daily life, favors the right-handed pupil. In general, assessment of writing by left-handers can proceed much as it will for right-handed students. However, teachers should expect some writing variance as a result of the change in writing posture. In particular, the left-handed student must be permitted more latitude in developing a comfortable posture and slant. Legibility as well as speed should still be assessed.

A final consideration in handwriting assessment concerns differences between manuscript and cursive writing forms. When students are introduced first to manuscript and then to cursive writing, they are required to make adjustments in (1) paper positioning (in cursive, the paper is tilted toward the midline); (2) letter slant; (3) spacing between letters (spaces are filled by connecting strokes); (4) letter appearance and formation; and (5) hand movements. During transition, one or more elements of handwriting may suffer a setback. To counteract these periods of lower skill achievement, teachers should clarify instructional goals and choose assessment questions most likely to provide them with usable information. For example, during transition to cursive writing, speed and accuracy are likely to be diminished, more so for some students than for others. In such a situation, requiring cursive writing in learning tasks designed to assess *other* aspects of written expression might seriously interfere with the teacher's ability to draw legitimate inferences from observed performance. Therefore, it would be more reasonable for teachers to assign students to write in a handwriting style in which they are most proficient if the intention is to assess written expression, writing mechanics, or spelling.

Types of Handwriting Assessment Measures

Informal Measures

Standardized and technically adequate instruments for assessing handwriting do not exist. However, informal techniques can be very informative. In general, assessment consists of observing students while they are writing or evaluating their finished products. Observations can be coded by the use of checklists, rating forms, and graphs.

Checklists

The various elements of handwriting can easily be used to construct a mastery checklist. Figure 8.5 presents an illustrative checklist. Using this format, teachers simply note the presence or absence of a particular writing element. Each element can be measured as follows:

1. **Size** can be measured with reference to horizontal guidelines on standard school writing paper. For example:

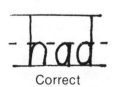

Correct

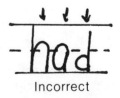

Incorrect

If consistency of size is preferred to conformity within paper guidelines, teachers can draw horizontal lines across the tops of small letters and ascenders. This solves the problem of a child who fails to conform with size guidelines on writing paper but who produces letters whose size relationships are very consistent.

2. **Slant** measurement may be accomplished in much the same way. Draw a line to bisect a series of sampled letters. For manuscript, these lines should be consistently vertical. For cursive, they should be slanted to the right, though the amount of slant is flexible. Teachers

	Size	Slant	Form	Space	Line	Alignment	Consistency

Name _____ Date _____ manuscript _____ cursive _____

a
A _____

b
B _____

c
C _____

d
D _____

e
E _____

f
F _____

g
G _____

h
H _____

i
I _____

j
J _____

k
K _____

l
L _____

m
M _____

n
N _____

o
O _____

Figure 8.5. Sample of mastery handwriting elements.

p
P _____

q
Q _____

r
R _____

s
S _____

t
T _____

u
U _____

v
V _____

w
W _____

x
X _____

y
Y _____

z
Z _____

should examine cursive slant for consistency across individual letters
and letters in words: For example:

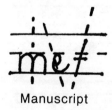
Manuscript

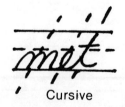
Cursive

3. **Letter form** can be checked against a commercially or teacher-
prepared standard. By making a transparency of the standard and
laying it over the student's word, teachers can judge to what degree

sample letters are acceptable. The various strokes in a letter should be proportionate to one another, and when implicit stroke length relationships are severely violated, the letter is distorted. For example:

Manuscript   Cursive

4. **Spacing** in manuscript defines the equal intervals between letters within and between words. If spacing within a word is variable and greater than that between words, readability suffers. Again, consistency is one of the important qualities being assessed. For example:

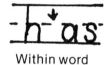   

Within word   Between words

5. **Line quality** refers to the evenness of pressure applied to the strokes in letter formation as well as to the amount of control exhibited. Poor grasp of the pencil can produce uneven and wavy lines. For example:

Manuscript   Cursive

6. **Alignment** refers to the consistency with which letters touch a common baseline and do not appear to float. As with the assessment of size, teachers can draw appropriate baselines if students' letters, though otherwise acceptable, fail to use paper guidelines. For example:

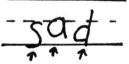

Misaligned letter   Misaligned word

Rating Forms

The same categories found in various checklists may be used to construct rating forms. Rating forms, as mentioned earlier, allow teachers to categorize their observations of a student's writing in a quasi-quantitative form along a mastery continuum of "below average," "average," or "above average" performance. Figure 8.6 presents a simple form for conducting this type of assessment.

Ratings are derived from a direct comparison of a student's writing sample with samples taken from those in a "reference" group (e.g., all students in the same group, class, or grade level). The teacher may begin by dividing writing samples into categories such as below average, average, and above average groupings. In order to assess more objectively, several teachers may be asked to rate a student's work using the same samples from a reference group. Each teacher should be permitted to categorize the reference group's work inde-

Rate: (for each of the following categories unless otherwise indicated)

1. Good
2. Average
3. Fair
4. Poor

	Oct.	Dec.	Feb.	Apr.	June

I. Neatness
  a. appearance of work
  b. cleanliness of paper
  c. organization of margins

II. Legibility
  a. size
  b. slant
  c. form
  d. spacing
    - letters within words
    - between words and sentences
    - paragraphs
  e. line quality
  f. alignment

III. Rate of writing
  (mark (s) slow or (f) fast)

IV. Writing position
  a. posture
  b. pencil grip
  c. slant of paper

Figure 8.6. Sample of handwriting evaluation scale. *Source*: Cohen, S. B., & Plaskon, S. P. (1980). Language arts for the mildly handicapped. Columbus, OH: Charles E. Merrill, p. 264.

pendently. Teachers may also be given a list of assessment criteria to improve interteacher reliability. Occasionally, especially in upper grades, students may be enlisted to act as "blind" judges once names have been removed from samples.

Commercial handwriting scales such as the very popular standards published by the Zaner-Bloser Company and the *Denver Handwriting Analysis* (Anderson, 1983) are developed in a similar way. These scales allow reference to some larger reference group—such as all students at a particular grade level. Technically adequate standardization procedures have not been used in the development of such scales, but if teachers feel a comparison to national standards is warranted, they may use a commercial scale as a quick check on the quality of their student's handwriting.

Locally developed norms, of course, do not permit teachers to generalize their estimates of quality beyond the local reference group. The teacher-ranked handwriting samples of five first-graders (see Figure 8.7) illustrate this point. The "best" handwriting sample is only the best of this particular group, and may only be average for first-graders elsewhere.

A portion of Zaner-Bloser's handwriting evaluation scale for grade 1 is presented in Figure 8.8 as a comparison to the rankings in Figure 8.7.

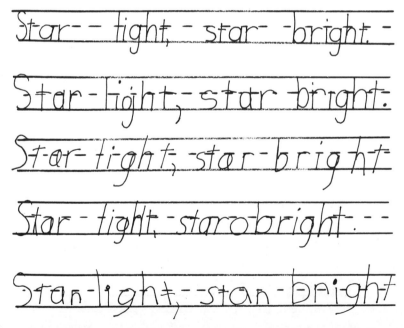

Figure 8.7. Teacher-ranked handwriting samples of five first-graders. (Excellent, good, average, fair, poor.)

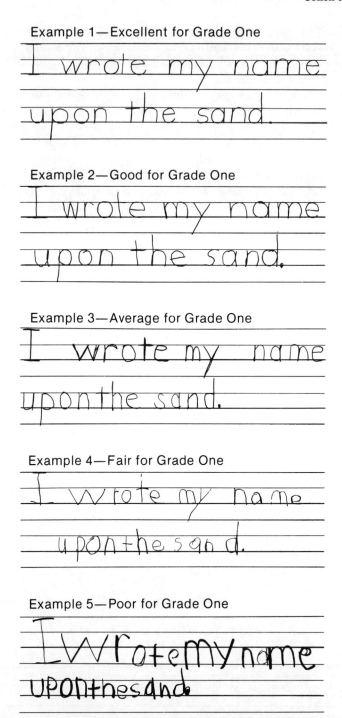

Figure 8.8. First Grade Manuscript Writing Evaluation Scale. *Source: Creative Growth with Handwriting.* Evaluation scale, first grade. (1979). Columbus, OH: Zaner-Bloser, Inc.

CASE STUDY

Part II

Present Testing

Intelligence

The *Wechsler Intelligence Scale for Children—Revised* (WISC-R) was given to assess Kay's intellectual capabilities. She attained a Verbal IQ of 101, a Performance IQ of 102, and a Full Scale IQ of 101. All of her subtest scores fell within the normal range. It should be noted that her weakest skill was on the Coding subtest. A summary of her subtest scaled scores follows:

Verbal		Performance	
Information	10	Picture Completion	11
Similarities	11	Picture Arrangement	13
Arithmetic	10	Block Design	11
Vocabulary	11	Object Assembly	10
Comprehension	9	Coding	7
(Digit Span)	(9)		

Academic

The *Peabody Individual Achievement Test* (PIAT) was administered to Kay as a means of measuring her academic skill levels. She is achieving at grade level in Reading and Math. In contrast, she is achieving just below grade level in Spelling and General Information. The following is a summary of her subtest scores as determined by grade norms:

Subtest	Grade Equivalent	Percentile Ranks	Standard Scores
Mathematics	3.5	50	100
Reading Recognition	3.6	53	101
Reading Comprehension	3.5	50	100
Spelling	3.2	41	97
General Information	3.2	43	97
Total Test	3.2	45	98

Psychomotor

The *Bender Gestalt Test* was given as a procedure to assess Kay's psychomotor development. She made six errors according to the Koppitz scoring system. Her drawings resulted in a developmental age equivalent of 6 years, 6 months to 6 years, 11 months. Kay was slow in drawing the designs; however, her perception of the forms was adequate.

Handwriting Analysis

The *Denver Handwriting Analysis* was given to Kay to identify handwriting strengths and weaknesses. The test assesses skills in near-point copying, writing the alphabet from memory, far-point copying, and writing cursive equivalents for manuscript letters and dictation. The results revealed that Kay has significant weaknesses in all areas. Kay demonstrated poor attentional skills in copying both near-point and far-point stimuli. The readability of her writing samples was problematic due to poor letter formation. Frequently emitted errors included overlooping the letter "o," squaring the letter "s," and a lack of letter closure. Kay had trouble with writing the alphabet from memory due to poor letter formation and transition errors. She has a slow writing pace, which prevented her from completing two out of five of the timed subtests. Kay's spatial organization, slant, and general appearance were all judged to be deficient. A summary of her mastery level scores on the subtests follows:

Subtests	Mastery Level
Near-Point Copying	46%
Writing Capital Letters	40%
Writing Lowercase Letters	40%
Far-Point Copying	44%
Manuscript-Cursive Transition	46%
Dictation	35%

Summary and Recommendations

Kay is a third-grade student who is functioning in the normal range of intelligence according to her WISC–R test scores. A noted weakness on the Wechsler Coding subtest was evident. Academically, as measured by the PIAT, Kay is functioning at grade level in Reading and Math, whereas she is slightly below grade level in Spelling and General Information. Psychomotor testing revealed some visual motor weaknesses. Results from the *Denver Handwriting Analysis* indicate significant handwriting deficits. It is recommended that Kay receive special resource services in handwriting training. Remedial suggestions are listed below.

Letter Formation

1. Dot-to-dot exercises.
2. Tracing letters on worksheets. Vary the tracing by having Kay use different colored pencils or markers.
3. Practice on closing the letters "a," "g," "p," "b," and "d".

Copying

1. Numbering words: On copying assignments have Kay write consecutive numbers above each word.
2. Have Kay break down words into syllables and copy each part separately.
3. Multicolor copying: For chalkboard work, use colored chalk as an aid by writing the words within a story in different colors.

Spatial Organization

1. Letters out-of-line: Have Kay mark all letters that are not proportional or correctly aligned in a story task and let her explain what is wrong.
2. Estimating space: Have Kay estimate how much room she will need on her paper to copy sentences on the chalkboard that vary in length.

Speed

1. Time trials: Have Kay keep a record of the time it takes her to finish a daily writing task. Remind her before the task to try and beat her previous time.

Appearance

1. Reworked letters: Have Kay circle reworked letters. Remind her that reworked letters reduce appearance quality.
2. Erasures: Have Kay circle any erased words or letters. Have her keep a chart on the number of erasures per assignment. Reward her for decreases in the frequency of erasures.

Slant

1. Paper position: Have Kay position her paper in an area on her desk marked for correct position.
2. Parallelogram boxing: Have Kay draw parallelograms around her words. Remind her that slanted words should take the form of a parallelogram.

Systematic Observation

Graphing aspects of handwriting performance by systematically recording repeated observations has major instructional benefits. Both naturally occurring and instructionally induced changes in performance over time can be closely monitored and evaluated.

To graph handwriting performance, teachers should carefully define one or more elements or behaviors of concern. For example, handwriting speed may be defined as the number of correctly written letters per minute. "Correctly" can be further defined with reference to the elements of size, slant, and so forth. To observe performance, standard conditions can be created by the teacher so that changes will not be caused by unknown variables. For example, teachers might assign a short passage to be copied or written from memory each day for a number of days. Consequently, each day's measure of handwriting speed will be directly comparable to each other day's performance.

Systematic observation of handwriting may also be achieved by asking a student to write the same passage on three different days, with slight variations in the writing directions. On day 1 ask the student to write using his or her best handwriting. On day 2 ask for the most natural handwriting, and on day 3 direct the student to write under a time constraint (Mann, 1981). A comparison of these three samples allows the teacher to:

1. Set appropriate handwriting goals through an analysis of the student's best product.
2. Determine a need for remedial instruction based upon an analysis of the natural writing sample.
3. Recognize when the student is performing under perceived pressure and therefore not producing at the level he or she should.

Systematic observation, as well as all other informal assessment techniques, requires some standard against which handwriting will be compared. If possible, this standard should be as nonarbitrary and instructionally relevant as possible. In systematic observation, the students may be compared to themselves, with each student acting as a personal standard by which to measure improvement. If some sense of absolute quality is necessary, ranking procedures using multiple teacher judges help to establish local standards. These standards can also be used to evaluate performance when using systematic observation and graphing. When using rankings, the teacher is concerned not with improvement but rather with the degree to which students approach a given standard. In either qualitative improvement or mastery, systematic observation techniques allow teachers to see the direct effects of their instruction upon their students' handwriting performance. As a result, instruction can be modified to achieve desired outcomes.

Summary

Ability in written expression is a composite of many interlocking skills that result in a complex product. Consisting of spoken language, reading, handwriting, vocabulary, writing conventions, and spelling, written expression is the most difficult language arts content area for students to master. In a parallel fashion it is one of the most difficult for teachers to assess. Although the separate factors within written expression may be objectively evaluated, the composite product is often analyzed in a more subjective manner.

Assessment of written expression begins with an understanding of the influence of spoken language upon written language. The speaker whose phrases are characterized by incomplete thoughts, poor vocabulary, sound omission, or inappropriate use of pauses may demonstrate these same elements when writing. The correct use of the various writing mechanics is often the focus of writing assessment. This chapter delineated strategies for both informal and formal written assessment. The reader is cautioned when using formal techniques to examine the aim of the assessment and the relevance of the assessment instrument for that concern. Three standardized diagnostic measures (TOWL, PSLT, and DEWS) were reviewed along with the most commonly used achievement tests. Informal evaluation strategies were more thoroughly reviewed, with an emphasis placed upon systematic procedures.

Handwriting instruction is given a great deal of attention in the basic elementary curriculum; however, handwriting assessment has not been given equal time. As a result, handwriting evaluation is primarily done informally with teachers often devising their own procedures. Several specific strategies for handwriting assessment were explained in this chapter.

Finally, the ultimate purpose of assessment in written expression is to guide the instructional program. It should be evident that assessment is the beginning of systematic instruction. The teacher must be able to recognize the writer's strengths and weaknesses, establish reasonable objectives, and implement an instructional program that will result in the learner's ability to communicate clearly in written form.

Educational Suggestions for Students with Written Expression and Handwriting Difficulties

The most crucial educational consequence of a student's difficulty in written expression and handwriting is their inability to communicate ideas or skill knowledge in written form. The following suggestions can assist students in their written communication in the instructional or assessment situations. However, the suggestions are not exhaustive, and teachers should design their own techniques based upon the student's needs, academic levels, and interests (Anderson, 1983).

It is best to teach letter formation by grouping problematic letters based on error type.

Students are less frustrated when instructed on letter formation based on a stroke-by-stroke strategy. This strategy allows the teacher to assess where the student is making an error.

Students who reverse letters occasionally can be instructed to look at partner letters in the alphabet.

Teachers can facilitate a student's memory for letters by having the student "air-write" the letters with exaggerated gestures.

Teachers can train students in self-evaluation of their handwriting by having them copy a story from the chalkboard, then circle in red those beginning word letters that are poorly formed while circling in blue adequately formed beginning word letters.

Teachers can use language experience writing to allow students to practice letters with which they are having difficulty. For example, if a student enjoys participating in Cub Scouts, have him write a story about a recent Cub Scout outing, but instruct the student to use words beginning with specific letters that he has difficulty forming.

Students who have connection difficulty when forming particular letters often benefit from instructional writing that stresses flowing fine-motor movements.

Before identifying an older student as having a problem in transition from printed to cursive writing, make sure that the student does not prefer to print.

For students who have been identified as making omission, insertion, and substitution errors, direct the student's attention on the written copy while reinforcing self-checking of work.

Students with an identified directional dictation difficulty can benefit from instructional tasks that emphasize clarifying spatial relationships.

Students who have been assessed as having spatial organization problems can benefit from classroom activities that emphasize spatial planning and awareness of spatial boundaries.

At times students who have slant handwriting difficulties can benefit from directions on positioning their paper correctly, maintaining a good sitting posture, and keeping their feet on the floor.

Study Questions

1. Discuss the importance of a child's motivation for written expression. List ways of increasing a child's motivation to write.
2. Discuss the positive and possible negative effects of corrective feedback for the written expression of a student.
3. Discuss the components of spontaneous writing assessment. How does this differ from contrived writing assessment?
4. Delineate the procedures for using type-token ratio technique for vocabulary assessment. Calculate the type-token ratio for the following: "The building on the square is the smallest building in town."
5. List the preskill behaviors required before instruction and assessment of handwriting can proceed.
6. Delineate procedures to measure size, slant, letter form, spacing, line quality, and alignment in handwriting assessment.
7. Specify the components that a teacher would use in a systematic observation procedure to assess handwriting.

Suggested Readings

Collins, R., Baer, G., Walls, N., & Jackson, M. (1980). The development of a behavioral assessment technique for evaluating gradual change in handwriting performance. *Behavioral Assessment, 2*, 369–387.

Moran, M. R. (1982). Analytic evaluation of formal written language skills as a diagnostic procedure. *Diagnostique, 8*(1),, 17–31.

Temple, C., & Gillet, J. W. (1984). *Language arts: Learning processes and teaching practices.* Boston: Little, Brown.

Towle, M. (1978). Assessment and remediation of handwriting deficits for children with learning disabilities. *Journal of Learning Disabilities 11*, 370–377

Wiederholt, J. L., Hammill, D. D., & Brown, V. (1983). *The resource teacher: A guide to effective practices.* Austin, TX: PRO-ED.

References

Anastasiow, N. (1972). The picture story language tests, 1972. In O. K. Buros (Ed.), *The seventh mental measurements yearbook.* Highland Park, NJ: Gryphon Press.

Anderson, P. (1983). *Denver handwriting analysis manual.* Novaro, CA: Academic Therapy Publications.

Beaver, M. H. (1977). Individualized goal setting, self-evaluation, and peer evaluation. In C. Cooper & L. Odell (Eds.), *Evaluating writing: Describing, measuring, judging.* Urbana, IL: National Council of Teachers of English.

Braddock, R., Lloyd-Jones, R., & Schoer, L. (1963). *Research in written composition.* Urbana, IL: National Council of Teachers of English.

Breland, H. M., & Gaynor, J. L. (1979). A comparison of direct and indirect assessments of writing skills. *Journal of Educational Measurement, 16*, 119–128.

Carroll, J. B. (1938). Diversity of vocabulary and the harmonic series law of word-frequency distribution. *Psychological Record, 2*, 379–386.

Chase, C. I. (1979). The impact of achievement expectations and handwriting quality on scoring essay tests. *Journal of Educational Measurement, 16*, 39–42.

Cartwright, G. P. (1969). Written expression and spelling. In R. M. Smith (Ed.), *Teacher diagnosis of educational difficulties.* Columbus, OH: Charles E. Merrill.

Cohen, S. B., & Plaskon, S. P. (1980). *Language arts for the mildly handicapped.* Columbus, OH: Charles E. Merrill.

Diederich, P. B. (1974). *Measuring growth in English.* Urbana, IL: National Council of Teachers of English.

Farnham-Diggory, S., & Simon, H. A. (1975). Retention of visually presented information in children's spelling. *Memory and Cognition, 3*, 599–608.

Hall, J. K. (1981). *Evaluating and improving written expression.* Boston: Allyn & Bacon.

Hammill, D. D., & Bartel, N. R. (1982). *Teaching children with learning and behavior problems.* Boston: Allyn & Bacon.

Hammill, D. D., & Larsen, S. C. (1983). *Test of Written Language*. Austin, TX: PRO-ED.

Hogan, T. P., & Mishler, C. J. (1979). Judging the quality of students' writings: When and how. *Elementary School Journal, 79*, 142–146.

Johnson, W. (1974). Studies in language behavior: A program of research. *Psychological Monographs, 56*(2).

Lundsteen, S. (1976). Help for the teacher of written composition: *New directions in research*. Urbana, IL: National Council of Teachers of English.

Mann, P. (1981). *Informal assessment of academic skills*. Paper presented for the Culpepper City Schools, Culpepper, Virginia.

Myklebust, H. R. (1965). *Development and disorders of written language, volume 1: Picture story language test*. New York: Grune & Stratton.

Personke, C., & Yee, A. H. (1966). A model for the analysis of spelling behavior. *Elementary English, 45*, 32–37.

Poteet, J. A. (1980). Informal assessment of written expression. *Learning Disabilities Quarterly, 3*(4), 88–98.

Weiner, E. S. (1980a). Diagnostic evaluation of writing skills. *Journal of Learning Disabilities, 13*, 43–48.

Weiner, E. S. (1980b). The diagnostic evaluation of writing skills (DEWS): Application of DEWS criteria to writing samples. *Learning Disabilities Quarterly, 3*(2), 54–59.

9

Assessment of Spelling Skills

Michael M. Gerber
Sandra B. Cohen

OBJECTIVES

After completing this chapter the teacher will be able to:

1. Determine appropriate spelling assessment questions to help guide test development or selection.
2. State the dimensions of spelling assessment and describe each component as it relates to informal test construction.
3. Discuss the use of the following assessment measures: Informal Spelling Inventories, direct observation of spelling errors, error analysis, correct letter sequences, and systematic observation of spelling achievement.
4. Analyze spelling samples using a variety of informal measures.
5. Debate the use of formalized tests in spelling assessment.

Considerations in Spelling Assessment

Two major assessment questions are often easily confused (e.g., Shores & Yee, 1973). The first concerns the student's ability to spell particular words correctly. The second question, and one that requires more inference, involves the student's general ability to solve spelling "problems" as they naturally occur in writing. Spelling problems occur whenever the speller has some initial uncertainty about how to represent the correct spelling. In such a circumstance the student is required to employ problem-solving strategies that make optimal use of previously acquired information about both the specific word and orthographic principles in general.

When a student responds to a weekly test by correctly spelling 20 words, the teacher assumes that the student can devise a strategy for recalling *those* particular words in *that* particular task situation. However, the teacher may not have learned anything about the student's abilities to spell those same words in another context (e.g., personal writing) or to spell words not tested.

Results of a standardized achievement test are interpretable in much the same way. If the student spells a number of words correctly, the achievement norms provided by the test developers will inform the teacher how the student's performance compares with that of a normal group on *that* particular set of words. It is an inescapable fact of spelling assessment that correct spellings only indirectly inform teachers about students' understanding and capacity to use spelling instrumentally in their writing. The teacher's knowledge and skill in assessment *must* fill the inevitable gaps.

Consequently, teachers must be clear in their own minds about what questions they expect a spelling assessment to answer for them. Next they need to consider the limitations inherent in assessment instruments when asking these questions. Table 9.1 presents some critical concerns that need to be resolved before time and effort are invested in any spelling assessment.

Work on this chapter by the senior author was supported in part by a contract (300-80-0623) from the U. S. Department of Education, Office of Special Education, for the University of Virginia Learning Disabilities Research Institute.

TABLE 9.1 Critical Concerns of Spelling Assessment

Step 1: Who requires assessment?
     a. Grade level or school
     b. Class
     c. Individual child/children

Step 2: What is the justification for assessment?
     a. To compare achievement with local, state, or national norms
     b. To evaluate the effects of unit of instruction recently completed
     c. To set priorities for new instructional period
     d. To monitor progress on some qualitative/quantitative variable
     e. To help to delineate learning problem

Step 3: What information should the assessment yield?
     a. Number and/or type of words spelled correctly
     b. Number and/or type of words spelled incorrectly
     c. Frequency or rate of error-making
     d. Types of orthographic features spelled correctly/incorrectly
     e. Number and/or type of words recognized as correctly/incorrectly spelled
     f. Number, type, and/or quality of self-corrections
     g. Specific rule knowledge and/or use
     h. Don't know? _____
                                        seek assistance

Step 4: What measurement instruments are available?
     a. Standardized
     b. Non-standardized, commercially available
     c. Non-standardized, teacher constructed
     d. Don't know? _____
                                        seek assistance

Step 5: What evidence of measurement validity is sufficient?
     a. Score is stable if retested after short interval
     b. Score is stable for items
     c. Score is related to other trustworthy measure
     d. Score closely predicts future or other important measure
     e. Score is interpretable to yield information desired
     f. Items reasonably and adequately sample the behavior of interest
     g. Items are not biased for children being assessed
     h. Don't know? _____
                                        seek assistance

CASE STUDY

Part I

Name: Jimmy H.   Age: 9 years, 11 months
Date of Birth: August 28, 1972   Grade Level: 4
Date of Evaluation: July 28, 1981

Background Information

Jimmy is a white, upper-middle-class student in Ms. G's fourth-grade class in a small town on the Atlantic Coast. He is 9 years, 11 months old and has been retained one school year. He appears to be having particular problems with written expression. Ms. G. requested a series of assessments and trial interventions in order to boost his achievement in various writing skills. He labored over each writing task, and although the written products showed imaginative thought sequences, there was little evidence of standard writing conventions. As a result, his papers were often "red-marked" and he seemed to be losing interest in writing.

Observation

Observation of Jimmy during spelling and other writing tasks revealed that he was frequently off task. When he wrote, his writing was slow, deliberate, and labored. However, he was very responsive to the teacher or examiner on a one-to-one basis. His behavior showed greatly improved attention to task as well as some observable increase in writing efficiency. His response to dictation and instruction revealed nothing remarkable about either his visual or his auditory skills. He could imitate dictated words correctly and easily identified obvious writing errors when prompted. His speech, vocabulary, and articulation all appeared to be normal for his age.

Past Test Results

Test	Date	Results
WISC–R	Sept. 1980	Full scale IQ: 110
		Verbal IQ: 112
		Performance IQ: 106
Woodcock-Johnson	Sept. 1980	
Psychoeducational Battery		
Reading Achievement		Scaled Score: 85
Written Language Achievement		Scaled Score: 74

Spelling Assessment Measures

Dimensions of Formal Measures

Formal measures of spelling include commercially prepared tests of achievement and/or ability. These tests are usually standardized on a sample of children who, it is hoped, are representative of the natural variation of characteristics found in the national population. Technical adequacy of formal assessment instruments is critical.

From the teacher's standpoint, technical adequacy translates into "interpretability" and "believability." The benefit of standardized spelling tests and their ability to compare performance under standard conditions with a particular reference group is seriously jeopardized when instruments are technically inadequate. A spelling score is meaningful only when it can be trusted to reliably measure some specific, well-defined spelling skill or ability and when measurement is comparable to performance measures of similar test takers.

Unfortunately, formal spelling measures that are highly reliable and valid are generally not available, or if they exist they are part of a more extensive achievement battery in which spelling assessment plays only a minor role (Shores & Yee, 1973). The remainder of this section will briefly describe 10 frequently cited standardized measures of spelling achievement or ability (see Table 9.2).

Standardized Tests

The tests reviewed briefly in Table 9.2 were chosen because they are frequently cited, widely used, and normed after 1968. To assist teachers who wish to compare these assessment instruments, the authors have assigned to each a technical adequacy "grade." If an instrument's technical manual or examiner's manual fails to provide clear and full information concerning characteristics of the norming population, validity of items and format, or reliability of scores across items, time, or alternate forms, the test was assigned an unsatisfactory (U) rating. If information was provided and discussed in a manner that would be clear and useful to teachers, the instrument was assigned a rating of excellent (E). Instruments with satisfactory (S) or good (G) ratings provided at least adequate information for a knowledgeable teacher to make reasonable decisions; instruments rated as good tended to provide more information or clearer information than those rated as satisfactory.

The evaluative judgments are intended to compare test construction and characteristics, as they are described in teachers' manuals, to an "ideal" spelling test (Shores & Yee, 1973). Though a test may not be ideal, this does not mean that it should not be used. Teachers need to

TABLE 9.2 Evaluations of Standardized Spelling Tests

Test	Format/Procedures	Standardization
California Achievement Tests (CTB/McGraw-Hill, 1978); grades 1.5–12	5 levels, 2 forms Multiple choice Timed Group administration	S Norm sample not well-defined
Comprehensive Tests of Basic Skills (CTB/McGraw-Hill, 1977); grades 2.5–12	4 levels, 2 forms Multiple choice Timed Group administration	S
Iowa Tests of Basic Skills (Hieronymous, Lindquist, & Hoover, 1982); grades 1–8	No levels Multiple choice Untimed Group or individual administration	S Norm sample characteristics insufficient
Iowa Tests of Educational Development—SRA Assessment Survey (Lindquist, Feldt, & Neckere, 1972); grades 9–12	No levels, 2 forms Multiple choice Timed Group administration	S Sampling not well described
Metropolitan Achievement Tests (Balow, Hogan, Farr, & Prescott, 1978); grades 2.5–9.5	4 levels, 3 forms Dictation Timed Group administration	S Sampling inadequate
Peabody Individual Achievement Test (Dunn & Markwardt, 1970); grades K–12	No levels Multiple choice Untimed Individual administration	G
SRA Achievement Series (Naslund, Thorpe, & Lefever, 1978); grades 1.5–10	5 levels, 2 forms Multiple choice Timed	G
Stanford Achievement Test (Gardner, Rudman, Karlsen, & Merwin, 1982); grades 1.5–9.5	6 levels, 3 forms Multiple choice Timed Group administration	E
Test of Written Spelling (Larsen & Hammill, 1976); grades 1–9	No levels, 1 form Dictation Untimed Individual administration	S

Reliability	Validity	Interpretability (Strengths and weaknesses)
S Stability in doubt No test/retest data	S Insufficient data and rationale	No specific error or word-type information (−) Grade norms by time of year tested (+)
S	S	Requires administration of other subtests for clear interpretation (−)
S Stability in doubt No test/retest data	S Insufficient data and rationale	Grade norms by time of year (+) Individual testing (+)
S	S Insufficient data and rationale	Special group norms (+) Specific for high school (+) Scoring service (+)
S Stability in doubt Test/retest and alternate forms	S Insufficient data and rationale	Dictation format (+) Multiple forms (+)
U Reliability low or insufficient	U Inadequate evidence	Individual testing (+) Ability not assessed (−) Questionable validity (−)
S Stability in doubt No test/retest, alternate forms data	S Inadequate criterion for items above primary level	Error analysis for primary level (+) Validity unclear above primary level (−)
G	G	Error analysis (+) Teaching objectives (+) Requires publisher scoring (−)
E	E	No alternative forms (−) Individual testing (+) Word-type error analysis (−)

TABLE 9.2 *(continued)*

Test	Format/Procedures	Standardization
Wide Range Achievement Test (Jastak & Jastak, 1978); ages 5–adult	2 levels, 1 form Dictation Untimed Individual administration	U No standardized information

be aware, however, of each test's limitations and the need to be cautious in making interpretations of the scores they yield. Moreover, many of these instruments are part of much more extensive achievement batteries; consequently, judgments of adequacy recorded in Table 9.2 apply only to *spelling* portions or subtests of these batteries.

Multiple Choice Format

Multiple choice tests have been criticized by Shores and Yee (1973) as being of questionable validity as *spelling* tests. They argue that this format tests word recognition skills but not the encoding process thought to be central to the production of correct spelling. Most achievement batteries include a spelling subtest that is multiple choice, multileveled, timed, and designed to be administered to groups (e.g., *California Achievement Tests, Comprehensive Tests of Basic Skills, Iowa Tests of Educational Development, SRA Achievement Series, Stanford Achievement Test*).

All of these instruments have received at least satisfactory standardization. The *Stanford Achievement Test* (Gardner, Rudman, Karlsen, & Merwin, 1982) was the most carefully normed of the entire group. However, other instruments, such as the *Iowa Tests of Educational Development—SRA Assessment Survey* (Lindquist, Feldt, & Neckere, 1972), provide special standardization information for subpopulations. This type of information is useful for teachers who must always decide whether their students are similar to the standardization population chosen by test developers. No instrument provided norms based on the performance of handicapped populations, thereby limiting their *diagnostic* value for teachers of exceptional students.

All of the above-mentioned multiple choice tests are meant to be used within a comprehensive achievement testing program. Often the spelling subtest cannot be separated from the battery because scores represent composite performance on several subtests. Also, although most provide two or more forms for pretesting/posttesting, many do not offer clear evidence that the alternate forms are equivalent. They

(cont'd)

Reliability	Validity	Interpretability (Strengths and weaknesses)
U	U	Individual testing (+)
Insufficient data	Clinical data only	Only one form (−)
		Dictation (+)

also fail to provide test-retest data for individual forms to show that scores are reliable indicators of a student's ranked performance relative to that of his or her peers.

Dictation Format
Relatively few achievement batteries contain subtests that are administered with a dictation format. The *Metropolitan Achievement Tests* (Balow, Hogan, Farr, & Prescott, 1978) is multileveled, group-administered, timed, and has multiple forms. However, the standardization, reliability, and validity of the instrument are just adequate. Because the test is timed (i.e., students have a fixed amount of time in which to respond to the dictated words), this instrument is not directly comparable to other dictation tests, which are usually untimed. (The effects of time constraints in an assessment device are discussed more fully in the following section on informal measures.)

The *Wide Range Achievement Test* (Jastak & Jastak, 1978) includes a popular and widely used spelling subtest. The WRAT has been especially popular in clinical assessments where a quick estimate of a student's current level of achievement is required. Unfortunately, the test developers have provided inadequate information about standardization, reliability, and validity of the spelling test. Furthermore, the instrument consists of only one form, making interpretation of gains very difficult.

A much more satisfactory dictation test is the *Test of Written Spelling* (TWS; Larsen & Hammill, 1976). The TWS also consists of only one form. However, interpretability is enhanced by the care taken in the test's development. The test consists of 60 hierarchically arranged words, 35 designated as "predictable" spellings and 25 as "unpredictable" spellings. Predictability was determined by the success or failure of a computerized algorithm, such as used by Hanna, Hanna, Hodges, and Rudorf (1966), to produce a correct spelling for each word. If the computer was unsuccessful in producing a correct spelling, the word was designated as "unpredictable." The validity, as well as the interpretability, of the instrument is also aided by the fact that each word appears in the 10 major commercial spelling programs. In addition, the manual provides the percentage of students in the norming sample who correctly spelled each word. These various features make the TWS a very versatile instrument for individual assessments as well as group achievement estimates.

As with most standardized tests, the scores derived from a student's performance are comparable to the scores of the standardization sample, which does not include handicapped students. Also, extensive use of this instrument by the first author with both learning disabled and normally achieving elementary school students has revealed an unexpectedly large percentage of normally achieving public school students who scored beyond the standardization range. It is possible that these students represent an unusual, though normal, clustering of very good spellers. However, it might also be the case that the standardization population is not as representative of "typical" achievement or ability as it claims. Inspection of the standardization data provided in the teacher's manual suggests that the demographic variables describing the norm sample are only adequate since the characteristics of the communities and schools sampled are not documented.

Despite the need for caution in using the TWS with exceptional (and perhaps high-achieving normal) students, it is a flexible, easy-to-use, and interpretable instument. When used in conjunction with various informal measures, the TWS can be a very informative assessment tool.

CASE STUDY

Part II

Present Testing

Jimmy was administered the *Test of Written Spelling* (TWS; Larsen & Hammill, 1976). Jimmy's total score age equivalent was 7 years, 6 months (spelling quotient = 77; grade equivalent = 2.2). He correctly spelled 14 out of 35 "predictable" (i.e., phonetically regular) words but none of the 25 "unpredictable" (i.e., phonetically irregular) words.

Ms. G. also examined a set of words from Jimmy's spelling series. She wanted some qualitative information about how Jimmy attempted to spell words he did not know. A list of these words, along with Jimmy's fall and spring spellings, follows.

Actual Words	Jimmy's Fall Spelling	Jimmy's Spring Spelling
1. united	1. unitit	1. unitited
2. dressing	2. dressing	2. dressing
3. hiked	3. hitit	3. hiked
4. human	4. humm	4. hummn
5. eagle	5. igl	5. egil
6. closed	6. closted	6. closed
7. peeked	7. peeked	7. peked
8. eighty	8. atey	8. atey
9. type	9. tiped	9. tipe
10. elevator	10. lzate	10. elivatrr
11. swimming	11. swiming	11. simming
12. toad	12. tode	12. toted
13. traded	13. traded	13. tated
14. flipper	14. flipper	14. fiper

Using the quality rating system devised by Gerber & Hall (in press), Ms. G. determined that Jimmy's average spelling quality was equal to 2.9 on a scale from 1 to 5 (1 = unintelligible; 2 = some but not all phonemes represented; 3 = all phonemes represented but some by using letter names instead of letter "sound"; 4 = all phonemes legally represented with evidence of correct vowel marking and past tense marking; 5 = correct spelling).

Following the administration of the 14-word teacher-prepared diagnostic test, Ms. G. attempted to assess Jimmy's word recognition and orthographic knowledge informally. She noted that he failed to spell any words on the TWS that were not predictable on the basis of sound-symbol relationship and wondered how he went about "problem-solving" with this type of word.

Jimmy was shown a card that contained the correct spelling of each word plus seven misspellings made by both Jimmy and other students in the class. The card looked like this:

1. kit	3. r5hh	5. hiekd	7. hikeb
2. hiaked	4. bucket	6. hiked	8. hite

Jimmy was asked to find two spellings that he felt could not be correct. Then he was asked to find two spellings that might be correct. Finally, he was asked to choose the one spelling that was probably correct. After each choice Jimmy was asked to justify his decision. The following is an excerpt from a taped exchange between Jimmy and his teacher over the spelling of the word *hiked*.

Teacher: Which two spellings do you think are possible for spelling *hiked*?
Jimmy: Number 6 and number 8.
Teacher: Which is the best?
Jimmy: Number 6.
Teacher: Why do you think so?
Jimmy: It's got a *-ed* at the end.
Teacher: What's good about that?
Jimmy: It spells /d-/.
Teacher: Huh?
Jimmy: Yeah, which spells "hike-duh." Like "He hike-duh." Hear it at the end? "Duh."
Teacher: No, I don't, actually. When I say it, I hear a /t-/ at the end. "Hiked."
Jimmy: Oh, I though it was "hike-duh." Oh, it was "hiked."
Teacher: [subvocalizing] Hiked. Hiked. [normal voice] Well, maybe that's all right. Some people might say it that way. But suppose I'm right and the correct way to say it is "hiked." Do you still like the same spelling even though it sounds different?
Jimmy: Well . . . hiked . . . I, uh, I know "hiked" is spelled that way.
Teacher: You know it's spelled that way? You mean, even if it doesn't sound right, you know it's spelled that way?
Jimmy: Yeah, some words aren't . . . don't sound like they're spelled.
Teacher: O.K. Very good.

Dimensions of Informal Measures

Informal spelling measures are either commercially or locally prepared (e.g., teacher-made). They are "informal" in the sense that administration procedures and assessment materials are somewhat adaptable to each teacher's circumstances. They are also "informal" in that they lack standardization and comprehensive technical development, thereby reducing their adequacy and restricting the sort of information they are likely to yield. However, depending upon the question being posed, informal measures of spelling may be more suitable and contain greater practical value in terms of time, effort, and usefulness than formalized measures.

Figure 9.1 presents a schematic diagram of the major dimensions of spelling assessment. Most procedures, whether teacher-designed, commercially prepared, or formally standardized, can be defined in terms of these dimensions.

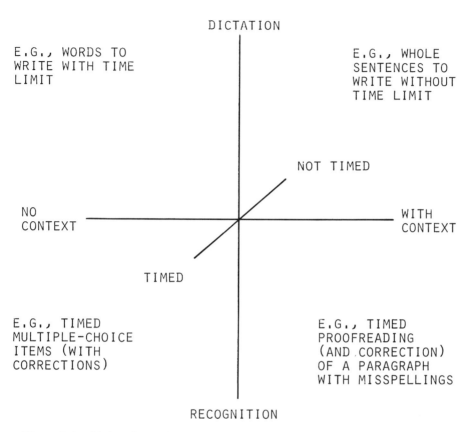

Figure 9.1. Major dimensions of spelling assessment.

Dictation versus Recognition Tests

The simplest, most effective, and most valid type of spelling assessment is the traditional spelling list dictation (Cartwright, 1969; Peters, 1967). Words can also be dictated within the context of sentences where children are required to write the entire sequence. Recognition tests (sometimes called proofreading) typically present the student with spelling alternatives either within sentences or as single or multiple word items. Students can be required to correct errors as they find them or simply to mark words as either correct or incorrect. Multiple choice spelling tests usually involve either (1) alternative spellings of the same word or (2) one misspelling and several correct spellings of different words. Both dictation and recognition tests can be either timed or untimed.

Deno, Mirkin, Lowry, and Kuehnle (1980) and Shores and Yee (1973) have criticized both dictation and recognition formats. Shores and Yee (1973) assert that dictation tests lack construct validity in that they do not relate to any particular model of the spelling process. For this reason, as was emphasized earlier, dictation tests may only tell teachers about students' ability to recall certain words in certain situations. Recognition tests are criticized for similar reasons. Moreover, although performance on recognition tests generally correlates with dictation test performance (Freyberg, 1970), proofreading is only one of the subskills underlying good spelling. In natural circumstances, spelling involves actually producing a letter string. Production of a response results from the composite of all spelling subskills. Normally when students proofread what they have written, they do not know in advance that a given spelling will be incorrect, nor are they provided with a set of alternatives, one of which they are certain will be correct.

Context Versus No-Context Tests
The most natural spelling assessment format is the spontaneously written passage. Simple measures of spelling accuracy and ability can be easily developed for such "natural" writing samples using these criteria:

1. Percentage of total number of words spelled correctly.
2. Percentage of total number of different words spelled correctly.
3. Percentage of errors that are spontaneously self-corrected (or improved).
4. Average number of sounds, letters, or syllables per word attempted correctly.
5. Number of correct words per minute.

It is traditional to allow students the opportunity to hear dictation words in context since meaning and syntactical function may help to differentiate homophones (e.g., peak, peek; read, red) or to assist recall of orthographic conventions such as -s, -ing, -ed, -er, and -ble. Students may also be required to write entire sentences rather than single words, placing the assessment in a more natural context. However, Allred (1977) concluded that the overwhelming evidence supports the superiority of words over sentences for assessment purposes. This finding may be due to the fact that the student more clearly understands the task goal—to spell correctly—and that the word list is free of confounding language variables.

Timed Versus Untimed Tests
There are basic differences between timed and untimed spelling assessment measures that affect interpretation of performance. The teacher must decide whether it is important to know (1) how well the student will spell compared to another student when all are given the

same amount of time or (2) what the student's maximum performance is when time is not a factor. The first question implies a timed, or "speed," test; the second calls for an untimed, or "power," test. In general, as time limits increase, the spelling performance should become more representative of ability, as opposed to relative achievement. The teacher must decide, as always, what assessment procedures fit the instructional questions being posed.

Examples of Informal Measures

Spelling Words from Lists

Assessment of spelling from lists is very straightforward. Students are simply asked to spell each of the words on the list, and the number or percentage correct is calculated. This measure adequately and directly represents the students' degree of mastery for that particular list.

This type of assessment is appropriate when spelling particular lists can be justified as an educational objective. Lists contain three types of spelling words: (1) "survival" words, (2) core vocabulary words, and (3) rule exemplar words. *Survival words* include words of such high utility or importance for a student that their spelling constitutes minimal competency. Words such as the student's full name, full address, danger and warning words, or vocationally related terms might comprise a "survival" list.

Many commercial spelling series and local curriculum guides make use of a *"core" spelling vocabulary* of several hundred to several thousand words. High-frequency words are taught because it is expected that such words will have special utility for students and will facilitate their written expression. The core list is often graded so that parts of it will be taught during each of several instructional years. Items on the list are generated from frequency counts of words appearing in students' reading or writing at different ages. All grading of such lists is not the same; the same or similar words will be targeted for teaching at different grade levels in different series. Moreover, depending upon the instructional philosophy of the authors, different series will vary slightly in the skills and sequence presented.

In other curriculum cases, high frequency of word use or even high utility might be sacrificed in favor of words that serve as *spelling rule exemplars*. For example, words like *fin*, *bin*, and *tin* might not be very useful in the spontaneous written expression of young students, but they may be very useful in teaching the particular spelling pattern "consonant, consonant blend, or digraph plus /in/." When assessing spelling mastery of such linguistically analyzed lists, teachers are interested in making inferences about the student's ability to generalize knowledge and skills to the spelling of words. A correct response, therefore, undergoes a subtle shift in meaning compared to correct spelling on the other two lists. Rule exemplar lists, it is hoped, allow teachers to make evaluative judgments about students' abilities to solve a class of orthographic problems involving words or syllables with the same characteristics. One possible advantage of this type of list is that errors may have instructional implications beyond revealing a need to reteach specific words. Spellers may manifest difficulties with specific patterns easily detachable by rule exemplar lists.

It is important to remember that interpretations of students' spelling ability from exemplar lists may or may not be adequately supported. Teachers will have to decide whether the speller's performance accurately reveals that rule knowledge has been acquired and will be used in natural writing. A conservative approach, if rule generalization is the skill being assessed, would be to conduct multiple assessments in different formats. For example, after a word list is administered, assessment of the student's natural writing might be examined for evidence of rule mastery.

Informal Spelling Inventory (ISI)
The ISI, suggested by Mann and Suiter (1974), is really an extension of the dictated list type of assessment. With the ISI teachers can construct their own lists to answer any assessment question they might have. The test is usually constructed by randomly selecting words from some larger corpus of words (e.g., a basal spelling program) by grade level. A standard dictation test is administered beginning with the subset of 20 words that are two grade levels below current placement. The test continues until seven errors are recorded. The ISI can be used for estimating grade placement and/or skills profiles, depending upon the nature of the corpus from which it was composed. Its limitations are similar to those already discussed for dictation lists. The obvious advantage is that it can be tailor-made to fit a set of instructional materials as a gross measure of achievement and progress.

Rule exemplar lists can be similarly constructed. But since teachers would require that such a list have some interpretability in terms of specific skills, words should not be randomly selected. The scope and sequence chart provided by basal spelling program publishers, or one devised by the teacher, serves as a guide to the word types that must be included. At least two word exemplars should be selected for each orthographic pattern to be assessed; more than two is preferable if the teacher wishes to increase reliability and does not mind increasing test length. Word exemplars should be presented in random order and performance scored for each pattern as: mastered (all exemplars correct), questionable (half of exemplars correct), or failed (no exemplars correct). Word difficulty, described as the grade level at which at least 50% of students will spell a word correctly, should also be controlled. The list can be "graded" by referring to other graded lists or by throwing out all words that every student either fails or passes and adding more discriminating exemplars.

CASE STUDY

Part III

Present Testing (Continued)

The following is an example of Jimmy's spontaneous writing:

Jan. 2.

a bee

A bee name is Lee.

He is a good bee

He Like Bears Lee

One day Lee saw a pie

a man came outside

and picked up The pie

and Lee Saw The man

Pick up the Pie and

Came to the man and

Lee stung The man.

The *Written Assessment Rating Scale* was applied to Jimmy's spontaneous writings, and vocabulary was assessed using a type-token ratio. Ms. G. also examined his handwriting against standards she established by her class rankings and found his penmanship to be below average for his peer group. The type-token ratio of .43 showed a repetitive use of common and key words. The writings along with the contrived statement responses (see below) determined that Jimmy had little understanding of capitalization and punctuation.

Directions: Capitalize the appropriate words in each sentence below:

1. Sue is a girl's name.
2. li will ride the pony to my house.
3. when can i speak to doctor jones?
4. you are in virginia.

Directions: Punctuate each of the sentences below:

1. This book isnt mine •
2. The flag is red white and blue.
3. Who is the teacher in this class
4. Mr Alan said Come here and eat with me •

Summary and Recommendations

It was concluded from the spelling assessment information that Jimmy had the ability to recognize correct spellings but apparently did not use this information when he spelled. His spellings were characterized by the use of the letter names instead of the letter sounds or correct orthographic patterns such as -ed, particularly in words like *eagle* (igl), *eighty* (atey), *elevator* (lzate), *united*, (unitit), *hiked* (hitit). Instructional objectives should be written to target vowel marking and past tense endings. Also useful will be teaching Jimmy to proofread his spellings to find parts about which he is doubtful, and then encouraging him to attempt to improve the spelling.

Based upon the writing assessments a program was planned to meet the following objectives:

1. Jimmy will begin each sentence with a capital letter and end each sentence with a punctuation mark.
2. In his spontaneous writings, Jimmy will capitalize all proper names and the pronoun *I*.
3. Jimmy will discriminate between uppercase and lowercase manuscript letters and will use only lowercase letters unless the instance calls for capitalization.
4. Jimmy will demonstrate the appropriate use of the comma when listing a series and setting off quotations.
5. Jimmy will choose a greater variety of words to express himself in writing. This will be noted by an increasing type-token ratio, with a long-term goal approaching .8.

Jimmy was given the opportunity to write something every day. These writing samples were evaluated through a conference with the teacher on four out of five days. Jimmy's progress was regularly charted on the General Progress Profile for Written Expression, and at the end of 9 weeks the objectives were reevaluated.

Program modifications and/or new instructional objectives were then determined at the end of each 9-week period.

Direct Observation

Observation of spelling performance may focus on the spelling product itself or on those behaviors thought to be representative of spelling subskills. Observational assessment techniques fall into two broad categories: (1) summary observations, which rate, rank, or judge the presence or absence of skills and behaviors thought to be important for good spelling and (2) systematic observations of instructional effects over time.

Summary observations depend upon checklists or rating forms designed to profile the presence, absence, or relative strengths and weaknesses of various skills or behaviors. The scope and sequence descriptions in most commercial spelling series are a good source of

TABLE 9.3 Spelling Rules and Principles

Final *e* rule	When a word ends in *e* and you add a morphograph that begins with a vowel letter, drop the *e*.
Doubling rule	When a short word ends cvc and the next morphograph begins with a v, double the final c.
Vowel-consonant	*Y* at the end of a morphograph is a vowel letter.
Y to *i* rule	Change the y to i when a word ends with a consonant-and-y, and the next morphograph does not begin with *i*.
Plural variation	If a word ends in *s, z, sh,* or *ch,* you add *es* to make the plural word.
Plural variation	If a word ends in *s, z, sh,* or *x,* you add *es* to make the plural word. The letter *x* acts like two consonant letters.
Contractions	A contraction is made from two words, and a contraction has a part missing. We show that the part is missing with an apostrophe.
Plural variation	If a word ends with a consonant-and-*y*, you add *es* to make the plural word.
Vowel-consonant	If *w* is at the end of a morphograph, then it is a vowel letter.
-En variation	When the word ends in the letter *w* and you add *en*, drop the *e*.
-Al insertion	When the word ends in the letters ic you must add the morphograph *al* before adding *ly*.
Plural variation	Some words that end in the sound *fff* have the letters *ves* in the plural. You can always hear the sound *vvv* in the plural.
Doubling rule	When the word ends in a short cvc morphograph, use the doubling rule.
O-r ending	Use *o-r* if a form of the word ends *i-o-n*.

From *Corrective spelling through morphographs* by R. Dixon & S. Engelmann (1979), Palo Alto, CA: SRA.

categories for observational assessment. Table 9.3 illustrates the scope and sequence information from a commercial series which can be used to generate an observation record. This type of assessment can be used to profile skills, to show progress, and to plan instruction.

Summary observation assessments are usually based on the teacher's cumulative observation of and experiences with the student. Occasionally teachers may not have any recent memory of the student performing a spelling task that demonstrates the specific skill being assessed and will thus be unsure of an item's rating. In this situation, teachers can create a minitest of the specific skill question. In doing so, they should be aware of the requirements for technical and conceptual adequacy previously discussed. Teachers should design tasks that will yield objective evidence *as if* other teachers were going to evaluate the results. Briefly stated, the procedures meet the following criteria:

1. Sample the targeted skill or behavior with enough items to probe the range of a student's likely responses.
2. Make sure the test items are both fair and relevant to the assessment question.
3. Tell the students explicitly what you are doing and why; they may provide you with information that their performance alone will not reveal, or their performance may be more representative when they know precisely what is being assessed.

Partoll (1976) prepared an error analysis checklist that is quite extensive. Teachers may choose to design similar lists to suit their own purposes. Partoll's list includes items related to error type (e.g., sounds omitted at the beginning of words, reversals of whole words, and mixing of uppercase and lowercase letters) as well as observable behaviors contributing to or indicative of poor spelling (e.g., laborious spelling, poor writing and letter formation, and spelling, erasing, and trying again to no avail). An example of a summary observation checklist is illustrated by the Spelling Observation Form shown in Figure 9.2. This assessment focuses on more global behaviors. However, each behavior may be an important indicator of strengths or weaknesses. Some examples that show potential outcomes of this assessment follow. Students who are observed to pause and think before they write from dictation, proofread before handing in papers, and spell over 80% of the words correctly on a dictation test are exhibiting behaviors usually associated with high performance. The same students who spell well on dictation tests and display task orientation and a positive attitude by their behavior may not show the same desirable behaviors when spelling in other contexts. They may fail to complete assignments or self-initiated projects, to proofread, or to ask for spellings of unknown words. Other students might be observed to behave in a very stereotypical way when faced with any

Name _____   Current spelling placement:
                                   Level _____
Date _____   Series _____
                                   Lesson # _____

I. General orientation towards spelling: Too seldom   Too often

a. Attends to teacher appropriately	1	2	3	4
b. Follows directions	1	2	3	4
c. Asks appropriate questions when directions are not understood	1	2	3	4
d. Pronounces words accurately	1	2	3	4
e. Repeats seven word sentences	1	2	3	4
f. Average speaking vocabulary	1	2	3	4
g. Copies letters accurately	1	2	3	4
h. Copies words accurately	1	2	3	4
i. Knows alphabet	1	2	3	4
j. Spells name:				
- first	1	2	3	4
- last	1	2	3	4
k. Spells some words from memory	1	2	3	4
l. Asks how to spell new words	1	2	3	4
m. Handwriting is legible:				
- manuscript	1	2	3	4
- cursive	1	2	3	4

II. Behavior during dictation   Average % correct words _____

a. Pauses to think before spelling	1	2	3	4
b. Spells word completely without pause	1	2	3	4
c. Response to error-making				
- recognizes most errors immediately	1	2	3	4
- backtracks to check/correct	1	2	3	4
- changes letters in the course of spelling word	1	2	3	4
- erases errors	1	2	3	4
- crosses out errors	1	2	3	4
- writes over errors	1	2	3	4
- rewrites whole word	1	2	3	4
- frequent partial spellings before complete spelling	1	2	3	4
d. Repeats words/letters before writing	1	2	3	4
e. "Sounds out" while spelling	1	2	3	4
f. Asks for repetition frequently	1	2	3	4
g. Cheats or continuously watches others	1	2	3	4
h. Rubs/closes eyes, becomes restless, looks fatigued	1	2	3	4
i. Negative emotional outbursts	1	2	3	4
j. Writes whole sentences when asked	1	2	3	4
k. Content with performance	1	2	3	4

Figure 9.2. Summary Spelling Observation Checklist.

III. Behavior during natural writing   Average % correct words _____

    a. Initiates, stories, poems, picture captions,   1   2   3   4
       etc.
    b. Writes more than one sentence   1   2   3   4
    c. Response to error-making:
       - recognizes most errors immediately   1   2   3   4
       - backtracks to check/correct   1   2   3   4
       - changes letters in the course of spelling
         words   1   2   3   4
       - erases errors   1   2   3   4
       - crosses out errors   1   2   3   4
       - writes over errors   1   2   3   4
       - rewrites whole word   1   2   3   4
       - frequent partial spellings before complete
         spelling   1   2   3   4
    d. Uses words learned in other areas of
       curriculum (e.g., reading, math, social
       studies, etc.)   1   2   3   4
    e. Attempts to read finished written work to
       self, friends, teacher, parents   1   2   3   4
    f. Proud of work   1   2   3   4
    g. Finishes writing projects   1   2   3   4
    h. Sought by others for spelling help   1   2   3   4
    i. Asks teacher for help   1   2   3   4
    j. Rubs/closes eyes, becomes restless, looks
       fatigued   1   2   3   4
    k. Negative emotional outbursts   1   2   3   4

Figure 9.2 *(continued)*

sort of writing or spelling task. They may react negatively to errors when they are pointed out, fail to self-correct, fail to finish self-initiated writing projects, and show general complacency about their poor performance. Such students may require behavior management in addition to, or instead of, remedial spelling instruction. Spelling observations along with other assessment measures (e.g., behavioral assessment) will help to clarify the problem areas.

   Systematic observations involve monitoring some particular spelling behavior or skill over time through repeated observations and recordings. Observations may be made for several months or for only a few weeks. Systematic observation methods are usually designed by the teacher to measure how well a specific aspect of spelling performance responds to instructional change. For example, teachers can systematically manipulate their teaching instruction and observe changes in word studying, proofreading, assistance seeking, test taking, and self-correction.

Teachers often wish to monitor a student's cumulative mastery of a specific list of words, such as the core list in a spelling series. If instruction is individualized, each student's progress through the list may vary somewhat. By graphically recording cumulative learning (using some criterion of mastery such as five correct spellings on each of five attempts), the teacher is provided with a visual representation of the student's rate of progress compared to others' or to some defined expectation.

Another example of systematic observation involves examining the effects of different instructional techniques. Under a "baseline" condition, students are assigned a story-writing activity and are told that the teacher will be available to spell any words with which they may need help. After several days of observing the written products, the teacher may decide to modify the approach by telling students that the number of correct spellings of different words will earn varying amounts of some specified reward (e.g., minutes of free time). Having tried this procedure for several days, the teacher withdraws the "experimental" instructions and returns to baseline conditions. This return to original conditions provides the teacher with direct evidence that the instructional modifications, and not some other unknown factor, were responsible for any observed improvements. Following a return to the "no reward" condition, the teacher reinstates contingent reward procedures. This is done (1) to confirm that the teacher's instructional manipulation controls the level of pupil response and (2) to maintain the conditions that have proven to be most effective. Notice that the teacher is careful not to change a procedure until several observations appear to show stability in students' behavior— or little change from day to day. Furthermore, the teacher only changes one well-defined aspect of instruction at a time, so that interpretation of what then occurs is as clear as possible. Finally, using a system such as this, academic and social behaviors can be observed concurrently—for instance, on-task behavior during story-writing (measured as the percentage of time on task).

Correct Letter Sequences

Deno et al. (1980) have researched formative evaluation methods useful for systematic observation, program monitoring, assessment of effects from instruction, and forecasting achievement. They have shown that the number of correct letter sequences (CLS) on dictated spelling tests will reliably predict *standardized* achievement test performance, regardless of the words chosen for dictation. Their finding was shown to hold true for learning disabled as well as for normally achieving students. Consequently, CLS measurement can be a rapid and useful estimator of students' spelling progress when measured directly and systematically over a period of time.

CLS is scored by counting correct letter pairs. Students are also allowed credit for letters correctly beginning and ending words. The remaining correct letter sequences are counted in pairs. For example:

1 2 3 4 5 6 7

Spelling 1   d o n k e y   = 7 correct

1   2   3

Spelling 2   d u n k a y   = 3 correct

1 2 3 4

Spelling 3   d o n k i e   = 4 correct

Each caret represents a correct "sequence" (recall that the initial and final letters, when correct, are counted as a sequence). This simple measure was found to correlate at well above .80 with a standardized achievement test when used with a variety of randomly generated lists (Deno et al., 1980).

Error Analysis

As discussed at the beginning of this section, error analysis may be more informative than a simple tally of the percentage of correct spellings. Unfortunately, although there are many clinical theories about the significance of error-making (e.g., Johnson & Mykelbust, 1967; Boder, 1970), no formal instrument of sufficient technical quality exists to guide teachers in this process. Nevertheless, teachers desiring to interpret spelling errors for instructional purposes may find error analysis useful. The remainder of this section describes some experimental and clinical techniques to illustrate the possibilities of this approach for spelling assessment. Teachers should consult the sources cited and make up their own minds about the practicality and usefulness of these procedures. Furthermore, they should not hesitate to develop their own analytical procedures if due caution is exercised in interpreting results.

Boder (1970) has proposed that severely deficient spelling, when analyzed in conjunction with word recognition abilities, represents diagnostic signs of three types of dyslexia: dysidetic, dysphonetic, and alexic. *Dysidetic* spellers can produce good "phonetic" spellings of words that they cannot read, but cannot spell familiar, irregularly formed words. *Dysphonetic* spellers present somewhat the opposite pattern. They fail to produce phonetic spellings of familiar, regularly spelled words but are able to spell correctly many irregularly spelled words. *Alexic* spellers are deficient in both phonological and visual abilities and therefore produce few correctly spelled words of any type and tend to create severely distorted and unintelligible spellings.

Holmes and Peper (1977) found that an analysis of error types failed to reveal error patterns in retarded readers similar to those predicted by Boder (1970). They categorized errors as (1) phonetically unacceptable, (2) vowel deletion, (3) vowel substitution or addition, (4) consonant deletion, (5) consonant substitution, (6) consonant addition, (7) incomplete processing (middle letters missing), (8) transposition and inappropriate doubling, and (9) garble (unclassifiable). Although retarded readers made more errors of every kind, the percentage of errors in each category was almost identical for both retarded and normally achieving readers. The categories used by Holmes and Peper (1977) might be useful for objectively assessing the type and extent of spelling errors.

Gerber and Hall (1981) approached error-making in another way. Based on the work of Henderson & Beers (1980), spelling errors of learning disabled students were examined to study evidence on developmental trends. The results showed that, when spelling errors are categorized developmentally, the types of errors made by learning disabled students were no different from those made by normally achieving students who were 3 to 4 years younger. The categories used to classify errors were: deviant, prephonetic, phonetic, and transitional. *Deviant errors* are strings of letters, numerals, or pseudoletters having no obvious relationship to the intended word (e.g., *drlg* for *human*). *Prephonetic spellers* represent some, but not all, of the phonemes in the word (e.g., *jes* for *dressing*). *Phonetic spellers* represent all phonemes, but choose a letter whose *name* is similar in place of articulation to the *phoneme* of the target word (e.g., *egl* for *eagle* or *luvtr* for *elevator*). *Transitional spellers* produce letter strings that are legal in English and generally represent the sounds of the word, but are nevertheless incorrect (e.g., *traided* for *traded*, *younighted* for *united*). The results of this analysis suggested that many errors are systematic and logical given the student's cognitive maturity and that spelling errors develop in a progressive sequence toward better approximations of conventional orthography. By assigning arbitrary development ratings (1 = deviant, 2 = prephonetic, 3 = phonetic, 4 = transitional, 5 = correct) to misspellings, teachers may be able to gauge the relative maturity of the students' abilities to solve orthographic problems.

Teachers should be cautious about overgeneralizing these experimental and clinical findings. However, they may find it useful to examine students' spelling errors for evidence of systematic misspellings, such as Gerber and Hall's (1981) "phonetic" errors or

Holmes and Peper's (1977) error classification types. These analysis techniques have instructional implications because they suggest that the student has not learned either some general principle about spelling or a specific skill. In addition, it is more appropriate for teachers to focus on the instructional implications of errors than on highly inferential diagnostic categories for the speller; error analysis should be done with this in mind. Misspellings may follow general patterns but may also reflect idiosyncratic knowledge and ability or disability on the part of the speller. At this time, researchers are only beginning to learn which is which.

CASE STUDY

Part IV

Follow-up

Six months later Ms. G. gave Jimmy another assessment battery, when he was 10 years, 5 months old. His scores on the TWS had improved somewhat (i.e., spelling age = 8 years, 2 months; spelling quotient = 79; grade equivalent = 2.8). He now spelled 18 predictable words and 1 unpredictable word correctly. On the teacher-made diagnostic test, he received an average rating of 3.8. Although achievement was moderate on the TWS, Ms. G. felt that qualitative gains were evident on the diagnostic retest. Not only did Jimmy spell vowels and markers better; he attempted to correct errors more frequently. Unfortunately, Ms. G. felt that Jimmy was overgeneralizing the use of the past tense marker -*ed* to spell sound-alike phonemes, and so began to reteach not only the spelling of the marker but also the concept of past tense.

   Ms. G. followed through with her planned program to increase Jimmy's written expression abilities. After three nine-week cycles, Ms. G. observed that Jimmy had mastered the fundamental elements of capitalization and punctuation and had increased his vocabulary to a ratio of .64. Allowing Jimmy to write each day and to select his conference versus nonconference (editing) days with the teacher provided him with enough writing practice and motivation. He seemed to enjoy expressing himself and seeing his own improvement. Ms. G. recognized that Jimmy had more progress to make, but she felt the systematic use of assessment, objectives, intervention, and reassessment was the significant factor in his increasing achievement.

Summary

Spelling results from the skillful applications of linguistic and orthographic knowledge, rules, and strategies. Skillful spellers are able to sequence letters correctly to form words. When spelling is skillful, the writer is free to attend to other aspects of written communication such as clarity, logic, and substance. Moreover, skillful spelling is analogous to problem solving in that students must generate an organized and strategic approach to reducing their uncertainty about orthography.

Spelling and reading are not simple inverses of one another. In fact, there has been mounting evidence that early spelling experiences facilitate reading ability because (1) print is understood to be systematic and meaningful; (2) the interior of words is examined closely; and

TABLE 9.4 Summary of Spelling Assessment Procedures

Name	Type	Format	Administration
California Achievement Tests	Formal	Proofreading	Group
Comprehensive Tests of Basic Skills	Formal	Proofreading	Group
Correct Letter Sequence	Informal	Any spelling sample	Individual
Direct Observation a. checklists b. ratings c. systematic observation	Informal	Any spelling sample	Individual
Error Classification a. Boder's b. Holmes & Peper c. Gerber & Hall	Informal	Selected spelling sample	Individual
Spelling Lists/ISI a. survival b. core vocabulary c. exemplar	Informal	Selected spelling sample	Group/Individual
Iowa Tests of Basic Skills	Formal	Proofreading	Group
Iowa Tests of Educational Development	Formal	Proofreading	Group
Metropolitan Achievement Tests	Formal	Dictation	Group
Peabody Individual Achievement Test	Formal	Multiple choice	Individual
SRA Achievement Series	Formal	Proofreading	Group
Stanford Achievement Test	Formal	Proofreading	Group
Test of Written Spelling	Formal	Dictation	Group/Individual
Wide Range Achievement Test	Formal	Dictation	Individual

(3) spelling draws on the student's implicit knowledge of (oral) language. Therefore, increased attention to spelling assessment may yield valuable instructional information about emerging language ability apart from the numbers of words that a student spells correctly.

A variety of formal and informal procedures can be used to assess spelling ability and achievement. A summary of these measures is shown in Table 9.4. Teachers must be clear about their reasons for conducting an assessment and what type of instructional information they desire. Basic technical adequacy, regardless of how formal an assessment procedure is, helps to make results both believable and interpretable. Unfortunately, few formal tests are adequate for making broad inferences about ability. Several highly adaptable informal procedures, however, have been shown to be useful for evaluating, planning, and monitoring instruction. These include the use of qualitative analysis of spelling errors, direct observation of spelling behavior and performance, and construction of special-purpose lists.

Educational Suggestions for Students with Spelling Difficulties

Frequently the errors of students with spelling difficulties follow a repeated pattern. As students' errors are identified through assessment procedures, remedial approaches can be initiated. The following procedures are suggested to help reduce a variety of spelling errors (Cohen & Plaskon, 1980).

If students' errors are diagnosed as the result of poor auditory discrimination, teachers can give these students practice in hearing likenesses and differences in words that are similar.

Students whose errors are diagnosed as resulting from poor visual imagery can benefit from exercises that expose the words for short periods of time and then have the students reproduce them in writing from memory.

At times, spelling assessment data reveal that students have not mastered rules for formation of derivatives. Such students can benefit from sessions that teach generalizations for forming tenses and adding suffixes.

If the assessment procedures reveal that errors are due to poor attention to letter sequence in certain words, the students can benefit from sessions concerned with pronouncing the words carefully while stressing the sequence of sounds and letters.

If errors are identified as due to carelessness, then the students should be encouraged to carefully proofread all their writing.

When assessment results indicate that errors are due to a lack of phonics ability, the students can benefit from a multisensory strategy in which the students see the word, hear the word, spell the word orally, and copy the word.

Study Questions

1. What is meant by the phrase "problem-solving ability" in spelling?
2. Distinguish between technical adequacy of a test from a test publisher's perspective and a teacher's perspective.
3. List standardized spelling tests that are part of well-developed achievement batteries.
4. What are the advantages of the TWS over the WRAT?
5. How do informal measures of spelling differ from formal measures?
6. How is error analysis used in spelling assessment?

Suggested Readings

Boder, E. (1971). Developmental dyslexia: A diagnostic screening procedure based on three characteristic patterns of reading and spelling. In: B. Bateman (Ed.), *Learning disorders* (Vol. 4). Seattle: Special Child Publications.

Beers, J. W., Beer, C. S., & Grant, K. (1977). The logic behind children's spelling. *Elementary School Journal, 77,* 237–242.

Frith, U. (1980). Unexpected spelling problems. In: U. Frith (Ed.), *Cognitive Processes in Spelling.* London: Academic Press.

Gentry, J. R. (1978). Early spelling strategies. *Elementary School Journal, 79,* 88–92.

Personke, C. R., & Yee, A. H. (1971). *Comprehensive spelling instruction: Theory, research, and application.* Scranton, PA: Intext.

Temple, C., & Gillet, J. W. (1984). *Language arts: Learning processes and teaching practices.* Boston: Little, Brown.

References

Allred, R. A. (1977). *Spelling: The application of research findings.* Washington, DC: National Education Association.

Balow, I., Hogan, T., Farr, R., & Prescott, G. (1978). *Metropolitan Achievement Test: Survey Battery.* New York: Psychological Corporation.

Boder, E. (1970). Developmental dyslexia. *Journal of School Health, 40,* 289–290.

Cartwright, G. P. (1969). Written expression and spelling. In R. M. Smith (Ed.), *Teacher diagnosis of educational difficulties.* Columbus, OH: Charles E. Merrill.

Cohen, S. B., & Plaskon, S. P. (1980). *Language arts for the mildly handicapped.* Columbus, OH: Charles E. Merrill.

Deno, S. L., Mirkin, P. K., Lowry, L., & Kuehnle, K. (1980). *Relationships among simple measures of spelling and performance on standardized achievement tests* (Research Report No. 21). Minneapolis: University of Minnesota, Institue for Research on Learning Disabilities.

Freyberg, P. S. (1970). The concurrent validity of two types of spelling test. *British Journal of Educational Psychology, 40,* 68–71.

Gardner, E. F., Rudman, H. C., Karlsen, B., & Merwin, J. C. (1982). *Stanford Achievement Test* (7th ed.). Cleveland: The Psychological Corporation.

Gerber, M. M., & Hall, R. J. (1981, April). *Development of orthographic problem-solving strategies in learning disabled children.* Paper presented at the annual meeting of the American Educational Research Association, Los Angeles.

Hanna, P., Hanna, J. D., Hodges, R., & Rudorf, E. (1966). *Phoneme-grapheme correspondence as cues to spelling improvement.* Washington, DC: Government Printing Office.

Henderson, E. H., & Beers, J. W. (1980). *Developmental and cognitive aspects of learning to spell—A reflection of word knowledge.* Newark, DE: International Reading Association.

Holmes, D. L., & Peper, R. J. (1977). An evaluation of the use of spelling error analysis in the diagnosis of reading disabilities. *Child Development, 48,* 1708–1711.

Jastak, J. R., & Jastak, S. (1978). *Wide Range Achievement Test.* Wilmington, DE: Jastak Associates.

Johnson, D. J., & Myklebust, H. R. (1967). *Learning disabilities: Educational principles and practices.* New York: Grune & Stratton.

Larsen, S., & Hammill, D. (1976). *Test of Written Spelling.* Austin, TX: PRO-ED.

Lindquist, E. F., Feldt, L. S., & Neckere, E. D. (1972). *Iowa Tests of Educational Development: SRA Assessment Survey.* Chicago: Science Research Associates.

Mann, P. H., & Suiter, P. (1974). *Handbook in diagnostic teaching: A learning disabilities approach.* Boston: Allyn & Bacon.

Partoll, S. F. (1976). Spelling demonology revisited. *Academic Therapy, 11,* 339–348.

Peters, M. L. (1967). *Spelling: Caught or taught?* London: Routledge & Kegan Paul.

Shores, J. J., & Yee, A. H. (1973). Spelling achievement tests: What is available and needed? *Journal of Special Education, 7,* 301–309.

10

Assessment of Behavior Disorders

Douglas Cullinan
Herbert Root

OBJECTIVES

After completing this chapter the teacher should be able to:

1. Discuss the implications for assessment of behavior problems given a usable definition of behavior disorders.
2. List common behavior patterns exhibited by behaviorally disordered children and adolescents.
3. List two considerations in measurement when assessing patterns of the behaviorally disordered.
4. Discuss three general ways of obtaining assessment information for the behaviorally disordered.
5. List assessment procedures to identify children and adolescents with problematic behavior patterns.

Recent polls indicate that discipline and behavior problems in school are perceived by citizens as major obstacles to appropriate education (e.g., Gallup, 1983). We all know of spectacular incidents of vandalism, assault, and disorderliness, because such antisocial acts tend to be reported in local newspapers. Far more common in many schools— though less dramatic—are continuing patterns of disruption, involving students' aggression, disobedience, excessive classroom activity, disrespect for teachers and the administration, and other problem behaviors. Additionally, many teachers are deeply concerned over children and adolescents who do not disrupt but behave in self-defeating ways: causing peers to shun them, showing no skills or inclination to interact socially, exhibiting fearfulness, failing to stand up for their own rights, or expressing chronic sadness and apathy. These are some of the main behavior problems that most teachers, sooner or later, have to deal with.

The term behavior disorders (or "emotional disturbance," "maladjustment," and various other descriptors) refers generally to extreme instances of behavior problems that demand substantial variations from usual procedures in order to provide appropriate education. There are many thorny problems in establishing a usable definition of behavior disorders (Kauffman, 1981), but the term can perhaps be most concisely defined as follows:

> Behavior disorders of a pupil are behavior characteristics that (a) deviate from educators' standards of normality, and (b) impair the functioning of that pupil and/or others. These behavior characteristics are manifested as environmental conflicts and/or personal disturbances, and are typically accompanied by learning disorders. (Cullinan & Epstein, 1982)

The key phrases in this definition have implications for assessment of behavior problems and behavior disorders of pupils, so it is worthwhile to examine them.

First, the term behavior characteristics indicates that educators must be most concerned with the pupil's behavior—what the pupil does and says. Also of interest are the effects those behaviors have on people and things in the school environment. Some theories of pupils' behavior disorders put heavy emphasis on disturbances of personality, emotions, or mental functioning, but, even so, such internal problems are suggested by the pupil's observable behavior. Certainly in the process of assessing students' behavior problems, the main focus must be on behavior characteristics. Second, deviations from educators' standards of normality remind us that there is no clear dividing line between normality and abnormality. All teachers have expectations about the range of behavior that is "normal" in most school situations, and these expectations often vary according to the pupil's age, sex, and other characteristics. The behavior that falls outside this range of expectations is the one that causes teachers concern, especially if it is drastically different, has persisted beyond a reasonable period of time, or is clearly worsening.

Behavior problems that impair the functioning of that pupil include those that suggest the pupil is experiencing substantial distress (unrealistic fears, sadness and moodiness, inability to make friends, and so on). Also included here are stumbling blocks to the child's personal and educational development (e.g., a maladaptively short attention span or excessive dependence on adults). Behavior characteristics that impair the functioning of others are quite familiar to most teachers: disrupting groups of task-oriented peers, interfering with the appropriate functioning of individual classmates, and rule violations that are disruptive to the school as a whole are three common examples.

Finally, while regular and special educators are confronted with a wide variety of maladaptive behavior patterns of students, research and informal school observation suggest that certain categories of problems are more common than others. It is informative to consider these *environmental conflicts, personal disturbances,* and *learning disorders* most often exhibited by students with behavior disorders (Cullinan, Epstein, & Lloyd, 1983).

CASE STUDY

Part I

Name: Cecil D.
Date of Birth: June 3, 1973
Date of Evaluation: January 10, 1982

Age: 8 years, 7 months
Grade: 3

Background Information

Cecil was referred for evaluation by his classroom teacher, Ms. G., who described him as disruptive and unmanageable. Specific complaints included frequent interruptions of the work of others, refusal to complete assigned activities, rude and defiant responses to simple requests, and occasional violent outbursts to seemingly minimal provocation. Cecil was frequently sent to the office of Mr. S., the principal. Mr. S. requested an expeditious evaluation and disposition of Cecil's case. He candidly admitted that he was at a loss to know how he could bring Cecil's behavior under control. Mr. S. believes that Cecil is a prime candidate for placement in a special class for children with behavior disorders.

Observations

Home

Cecil is the second of four children of Ms. D. He has an 11-year-old brother who is currently in a special class for mildly retarded children located in the same school that Cecil attends. He also has two sisters of preschool age. Cecil's mother never married. She lives with her own mother, who cares for the girls during the day and works evenings as a clerk in a neighborhood market. Ms. D. works as a housekeeper at the local university. She has held this job for 3 years.

Ms. D. insists that Cecil is not a problem at home. She often relies on Cecil and his brother to mind their sisters at home on those evenings when she visits friends or goes out socially. Cecil's grandmother stated that she finds the girls unattended about once a week when she returns from work at 10:30, Cecil and his brother being out with friends in the neighborhood. She also admitted that Cecil had been returned home by the police on four evenings during the preceding year, but would not share the details of those episodes. There apparently has been no official record of these incidents, and the police have never filed a petition on Cecil.

Medical

Cecil's hearing and vision were screened at the end of first grade, and the results indicated normal acuity in both senses. A medical evaluation completed at the public health department on the request of the school (October 25, 1981) revealed no abnormal conditions or other sources of concern. The examining physician indicated that there were no physical reasons why this child might not be able to perform acceptably in school. Otherwise, medical data are not available. Cecil's mother remembers no illnesses for which medication was prescribed during her pregnancy with Cecil and recalls that his delivery, after 3 hours of labor, was not unusual in any way.

School

Cecil's quarterly grade reports reflect fair to poor performance throughout his school career. His grades have been mostly C's and D's, with an occasional B. He has received unsatisfactory marks on deportment for 8 of the 10 grading periods he has completed. The two satisfactory ratings were recorded last year as a second-grader.

Cecil's first-grade teacher recommended that he be retained in the first grade on the basis of his "atrocious work habits and largely uncivilized behavior." The principal overruled this recommendation, citing Cecil's acceptable performance on the end-of-year group achievement test and the fact that he is big for his age as justification for the promotion.

Cecil's second-grade teacher left the employ of the system at the end of last year and could not be reached for consultation. However, her report at the end of the year stated, "Cecil is inclined to recalcitrance but can be very agreeable when given the opportunity to perform special duties, such as taking attendance or leading the lunch line." When the present teacher was asked about changes in Cecil's behavior when given special tasks, she replied that such tasks were reserved for children who completed their work and behaved properly. Mr. S. said that sometimes he gave Cecil small jobs "to keep him out of the secretaries' hair" when he was sent to the office and that the secretaries reported these tasks to be completed efficiently and agreeably.

Past Testing

Achievement
SRA Achievement (Primary) administered 5-15-81:
  Reading, Grade Equivalent = 2.5, 38th percentile on national norms
  Language Arts, GE = 3.0, 46th percentile
  Mathematics, GE = 2.4, 35th percentile
  Composite, GE = 2.6, 42nd percentile
Peabody Individual Achievement Test, administered 11-5-81:
  Math, Grade Equivalent = 3.3, 55th percentile on national norms
  Reading Recognition, GE = 3.1, 49th percentile
  Reading Comprehension, GE = 3.6, 61st percentile
  Spelling, GE = 2.8, 40th percentile
  General Information, GE = 3.5, 57th percentile

Ability
Wechsler Intelligence Scale for Children—Revised, administered 11-5-81:
  Verbal IQ: 125
  Performance IQ: 120
  Full Scale IQ: 123

Types of Behavior Problems

Aggression-Disruption

Aggression is a common behavior pattern of children and adolescents, and in many forms (e.g., assertiveness in pursuing objectives) it is generally admired and encouraged. But it is also clear that cruelty, bullying, fighting, tantrums, disobedience toward the teacher, and other behaviors cause destruction, pain, and disadvantage to others. Aggression-disruption is the most common behavior problem of nonhandicapped students (Quay, 1979) as well as behaviorally disordered students (Bullock & Brown, 1972; Cullinan, Epstein, & Kauffman, 1984).

Hyperactivity

Hyperactivity refers to a behavior pattern that invovles inappropriate overactivity (restlessness, moving around without permission), attention deficits (inability to remain engaged in a task, tendency to be easily distracted from a task by irrelevent events), and impulsivity (interrupting and interfering with others, hasty and inaccurate decision-making). These problems are most apparent in situations that require attention to and compliance with instructions, rules, and other highly structured expectations. Not surprisingly, then, teachers are more likely than parents or physicians to identify children as hyperactive (Bosco & Robin, 1980). Some children with hyperactivity also show aggression, learning disabilities, and/or debatable evidence of brain damage or dysfunction ("MBD" or "soft neurological signs"), but these are probably not central features of hyperactivity (Routh, 1980). Fewer than 5% of elementary-aged pupils are hyperactive (Bosco & Robin, 1980), but hyperactivity accounts for a large proportion of referrals to child guidance clinics (Paternite & Loney, 1980). The disorder is usually first noted before 7 years of age, and adolescents are rarely identified as hyperactive. Yet most hyperactive children continue to have significant adjustment problems (Whalen, 1983) as they get older.

Social Maladjustment

This term refers to behavior that violates laws or deviates from conventional standards of the school or community but conforms to the standards of a peer group. Truancy, fighting, vandalism, drug or alcohol abuse, early sexual activity, and an attitude of contempt for conventionally valued goals and institutions fits the pattern of social maladjustment if such deviance is accepted or encouraged by members of the young person's peer group (gang, clique), neighborhood, or subculture. Changing standards for some of these behaviors make this characteristic especially difficult to identify and assess in many cases. Yet this is a particularly troubling variety of disorder for schools to handle.

Anxiety Disorders

The child or adolescent presenting an anxiety disorder generally experiences a strong anticipation of danger, feels physiological arousal and discomfort, becomes disorganized in thinking, and avoids the feared situation(s). Such students may become ill before school or in class, exhibit nervousness when given an assignment, refuse to speak when called on, and express a total lack of self-confidence in performing an educational, social, or other act that ought to be easily accomplished. Usually included within anxiety disorders is school phobia: a refusal to attend school often accompanied by pains, symptoms of physical illness, and extreme expressions of fear.

Social Withdrawal

Students who rarely communicate, appear extremely shy and self-conscious, seldom play or interact with peers, and resist joining in educational activities are characterized as socially withdrawn. Some of these youngsters are "isolated": they have poorly developed social skills, fear interactions with peers or adults, and seem to prefer solitary activities. Other socially withdrawn students initiate social interactions but in such aggressive, immature, or otherwise inappropriate ways that they turn off other people, so that interaction with them is avoided thereafter by peers and adults alike (that is, they are "rejected").

Learning Disorders

Students with behavior problems are usually below average in learning abilities and/or school achievement (Kauffman, 1981; Roberts & Baird, 1972). Teachers of the behaviorally disordered correctly see their students' academic retardation as a significant problem (Morse, Cutler, & Fink, 1964). Learning disorders of the behaviorally disordered appear to be similar to those experienced by pupils with other mild to moderate educational handicaps.

These are the major—although certainly not the only—kinds of behavior problems shown by students. Special and regular education teachers, individually or together, are often expected to deal with and correct such situations. Often a key ingredient in successful efforts is the teacher's ability to measure important aspects of the problem.

Measuring Behavior Problems

Measurement is the process of assigning a number to some characteristic so that the number accurately represents the characteristic. In this chapter the characteristics of most interest are behavior problems and disorders—such as those just described—that the educator sees as needing change. Once a characteristic is selected, it is measured by deciding (1) how the characteristic can be recognized and observed, and (2) how different numbers will be used to represent more and less of the characteristic. For example, suppose the characteristic of concern is "restlessness." Let's say this characteristic is observed when the pupil either leaves her seat without permission, turns her head to face the rear wall of the classroom, or taps her pencil on the desk so the teacher can hear at least two taps. A simple way to assign numbers to this characteristic would be to tally each instance of seat-leaving, head-turning, and pencil-tapping. This would permit daily totals that represent that day's "restlessness" (hourly, weekly, and other totals could be used, as could averages and other numbering rules). Of course, the developers of standardized measurement procedures have already made decisions (1) and (2) above. The educator must still select the characteristics to be measured, pick an appropriate test or other measurement procedure, and follow instructions in the manual for using the procedure properly.

The importance of measurement in the educator's efforts to reduce behavior problems can hardly be overstated. Few people would attempt to lose weight without careful, frequent measurement of their weight; yet all too often teachers who deal with pupil behavior problems pay little or no attention to measurement. Although it is obviously unfeasible for classroom teachers to measure all aspects of students' learning and behavior problems, some measurement of selected behavior characteristics is reasonable, and will usually justify the time and effort required. Measurement is especially needed for students who exhibit behavior disorders.

Measurement Methods

There are many specific procedures for measuring behavior and emotional problems of students. For the most part, however, they boil down to three general ways of obtaining information: (1) reported functioning, (2) actual functioning in an artificial setting, and (3) actual functioning in a natural setting.

Reported Functioning

An obvious way to obtain information about the social, personal, academic, or other functioning of a student is to ask someone—a teacher, parent, classmate, or the student. There are several variations of this general method.

Interviews
In an assessment interview, the questioner asks for information that may clarify the nature and severity of a behavior problem, help plan and carry out intervention, or achieve other purposes. One major way assessment interviews differ is along a dimension of structure. In highly structured formats, the interviewer presents a standard list of questions and records the interviewer's responses, but has little or no freedom to ask follow-up questions about interesting topics suggested by those responses. At the other extreme, unstructured interviews allow almost unlimited flexibility in what and how information is sought, and the interviewer is free to pursue any lines of inquiry he or she suspects may yield valuable clues. The level of structure may, of course, fall somewhere in between these extremes, as when the

interviewer looks for certain specific information but does not strictly follow a standard question format. Structured interviews have powerful advantages over unstructured ones: (1) they usually require less training and experience; (2) they are generally much more reliable (consistent across interviewers and over time), and (3) they produce information that permits comparisons that are important in understanding and treating behavior disorders (e.g., the student's functioning on two occasions, to check for progress; this student's functioning versus that of others, to establish relative severity of the disorder). Generally, structured interviews would seem to be more appropriate than unstructured ones for educational purposes, but efforts are needed for development and validation of such educational interviews.

One example of the structured interview format was used by Herjanic & Campbell (1977) with child psychiatric patients. It involved more than 200 questions, most of which the child was to answer with a "yes" or "no." Included were questions about learning problems, social problems at home, school, and play, as well as behavior and personal disorders of special interest to psychiatrists (e.g., phobias, depression, bed-wetting, body pains). Table 10.1 presents a few items from the latest revision of this structured interview (Herjanic, 1981). Herjanic and Campbell (1977) found that it could distinguish between behaviorally disordered and nondisordered youngsters. Other structured interview formats are listed in Appendix A (see page 309).

Behavior Rating Scales

The behavior rating scale is a standard collection of items, each of which describes a behavior pattern (usually, a *problem* behavior pattern). For each item there is a scale of 2 or (preferably) more points indicating the degree to which a youngster exhibits that behavior. The teacher (or other rater) marks this scale according to how he or she perceives the student's functioning on that behavior. For example, an

TABLE 10.1: Illustrative Sample of a Structured Assessment Interview for Youngsters with Behavior Disorders

Instructions: Ask the child or adolescent the question, then follow-up and/or code the response.

13. B. Do you often start on your school work and then not finish it, even if you know how to do it?
32. Do you often do just the opposite of what you were told, because you don't like being told to do anything?
58. C. Have your parents or teachers punished you frequently because they thought you were lying?

Adapted from Herjanic, 1981.

item about classroom aggression might have to be rated as either "no problem," "mild problem," or "severe problem," depending on the teacher's judgment about how much the pupil shows classroom aggression. Most behavior rating scales contain items that survey a wide range of problems. These items are often clustered into narrower categories of behavior disorder. As a result, some of these instruments yield an overall score along with category subscores.

For example, the *Behavior Rating Profile* (BRP; Brown & Hammill, 1983) has a Teacher Rating Scale that lists 30 problems. Each problem is rated on a 4-point scale according to the extent to which the teacher judges that the problem accurately describes the rated student (see Table 10.2). Based on these teacher ratings, a total score for the student can be derived. This score may be compared to national norms available in the manual and to other information on socioemotional development (e.g., self-perception of the problem or parent views; see Brown & Hammill, 1983).

Some rating scale instruments have a narrower focus. The *Conners Parent-Teacher Questionnaire* (PTQ; Conners, 1973) was devised to measure hyperactivity. Eyberg (1980) published a brief rating scale of aggression-disruption. It is also possible to devise individually tailored rating scales for particular problems and/or particular youngsters. Finch, Deardorff, and Montgomery (1974) developed such a rating scale to evaluate a treatment program for a highly aggressive 9-year-old boy in a residential facility. Items were based on problem behaviors as described by the ward staff and by the boy himself. Finch et al. (1974) reported that such a scale is simple and inexpensive to construct and use. Its reliability was adequate, and results accurately

TABLE 10.2: Illustrative sample of the *BRP* Teacher Rating Scale

Instructions: Indicate the extent to which you view each item as describing a problem for this student.

Item	Very much like the student	Like the student	Not much like the student	Not at all like the student
7. Disrupts the classroom	_____	_____	_____	_____
12. Is passive and withdrawing	_____	_____	_____	_____
13. Says that other children don't like him/her	_____	_____	_____	_____
16. Is overactive and restless	_____	_____	_____	_____

Adapted from Brown and Hammill, 1983.

reflected the boy's improvement once treatment was implemented. Other rating scales that can be used easily by teachers are listed on page 309 (Appendix A).

CASE STUDY

Part II

Present Assessment

Classroom Behavior

A psychometric assistant visited Cecil's classroom to collect further information on his situation. The assistant observed the occurrence of three of Cecil's main referral problems: "talkouts" (speaking without the permission of the teacher during instructional time), "physical" (hitting, pushing, or otherwise touching other students, except for allowed exchanges such as passing papers), and "noncompliance" (indicating to Ms. G. that her instructions would not be followed—often in a rude way such as "Forget it," "Screw you," or "No way"). These behavior problems were recorded for Cecil and two other boys in his class selected at random by the assistant. On each of the five observation days, the aide recorded these behaviors during one 60-minute period. The aide watched each boy for 1 minute on a rotating basis (20 minutes per boy per day) and tallied the number of times each of the three behavior problems occurred. Results are reported in the table below:

Behavior/Student	Observation Day				
	1	2	3	4	5
Talkouts					
Cecil	6	2	7	10	8
Boy A	5	0	0	4	3
Boy B	1	0	1	0	0
Physical					
Cecil	1	0	2	2	0
Boy A	0	0	0	0	0
Boy B	0	0	1	0	0
Noncompliance					
Cecil	0	1	1	3	1
Boy A	1	0	0	0	0
Boy B	0	0	1	0	0

The aide also kept a record of the number of times that Ms. G. responded to these three behaviors (usually by criticizing or giving a rule reminder). For Cecil she responded 37 times out of the 44 occurrences, or 84% of the time.

Ms. G. keeps a record (a prominently posted chart) of weekly assignments completed by each student. According to this chart, Cecil completed 6 of 30 assigned exercises during the current week, fewer than anyone else (average = 23, range = 14–30, excluding Cecil).

Ms. G. completed the Teacher Rating Scale of the BRP by rating how severely Cecil exhibits 30 school problems. Cecil's score on this instrument placed him at percentile rank 2 (i.e., among the most deviant 2% in comparison to national norms). Inspection of the teacher's responses indicated that Cecil has serious problems related to discipline, compliance, restlessness, and disruptiveness, but shows few problems in other possible problem areas (e.g., social withdrawal, anxiety disorders).

Finally, Bower's "A Class Play" sociometric procedure was administered to all the children in Cecil's class. Cecil was chosen more frequently than any other boy or girl in the class for negative roles. This indicates that he is actively rejected more than any other child. However, he was also quite often selected for positive roles.

Sociometrics

Sociometric procedures obtain information on each member of a group by measuring the interpersonal preferences of all members. For example, each class member may be required to nominate privately one or more classmates liked, disliked, sought out, avoided, respected, and so on. By comparing all students' responses, it is possible to identify a few students who are generally admired, some who are actively rejected, and others who are simply ignored. Such information may be useful in identifying candidates for special attention and for grouping students for social or other purposes.

One sociometric procedure is Bower's (1969) "A Class Play." In one part of this procedure, each student writes the name of a classmate who would best fit each of a number of roles to be acted in an imaginary class play. An example of roles (items) is presented in Table 10.3. When completed, the procedure is scored by counting how many times each student was picked for positive roles (odd-numbered items) and negative roles (even-numbered items). This procedure may help

TABLE 10.3: Illustrative Sample of "A Class Play" Procedure

Instructions: On the line beside each description, have the student write the name of a classmate who could best play the part.

_____ 1. A true friend.
_____ 2. Somebody who is often afraid and who acts like a little boy or girl.
_____ 3. A class president.
_____ 4. Somebody who is stuck-up and thinks he's better than everyone else.
_____ 5. A girl to act the part of a teacher of small children.
_____ 6. A mean, cruel boss.

Adapted from Bower, 1969.

identify rejected students (frequently picked for negative roles) and isolated students (rarely or never picked for any role).

Other sociometric procedures vary as to kind of item, manner of response, and age of respondent targeted for measurement. In the sociometric portion of the *Test of Early Socioemotional Development* (Hresko & Brown, 1984), a simple item is presented to young children (ages 3 through 7 years) to solicit the names of three friends (no negative nominations). A child's score depends on the number and priority of his or her selection as a friend by his or her peers. In another variation, students may be given a grid that lists behavior items on one side and the names of peers to be evaluated along the top. For each item, the student is to indicate all those peers accurately described by the item. Table 10.4 presents a few items from such an instrument, the *Adjustment Scale for Sociometric Evaluation of Secondary-School Students (ASSESS*; Prinz, Swan, Liebert, Weintraut, & Neale, 1978). A similar procedure instrument for younger pupils was described by Pekarik, Prinz, Liebert, Weintraut, and Neale (1976).

Self-Completed Personality Tests
Adult personality traits are commonly measured by having the individual examine a series of statements and indicate how self-descriptive each one is. This self-report method is also used in a few personality tests for children, including ones for self-concept (e.g., Coopersmith, 1967; Fitts, 1965; Piers & Harris, 1969), anxiety level (e.g., Castaneda, McCandless, & Palermo, 1956), and locus of control (e.g., Nowicki & Strickland, 1973).

For example, in the *Piers-Harris Children's Self-Concept Scale* (Piers & Harris, 1969), children indicate whether or not they think each of 80 statements is true about them (see Table 10.5). This instrument is designed for children who read at the third-grade level, but items can be read to less skillful readers. Other self-completed personality tests are listed on page 309 (Appendix A).

Actual Functioning in an Artificial Setting

Some characteristics of students can be measured by observing their performance on tasks selected as representative of how they function in everyday life. Standardized tests of abilities and educational achievement are major examples of this measurement procedure. For instance, general intellectual ability is usually measured by observing the individual's performance on a standard set of tasks that have been designed to be representative of intellectual ability in various real-world situations. The results are compared to the performance of other similar individuals to yield an estimate of (among other things) the individual's future school success. Likewise, standard collections of representative tasks administered in a standardized way within

TABLE 10.4: Illustrative Sample of ASSESS Format

Instructions: For each description, the student puts an X under the name of every classmate who fits the description.

Students

Description	Shawn	Karen	Tom W.	Steve	Thomas S.	Faye	Michael	Rick	Delores	Crystal	Paula	Janet	Sam	Bobby F.	Karla	Tod	LaVerne	Bobby A.
Those who do nervous things.																		
Those who push other people around.																		
Those who are sort of ignored.																		
Those who have confidence in themselves.																		
Those who usually botch an assignment.																		
Those who act phony.																		

Adapted from Prinz, Swan, Liebert, Weintraub, & Neale, 1978.

TABLE 10.5: Illustrative Sample of the Piers-Harris Format

Instructions: The student circles the "yes" or "no," depending on whether he or she decides each item applies.

It is hard for me to make friends	yes	no
I am smart	yes	no
I am shy	yes	no
My looks bother me	yes	no
When I grow up, I will be an important person	yes	no
I am well behaved in school	yes	no
It is usually my fault when something goes wrong	yes	no
I have good ideas	yes	no

Adapted from Piers, 1969.

artificial settings are the basis for tests of other individual abilities (e.g., perceptual-motor, memory, language processing) and educational achievement (general, reading comprehension, arithmetic fundamentals). These ability and achievement tests are often administered to students with behavior disorders as well as others who may need special education.

In addition, measurement of actual functioning in an artificial setting can be directed more specifically toward behavior problems. To measure children's "assertiveness deficits"—a lack of social skills needed to effectively communicate positive and negative feelings—Bornstein, Belleck, and Hersen (1977) devised the *Behavioral Assertiveness Test for Children* (BATC). It consists of nine different scenarios in which a peer violates the rights of the assessed child (one scenario is described in Table 10.6). Each scenario is first described to the child, then a model plays the part of the peer. The child's reactions to the model can be measured in terms of four aspects of behavior believed to represent everyday assertiveness: (1) amount of eye contact with the model; (2) loudness of the child's spoken response; (3) requests that the model do something different; and (4) a judgment as to the overall assertiveness of the child's reaction. (The treatment for assertiveness deficits involves instructions, modeling, and feedback to the child; see Bornstein et al., 1977).

TABLE 10.6 *BATC* Scenario 8

You're in school and you brought your chair to another classroom to watch a movie. You go out to get a drink of water. When you come back, Mike is sitting in your seat.

Mike (model): "I'm sitting here."

Adapted from Bornstein, Bellack, & Hersen, 1977.

Actual Functioning in a Natural Setting

Most behavior problems of students involve the things they say and do in classrooms and other ordinary school environments. Their functioning in artificial assessment sessions may not reflect the behavior problems they show in typical ("natural") settings. Therefore, measurement procedures suitable for use in natural settings may most accurately portray the behavior problems of practical concern to teachers. Two general procedures of this kind are (1) target behavior recording and (2) measurement of behavior products.

Target Behavior Recording
Behavior problems of students are often phrased in general terms that mean different things to different people. For example, "hyperactivity" might mean (1) impulsive failure to take turns or follow other rules; (2) excessive movements of the arms, trunk, head, fingers, feet, or other body parts while seated; (3) frequent and unpermitted seat-leaving and other locomotion; or (4) failure to keep the eyes and pencil engaged in an assigned task for more than a few seconds. Other possible meanings could also be listed. To perform target-behavior recording, it is necesary first to decide exactly which *observable* behaviors are of primary concern ("target behaviors"). Each target behavior is then defined in such a way that there can be little or no doubt as to whether it did or did not occur. Table 10.7 illustrates a target behavior definition used in recording disruptive behavior. In some cases, environmental events that precede or follow the target behavior are also important to record. Observable environmental events can be measured in the same way as observable behaviors.

The next step is to select, for each target behavior, a recording strategy that (1) will result in data that accurately reflect the extent to which the behavior problem occurs and (2) is practical to use in the educational setting. There are several target behavior recording strategies available (see, e.g., Kazdin, 1984; Sulzer-Azaroff & Mayer, 1977). Each recording strategy is intended to be used regularly (if

TABLE 10.7: Target-Behavior Definition Used to Assist a Teacher's Recording of Disruptive Behavior

Disruptive behavior . . . included the occurrence of any of the following behaviors: (a) out-of-seat—the student leaving his seat (i.e., buttocks not in contact with the chair seat) for more than 2 s; (b) talking-out—any off-task vocalization (i.e., not germane to academic task, such as speaking out loud without being called on); (c) excessive physical movement—any off-task physical movement (e.g., waving arms, turning around in his chair); and (d) any other behavior that required a teacher reprimand.

From Stevenson & Fantuzzo, 1984.

possible, every day) so that it will provide an ongoing record of the student's behavior. Some of the strategies that are more practical for teacher use are briefly described below.

In the *frequency* method, the teacher notes each occurrence of the target behavior by making a pencil mark (or by some other means of tallying). These marks are totaled at the end of the recording session (day, morning, math period, or some other length of time) to yield a frequency of the target behavior. If sessions vary in length, frequency can be divided by the number of minutes in that session. The result—rate per minute—permits measurement results from different sessions to be more accurately compared. The frequency method is suitable if the target behavior (1) is a discrete event (has a definite beginning and end) and (2) does not happen too often. Inappropriate greetings to a peer, spitballs, rule violations, and inappropriate questions are just a few of the target behaviors suitably recorded through the frequency method.

In the *duration* method, the teacher uses a clock or stopwatch to record how long a target behavior continues each time it occurs. These individual durations are summed to yield a total duration for the recording session. For sessions that vary substantially from day to day, each session's total duration can be divided by its length in minutes to yield percentage duration. The duration method is especially suitable if a target-behavior (1) is continuous rather than discrete (e.g., crying) or (2) is too long (e.g., too great a delay before obeying the teacher) or (3) too short (e.g., insufficient time spent working on an assigned task).

In the *time sampling* method, the recording session is divided into smaller units of time. For example, a 75-minute math period could be broken into 15 units of 5 minutes each. At the end of each unit, the teacher observes for an instant, decides whether or not the target-behavior is occurring, and records this decision ("yes" or "no"). Summing these decisions yields a total of time samples in which the target behavior was occurring. The units of time need not be equal, but must be set beforehand and cannot be changed during the session. The time sampling method is particularly suitable for the continuous type of target behavior (e.g., not paying attention to the teacher, talking without permission) and very frequent behaviors. Because this method can be arranged to require a minimal amount of the teacher's time and effort, it is especially useful when target behaviors must be monitored during times of intensive teaching.

Measurement of Behavior Products

Many important behaviors in natural settings are best measured indirectly through the products they generate. For instance, it would be difficult to observe directly the lung, throat, tongue, and other body parts that generate speech, but usually the product of these behaviors—speech—can be measured. The frequency method could be used to directly observe a student balling up his or her arithmetic worksheets, but it may be easier and more accurate to simply count the products of this behavior (balled-up worksheets). Other examples of behavior products include words written, books left unshelved, reports turned in, crayons broken, garbage left on lunchroom tables, and comprehension questions correctly answered. If a target behavior definition involves such a behavior product, the teacher can arrange to measure that product daily as it is generated in the classroom or other educational setting. The results of this measurement procedure represent the target behavior.

The discussion of measurement methods has concentrated largely on measurement of the behavior and emotional problems of students. This is not to say that other phenomena are unimportant in understanding and treating behavior disorders of children and adolescents. It is worthwhile, for instance, to understand the student's strengths (e.g., competencies, interests, and other resources) as well as problems. It can be critical to know the depth and spread of a problem—how long it has been a problem, how many environments or people are involved, and what response systems (motor actions, verbal responses, attitudes and feelings, physiological reactions) are associated with a particular problem. Furthermore, certain intervention practices call for particular assessment information: For example, contingency contracting and other forms of behavior modification benefit from the identification of present and potential consequences so that reinforcers for maladaptive behavior can be eliminated and other reinforcers applied to selected appropriate behaviors (Tharp & Wetzel, 1969). Numerous comprehensive plans for assessing disorders have been put forward (e.g., Bandura, 1969; Nay, 1979), but many are suitable for use only in situations with exceptionally good resources. In more typical educational assessment situations, priorities often dictate that all desired assessment information cannot always be obtained.

Purposes of Measurement

Measurement methods such as those just described are put to various uses that are related to the education of pupils with behavior disorders. For example, measurement and measurement issues are fundamentally important in research on behavior disorders. There are many interesting ideas about causes, educational and other interventions, prognosis, and other issues related to behavior disorders of students. Scientific research can help evaluate the merit of these ideas, and professional educators must be informed consumers of research that addresses educational concerns. Measurement is vital to scientific research, and measurement is an important consideration for the consumer of research because the meaning of research results often depends on the way a characteristic has been measured. For example, "social withdrawal" can be measured in various ways, including sociometric assessment of a student's acceptability or popularity among peers as well as target behavior recording of the frequency of his or her social talk and play. But these two methods may be measuring very different aspects of social withdrawal because teaching procedures that increase social behavior may not affect popularity, and vice versa (see Gottman, Gonso, & Rasmussen, 1975). In order to interpret the value of an intervention for behavior disorders intelligently, a research consumer must carefully consider the method used to measure a behavior problem or other characteristic.

Of course, the most practically important purpose of measurement from the teacher's viewpoint is its contribution to the educational assessment process. As ordinarily practiced in the education of students with behavior disorders, this process consists of four main parts: (1) student selection, (2) problem identification, (3) program monitoring, and (4) outcome evaluation. Measurement plays an important role in each of these phases.

Student Selection

In most school districts, a child or adolescent must be officially identified as "behaviorally disordered" (or some similar term) in order to receive special education and related services targeted for such pupils (Epstein et al., 1977; Wood & Lakin, 1979). A major reason is that education officials have to account for how they allocate financial and other resources. The student selection process often involves two stages: (1) identifying candidates (locating students who may need help) and (2) selecting the behaviorally disordered (deciding which candidates actually do need assistance).

Identifying Candidates
Many students are identified as candidates through *referral*: a teacher who is reasonably confident that some degree of special help may be needed forwards the student's name and records to those in the school system empowered to take further official action (e.g., principal, special education supervisor).

A second way to identify candidates is through *screening*. One function of screening is to identify students likely to be missed by the referral process. Teachers are usually well aware of aggressive-disruptive and hyperactive pupils, but some youngsters can be experiencing social maladjustment or personal disturbances of which the teacher is unaware. Screening is also used to find students with characteristics that suggest a high risk for behavior disorders in the future. Such pupils might profit from preventative services. Furthermore, it is possible to screen an entire group of students (e.g., a classroom, school, or district) in order to quickly distinguish candidates from other students who definitely do not show behavior disorders.

Measurement procedures used in screening vary according to the object of the screening. If the object is to find pupils whose disorders are not readily evident to the teacher, teacher-reported functioning (e.g., behavior rating scales) will probably not help, but self-reported functioning (through interviews, objective personality tests, and so on) and peer-reported functioning (e.g., sociometrics) may be informative. For instance, the Bower-Lambert screening procedure for behavior disorders (Bower, 1969) utilizes information from teacher, peers, and the student's self-reports to select candidates who will receive more detailed assessment for behavior disorders. On the other hand, in screening large groups of students to find candidates for early prevention services, a main consideration is usually economy of time, effort, and resources. Therefore, brief teacher-completed behavior rating scales are often favored. For example, the AML is a short teacher rating scale used to find high-risk young pupils for special assistance in the Primary Mental Health Project (Cowen, 1980), which was designed to prevent serious educational handicaps through early detection and intervention.

Selecting the Behaviorally Disordered

Not all students referred or screened as candidates actually should receive special education for the behaviorally disordered. Selection decisions are often made by a team that may include the student's regular class teacher, building principal, the child's parents, the special education supervisor, a school psychologist, other professionals, and sometimes the student as well. Before making its decision the team usually has to consider the results of certain assessment procedures that are required by law or regulation for any student who may be behaviorally disordered. For example, many states or localities specify an individually administered intelligence test and a standardized achievement test; others require an examination by a psychiatrist or neurologist; still others call for additional forms of assessment. Based on this and other information—especially input from the regular class teacher—the team arrives at a selection decision, and the student may be placed in special education.

Problem Identification

In the process of student selection, some aspects of the behavior disorder are uncovered. However, the special education teacher of a pupil selected must usually collect more detailed information to understand the student's problems well enough to plan and carry out appropriate educational intervention. Collecting and assembling information for problem identification can be a two-step process: (1) gathering general information and (2) specifying the problem.

General Information
The first step is to understand generally what problems the child is experiencing in order to avoid wasting time and effort on characteristics that have little or no relevance to the student's problems. There is often useful information from the student selection phase. For instance, the regular teacher's referral information often describes the general nature of a pupil's behavior problems, and screening procedures can help establish some dimensions of the problem. The results from IQ, achievement, neurological, and other tests used by the selection team may point out some general problem. Often, however, important areas have not been addressed, so the special educator must measure them. For instance, achievement tests for particular learning problems, rating scales, interviews, and other measurement procedures can narrow the focus to problems that are most in need of special education.

Specifying the Problems
Once the student's most important problem areas have been picked, they must be specifically described. The most suitable methods are those that measure actual functioning in natural settings—that is, target behavior recording and measurement of behavior products. Behavior rating scales can also be helpful, especially brief, focused scales such as the PTQ or individually tailored rating scales.

Once measurement methods have been selected, the teacher must measure regularly and frequently—preferably every day. The benefits of direct and daily measurement of a student's behavior have been described by Lovitt (1975). One major benefit is that the status and trend of an educational problem is objectively described. This assists in specifying the problem; it also helps in stating the student's present functioning for the IEP.

With this specific information on problems, the teacher can select one or several problems as most appropriate for beginning the intervention program. This decision may be based on a desire to select the problem that is most frequent, most troublesome to others, most distressing to the student, easiest for parents to assist with, or some other consideration.

Program Monitoring

Once problems are specified and intervention is selected, the teacher should monitor the intervention program. Continuing the regular, frequent measurement practices used in specifying the problem will make the student's progress or lack of progress apparent. Daily results may be graphed to further clarify performance trends. This helps avoid the danger of using an intervention for too long (after it has been given a fair trial) when it still provides few or no gains. With the frequent and regular feedback from results of regular and frequent measurement, the teacher will be able to judge when an intervention technique or program ought to be changed.

Outcome Evaluation

There are many ways of evaluating program outcome. Most obviously the measurement procedures used in specifying the problem and monitoring student progress (especially target behavior recording and behavior products) can also be used to determine how well IEP goals are being met. Additionally, some of the methods used in general problem area identification can be used to evaluate outcome. For example, if after some time in special education the behaviorally disordered student shows substantial improvements in achievement test performance and sociometric evaluations, this is an indication that success is being achieved in the program.

Recently there has been increased interest in social validation, a concept with strong relevance to program outcome evaluation (Kazdin, 1984; Cullinan, Epstein, & Lloyd, 1983). Social validation includes procedures for examining whether measured changes in a student's functioning are appropriate and large enough to change the student's status in practically important ways. Two ways of socially validating intervention programs are (1) peer comparison and (2) subjective evaluation. In the peer comparison method, the target behavior recorded for the student with the behavior problem is also recorded on one or several other normal pupils (those not in need of intervention). These data provide a "normal" level of that target behavior against which the special student's measured behavior is compared. Peer comparisons not only help in program outcome evaluation but also give the teacher an objective way of determining when the behaviorally disordered pupil's target behavior is normalized, thus assisting judgments as to when reintegration with regular students may be likely to succeed.

The subjective evaluation method involves selecting persons who, by virtue of experience with the student or possession of special knowledge about the target behavior, can judge the practical importance of improvements in the target behavior. Such judgments are often given as responses to behavior rating scales, checklists, or other reported functioning measures.

CASE STUDY

Part III

Summary and Recommendations

It is clear that Cecil's acting out has become extensive and is disturbing to school personnel. His behavior may not be viewed as a problem in the home, but there are signs that insufficient home supervision may lead to norm violations with peers and perhaps official delinquency in time. It may be appropriate to refer this situation to Family Social Services. There is no reason to believe that medical conditions are involved in Cecil's behavior problems.

Cecil's academic achievement performance was substantially better on an individually administered test than on a test administered with the classroom group. Cecil shows achievement that is a little better than his average third-grade peer. Yet this is substantially below his potential as indicated by the WISC-R results which indicate that Cecil should be functioning among the top two or three students in his class.

The target behavior recording and behavior problem rating scale results verified the referral problem information and provided some specifics. Cecil behaves in an unruly manner, failing to follow rules or instructions. He tends not to complete assigned work. Sociometric results suggest that many children in the class don't think much of Cecil's behavior, but many also admire him and perhaps look up to him as a leader within the peer group.

The following points should be considered in planning for Cecil's educational program.

1. In any school program, assistance from Cecil's home should not be relied on at this time. The involvement of his mother and grandmother should be increased, if appropriate, commensurate with their desire and ability to be involved.
2. Cecil's improved response to individual rather than group achievement testing suggests that extra individual attention in class may yield good results. (Cecil appeared entirely at ease throughout the individual testing session, initiated friendly banter, cooperated with all directions given to him by the examiner, and worked at the tests diligently.)
3. Cecil's prosocial behaviors as well as his intellectual strengths referred to earlier need to be encouraged. At the same time, his disruptiveness and antisocial patterns must be discouraged. It may be that his teacher and principal are inadvertently reinforcing maladaptive behavior. Recall that many of his observed misbehaviors were followed by attention from his teacher. Cecil is also rewarded for extreme misbehavior by a trip to the office, where he often gets to perform special duties for the secretaries. It may be that his frequent nomination by peers for positive (as well as negative) roles indicates peer admiration and reinforcement of his rebellious behavior. In all probability the teacher and principal could benefit from consultation in contingency management in the school.
4. Special education placement does not appear justified at this time. Instead, the recommendations include extensive consultation in behavior management

procedures, increased individual attention during instruction and academic assignments, and perhaps some special assignments to challenge Cecil's high intellectual ability.

Summary

Behavioral, emotional, and other adjustment problems are exhibited by many students, including those officially identified as behaviorally disordered or handicapped in some other way. Definitions of behavior disorders can direct our attention to some key aspects that need to be considered in designing useful assessment methods for behavior disorders. Assessment methods were discussed under the categories reported functioning, actual functioning in an aritifical setting, and actual functioning in a natural setting. No particular methods are always advisable; to select a method, one needs to take account of the problems to be assessed, resources available for assessment and intervention, and other considerations. The educational assessment process includes different but interrelated purposes of measurement. Appropriate measurement practices that achieve these educational purposes are needed for helpful intervention that contributes to appropriate education for students with behavior disorders.

Educational Suggestions for Students with Behavior Disorders

There is extensive literature on intervention with students with behavior disorders. The recommended educational practices vary greatly by theoretical orientation, kind of disorder, age and other personal characteristics of student, and so on. However, the following points would appear to be worth consideration in attempting to move from assessment to intervention with behaviorally disordered students (Gardner, 1977; Rotatori, Kapperman, & Fox, 1981).

Be as specific as possible about the problem and intervention alternatives.

Formulate hypotheses about the conditions that are contributing to the problem, especially if these conditions can be changed in the effort to help the student.

Take account of curriculum, both the one to which the student is currently exposed and other possibilities that may help improve behavior adjustment.

In projecting IEP goals and objectives, be realistic and consider feasible assessment practices that will assist in monitoring progress toward goals and objectives.

Unless there are clear indications to the contrary, carefully structuring the time, physical environment, routines, rules, and other features of the education experience is likely to yield better results.

The teacher needs to be careful to model the behaviors that he or she wishes the student to emulate while carefully avoiding displays of inappropriate behavior.

Consistency is very important, but the teacher needs to know how to be adaptable when exceptions to the rule are in order.

Teachers of the behaviorally disordered need to understand the hopes, frustrations, strengths, and weaknesses of parents so that they can be involved, as feasible, in the intervention plan for their handicapped child.

Once an intervention strategy has been selected and implemented, it must be carried through consistently until it is clear that negligible progress is being achieved. Then the teacher must be ready with an alternative action.

Study Questions

1. Briefly describe key features of the patterns of behavior disorders exhibited by students (aggression-disruption, hyperactivity, social maladjustment, social withdrawal, and anxiety).
2. For each pattern, describe several measurement methods that could be used to assess it. Be specific in the details of each method. What information would be desired as an outcome of each procedure?
3. Describe an "actual functioning in an artificial setting" scenario that could be used to measure a student's reaction to criticism. List the responses that would be of interest for a measurement procedure. Describe how each response would be measured.
4. Establish an assessment system for students with behavior disorders that encompasses the various steps of the educational assessment process. For each step, note which measurement methods are to be used, which professionals are responsible, and what information is to be obtained through the use of these methods. How are the various steps of the educational assessment process coordinated with one another and with the student's IEP?

Suggested Readings

Hersen, M., & Bellack, A. S. (Eds.) (1981). *Behavioral assessment* (2nd ed.). New York: Pergamon.

Hall, R. V., & Van Houten, R. (1983). *Managing behavior 1: Behavior modification: The measurement of behavior* (2nd ed.). Austin: PRO-ED.

Howell, K. W., Kaplan, J. S., & O'Connell, C. Y. (1979). *Evaluating exceptional children.* Columbus, OH: Charles E. Merrill.
Mash, E. J., & Terdal, L. G. (Eds.) (1981). *Behavioral assessment of childhood disorders.* New York: Guilford Press.
Ollendick, T. H., & Hersen, M. (Eds.) (1984). *Child behavioral assessment.* New York: Pergamon.
Wahler, R. G., House, A. E., & Stambaugh, E. E. (1976). *Ecological assessment of child problem behavior.* New York: Pergamon.

References

Balow, B., & Rubin, R. (1970). *Manual of directions for the school behavior profile.* Minneapolis, MN: University of Minnesota.
Bandura, A. (1969). A social learning interpretation of psychological dysfunctions. In P. London & D. Rosenhan (Eds.), *Foundations of abnormal psychology.* New York: Holt, Rinehart, & Winston.
Barker, W., Sandler, L., Bornemann, A., Knight, G., Humphrey, F., & Risen, S. (1971). *Psychiatric Behavior Scale.* Philadelphia: Franklin Institute Research Laboratories.
Behar, L., & Stringfield, S. (1974). A behavior rating scale for the preschool child. *Developmental Psychology, 10,* 601–610.
Borgatta, E. F., & Fanshel, D. (1970). The child behavior characteristics form: Revised age-specific forms. *Multivariate Behavioral Research, 5,* 49–82.
Bornstein, M. R., Bellack, A. S., & Hersen, M. (1977). Social-skills training for unassertive children: A multiple-baseline analysis. *Journal of Applied Behavior Analysis, 10,* 183–195.
Bosco, J. J., & Robin, S. S. (1980). Hyperkinesis: Prevalence and treatment. In C. K. Whalen & B. Henker (Eds.), *Hyperactivity: The social ecology of identification and treatment.* New York: Academic Press.
Bower, E. M. (1969). *Early identification of emotionally handicapped children in school* (2nd ed.). Springfield, IL: Charles C. Thomas.
Brown, L. L., & Hammill, D. D. (1983). *Behavior Rating Profile: An ecological approach to behavioral assessment.* Austin: PRO-ED.
Bullock, L. M., & Brown, R. K. (1972). Behavioral dimensions of emotionally disturbed children. *Exceptional Children, 38,* 740–742.
Burks, H. (1968). *Manual for Burks behavior rating scale.* El Monte, CA: Arden Press.
Buros, O. K. (Ed.). (1972). *The seventh mental measurements yearbook* (2 vols.). Highland Park, NJ: Gryphon Press.
Castaneda, A., McCandless, B. R., & Palermo, D. S. (1956). The children's form of the Manifest Anxiety Scale. *Child Development, 27,* 317–326.
Christiansen, T. (1967). A method of identifying maladjusted children in the classroom. *Mental Hygiene, 51,* 574–575.
Collett, L. J., & Lester, D. (1969). The fear of death and the fear of dying. *Journal of Psychology, 72,* 179–181.
Conners, C. (1973). Rating scales for use in drug studies in children. *Psychopharmacology Bulletin,* Special Issue, Pharmacotherapy of children, 24–84.

Coopersmith, S. A. (1967). *The antecedents of self-esteem*. San Francisco: W. H. Freeman.

Cowen, E. L. (1980). The primary mental health project: Yesterday, today, & tomorrow. *Journal of Special Education, 14*, 133–154.

Cullinan, D., Epstein, M. H., & Kauffman, J. M. (1984). Teachers' ratings of students' behaviors: What constitutes behavior disorder in school? *Behavioral Disorders, 2*, 9–19.

Cullinan, D., Epstein, M. H., & Lloyd, J. W. (1983). *Behavior disorders of children and adolescents*. Englewood Cliffs, N.J.: Prentice-Hall.

Cullinan, D., & Epstein, M. H. (1982). Behavior disorders. In N. G. Haring (Ed.), *Exceptional children and youth* (3rd ed.). Columbus, OH: Charles E. Merrill.

Dunn, J., & Bergan, J. (1968). *School anxiety questionnaire*. Palo Alto, CA: American Institute for Research.

Eyberg, S. M. (1980). Eyberg Child Behavior Inventory. *Journal of Clinical Child Psychology, 9*, 29.

Epstein, M. H., Cullinan, D., & Sabatino, D. A. (1977). State definitions of behavior disorders. *Journal of Special Education, 11*, 417–425.

Finch, A. J., Deardorff, P. A., & Montgomery, L. D. (1974). Individually tailored behavioral rating scales: A possible alternative. *Journal of Abnormal Child Psychology, 2*, 209–216.

Fitts, W. H. (1965). *Manual for the Tennessee self-concept scale*. Nashville: Counselor Recordings and Tests.

Gallup, G. H. (1983). The 15th annual Gallup poll of the public's attitudes toward the public schools. *Phi Delta Kappan, 5*, 33–4.

Gardner, W. I. (1977). *Learning and behavior characteristics of exceptional children and youth: A humanistic behavioral approach*. Boston: Allyn & Bacon.

Gottman, J. M., Gonso, J., & Rasmussen, B. (1975). Social interaction, social competence, and friendship in children. *Child Development, 46*, 709–718.

Herjanic, B. (1981). *Diagnostic interview for children and adolescents*. Unpublished manuscript, Washington University School of Medicine.

Herjanic, B., & Campbell, W. (1977). Differentiating psychiatrically disturbed children on the basis of a structural interview. *Journal of Abnormal Child Psychology, 5*, 127–134.

Hresko, W. L., & Brown, L. (1984). *Test of Early Socioemotional Development*. Austin: PRO-ED.

Kauffman, J. M. (1981). *Characteristics of children's behavior disorders* (2nd ed.). Columbus, OH: Charles E. Merrill.

Kazdin, A. E. (1984). *Behavior modification in applied settings* (3rd ed.). Homewood, IL: Dorsey Press.

Kipnis, D. (1971). *Character structure and impulsiveness*. New York: Academic Press.

Lambert, N. (1974). *Technical report supplement: The development of instruments for the nonintellectual assessment of effective school behavior*. Berkeley, CA: University of California.

Lanyon, B. (1969). *Development of a sentence completion test for children. I: Construction of criterion measures*. Unpublished master's thesis. Pittsburg, PA: University of Pittsburg.

Long, N. J. (1979). Lecture series, American University, Washington, DC.

Lovitt, G. C. (1975). Applied behavior analysis and learning disabilities. *Journal of Learning Disabilities, 8*, 42–43.

Maccoby, E. E., & Maccoby, N. (1954). The interview: A tool of social science. In G. Lindzey (Ed.), *Handbook of social psychology* (Vol. 1). Cambridge: Addison-Wesley.

Morrison, E. (1969). Underachievement among preadolescent boys considered in relationship to passive aggression. *Journal of Educational Psychology, 60*, 168–173.

Morse, W. C., Cutler, R. I., & Fink, A. H. (1964). *Public school classes for the emotionally handicapped: A research analysis*. Washington, DC: Council for Exceptional Children.

Mundy, J. (1972). The use of projective techniques with children. In B. B. Wolman (Ed.), *Manual of Child Psychopathology*. New York: McGraw-Hill.

Nay, W. R. (1979). *Multimethod clinical assessment*. New York: Gardner Press.

Nowicki, S. & Strickland, B. R. (1973). A locus of control scale for children. *Journal of Consulting and Clinical Psychology, 40*, 148–154.

Paternite, C. E., & Loney, J. (1980). Childhood hyperkinesis: Relationship between symptomotology and home environment. In C. K. Whalen & B. Henker (Eds.), *Hyperactive children: The social ecology of identification and treatment*. New York: Academic Press.

Pauker, J. D., Sines, J. O., & Sines, L. K. (1966). *Missouri Children's Picture Series*. Iowa City, IA: Psychological Assessment and Services.

Pekarik, E. G., Prinz, R. J., Liebert, D. E., Weintraut, S., & Neale, J. M. (1976). The pupil evaluation inventory: A sociometric technique for assessing children's social behavior. *Journal of Abnormal Psychology, 4*, 83–97.

Piers, E. V., & Harris, D. (1969). *Manual for Piers-Harris children's self-concept scale*. Nashville: Counselor Recordings and Tests.

Prinz, R. J., Swan, R., Liebert, D., Weintraut, S., & Neale, J. M. (1978). ASSESS: Adjustment scales for sociometric evaluation of secondary-school students. *Journal of Abnormal Child Psychology, 6*, 493–501.

Prior, M., & MacMillan, M. B. (1973). Maintenance of sameness in children with Kanner's Syndrome. *Journal of Autism and Childhood Schizophrenia, 3*, 154–167.

Quay, H. C. (1977). Measuring dimensions of deviant behavior: The behavior problem checklist. *Journal of Abnormal Child Psychology. 5*, 277–287.

Quay, H. C. (1979). Classification. In H. C. Quay & J. F. Werry (Eds.), *Psychopathological disorders of childhood* (2nd ed.). New York: John Wiley & Sons.

Quay, H. C., & Peterson, D. R. (1975). *Manual for the behavior problem checklist*. Unpublished manuscript.

Roberts, J., & Baird, J. T. (1972). *Behavior patterns of children in school* (DHEW Publication No. (HSM) 72-1042). Washington, D.C.: U.S. Government Printing Office.

Rorschach, H. (1942). *Psychodiagnostics: A diagnostic test based on perception* (4th ed.). New York: Grune & Stratton.

Rotatori, A. F., Kapperman, G., & Fox, R. (1981). A behavioral analysis approach to the vocational assessment of severely handicapped. *Illinois Council of Exceptional Children Quarterly, 30*, 7–11.

Routh, D. K. (1980). Developmental and social aspects of hyperactivity. In C. K. Whalen & B. Henker (Eds.), *Hyperactive children: The social ecology of identification and treatment.* New York: Academic Press.

Rubin, E., Simson, C., & Betwee, M. (1966). *Emotionally handicapped child and elementary school.* Detroit: Wayne State Press.

Salvia, J. & Ysseldyke, J. E. (1981). *Assessment in special and remedial education.* (2nd ed.). Boston: Houghton Mifflin.

Simon, A., & Ward, L. O. (1974). Variables influencing the source, frequency and intensity of worry in secondary school pupils. *British Journal of Social and Clinical Psychology, 13,* 391–396.

Sines, J. O., Pauker, J. D., Sines, L. K., & Owen, D. K. (1969). Identification of clinically relevant dimensions of children's behavior. *Journal of Consulting and Clinical Psychology, 33,* 728–734.

Spaulding, R. (1970). *Classroom behavior analysis and treatment.* San Jose, CA: San Jose State College.

Stevenson, H. C., & Fantuzzo, J. R. (1984). Application of the "Generalization Map" to a self-control intervention with school-aged children. *Journal of Applied Behavior Analysis, 17,* 203–212.

Sulzer-Azaroff, B., & Mayer, G. R. (1977). *Applying behavior-analysis procedures with children and youth.* New York: Holt, Rinehart and Winston.

Tharp, R. G., & Wetzel, R. J. (1969). *Behavior modification in the natural environment.* New York: Academic Press.

Van Vleet, P. (1973). The A-M-L: A quick-screening device for early identification of school maladaption. *Journal of Community Psychology, 1,* 12–25.

Walker, R. (1967). Some temperament traits in children as viewed by their peers, their teachers and themselves. *Monographs of the Society for Research in Child Development, 32,* 1–10.

Werry, J., Weiss, J., & Peters, J. (1968). Developmental hyperactivity. *Pediatrics Clinics of North America, 15,* 581–599.

Whalen, C. K. (1983). Hyperactivity, learning problems, and the attention deficit disorders. In T. H. Ollendick & M. Hersen (Eds.), *Handbook of child psychopathology.* New York: Plenum.

Wood, F. H., & Lakin, K. C. (Eds.). (1979). *Disturbing, disordered, or disturbed?* Minneapolis: Advanced Training Institute (Department of Psychoeducational Studies), University of Minnesota.

APPENDIX A. Rating Scales, Questionnaire and Checklist Which Assess Behavioral Characteristics

Name of Test	Type of Measure	Age/Grade	Assessment Areas
AML Behavior Rating Scale (Van Vleet, p. 1 1973)	Rating scale	Preschool to high school	Aggression, outgoing, moody, withdrawn, internalized behavior
Behavior Checklist (Rubin, E., 1966)	Checklist	Grades 1–8	Assertiveness, aggression, sensitivity, independence
Burks Behavior Rating Scale (Burk, H., 1968)	Rating scale	Grades 1–9	Excessive self-blame, anxiety, withdrawal, dependency, suffering, sense of persecution, aggresiveness, resistance, ego strength, impulse centered, anger control
Checklist for the Classification of School-aged Maladjusted Children (Christiansen, T., 1967)	Checklist	Grades 1–12	Anxiety, fearfulness, tenseness, depression, unhappiness, withdrawal
Child Behavior Characteristic Form (Borgatha, E., & Fanshel, D., 1970)	Rating scale	Infancy to 17	Defiance-hostility, emotionality-tension, infantilism, withdrawal, sex precociousness, overcleanliness, sex inhibition, assertiveness
Child's Behavior Traits (Levenstein, P., 1971)	Likert-type scale	2 to 12 yrs	Self-responsible independence, social cooperation, cognitively related skills, emotional stability, and task orientation
Children's Temperament Questionnaire (Walker, R., 1967)	Questionnaire	Grades 3 to 7	Energy, stability, aggressiveness, fearfulness, socialness, cheerfulness
Collett-Lester Fear-of-Death Scale (Lester, D., & Collett, L., 1969)	Self-Report Inventory	6 and up	Fears about death

Instrument	Type	Age	Behaviors
Compliant, Aggressive, Detached Interpersonal Anxiety Inventory (Tinkham, S., 1973)	Rating scale	Adolescence and up	Aggression, anxiety, and compliance
Coping Analysis Schedule for Educational Settings (Spaulding, R., 1970)	Behavior Rating Scale	Preschool to high school	Aggression, negativism, manipulating, resisting, withdrawal, nonconforming dependency, self-direction
Insolence-Impulsiveness Scale (Kipnis, D., 1971)	Questionnaire	15 years and up (males only)	Risk-taking, impulsiveness, interest in sex, drinking, gambling
Lanyen's Incomplete Sentences Task (Lanyen, B., 1969)	Sentence Completion Scale	7 to 9 years	Hostility, anxiety, and dependency
Missouri Children's Behavior Checklist (Sines, J., Parker, J., Sines, L., & Owen, D., 1969)	Checklist	5 to 16 years	Inhibition, withdrawal, activity level, sleep disturbance, and sociability
Missouri Children's Picture Series (Sines, J., Parker, J., & Sinse, L., 1966)	Sorting	5 to 16 years	Conformity, maturity masculinity, femininity, aggression, inhibition, activity level, and sleep disturbance
Morrison's Passive Aggression Scale for Pupils (Morrison, E., 1969)	Likert-type Rating	Middle grade to high school	Passiveness, aggression, procrastination, stubbornness, obstructionism, and intentional inefficiency
Preschool Behavior Questionnaire (Behar, L., & Stringfield, S., 1974)	Rating scale	3 to 6 years	Hostility, anxiety, fearful, aggressiveness, hyperactive, and distractibleness
Prior Sameness Behavior Questionnaire	Questionnaire	Autistic children 2 to	Obsessive behavior, desire for sameness

(continued)

APPENDIX A. *(continued)*

Name of Test	Type of Measure	Age/Grade	Assessment Areas
Questionnaire (Prior, M., 1973)		18 years	
Psychiatric Behavior Scale (Barker, W., Sandler, L., Bornemann, A., Knight, G., Humphrey, F., & Risen, S., 1971)	Rating scale	2½ to 6½ years	Aggression, independence-dependence, impulse control, and reaction to stress
Pupil Behavior Rating Scale (Lombert, N., 1964)	Rating	Grades K to 8	Motivation, distractibility, aggressiveness, immaturity, unhappiness, withdrawal
School Anxiety Questionnaire (Dunn, J., & Bergan, J., 1967)	Self-rating question-	Grades 4 to 12	Anxiety due to report card, failure, test, achievement, and recitation
School Behavior Profile (Balow, B., & Rubin, R., 1970)	Rating scale	5 to 18 years	Poor self-control, immaturity, anxiety, neurotic tendencies
Simon's Worry Response Survey (Simon, A., 1974)	Questionnaire	11 to 16 years	Children's worries
Werry-Weiss-Peters Activity Scale (Werry, J., Weiss, J., & Peters, J., 1968)	Parent rating scale	5 to 12 years	Activity level of children

11

Assessment of Adaptive Behavior

Harvey N. Switzky
Anthony F. Rotatori
Robert Fox

OBJECTIVES

After completing this chapter the teacher should be able to:

1. Select appropriate screening devices for estimating adaptive skill levels.
2. Select comprehensive adaptive devices for measuring specific adaptive skills.
3. Match up appropriate adaptive devices for specific levels of retardation.
4. Discuss various definitions of adaptive behavior.
5. List the typical skill areas that are commonly included in adaptive behavior devices.
6. Identify the primary areas of concern in regard to adaptive behavior assessment in early childhood, adolescence, and adulthood.

Definitions of Adaptive Behavior

Adaptive behavior refers to the skills an individual uses to cope with the demands of the environment (Leland, Nihira, Foster, Shellhaas, & Kugin, 1968). The concept of coping consists of three major components:

1. **Independent function**, which refers to the ability of the individual to successfully accomplish these tasks or activities demanded of him or her by the general community in terms of specific age expectations.
2. **Personal responsibility**, which refers to the willingness and accomplishments of the individual assuming responsibility for his or her personal behavior. This ability is reflected in decision-making and choice of behaviors.
3. **Social responsibility**, which refers to the ability of the individual to accept responsibility as a member of a community by demonstrating social adjustment, emotional maturity, and civic responsibility leading to complete or partial economic independence and other expectations of the community.

This point of view parallels the early work of Binet, who considered individuals to be normal if they were able to conduct their affairs of life without having need of supervision of others, if they were able to do work sufficiently renumerative to supply their own personal needs, and if their intelligence did not unfit them for the social environment of their parents.

Jane Mercer, a sociologist and co-author of *The System of Multicultural Pluralistic Assessment* (SOMPA; Mercer & Lewis, 1977) stresses the social context of adaptive behavior rather than the fit of the individual to environmental demands as does Leland et al. (1968). Mercer (1973) defines adaptive behavior as the child's ability to perform the social roles appropriate for a person of his or her age and sex in a manner that meets the expectations of the social systems in which he or she participates. Thus social role performance is viewed in relation to specific social systems and their roles. Adaptive behavior in the young child is the extent to which he or she has acquired the self-help and social skills upon which more complex role performances can be built. Adaptive behavior for the older child and adult is the extent to which that person is playing a full complement of social roles appropriate to his or her age and is performing in those roles in a manner comparable to that of other persons of his or her age in society.

The most widespread definition of adaptive behavior is the one used by the American Association on Mental Deficiency (Grossman, 1983), which was built upon these earlier conceptions. Adaptive behavior is defined as the effectiveness or degree to which the individual meets the standards of personal independence and social responsibility expected of his or her age and cultural group. Since these expectations vary considerably for different age and cultural groups, deficits in adaptive behavior will vary at different ages (and in different cultural groups).

During infancy and early childhood, deficits in adaptive behavior may be primarily in the areas of sensorimotor skill development, communications, self-help skill development, and socialization skill development. During the elementary school years and in early adolescence, deficits in adaptive behavior may include not only academically important school activities such as reading and writing, but also such functional skills as mailing a letter, purchasing food, time and money skills, and social responsiveness. During late adolescent and adult years, deficits in adaptive behavior may consist of vocational and social responsibilities, the individual's ability is to maintain himself or herself independently in the community, and the ability to earn a living and to meet and conform to local community standards.

CASE STUDY

Part I

Name: Debbie
Date of Birth: August 19, 1965
Date of Evaluation: June 19, 1984

Age: 18 years, 10 months
Grade: Senior High Special
Education Class

Background Information

Debbie was referred by her mother for consideration regarding placement in a community group home for the retarded. Presently, she is a student and resident of St. Vern's Residential School. Noted on a recent health history report were the following difficulties: poor coordination, which necessitates the participation in specific exercises; frequent falling and minor injuries due to poor visual perception and moderate seizure activity; and periodic psychomotor seizures. Social reports from school and from her mother reveal that Debbie is an enjoyable individual who likes being with peers, staff, and family. She does have a tendency to be authoritarian and bossy, and it is necessary to redirect her behavior at these times.

Observations

Debbie, who stutters at times, entered the testing and interview situation with some reservations. However, after only a few minutes she willingly engaged in spontaneous conversation. Noticed during the initial minutes was Debbie's frequent blinking. According to Debbie's mother, the blinking occurs initially after Debbie comes into a building from outside. The mother thought that Debbie was readjusting to the light, as she seems to be somewhat sensitive to it. This individual tried extremely hard throughout the testing. Her attention to task was adequate, and she was quite responsive to praise for her efforts as well as encouragement to continue on the more difficult ones.

Past Testing

Test	Date	Results
Stanford-Binet Intelligence Scale (Form L-M)	9/2/81	Mental Age, 5–7 years IQ: 32
Peabody Picture Vocabulary Test	9/2/81	Mental Age, 5–8 years IQ: 33

The Measurement of Adaptive Behavior

The use of adaptive behavior assessments has two purposes (Oakland & Matuszek, 1977): (1) classification/labeling and (2) educational intervention/programming. For instance, mental retardation is defined (Grossman, 1983) as significantly subaverage general intellectual functioning existing concurrently with deficits in adaptive behavior as manifested during the developmental period. "Deficits in adaptive behavior" as well as "subaverage general intelligence" have to be substantiated before a student can be labeled mentally retarded.

The measurement of adaptive behavior for the purposes of educational intervention and programming is part of the individual-ized educational program (IEP) process for all categories of handi-capped children, but it is a *major* program emphasis for severely handicapped students (Sontag, 1975). The use of adaptive behavior scales becomes part of the assessment/curricular process. The mea-surement and definition of adaptive behavior for the purposes of educational intervention is a complex and sometimes confusing enterprise that may reflect conflicting philosophical points of view as determined by the values and expectations of parents, teachers, the community, and educational curriculum theorists (Brown, Nietupski, & Hamre-Nietupski, 1976; Tawney & Smith, 1981). These contro-versies revolve around educational programming for severely handi-capped students and involve questions of ecologically relevant educa-tional goals based on the chronological age of the child, rather than on the child's mental age, and on the use of natural community settings in which to teach these educational goals rather than in artificial classroom settings.

Formal Assessment Instruments

Assessment instruments vary along a continuum of comprehensiveness in terms of their thoroughness of assessment and the time needed for their administration. *First-position* instruments are basically screening systems that are completed quickly and present an overview of the student's current level of skills across various content domains. *Second-position* instruments are more systematic and detailed than first position instruments. *Third-position* instruments are fully detailed and comprehensive assessment instruments.

First-position instruments include such tests as the *Camelot Behavioral Checklist* (Foster, 1974); the *TARC Assessment System* (Sailor & Mix, 1975); the *Fairview Self-Help Scale* (Ross, 1970); the *Portage Project Guide to Early Education: Instructions and Checklist* (Shearer, Billingsley, of Frohman, 1970); the *Cain-Levine Social Competency Scale* (Cain, Levine, & Elzey, 1977); and the *Vineland Social Maturity Scale* (Doll, 1965).

Second-position instruments include such tests as the *Pennsylvania Training Model: Individual Assessment Guide* (Somerton & Turner, 1975); the *APT: A Training Program for Citizens with Severely or Profoundly Retarded Behavior* (Brady & Smilovitz, 1974); the *Uniform Performance Assessment System* (Bendersky, Edgar, & White, 1976), and the *Comprehensive Test of Adaptive Behavior* (Adams, 1983).

Third-position tests include such devices as the *Balthazar Scales of Adaptive Behavior* (Balthazar, 1971, 1973, 1976); the *AAMD Adaptive Behavior Scale* (Nihira, Foster, Shellhaas, & Leland, 1974); the *AAMD Adaptive Behavior Scale—Public School Version* (Lambert, Windmiller, Cole & Figueroa, 1975); the *Adaptive Behavior Inventory for Children* (Mercer & Lewis, 1977); the *Behavioral Characteristics Progression, the Santa Cruz Special Education Management System* (Office of the Santa Cruz County Superintendent of Schools, 1973); and the *TMR Performance Profile for the Severely and Moderately Retarded* (DiNola, Kaminsky, & Sternfeld, 1970). Selected instruments for each position are described below.

First-Position Instruments

The *Fairview Self-Help Scale* (Ross, 1970) is designed to be used to assess various aspects of adaptive behavior in severely and profoundly retarded students. It is short, easy to use by parents, caregivers, or teachers, and easy to score. The scale is composed of 34 specific kinds of behavior measures in five content domains: (1) motor dexterity; (2) self-help (toilet training, dressing, eating, and grooming); (3) communications skills; (4) social interaction; and (5) self-direction. The checklist is scored by an observer who is familiar with the behavior of the student and who rates the student as to his or her current proficiency.

The Ambulation score is found by adding scores for standing and walking. The Motor Dexterity score is found by adding scores for standing and walking, arm-hand use, and muscular coordination. The Self-Help score is the sum of scores for toilet training, dressing, eating, and grooming. The total score can be converted to an age equivalent in months—the Behavioral Age. The test covers a Behavioral Age up to 120 months.

The Fairview Self-Help Scale provides information as to the present level of skill proficiency in adaptive behavior for severely and profoundly retarded children. Training targets can be selected that will expand on the individual's behavioral repertoire by examining the student's profile on the subcontent and content domains. If the student's Mental Age is known, the *Fairview Self-Help Scale* can provide self-help scale expectancies to help the teachers determine a realistic and appropriate set of training targets.

The test-retest reliability of the *Fairview Self-Help Scale* as reported in the manual varied between .79 and .96 over a 3-month period. Interrater reliability varied between .72 and .93 for a sample of 105 retarded children. The Fairview Self-Help Scale appears to measure the same kinds of adaptive behavior domains as the *Vineland Social Maturity Scale* ($r = .94$) and the *Cain-Levine Social Competency Scale* ($r = .97$).

The *Cain-Levine Social Competency Scale* is designed to assess domains of adaptive behavior in moderately retarded school-age children 5 to 13 years of age. The scale consists of 44 items consisting of brief one- to four-word phrases followed by four or five sentences 3 to 16 words long describing four or five levels of increasingly independent performance. A score of 1 on an item reflects the most dependent level of functioning, a score of 2 or 3 reflects the transition from dependence to independent functioning, and a score of 4 or 5 reflects the most independent level of functioning. The items form five subdomains of adaptive behavior: (1) communication, (2) personal care, (3) interpersonal skills, (4) general tasks and responsibility, and (5) mealtime skills. These subdomains form four content domains of adaptive behavior: (1) self-help, (2) initiative, (3) social skills, and (4) communication. There are 14 items in the self-help domain and 10 each in the initiative, social skills, and communication domains. Informants may be interviewed and may be asked to describe the present level of adaptive behavioral functioning of the student. The rater must judge which sentence under the item best describes the informant's description of the behavioral functioning of the student. Scores are determined for each of the four content domains—self-help, initiative, social skills, and communication—as well as a total score. Scores can be converted to percentile ranks, which allow the rater (teacher) to determine the moderately retarded student's relative standing in relation to other moderately retarded students (716 moderately retarded children varying in age from 5 to 13 years in the standardization sample) in each of the four domains of adaptive behavior measured by the test and in overall social competency. The *Cain-Levine Social Competency Scale* has good test-retest reliability over a 3-week period (*r* varied between .88 and .97). Split-half reliability is moderate and varied between .50 and .96.

The *Vineland Social Maturity Scale* is an adaptive behavior scale measuring children's progressive capacity for independent functioning and for participating in activities that lead toward ultimate independence as adults. The scale, which can be used for mildly, moderately, and severely handicapped children, is arranged in order of increasing difficulty and represents continuous development in six areas: (1) self-help, (2) self-direction, (3) locomotion, (4) occupation, (5) communication, and (6) social relations. The self-help area is divided into three parts: (1) general, (2) eating, and (3) dressing. This developmental scale in social independence is taken as a measure of maturation in social capabilities. The scale was standardized on 620 nonhandicapped individuals from birth to 30 years of age. Each item on the scale is scored on the basis of information obtained from an informant who knows the skill abilities of the person scored (e.g., mother, a close relative, attendant, teacher, teacher's aide). A major emphasis of the scale is on interviewing the parents and other family members in order to assimilate them into the assessment process and eventually into the process of academic and skill training.

The Vineland provides (1) a continuum of normal maturation that can be used repeatedly for the measurement of growth or change; (2) a measure of individual differences as well as extreme variance; (3) an index of variation in development in abnormal persons; (4) a measure of skill development following skill training, and (5) a guide for reviewing developmental histories. The items are short phrases explained by short sentences in the manual. Each item is rated by the tester, who is required to judge and describe how much, to what extent, and in what ways the individual typically acts. The tester gathers as much detail as possible regarding the skill assessed. Ratings are made based upon the criteria listed in Table 11.1.

A Social Age is calculated by adding to the basal score the additional scattered credits beyond the basal score until two consecutive minus scores are encountered. Any additional (+) counts as 1 point, (+F) counts as 1 point, (+N.O.) counts as 1 point, (±) counts as .5 points. A Social Quotient (SQ) can be determined by dividing the subject's Social Age score by his or her Life Age and multiplying by 100. The degree to which an individual's Social Age is below his or her Life Age is the extent to which the individual is considered socially

TABLE 11.1 Criteria for Ratings on the *Vineland Social Maturity Scale*

Rating Category	Criterion
+ (plus)	Individual demonstrates behavior consistently
+F	Individual has skill, but skill was not performed at the time due to special restraint
+N.O. (no opportunity)	Individual has not performed behavior due to lack of opportunity; if opportunity were present the individual could perform behavior or learn to perform it quickly
± (plus/minus)	Individual does not consistently perform behavior with full success, yet performances are more than superficial acts
− (minus)	Individual does not perform behavior because of inability to do so

immature. Test-retest reliability for 400 retarded children varied from .94 to .96 over a 2-year period; interrater reliability for retarded children is reported to be good (r = .92). Data from the *Vineland Social Maturity Scale* can provide an estimate of social functioning as well as act as a rapport-building system with the parents and significant others. Unfortunately, the data cannot easily be used for programmatic purposes by teachers.

Second-Position Instruments

The *APT* (Assessment Program Team): *A Training Program for Citizens with Severely and Profoundly Retarded Behavior* consists of an assessment scale, training programs, and progress forms. The system is based on behavioral assessment whereby the teacher evaluates by direct observation the student's performance on the 50 items of adaptive behavior skills presented in the *APT Skill Assessment Scale*. For skills that are present in the repertoire of the student, the teacher then uses the APT Training Procedures and the Individual Program Plan to record behavioral changes.

The APT materials (assessment scales, training programs, and progress forms) were created by an interdisciplinary team of professionals at the Pennhurst State School in Pennsylvania. The APT is an example of a less formal (informal) assessment/curricular technique. It recognizes that not all adaptive behavioral skills can be provided for and that the assessment component of such a device will be incomplete. Thus teachers are encouraged to come up with their own assessment/curricular programs, which are in essence criterion-referenced measures.

The *APT Skill Assessment Scale* consists of 50 items of adaptive behavior skill goals that are well defined and organized into seven adaptive behavior domains: (1) motor (reaching and grasping, sitting, walking, climbing stairs, hopping); (2) communication (attending behavior, basic instructions, environmental concepts, imitation, sign language, verbal ability, spatial orientation); (3) self-help skills (eating, using fork, drinking, dining room procedures, routine trained, toilet trained, washing, showering, dressing, shoe-tying, toothbrushing, hair brushing, menstruation, shaving, clothing care, housekeeping, bed making); (4) prevocational (stringing beads, cobbler's bench, stacking rings, color matching, matching forms, sorting assembly, time, money/counting); (5) social skills (grounds orientation, independence, basic cooperative interaction, intermediate cooperation); (6) behavior problems (bites or assaults others, bites or assaults self, destroys or steals); and (7) visual impairment (walking with a sighted guide, going through doors, going up and down stairs, trailing and taking directions). The *APT Assessment Scale* is based on "yes" and "no" answers reflecting whether the student has mastered the goal item. For unmastered items, the teacher consults the APT Training Procedures, which present the assessment item, general instructions, the recommended behavior objectives, and the possible methods and materials needed to master each behavior objective, and plot the student's progress on the individual program plan.

Third-Position Instruments

The *AAMD Adaptive Behavior Scale* is divided into two sections: independence skills for daily living (Part I) and measures of maladaptive behavior (Part II). The Scale was standardized on 4,000 residents of institutions for the retarded across the United States. The sample population included children and adults at all levels of mental retardation. The scale is typically administered by a first-party assessment; however, third-party or direct interview methods can be used. The following uses of the scale have been indicated by Nihira et al. (1974): (1) identifying the area of deficiency; (2) providing an objective basis for the comparison of a resident's ratings over time; (3) comparing ratings of a resident under different environmental situations; (4) providing a standardized reporting system for use by teachers, psychologists, social service agencies, or school administrators; and (5) providing descriptions of a resident's behavior to be used for program and/or treatment planning.

The scale items for Part I are arranged along developmental levels of independence in daily living. It consists of 10 domains: (1) independent functioning, (2) physical development, (3) economic activity, (4) language development, (5) numbers and time, (6) domestic activity, (7) vocational activity, (8) self-direction, (9) responsibility, and (10) socialization.

Part II is divided into 14 areas: (1) violent and destructive

behavior; (2) antisocial behavior; (3) rebellious behavior; (4) untrust-
worthy behavior; (5) withdrawal; (6) stereotyped behavior and odd
mannerisms; (7) inappropriate interpersonal manners; (8) unacceptable vocal habits; (9) unacceptable or eccentric habits; (10) self-
abusive behavior; (11) hyperactive tendencies; (12) sexually aberrant
behavior; (13) psychological disturbances; and (14) use of medica-
tions. The data from Part II provide a measure of maladaptive
behaviors that can be correlated to the resident's emotional and social
status.

Scale items on Part I are of two forms. One form specifies that the
rater select only one description of several possible responses for an
item. The responses are arranged in a hierarchical order, and the rater
circles the level that the resident is presently exhibiting. The second
form specifies that the rater check all descriptions of behavior that the
resident has within his or her behavior repertoire in regard to that
item.

The data can be converted into percentile ranks and plotted
according to age levels. The plotted data reveal a profile of "hills" and
"valleys" depicting strengths and weaknesses. Areas that reveal
weaknesses can then be identified as curriculum components where
intervention is needed.

The *AAMD Adaptive Behavior Scale—Public School Version* (Lambert, Windmiller, Cole, & Figueroa, 1975) is an extension of the *AAMD
Adaptive Behavior Scale* (Nihira, Foster, Shellhaas, & Leland, 1974) to
public school populations of mildly and moderately retarded elementary school children. The public school version of the AAMD Adaptive
Behavior Scale was developed as a response to legislative mandates
within the state of California in order to more precisely define school-
age populations that were in need of special education services. The
AAMD Adaptive Behavior Scale—Public School Version is identical to
the *AAMD Adaptive Behavior Scale* except that, in the former, the
Domestic Activity domain was deleted from Part I, and the domains of
Self-Abusive Behavior and Sexually Aberrant Behavior were deleted
from Part II.

Part I and Part II are scored as norm-reference tests, based upon a
standardization sample of 2,800 children. Approximately equal numbers of nonretarded, mildly retarded, and moderately retarded students were sampled. Sampling was also sensitive to the sex and ethnic
status (black, white, Asian, and Spanish-speaking) of the students. The
objective of the sampling procedure was to produce representative
groups of male and female children from different ethnic backgrounds
in the second through the sixth grade in several classification
groups.

Parents and teachers were found to be equally reliable and valid as
informants for the assessment of adaptive behavior. Lambert, Wilcox,
and Gleason (1974) found no significant differences in the ratings

obtained from parents and teachers, whether the population being assessed was nonhandicapped children or mildly retarded children. There were also no systematic biases in scores attributable to the sex or ethnic status of the informants. Thus teachers were used as the most expedient informants of adaptive behavior within the standardization sample (Lambert, Windmiller, Cole, & Figueroa, 1975). The results of these studies show that it is not necessary to have extraschool information regarding the adaptive behavior of students; this is an extremely valuable and useful finding.

Lambert, Windmiller, Cole, and Figueroa (1975) determined the item validities of the *AAMD Adaptive Behavior Scale—Public School Version* in predicting adaptive behavior as a function of school classification status—regular or educable mentally retarded (EMR)—controlling for sex and ethnicity. These analyses showed that 80% to 90% of the Part I items were significantly related ($p < .01$) to classification status from ages 7 through 12, and that 12% to 75% of the items on the Part II were equally as valid. Part I assesses independence and responsibility aspects of adaptive behavior, whereas Part II assesses problems in social-emotional functioning that are not restricted to individuals with evidence of mental retardation. However, the number of valid items increased with age on Part II, suggesting a greater extent of behavior disorders as EMR children grow older.

Lambert (1979) also presented evidence that differences in domain scores on Parts I and II on the *AAMD Adaptive Behavior Scale—Public School Version* are very highly associated with the classification of regular and EMR pupils and can be considered valid for differentiating regular class pupils from those assigned to EMR programs.

There were few sex differences on the domain scores for Part I. Differences in socialization practices for boys and girls did influence Part II domain scores. Girls were judged to be less destructive, less nonconforming, and less hyperactive than boys at all ages. Thus, separate norms for boys and girls as well as the total sample in each age and classification group are provided for Part II domain scores.

There were few differences due to ethnic status on Part I domain scores when the effects of classification (regular or EMR status) are accounted for on Part I of the scale. Differences in cultural demands and expectations do affect Part II domain scores. Thus, separate norms for ethnic status are provided for Part II domain scores. These norms, along with the norms for the total sample and those by sex, provide the user with reference groups sufficient for adequate and fair interpretation of the results.

As might be expected, the mean scores for Part I domains for regular class pupils were always higher than those for EMR pupils, whose scores were higher than trainable mentally retarded (TMR) pupils, thus showing greater amounts of adaptive behavior in regular class students than in retarded students. The EMR students showed greater amounts of adaptive behavior than TMR students. Part II domain mean scores were lower for˜regular class pupils than for retarded pupils, showing better adaptation in all domains for regular class pupils. Both EMR and TMR students show complex differences in the patterns of their mean domain scores on Part II. These differences are not easily understood. Further research needs to be done on the interaction of the level of intellectual functioning and maladaptive behavior. Nevertheless, the *AAMD Adaptive Behavior Scale—Public School Version* is a valid instrument for differentiating among pupils from ages 7 through 12 assigned to regular, EMR, and TMR classes. The correlation between measured intelligence and adaptive behavior as measured by the domain scores is low to moderate (r = .1 to .6 for Part I domain scores and $-.01$ to $-.21$ for Part II domain scores), showing that the *AAMD Adaptive Behavior Scale—Public School Version* is not just a test of intelligence. Lambert and her collaborators have shown that there are no consistent ethnic status or sex effects interacting with the domain scores on Part I. Consequently it is possible to infer that differences found in adaptive behavior assessment reflect real differences in adaptive behavior functioning and provide assessment of adaptive behavior that can˙be applied fairly to boys and girls and to children of different ethnic groups.

The *AAMD Adaptive Behavior Scale—Public School Version* provides data expressed as an individual's percentile rank compared with age and classification peers. This information can be used to: (1) determine the student's level of adaptive behavior as inferred from performance on the domains associated with functional autonomy and social responsibility dimensions and (2) evaluate the potential for successfully meeting environmental demands of regular and special education classrooms based on evidence of social-emotional maladaptation.

The manual for the public school version of the *AAMD Adaptive Behavior Scale* provides norms for regular, EMR, and TMR subjects from 7 through 13 years of age and additional norms for sex and ethnic status for Part II of the scale.

In order to use this scale to facilitate the decision for special education placement, ideally teachers and parents should fill out the scale independently in order to measure the consistency of perceptions of the student in the school and home community environments. Part I and Part II domain scores are usually analyzed separately. The first step is to compare the student's domain scores percentile ranks in Part I to the norms for same-age special class peers. Do the student's scores resemble those of the same-age peers in regular class placement or those of same-age peers in special class placement? If a student scores between 10 and 20 raw score units on the Physical Development Scale, indicating that the child does not function within the normal limits of sensory and motor functioning, a special consultant needs to be brought in. The same sort of analysis can be undertaken for domain scores percentile ranks on Part II. If the student also scores at least 2 standard deviations below the mean in terms of measured intelligence, and the scores on the *AAMD Adaptive Behavior Scale—Public School Version* more closely resemble the adaptive behavior scores of the same-age handicapped peers as determined by the teacher (and confirmed by the parents), the student may be considered for special education placement.

The *Adaptive Behavior Inventory for Children* (ABIC; Mercer & Lewis, 1977) is part of the *System of Multicultural Pluralistic Assessment* (SOMPA), which Mercer and Lewis (1977) designed as a comprehensive system of nondiscriminatory assessment involving medical functioning, social system functioning, and academic functioning of elementary school children, especially children whose racial or cultural heritage is different from that of Anglo-Americans. The ABIC is designed to provide a cross-sectional view of the child's adaptive behavior or social-role performance in a variety of social systems in which the child is participating at a single point in time and which may include the family, the peer group, the community nonacademic social roles, self-maintenance roles, and academic school roles. The ABIC serves three primary functions in a system of pluralistic assessment: (1) it provides a multidimensional view of the child's performance in several social systems other than the school; (2) it provides systematic information about the child from the perspective of the family and its norms, meaning the child's performance in relation to the normative expectations for the statuses he or she occupies and the roles he or she plays; and (3) it operationalizes the AAMD's concern for adaptive behavior measurement in the diagnosis of mental retardation.

The ABIC contains 242 questions organized into six scales: (1) family relations (52 questions), (2) peer relations (36 questions), (3) nonacademic school roles (37 questions), (4) earner/consumer (26 questions), (5) community roles (42 questions), and (6) self-maintenance (49 questions). Examples of items from two of the scales follow:

Nonacademic school role performance: Behavior of the child in relation to teachers and peers at school and interaction with classmates. Nonacademic aspects of the school are included, such as holding class offices; serving as monitor or other type of helper in the classroom, office, or cafeteria; behavior on the playground; participation in social affairs and athletic activities at school; and participating in school competitions and projects.

Earner/consumer role performance: The child's economic behavior. Specifically, the questions ask about the child's understanding of money, knowledge of monetary values, shopping skills, and activities in which money is earned. Questions cover behavior in carrying, handling, borrowing, and spending money; knowledge of brand names and values of products; ability to accumulate money for desired purchases; and uses made of money in paying expenses.

In order to have some method for making an internal check on the probable veracity of the responses given by each respondent and estimating the extent to which a total score might have been inflated by a respondent routinely selecting the mastered response for each query, a veracity scale measure is included in the ABIC items. Twenty-four questions designed for children 11 years of age, having the highest difficulty level and not needed to maintain the ceiling, make up the veracity scale. These items are interspersed at frequent intervals among the other ABIC questions in the final version of the measure.

Raw scores are obtained for the child on each of the six subtests of the ABIC. The percentage of the variance in adaptive behavior scores of children in the standardization sample explained by scores on the sociocultural scales is substantially quite small. Consequently, the child's raw score is converted to a scaled score and plotted on the SOMPA profiles without reference to the child's sociocultural background. Conversion tables appear in the appendix of the Parent Interview Manual. The mean for each age group on each subtest is set at 50, the standard deviation at 15. Thus, it is possible to compare the performance of a child directly with a child of his or her own age and to plot profiles for the individual child so that scores on the various subtests can be compared with each other. Analysis of the scaled scores of the standardization sample indicate that the social roles played by 5- to 11-year-old children of different ages and ethnic backgrounds appear to be quite similar when viewed as a scaled score. However, there are internal differences among items of the subtests, so it is important for the assessor to look at responses to individual items as well. A respondent who is familiar with the student is interviewed, usually the parents. The interview can be conducted in either Spanish or English. The ABIC has 35 non-age–graded questions and 207 age-graded questions; i.e., items were placed in approximate chronological order from simplest to most difficult, based on the average age of the children for whom the role was for children 5 to 11 years of age. Questions were constructed that would apply equally to all ethnic and socioeconomic groups and both sexes (Mercer, 1979). Questions in each scale reflect the adaptation process within the social system—providing a secure base for exploration of new systems, transition agents for support, and a setting in which the child may experiment with materials and tools and master complex skills. Responses to the ABIC receive one of five scores: (1) latent role (child has not performed the activity); (2) emergent role (child is beginning to perform the role); (3) mastered role; (4) no opportunity/not allowed; and (5) respondent does not know. Raw scores for each of the six subtests of the ABIC are converted to standard scores and plotted on the SOMPA profiles without reference to the child's sociocultural background.

The ABIC is designed primarily to aid in decisions regarding diagnosis and classification for mental retardation services. The ABIC can also be helpful in determining whether a child is physically handicapped or emotionally disturbed. It was standardized on 2,080 children from three ethnic groups (Anglo, black, and Spanish-surname) from California who ranged from 5 to 11 years of age. Split-half reliabilities for average scores were .97.

CASE STUDY

Part II

Present Testing

Intelligence
The *Wechsler Adult Intelligence Scale* (WAIS) was administered as a means of measuring Debbie's present cognitive level. A calculation of the items correct resulted in a Verbal IQ of 56, a Performance IQ of 41, and a Full Scale IQ of 47. Debbie's best skills were in the areas of general information and comprehension of situations. Her weak areas were in memory, visual motor, and social awareness. Noted on the testing was a tendency for Debbie to perseverate on both motor and verbal responses. Also, she did much better when questions were repeated.

Academic
The *Peabody Individual Achievement Test* (PIAT) was given to measure Debbie's present academic skill levels. She is functioning at a beginning first grade level in Reading and Spelling, whereas she is at about a middle kindergarten level in Math and General Information. Debbie can correctly identify all the basic colors as well as numerals up to 50. A summary of her subtest scores follows:

Subtest	Raw Score	Grade Equivalent
Mathematics	13	.6
Reading Recognition	19	1.3
Spelling	18	1.4
General Information	12	.8

Psychomotor
The *Bender Gestalt Test* was given to assess Debbie's psychomotor skills. She made 19 errors according to the Koppitz scoring system. Her drawings resulted in a Developmental Age Equivalent below 5-0 years. The drawings were highly significant of visual motor deficits.

Adaptive

The *Vineland Social Maturity Scale* was used to assess Debbie's adaptive skills. She attained a Social Age of 7.2 years, which resulted in a Social Quotient of 38.

The Community Living Skills Assessment Inventory was completed by Debbie's mother. Debbie's skill levels on six adaptive areas are listed below. The information indicates that Debbie is functioning at an independent level in the majority of areas. Skills that she is presently deficient in but capable of learning with proper training include the following: buttoning, tying shoes, and nail care.

Performance Score Ratings: Please rate individual in regards to performance and independence.

6—Independent, perfect performance
5—Independent, imperfect performance
4—Supervised
3—Assisted partially

2—Assisted primarily
1—Cooperative
0—No participation
NA—Not applicable

I. Dressing and Undressing
  A. Selecting clothing
    1. Color combination   5
    2. Clean clothing   5
    3. Weather conditions   4
    4. For various occasions   4
    5. Gathering all clothing   4
  B. Puts on clothing
    1. Put on briefs   6
    2. Put on shirt
      a. pullover   6
      b. button   3
    3. Put on pants   5
    4. Fasten pants   5
    5. Zip pants   5
    6. Put on belt   5
    7. Put on suspenders   NA
    8. Put on socks   6
    9. Put on shoes   6
    10. Tie shoes   2
  C. Removes clothing
    1. Untie shoe   5
    2. Take off shoes   6
    3. Take off socks   6
    4. Unzip pants   5
    5. Unfasten pants   5
    6. Take off belt   6
    7. Take off suspenders   NA
    8. Take off pants   6
    9. Unbutton shirt   4
    10. Take off shirt
      a. pullover   6
      b. button   4

    11. Take off briefs   6
  D. Puts on outerwear
    1. Put on jacket   6
    2. Fasten jacket
      a. zips   4
      b. buttons   3
      c. snaps   4
    3. Put on hat   6
    4. Put on scarf   6
    5. Put on gloves or mittens   6
  E. Takes off outerwear
    1. Take off gloves or mittens   6
    2. Take off scarf   6
    3. Take off hat   6
    4. Unfasten jacket
      a. unzip   6
      b. unbutton   4
      c. unsnap   6
    5. Take off jacket   6

II. Personal Hygiene and Grooming
  A. Bathing or showering
    1. Gathers
      a. towel   6
      b. washcloth   6
      c. clean clothes   6
      d. pajamas   6
    2. Turns on water   5
    3. Regulates temperature   5

4. Turns off water	5
5. Lathers all parts of body	5
6. Rinses all parts of body	6
7. Dries all parts of body	5
8. Cleans bathtub, puts towel away	5

B. Brushing teeth
1. Open toothpaste	6
2. Apply toothpaste	6
3. Rinse mouth	6
4. Wipe mouth	6

C. Hair care
1. Wet hair	6
2. Shampoo	
a. open	6
b. pour	6
3. Lather entire head	6
4. Rinse	6
5. Dry hair	
a. towel	5
b. hairdryer	5

D. Washing up
1. Turn on water	6
2. Regulates temperature	5
3. Lather	6
4. Rinse	6
5. Dry	6

E. Toileting
1. Use urinal	6
2. Sits on toilet seat	6
3. Uses toilet tissue	6
4. Flush toilet after use	6
5. Readjusts clothing	6
6. Washes hands	6

F. Nail care
1. Clean nails	2
2. Cut nails	2

III. Eating
1. Spoon usage	6
2. Fork usage	6
3. Napkin usage	6
4. Glass drinking	6
5. Pours liquid	6
6. Passes food	6

IV. Housekeeping
1. Bed making	5
2. Changing sheets	5
3. Vacuuming	5
4. Dusting	5
5. Clean sink or tub	4
6. Clean toilet	4
7. Broom sweeping	5
8. Empty trash	6
9. Mop floor	4
10. Wax floor	4

V. Care of Clothing
1. Puts dirty laundry in appropriate place	5
2. Sort clothing	4
3. Load washing machine	4
4. Operate washing machine	4
5. Fold clothes	5
6. Iron clothing	2
7. Hangs clothes	4
8. Loads clothes dryer	5
9. Operates clothes dryer	5
10. Repairs torn clothing	2
11. Care for shoes (including lacing)	4
12. Sew buttons on	2

VI. Self-Medication
1. Knows when to take meds	5
2. Knows what pills are taken	5
3. Knows number of pills to take	5
4. Opens pill box	5
5. Puts pill(s) in hand	5
6. Puts pill(s) in mouth	5
7. Swallows pills	5
8. Gets drink of water	5

Informal Assessment Instruments

Informal assessment procedures used in the measurement of adaptive behavior are usually criterion-referenced, observational instruments that are tailor-made to the teacher's unique situation. These instruments, usually not standardized, are created because the more formal instruments available are not suitable to the particular situation confronting the teacher.

Ecological inventories strategies (Belmore & Brown, 1978; Falvey, Brown, Lyon, Baumgart, & Schroeder, 1980) and informal observational analysis of environments and adaptive behaviors necessary to function in those environments have been undertaken for severely handicapped students. These strategies can easily be adapted for mild and moderately handicapped students as well. The authors have had occasion to construct an informal measure of adaptive behavior when no formal adequate commercial measures of adaptive behavior were available, namely the *Community Living Skills Assessment Inventory* (Switzky, Rotatori, & Cohen, 1978).

The *Community Living Skills Assessment Inventory* was constructed to delineate an individual's functional living skills in areas considered essential for successful placement in a range of semi-independent community living facilities from an institutional setting. The inventory provides a description of an individual's functional living skills in eight areas: (1) dressing and undressing, (2) personal hygiene and grooming, (3) eating, (4) housekeeping, (5) care of clothing, (6) food preparation and culinary, (7) self-medication, and (8) functional/adaptive equipment.

The skills identified in the inventory were derived by discussion with the operators of alternative facilities (i.e., house parents, group home operators, nursing home operators, advocates, and by residents themselves when possible). Items relevant to skill areas were generated by the institutional staff, which included psychologists, occupational and physical therapists, social workers, physicians, and nurses. Items finally included in the inventory had to represent socially appropriate sequences of behavior that were both easily observed in the natural environment and relevant to an individual's functional adjustment into the community and the living facility.

The inventory was individually completed in the natural environment by persons who were thoroughly familiar with the handicapped individual to be observed (i.e., teachers, professionals, child-care workers, and volunteers). The observation periods were arranged at times when the functional living skills occur naturally, based on sequences of environmental patterns of behavior. Dressing skills were assessed in the handicapped person's bedroom when he or she was awakened in the morning and was getting ready for breakfast or when the person was leaving for school or work. Undressing skills were assessed when the handicapped person was preparing to go to bed or had arrived at school or work. All the skills were assessed in vivo in the natural setting. The observers rated the degree and the amount to which the handicapped person independently performed the behavioral items on a 7-point scale (e.g., 0 = no participation, 2 = assisted primarily, 4 = supervised, 6 = independent perfect performance). Individuals were usually observed and rated on three separate occasions so as to increase the reliability of the behavior observed.

CASE STUDY

Part III

Summary and Recommendations

Debbie is an 18-year-old young adult who had eye surgery for correcting a strabismus problem while she was a toddler. Intellectually, as assessed by the WAIS, Debbie is functioning in the moderately retarded range of intelligence according to the AAMD classification scheme. However, her verbal skills are more similar to an individual in the low mildly retarded range. Debbie has both visual-motor and depth perception difficulties, which interfere with her functioning on tests as well as in environmental situations. This difficulty, combined with her seizure problems, at times makes her appear clumsy and disoriented. Adaptively, as measured by the *Vineland Social Maturity Scale*, Debbie has skills similar to a 7- to 8-year-old child. Academically, as assessed by the PIAT, Debbie achieved at a middle kindergarten level in Math and General Information and at a beginning first grade level in Reading and Spelling. Psychomotor assessment, utilizing the *Bender Gestalt*, revealed significant visual-motor deficits. Socially, Debbie is an enjoyable person who apparently likes being with peers and staff. Behaviorally, she is easily managed, but she does have a tendency to be authoritarian and bossy.

1. Debbie would be a most appropriate candidate for a community living facility. The staff must be aware of her visual-motor, depth perception, and seizure problems so that her adjustment will be smoother.
2. Debbie should be evaluated by a physical therapist for suggestions regarding her motor difficulties.
3. Vocational assessment assignments should be those that deemphasize the need for fine-motor skills. Debbie would do much better with gross-motor tasks that involve discrimination or simple reacting skills.
4. Due to Debbie's seizure frequency, as well as the fact that she apparently has psychomotor seizures, it would be best for her to be placed at a facility that does not have a high auto traffic flow or involve going up and down two or three flights of stairs. As she adjusts to her new environment and as a reduction in seizures occurs, the above can be reevaluated.

5. Home visits should be encouraged as much as possible. This is a positive experience for Debbie and her family and should continue.

Summary

The concept of adaptive behavior is relatively new, yet already it has made a major impact on the field of education, particularly for children, adolescents, and adults with developmental disabilities. In fact, in many programs serving exceptional people, the importance attached to adaptive behavior has usurped the earlier emphasis given to an individual's IQ. Adaptive behavior requirements in society change as the individual matures, beginning with the attainment of developmental milestones and self-help skills in early childhood, leading next to successful performance in school, followed by increasing social and vocational responsibilities in adulthood. This progression, which is followed fairly well by most individuals, represents a major source of difficulties for persons with exceptional characteristics. As most educational programs hold independent functioning in society as one major goal, the concept of adaptive behavior serves as a useful mechanism for conceptualizing the steps comprising this important long-term goal. Further, the objective nature that has characterized the adaptive behavior literature permits continuous empirical measurement of these developmental phenomena.

Instruments used to assess adaptive behavior follow a continuum of comprehensiveness in terms of their thoroughness of assessment and the time needed for their administration: first-position instruments (screeners), second-position instruments (more systematic and detailed), and third-position instruments (fully detailed and comprehensive instruments). Additionally, informal procedures are available. The selection of instruments depends on the time constraints of the teacher or practitioner and the particular level of analysis of adaptive behavior that is required.

Educational Suggestions For Students with Adaptive Deficits

Assessment data from adaptive devices can assist teachers in program and curriculum planning, classification of students, deciding program resource allocations, grouping of students for instruction, and providing descriptive data for summary year-end reports. However, not all adaptive devices measure the same skill areas. Thus it is important that teachers select an appropriate adaptive device to answer their assessment questions. Some suggestions that can assist teachers in this matter are:

If information is needed to describe a student's current level of skills across a variety of content areas, then first-position adaptive devices should be selected.

If information is needed for program planning and the listing of objectives for a student's IEP, then second-position adaptive devices should be selected.

If comprehensive information is needed for program placement, curriculum organization, and classification concerns, then third-position adaptive devices should be selected.

When selecting an adaptive device, teachers should examine the manual to ensure that the standardization population for the device is appropriate for the students being assessed.

A large majority of adaptive devices have been normed on retarded individuals. When such devices are used with normal students, teachers must be cautious in their interpretations regarding student deviance because the norms incorporate deviance instead of normalcy.

Study Questions

1. What is adaptive behavior?
2. How do components of adaptive behavior change in (a) infancy and early childhood, (b) elementary and junior high school years, (c) high school and postschool years?
3. How do Jane Mercer and Henry Leland differ in their views concerning adaptive behavior?
4. When should first-position instruments be used? Give examples.
5. When should second-position instruments be used? Give examples.
6. When should third-position instruments be used? Give examples.
7. How should the teacher use informal assessment methods to measure adaptive behavior?

Suggested Readings

Doll, E. (1953). *Measurement of social competence: A manual for the Vineland social maturity scale.* Princeton, NJ: Educational Testing Service.
Leland, H. (1969). The relationship between "intelligence" and mental retardation. *American Journal of Mental Deficiency, 73,* 533–535.

Leland, H., Shellhaas, M., Nihira, K., & Foster, R. (1967). Adaptive behavior: A new dimension in the classification of the mentally retarded. *Mental Retardation Abstracts*, *4*, 359–387.

References

Adams, G. (1978) *Comprehensive Test of Adaptive Behavior*. Columbus, OH: Charles E. Merrill.

Balthazar, E. E. (1971). *Balthazar Scales of Adaptive Behavior, Section I: The Scales of Functional Independence (BSAB-I)*. Champaign, IL: Research Press.

Balthazar, E. E. (1973). *Balthazar Scales of Adaptive Behavior II: Scales of Social Adaptation (BSAB-II)*. Palo Alto, CA: Consulting Psychologist Press.

Balthazar, E. E. (1976). *Training the retarded at home or in school*. Palo Alto, CA: Consulting Psychologist Press.

Belmore, K., & Brown, L. (1978). A job skill inventing strategy for use in a public school vocational training program for severely handicapped potential workers. In N. G. Haring & A. Bricker (Eds.), *Teaching the severely handicapped* (Vol. III). Seattle: American Asssociation for the Severely and Profoundly Handicapped.

Bendersky, M., Edgar, E., & White, O. (1976). *Uniform Performance Assessment System* (UPAS). (Experimental Education Unit, Child Development and Mental Retardation Center, Working Paper 65). Seattle: University of Washington.

Brady, J. F., & Smilovitz, R. (Eds.). (1974). *APT: A Training Program for Citizens With Severely or Profoundly Retarded Behavior*. Spring City, PA: Spring City, Pennhurst State School.

Brown, L., Nietupski, J., & Hamre-Nietupski, S. (1976). Criterion of ultimate functioning. In M. A. Thomas (Ed.), *Hey don't forget about me*. Reston, VA: Council for Exceptional Children.

Cain, L. F., Levine, S., & Elzey, F. F. (1977). *Cain-Levine Social Competency Scale*. Palo Alto, CA: Consulting Psychologist Press.

Doll, E. A. (1965). *Vineland Social Maturity Scale: Condensed Manual of Instructions*. Circle Pines, MN: American Guidance Service.

DiNola, A. J., Kaminsky, B. P., & Sternfeld, A. E. (1970). *TMR Performance Profile for the Severely and Moderately Retarded*. Ridgefield, NJ: Educational Performance Associates.

Foster, R. W. (1974). *Camelot Behavioral Checklist*. Parsons, KS: Camelot Behavioral Systems.

Falvey, M., Brown, L., Lyon, S., Baumgart, B., & Schroeder, T. (1980). Strategies for using cues and correction procedures. In W. Sailor, B. Wilcox, & E. L. Brown (Eds.), *Instructional design for the severely handicapped*. Baltimore: Paul H. Brookes.

Grossman, H. (Ed.) (1983). Manual on terminology and classification in mental retardation, 1983 revision. Washington, DC: American Association on Mental Deficiency.

Lambert, N. M. (1979). Contributions of school classification, sex, and ethnic states to behavior assessment. *Journal of School Psychology*, *17*, 3–16.

Lambert, N. M., Wilcox, M. R., & Gleason, W. P. (1974). *The educationally retarded child*. New York: Grune & Stratton.

Lambert, N. M., Windmiller, M., Cole, L., & Figueroa, R. (1975). *Manual: AAMD Adaptive Behavior Scale, Public School Version.* Washington, DC: American Association on Mental Deficiency.

Leland, H., Nihira, F., Foster, R., Shellhaas, M., & Kugin, E. (1968). *Conference on measurement of adaptive behavior, III.* Parsons, KS: Parsons State Hospital and Training Center.

Mercer, J. E. (1973). *Labeling the mentally retarded.* Berkeley: University of California Press.

Mercer, J. R. (1979). *Technical manual. System of multicultural pluralistic assessment.* New York: Psychological Corporation.

Mercer, J. R., & Lewis, J. F. (1977). *Systems of multicultural pluralistic assessment.* New York: Psychological Corporation.

Nihira, K., Foster, R., Shellhaas, M., & Leland, H. (1974). *Adaptive Behavior Scale: Manual.* Washington, DC: American Association on Mental Deficiency.

Oakland, T., & Matuszek, P. (1977). Using tests in nondiscriminatory assessment. In T. Oakland (Ed.), *Psychological and educational assessment of minority children.* New York: Brunner/Mazel.

Ross, R. T. (1970). *Fairview Self-Help Scale.* Fairview, CA: Fairview State Hospital.

Sailor, W., & Mix, B. J. (1975). *The TARC Assessment System.* Austin, TX: PRO-ED.

Santa Cruz County Superintendent of Schools. (1973). *Behavior Characteristics progression: The Santa Cruz special education management system.* Palo Alto, CA: Santa Cruz County Schools.

Shearer, D., Billingsley, J., & Frohman, A. (1970). *A portage guide to early education: Instructions and checklist.* (Number 12). Portage, WI: Cooperative Educational Service Agency.

Somerton, M. E., & Turner, K. D. (1975). *Pennsylvania training model, individual assessment guide.* Harrisburg, PA: Pennsylvania Department of Education.

Sontag, E. W. (1975). Federal leadership. In M. A. Thomas (Ed.), *Hey don't forget about me.* Reston, VA: Council for Exceptional Children.

Switzky, H. N., Rotatori, A. F., & Cohen, A. (1978). The community living skills inventory: An instrument to facilitate the deinstitutionalization of the severely developmentally disabled. *Psychological Reports, 213,* 1335–1342.

Tawney, J. W., & Smith, J. (1981). An analysis of the forum: Issues in education of the severely and profoundly retarded. *Exceptional Children, 48,* 5–18.

12

Assessment of Vocational Skills

Paul Bates
Ernest Pancsofar

OBJECTIVES

After completing this chapter the teacher should be able to:

1. Describe a continuum of work options available to students upon leaving a vocational training program.
2. Describe the difference between static and dynamic vocational assessment procedures.
3. List the common ingredients of available work-sample evaluation systems.
4. Develop a job-skill inventory for determining the skills necessary for working in a nonsheltered competitive employment situation.
5. Describe four of the variables involved with criterion-referenced vocational assessment.
6. Define social validation.

Issues in Vocational Training

The role of the public schools in the career and vocational education of all students has been receiving considerable attention in the past few years. This interest stems in part from rising unemployment rates, an increased emphasis on accountability in educational programming, and the realization that school programs have inadequately prepared students for the world of work. In a study that was conducted as part of the National Association of Education Progress, Boyer (1978) reported that only 2% of a sample of 35,000 17-year-olds considered their school experiences as useful preparation for a future job. Additional data in support of an increased emphasis on career and vocational education in the public schools were provided by Kerr and Rosow (1979) as part of the Carnegie Council of Policy Studies in Higher Education. This report estimated that one-third of today's youth are ill-educated, ill-employed, and ill-equipped to make their way in American society. These estimates were supported by an overall dropout rate from school of 23%, with minority rates of 35% for blacks and 45% for Hispanics. There is also reason to believe that handicapped students have been inadequately prepared for productive lives beyond the school setting. According to data presented in a position statement on comprehensive vocational education for handicapped persons, only 42% of the handicapped population is employed as compared to 59% of the total population (*Federal Register*, September 25, 1978).

In support of increased vocational opportunities for handicapped students, recent legislation has given new prominence to the importance of vocational preparation. One of the major objectives of the Education for All Handicapped Children Act (PL 94-142) was to ensure the provision of an appropriate education for all handicapped persons (ages 3–21) so that they might obtain their maximum degree of self-sufficiency. Since our culture often measures self-sufficiency by a person's ability to hold a job, public school programs must be oriented toward providing students with skills that maximize their employability. According to PL 94-142 and other legislation (e.g., section 504 of the Rehabilitation Act and the education amendments of 1976, PL 94-482), vocational training programs must be developed for all handicapped persons of school age.

From the combination of forces cited above, a need has surfaced for training programs to expand and refine the present service delivery model to accommodate a full range of occupations and virtually all student populations. Teachers in these training programs must now assume the responsibility for preparing all students for community employment. Community employment can be conceptualized as a

The authors would like to acknowledge the assistance of Ernie Biller in preparing the tables on psychological tests and work sample evaluation.

series of options along a continuum of dependence to independence. According to Durand and Neufeldt (1980), these employment options include sheltered employment, sheltered industry, semisheltered industry, competitive work with support, individual competitive employment, and self-employment.

A comprehensive vocational training program will prepare each student to function as independently and self-sufficiently as possible on the continuum of community employment options. For a public school program to function optimally toward this end, vocational assessment activities are vital components in this process. In this chapter vocational assessment is discussed and specific assessment models are described. The initial discussion of vocational assessment is centered on the differences between static assessment methods and dynamic assessment techniques. This discussion is followed by a presentation of traditionally used vocational assessment models and alternative assessment techniques. The traditional models include psychological tests, work sample evaluation, situational assessment, and on-the-job tryouts. Alternative models include community assessment and criterion-referenced assessment. Throughout the discussions of assessment models and techniques, an emphasis is placed on how educators can use this information to develop a school's vocational education program. Tables of formal and informal vocational assessment tools are provided for the educator to assist in this process.

CASE STUDY

Part I

Name: Robert
Date of Birth: March 18, 1963
Date of Evaluation: March 30, 1981 to April 12, 1981

Age: 18 years, 1 month
Grade: Senior High Special Education Class

Background Information

Bob is an 18-year-old white male diagnosed as schizophrenic. His measured intelligence on the WAIS–R was a performance IQ of 73. He is enrolled in a high school special education program, and was referred by his rehabilitation counselor for vocational training evaluation. The counselor seriously questioned whether Bob was capable of competitive employment due to a previously unsatisfactory work record in the community. Typical work characteristics included low rates of production, high levels of off-task behavior, and poor interpersonal-social relationships with fellow workers.

Observation

Bob has normal vision and hearing, and his latest physical examination (3/10/80) indicated good overall fitness. In situations with new people, Bob does not initiate conversation and answers all request with short one- or two-word responses. It was also noted that Bob avoided direct eye contact when persons talked to him.

Past Test Results

On-the-job training efforts were initiated on three separate occasions for evaluating Bob's work behaviors.

January 5, 1979–January 16, 1979: Bus person at cafeteria
Duties: Clear, wash, and reset tables
Evaluation result: Bob would wash previously cleaned tables, remove materials from customers before they were finished with their meal, and stand idly by when work needed to be done.

March 3, 1980–March 20, 1980: Janitorial crew member
Duties: Vacuum carpets, sweep floors, and clean restrooms of large downtown office building
Evaluation result: Average time to clean restroom should have been 15 minutes, but Bob did not complete any restroom in less than 30 minutes. Verbal prompting and reinforcement did not influence rate.

September 22, 1980–September 26, 1980: Sheltered workshop
Duties: Recycle cans and sort bottles by color
Evaluation result: Bob made an unusually high number of discrimination errors when sorting bottles by color. He seemed to work as quickly as possible without regard to where items were placed. He maintained an unacceptable error rate even with continual reminders by supervisor.

Static Assessment versus Dynamic Assessment

Static assessment refers to the practice of collecting a limited sample of student behavior for the purpose of identifying characteristics that can be used to predict future performance. In static assessment, the student's characteristics are considered foremost, and the dynamic interplay between student behavior and environmental conditions are secondary. The classic example of a static assessment method is the traditional psychological evaluation. In principle and in practice, psychological tests have been directed toward identifying what goes on within the person (Forness, 1971). Unfortunately, many administrators of these tests have failed to appreciate the potential impact of environmental experiences. As a result, evaluation methods of this type often result in a condition described by Forness (1971) as the "paralysis of the analysis." This condition is evident in vocational assessment activities that fail to result in useful training recommendations. Gold (1980) has described this phenomenon as the gulf between "description and prescription."

Dynamic assessment includes techniques for evaluating a student's work performance in a variety of different situations and under several different environmental conditions (Bellamy, Horner, & Inman, 1979). These assessments are usually conducted over an extended period of time with repeated measurements of student behavior (Neff, 1970). Dynamic assessment is useful for measuring individual growth (Schalock & Karan, 1979), and it is well suited for assisting teachers in individualizing a student's vocational education.

Traditional vocational assessment activities have primarily relied on a limited sample of student behavior for the purpose of making predictions about an individual's work potential. Unfortunately, the emphasis of these assessment instruments has been directed toward the identification of static student characteristics rather than toward a better understanding of the dynamic interplay between a student's behavior and environmental conditions. However, if the instrument is used appropriately and the data considered in proper perspective, traditional vocational assessment methods should yield useful information for planning a school's vocational education program. This information will be even more valuable if it is strengthened by alternative assessment data that include information on student performance over time and under varying environmental conditions.

Traditional Vocational Assessment

Vocational assessment is a "comprehensive process involving an interdisciplinary team approach to assessing an individual's vocational potential and training and placement needs" (Brolin, 1976, p. 81). Traditionally, vocational assessment has consisted of (1) psychological tests of general ability/aptitude, (2) work sample evaluations, (3) situational assessments, and (4) on-the-job tryouts.

Psychological Tests

Psychological tests typically involve paper-and-pencil assessments of cognitive, attitudinal, and affective traits presumed to be functionally related to job performance. Frequently used psychological tests in vocational evaluation include: (1) achievement batteries and reading tests, (2) character and personality instruments, (3) intelligence measures, (4) multiaptitude batteries, and (5) vocational tests for clerical, interest, manual dexterity, and mechanical ability. Suggested psychological tests for each of these evaluation categories are included in Table 12.1. Three sample evaluation instruments will be discussed to provide examples of the specific content of psychological tests.

The *Kuder Occupational Interest Survey* (KOIS) is a vocational interest test designed to obtain general information about a student's work interests. The student is asked to indicate his or her most and least preferred activity from each of 100 triads. After completing the test, the student's score is determined by correlating the responses and "those of individuals involved in 37 occupations and 19 college majors (normed on female populations), and 20 additional occupations and 8 college major scales (normed on men)" (Miller, 1979, p. 573).

The *Vocational Capacity Scale* (VCS) is a multiaptitude test designed to evaluate the vocational potential of retarded young adults (Browning & Irvin, 1981). Developed by Pinkard, Gilmore, Ricker, and Williams (1963), the VCS is used to predict the most suitable vocational status within three broad groups: (1) competitive employment, (2) sheltered workshops, and (3) day care. Specific components of the VCS are administered to measure the areas of work habits, physical capacity, social maturity, general health, manual skills, arithmetic, motivation, and direction-following.

The *Nonreading Aptitude Test Battery* (NATB) purports to measure the areas of intelligence; verbal, numerical, spatial, and form perception; clerical perception; motor coordination; finger dexterity; and manual dexterity. Ten pen-and-paper tests and four performance tests are contained in the battery. Sample activities include coin matching, name comparisons, and finger and manual dexterity activities. Developed by the United States Training and Employment Services, the NATB is intended to replace the *General Aptitude Test Battery* for nonreaders.

The face validity of psychological assessments is weak because the tests do not assimilate in any way community employment conditions. Also, many students have exhibited low motivation and apathetic response in the testing situation due to previous experiences of failure with written evaluations. Many students have a difficult time associating their performance on these assessments with improved prospects of being employed. However, psychological test data can be a useful component in a comprehensive vocational evaluation when such data are used for general counseling purposes and for identifying areas in need of additional training.

Work Sample Evaluations

The work sample evaluation is a formal assessment technique that was developed, in part, due to the inadequacies in psychological testing. A work sample evaluation assesses a student's performance on a well-

TABLE 12.1. Psychological Tests in Vocational Evaluation[1]

Achievement Batteries and Reading Tests	Character and Personality	Intelligence Measures	Multi-Aptitude Batteries	Vocational-Clerical	Vocational-Interests	Vocational-Manual-Dexterity	Vocational-Mechanical Ability
Adult Basic Learning Exam	Edwards Personality Inventory	Culture Fair IQ Test	Differential Aptitude Test	General Clerical Test	AAMD Becker Reading Free Vocational Interest Inventory	Crawford Small Parts Dexterity Test	Bennett Mechanical Comprehension Test
California Achievement Tests	Edwards Personal Preference Schedule	Peabody Picture Vocabulary Test	USES General Aptitude Test Battery	Minnesota Clerical Test	Kuder Occupational Interest Survey	Hand-Tool Dexterity Test	Revised Minnesota Paper Form Board Test
Gray Oral Reading Test	Minnesota Multi-Personality Inventory	Revised Beta Examination	USES Non-Reading Aptitude Test Battery	SRA Typing Skills	Minnesota Importance Questionnaire	Purdue Pegboard	SRA Mechanical Aptitudes
Nelson-Denny Reading Test	Sixteen Personality Factor Questionnaire	SRA Pictorial Reading Test	Vocational Capacity Scale	Stenographic Aptitude Test	Ohio Vocational Interest Survey	Stromberg Dexterity Tests	
Peabody Individual Achievement Test	Work Environment Preference Schedule	SRA Verbal Form			Wide Range Interest-Opinion Test		
Test Adult Basic Education		Stanford-Binet or Weschler Adult Intelligence Scale			Strong-Campbell Interest Inventory		

[1]Based in part on Botterbusch (1978).

defined activity involving tasks, materials, and tools that are highly similar to those in a job or group of jobs located in the community (Neff, 1968). The *Vocational Evaluation Project Final Report* (Tenth Institute on Rehabilitation Services, 1975) recommends the work sample be (1) an actual job itself moved into an evaluation unit; (2) a trait sample designed to assess a single factor such as finger dexterity; (3) a simulation of an actual job operation; and (4) a cluster of trait samples that measure a group of traits for specific skills. The work sample evaluation should approximate the range of vocational behaviors that are important for success on a particular job or group of jobs.

The use of work sample assessments represents an attempt by teachers and rehabilitation personnel to apply the testing approach to actual job performance. Work sample evaluation requires that students actually manipulate real work materials. The work sample is usually a discrete task from a specific work area (e.g., small parts assembly, clerical work, food services). The format for evaluating these tasks is standardized. Student performance is measured in comparison to norm groups that have been evaluated previously. Often individual work samples are incorporated into more general test batteries. The Institute for the Crippled and Disabled (ICD) developed the first work sample battery in 1937. This system was the *Test Orientation and Work Sample System* (TOWER). Since the development of the TOWER, over 10 major work sample systems have been developed.

Included in Figure 12.1 are the more commonly used work sample evaluation systems. The approximate cost, reading level, validity reports, target audience, grade level, and special training needs are contained in this figure. Several authors have described the primary characteristics of commonly used work evaluation systems (Brolin & Kokaska, 1979; Browning & Irvin, 1981; Gold, 1973; Revell, Kriloff, & Sarkees, 1980; Revell & Wehman, 1978). Five of these systems are detailed in the following discussion.

In the *McCarron-Dial Work Evaluation System*, 17 individual instruments are used to assess five factors for each student. These factors include verbal-cognitive, sensory, motor ability, emotional, and integration-coping skills. Each of these skills is evaluated for a prediction that future programming should occur in a day care center, work activities center, extended sheltered employment, transitional sheltered employment, or community work environment. Developed primarily for assessing mentally retarded and behavioral disordered students, the McCarron-Dial system has been used with learning disabled and disadvantaged students and adults as well.

A unique feature of the *Singer Vocational Evaluation System* is the method of instruction for the student. Audiovisual instruction, via earphones and slides, is used to provide the testing cues for the

Vocational Evaluation Systems*	Approx. Cost	Reading Grade Level	Validity	Disability Group								Grade Level				Special Training Needed
				Learning Disability	Mildly Retarded	Moderately Retarded	Behavior Disorders	Hearing Impaired	Visually Impaired	Physically Impaired	Disadvantaged	Grades 7–9	Grades 9–12	Post Secondary	Adult	
Comprehensive Occupational Assessment & Training System	1,275 & up	7-8	Construct Data Avail.	•	•		•			•	•	•	•	•	•	No
HESTER Evaluation System	7,200	N/A	N/A	•	•	•	•	•			•			•	•	Yes 2 Days
McCarron-DIAL Work Evaluation System	1,415	N/A	Construct/ Concurrent Data Avail.	•	•	•	•				•	•	•	•	•	Yes 3 Days
Micro-TOWER	7,943 & up	3-4	Construct/ Concurrent Data Avail.		•					•	•	•	•	•	•	No
Philadelphia Jewish Employment and Vocational Service	7,975	N/A	N/A	•			•				•		•	•	•	Yes 5 Days
Pre-Vocational Readiness Battery	3,200	Minimal	N/A		•	•						•	•		•	No
Talent Assessment Programs	3,100 & up	None Required	N/A	•	•		•			•	•		•	•	•	Yes 1.5 Days
The Tower System	5,000	Minimum of 6th	Equivocal results				•			•		•	•	•	•	Yes 15 Days

Figure 12.1 Vocational evaluation systems guide.

continued next page

Vocational Evaluation Systems*	Approx. Cost	Reading Grade Level	Validity	Learning Disability	Mildly Retarded	Moderately Retarded	Behavior Disorders	Hearing Impaired	Visually Impaired	Physically Impaired	Disadvantaged	Grades 7-9	Grades 9-12	Post Secondary	Adult	Special Training Needed
				Disability Group								Grade Level				
Valpar Component Work Sample Series	495 to 990 each	Varied	N/A	•					•				•	•	•	No
Vocational Evaluation System (Singer)	Avg. cost per sample 1,544	N/A	Mostly Content	•	•		•	•		•	•	•	•	•	•	No
Vocational Information and Evaluation Work Samples	7,675	N/A	N/A	•			•			•	•	•	•			Yes 5 Days
Vocational Interest Temperament and Aptitude System		Minimal	N/A	•	•		•			•	•	•	•			Yes 5 Days
Vocational Skills Assessment and Development Program	5,950	N/A	N/A	•			•			•	•	•	•	•	•	No
Wide Range Employability Sample	1,698	N/A	High Correlation Reputed		•						•	•	•	•	•	No
VALPAR CUBE		None	N/A	•					•			•	•	•	•	No

*Information based, in part, from Botterbusch (1980).

Figure 12.1 *(continued)*

student. Each student can have the opportunity to work on 20 individual work samples including: (1) bench assembly, (2) carpentry, (3) cooking and baking, (4) cosmetology, (5) data calculation and records, (6) drafting, (7) electronic wiring, (8) engine service, (9) masonry, (10) medical services, (11) needle trade, (12) office and sales clerk, (13) photo lab technician, (14) plumbing and pipe fitting, (15) production machine operator, (16) refrigeration, heating, and air conditioning, (17) sample making, (18) sheet metal, (19) soil testing, and (20) soldering and welding. Each work sample is evaluated on a 5-point scale with no rigid time limitation per sample. Thus, the testing is conducted across a broad range of skills that are found in the *Dictionary of Occupational Titles* (U.S. Department of Labor, 1977).

The *Test Orientation and Work Sample System* (TOWER) was developed by the Vocational Rehabilitation Administration and the Institute for Crippled and Disabled Rehabilitation and Research Center in New York City. The TOWER system is used primarily with physically disabled and behavior disordered students. Ninety-three work samples are divided into 14 areas including: (1) clerical, (2) drafting, (3) drawing, (4) electronics assembly, (5) jewelry manufacturing, (6) leather goods, (7) lettering, (8) machine shop, (9) mail clerk, (10) optical mechanics, (11) pantograph engraving, (12) sewing machine operation, (13) welding, and (14) workshop assembly. In the TOWER system there is a weighted score obtained in terms of time and quality of work.

The *Valpar Component Work Sample Series* contains 16 work samples including: (1) clerical comprehension and aptitude, (2) drafting, (3) electrical circuitry and print reading, (4) eye-hand-foot coordination, (5) integrated peer performance, (6) money handling, (7) multilevel sorting, (8) numerical sorting, (9) problem solving, (10) range of motion: upper extremity, (11) range of motion: whole body, (12) simulated assembly, (13) size discrimination, (14) small tools, (15) soldering and inspection, and (16) tri level measurement. The student's total score is an indicator of the overall quality and quantity of work based on time and error calculations.

The *Vocational Information and Evaluation Work Samples* (VIEWS) was developed by the Jewish Employment and Vocational Service in Philadelphia. Sixteen work samples are included in the work areas of (1) clerical, (2) handling, (3) machine, and (4) manipulative crafts. In the VIEWS system students experience orientation, demonstration, training, and production work periods. During each work period the student receives tasks that range from least complex to most complex in difficulty. The evaluator uses verbal cues and demonstrations to provide the instructions for each work sample.

Several positive aspects of the work sample approach to vocational assessment should be noted. Work samples (1) represent a close approximation of actual employment tasks; (2) provide simulated exploration, exposure, and experience in a wide range of occupational areas; (3) give students the chance to improve their work performance on real jobs; (4) rely minimally on academic and cultural factors that may discriminate against certain learners; (5) identify areas of strength for particular students; (6) identify areas that need improvement for particular students; (7) enable students to respond favorable to the novelty of the work sample as opposed to paper-and-pencil assignments; and (8) have high face validity.

Potential disadvantages of work sample evaluations include: (1) the high cost of commercially prepared samples; (2) the time-consuming task of producing self-made samples; (3) the possibility of excluding students based solely upon the outcome measure of one work sample; (4) the length of time—1 to 2 weeks—for administering one work sample battery; (5) lack of availability for work samples for all jobs and the inability to stay abreast of a changing labor market once a system is purchased; (6) possibility of restricting the number of choices a student would have otherwise considered; (7) tendency to discourage teachers who are responsible for job training and employment from using the community as a major resource of exploration, training, and experience; and (8) weak validity outside of face validity.

Although there are several aspects of work sample evaluation that are not entirely positive, this method of assessment does provide data for a student's vocational program development beyond that which is available from pencil-and-paper assessments. Work sample assessments actually measure real work performance, albeit these assessments are usually conducted in artificial work environments and measure limited aspects of the total work repertoire required for success in community employment.

Situational Assessments

The situational assessment refers to the practice of conducting a 20- to 30-day evaluation of a student's performance in a structured setting (i.e., sheltered workshop or simulated work situation). In these assessment situations, the student is given an actual job to perform and information is collected on work skills and other work-related behaviors. Work skills include the time required to learn new tasks, speed of performance, and accuracy. Examples of work-related behaviors are direction following, frustration tolerance, safety, motivation, punctuality, dependability, perseverance, and social-interpersonal skills.

According to Brolin (1976), the emphasis of a situational assessment is on the student's general work personality. With the exception of work productivity data, the information collected in the situational assessment is primarily subjective and anecdotal. At the completion of the situational assessment period, a staffing is usually held and the student's vocational education program is modified according to individual needs. Although situational assessments do not follow any standard format, the reality of the job situation results in the collection of information that may closely approximate a student's performance in an actual employment situation. If student data can be collected across a variety of different situations, teachers are able to acquire extensive information regarding the relevance of their vocational preparation programs. The value of this data can be increased by efforts to quantify aspects of a student's work personality and by repeated measurement techniques. Potential limitations of situational assessment methods relate to the artificial nature of many evaluation settings and to logistical problems in collecting data across a large range of occupations. In response to these limitations, on-the-job tryouts have often been used to increase the reality factor of assessment and to expand a student's exposure to different jobs.

CASE STUDY

Part II

Present Testing

A situational assessment was conducted in a simulated sheltered workshop setting within the public school. The contract that was being produced in this simulated setting was a jump rope assembly. This assembly required stringing 1-inch plastic tubing on insulated wire and then affixing wooden handles on the ends by double knotting the wire through each handle end. The completed jump rope was packaged in a zip lock bag along with a 3-inch × 5-inch card upon which the word "completed" was printed. This task was selected because it was a real job and one of the most important subcontracts held by a community-based sheltered workshop from which the materials were borrowed.

The work schedule consisted of two 30-minute daily afternoon sessions separated by a 15-minute coffee break. The number of students present ranged from six to eight daily. There were usually between one and four staff members present.

Verbal instructions and modeling were given to Bob specific to assembling the jump ropes. A teacher observed Bob assemble the jump rope and, when required, assisted him through the various steps until he demonstrated competency. Competency was determined to be two consecutively completed jump rope assemblies without error.

Bob was informed that jump rope assembly was to be his job for a period of time and that he would be paid a stipend at the end of the week for regularly attending and working on his assigned job. He also received periodic praise for work on the jump rope assembly. Five days of baseline behavior were recorded during which the periodic praise and the stipend conditions were in effect.

Production time began as soon as Bob either started unwinding the rope or placed a wooden handle into an assembly board. It ended when Bob either left the work table for scheduled breaks or at the end of the day. The number of ropes completed per minute was recorded daily by dividing the number of completed ropes by the number of minutes worked.

Following the baseline period, an initial criterion performance level was selected. A criterion performance level is a contingency that requires a specific number of ropes to be finished in a particular time period. The initial criterion was based on the teacher's assumption that the work requirement was within Bob's capabilities. Simultaneously with the establishment of a work requirement, an additional contingency was implemented that consisted of a $1.00 bonus per day for meeting the new criterion. The daily bonus plus the $2.00 stipend was paid in lump sum at the end of the week. Red stars placed at the bottom of a daily check sheet were used to inform Bob that he had reached the criterion for that day and had thus earned his bonus. All criterion shifts were discussed thoroughly with Bob prior to their implementation.

A new criterion was established whenever Bob successfully matched the previous criterion for a minimum of 3 consecutive days. The magnitude of each subsequent criterion change was established at a rate slightly faster than Bob's previous production rates.

As the requirements became more stringent, Bob exhibited some reluctance in working at increased rates, yet his production output continued increasing. The terminal criterion rate was established at .166/minute and was compatible with normal employee competitive work standards. This criterion was established by assessing the jump rope assembly performance rates of several of the staff members.

Different teachers worked with Bob, but all followed the same procedure. At the beginning of the work day, Bob was informed of the criterion in effect. From that point on, he was given feedback on the average of every 10 minutes relative to whether or not he was on schedule.

Examination of Bob's work behavior revealed that, in a period of 24 sessions, his production increased over 100% through the gradual criterion changes and positive reinforcement. Production rates increased to a competitive employment level of .166/minute, and there was only 1 day in which a target criterion was not met.

Summary and Recommendations

The assessment data indicated that Bob has competitive employment potential, which rapidly became evident through relatively simple changes (contingent reinforcement and feedback) in the environment. However, without an extended situational assignment utilizing interaction techniques, Bob may have been excluded from consideration for further vocational training. On the basis of this demonstration of his work potential, Bob is presently being reconsidered for more advanced vocational training and community employment.

On-The-Job Tryouts

The on-the-job tryout provides the most realistic setting in which to assess vocationally relevant behaviors. This method of evaluation gives the educator an opportunity to determine a student's ability to work in different settings. Further, this method can be used to expose students to a variety of occupations.

Students are evaluated by the actual supervisory staff and by school personnel. On-the-job assessment typically includes these characteristics: (1) students are not usually paid, (2) placement is primarily for the student's benefit and not the employer's, (3) placement does not usually result in employment, (4) the student does not displace other workers, and (5) the student's performance is supervised and evaluated by the employer and education personnel.

Information that is typically collected includes work skill performance, social-interpersonal skills, vocational interests, and work habits (e.g., punctuality, compliance, dependability). From the student's exposure to a series of community employment experiences, school personnel are provided with assessment data from which they can further develop the relevance and quality of their vocational education program. For specific students, this information will be extremely useful in planning the vocational component of each student's individualized educational program (IEP).

Alternative Vocational Evaluation Techniques

The traditionally used vocational assessment methods may result in the identification of specific strengths and weaknesses in the vocational repertoire of school-age students (Gold, 1973). However, strict reliance on these methods to the exclusion of other data is inappropriate. Potential problems with some of the traditional assessment methods that should be considered are (1) poor predictive validity, (2) inappropriate norm groups, (3) confounding of acquisition and performance, (4) limiting feature of expectancies, and (5) individual differences in motivation levels.

Since vocational evaluation needs to be more sensitive to the interaction of student behavior and environmental conditions, alternatives are needed to traditionally used methods. These alternatives should be dynamic as opposed to static. Furthermore, these assessment techniques need to include repeated measurements across an extended period of time. As a first step in developing more appropriate vocational assessment techniques, a detailed analysis of employment situations in the community should be conducted. This assessment can be used to identify the criteria for successful vocational performance across a variety of occupational areas.

Community Job Assessment

Vocational preparation programs in the public schools must be responsive to an ever-changing job market. The content of these programs should reflect those occupations that are presently in demand and those that are projected to be available on the local, regional, and national levels. For handicapped students, vocational mobility beyond the local community may be limited. Consequently, vocational programs for handicapped students need to be closely aligned with those specific occupations that are realistically available in the student's home community.

Local job availability must be continually assessed by school personnel. Assessment activities include listings of employment situations where former students have succeeded, help-wanted ads in local newspapers, job service listings, consultation with rehabilitation counselors, telephone and written surveys, discussions with friends and service clubs, personal contacts with employers, and review of other vocational training programs.

For the employment options that have been identified for a student or group of students, a detailed assessment of the specific skills that are required to succeed should be conducted. This assessment should result in the identification of specific skills for the actual performance of the job(s) and of specific work-related behaviors that have been determined to be important for employment success. Two exemplary methods for identifying the actual behaviors that are required to attain community employment have been described in the literature. One of these methods was developed for sheltered employment (Mithaug & Hagmeier, 1978) and the other for nonsheltered competitive employment (Belmore & Brown, 1978).

Sheltered Employment

Mithaug and Hagmeier (1978) reported an analysis of the entry requirements for sheltered workshops in five Northwestern states. This analysis included the results of a questionnaire that was administered to sheltered workshop supervisors. The questionnaire contained approximately 400 behavior statements, each preceded by the statement, "For entry into sheltered employment, it is important that a client should . . . ."

The survey results of those behavior standards that were identified as important by 90% or more of the respondents are presented in Tables 12.2 and 12.3 for vocational and social survival skills, respec-

TABLE 12.2 Behavior Standards in Vocational Survival Skills Selected for Entry by 90% or More of Supervisors

Employees should be able to:

1. Participate in work environments for 6-hour periods
2. Move safely about the shop by:
   a. Walking from place to place
   b. Identifying and avoiding dangerous areas
   c. Wearing safe work clothing
3. Work continuously at a job station for 1–2-hour periods
4. Learn new tasks when the supervisor explains by modeling
5. Come to work an average of 5 times per week
6. Correct work on a task after the second correction
7. Want to work for money/sense of accomplishment
8. Understand work routine by not displaying disruptive behavior during routine program changes
9. Continue work without disruptions when:
   a. Supervisor is observing
   b. Fellow worker is observing
   c. Stranger is observing
10. Adapt to new work environment with normal levels of productivity in 1–5 days and with normal levels of contacts with supervisor in 30–60 minutes

Note. From *Vocational Training for Mentally Retarded Adults: A Behavior Analytic Approach* by F. R. Rusch and D. E. Mithaug, Champaign, IL: Research Press, 1980. Copyright 1980 by Research Press. Reprinted by permission.

tively. These results should be used by teachers in determining priorities for vocational training purposes.

Nonsheltered Competitive Employment

Since vocational training programs in the public schools are primarily geared toward preparing students for nonsheltered competitive employment, an analysis of requisite skills across a variety of occupations should be conducted. These analyses should result in the identification of behaviors that students will need to acquire for functioning successfully in competitive employment situations. Belmere and Brown (1978) developed the *Job Skill Inventory* for the purpose of identifying the specific skills required in competitive employment. This inventory, outlined in Table 12.4, consists of three major components. First, general information regarding the work and social requirements of the job is presented. This section should also include an evaluation of the realistic availability of employment for students in particular occupational areas. Second, specific work skills required for the targeted jobs are delineated. Many of these specific work skills can be task-analyzed into a series of component behaviors that

TABLE 12.3 Behavior Standards in Social Survival Skills Selected for Entry by 90% or More of Respondents

Employees should be able to:

1. Communicate basic needs such as those involving thirst, hunger, sickness, pain, and toileting
2. Communicate basic needs receptively by means of verbal expression, signs, or gestures
3. Communicate basic needs expressively by means of verbal expression or gestures
4. Respond to instructions requiring immediate compliance within 0–30 seconds
5. Respond appropriately to safety signals given verbally through signs or through signals
6. Initiate contact with supervisors when the employee:
   a. cannot do the job
   b. runs out of materials
   c. finishes job
   d. feels too sick or tired to work
   e. needs drink or to go to rest room
   f. makes a mistake
7. Maintain proper grooming by:
   a. dressing appropriately after using the rest room
   b. cleaning self before coming to work
   c. cleaning self after using the rest room
   d. cleaning self after eating lunch
   e. eating food appropriately at lunch
   f. displaying proper table manners at lunch
8. Reach place of work by means of:
   a. company-sponsored vehicle
   b. own arrangement
   c. public transit
9. Maintain personal hygiene by:
   a. shaving regularly
   b. keeping teeth clean
   c. keeping hair combed
   d. keeping nails clean
   e. using deodorant
10. Leave job station inappropriately no more than 1–2 times per day
11. Display or engage in major disruptive behavior no more than 1–2 times per week
12. Display or engage in minor disruptive behavior no more than 1–2 times per week

Note. From *Vocational Training for Mentally Retarded Adults: A Behavior Analytic Approach* by F. R. Rusch and D. E. Mithaug, Champaign, IL: Research Press, 1980. Copyright 1980 by Research Press. Reprinted by permission.

TABLE 12.4 Madison Job Skill Inventory

I. General Information
  A. Why considered
  B. Job description
  C. Description of social environment
II. Specific Work Skills Required
  A. Physical/sensory motor
  B. Basic interpersonal
  C. Language
  D. Functional academic
  E. Machine and tool use
  F. Hygiene
III. Supportive Skills and Other Required Information
  A. Transportation
  B. Work preparation
  C. Money management
  D. Time telling and time judgment

cumulatively result in competent vocational performance. One method for identifying and sequencing specific work skills is to directly observe successful employees and record the sequence of behaviors that they follow to complete the job. Finally, supportive skills and other information that may be pertinent to job success are described. Supportive skills have often been found to be the most crucial behaviors for long-term job effectiveness. From the *Job Skill Inventory*, teachers are provided with information from which to evaluate the relevance of their present curriculum. If certain behaviors appear consistently important across a range of occupations, these skills should be given a priority in the program's curriculum. Many of the behaviors that are identified with the *Job Skill Inventory* are relevant across vocational and academic programs. As a result, this technique can be used by school personnel to identify numerous areas where interdisciplinary planning and curriculum integration are needed.

Criterion-Referenced Assessment

Criteria for vocational performance should be established for all variables that are determined to be important for successful employment. These variables include acquisition of work skills and work-related behaviors, speed of performance (production rate), persistence on the job (attending to task), and quality or accuracy of vocational performance. Examples of criterion-referenced assessment activities are presented for each of these vocationally relevant behaviors.

Acquisition Assessment
Task analytic assessment is the criterion-referenced assessment technique that is particularly appropriate for evaluating acquisition of vocational skills. To appropriately use task analytic assessment, target behaviors are divided into a series of subcomponents (steps) that are then sequenced in a logical order. Task analyses can be generated in several different ways. Preferably these analyses are derived on the basis of observing currently employed workers performing the work tasks. Once task analyses are developed, the behavioral subcomponents or steps are then written in serial order on a recording form. After recording the task requirements on a data sheet, assessment situations are then structured. Assessment situations should be as similar as possible to those conditions that will be encountered at actual employment sites.

Attending to Task
In addition to the requirement that workers be able to perform all duties that are associated with a particular job, employers are also concerned about other related work habits. One of these work habits that is highly desired is persistence in job performance (i.e., attending to task). A definition of attending to task is "engaging in behaviors that are functional to task completion." The criterion for attending to task may be different from job to job. This criterion can be estimated by discussions with a work supervisor, but is best determined by direct observations of successful employees performing identical duties as are targeted for particular students. One method for conducting these direct assessments is to select a representative period of time from a work day (e.g., 30 minutes), divide the time period into a series of equal intervals (e.g., 30-second intervals), and record each interval during which the student was off task.

Production Rate Assessment
After a student demonstrates competence in performing the basic requirements of a job, attention often shifts to how proficiently the job is performed (Bates, Renzaglia, & Clees, 1980). One aspect of job proficiency is speed of task performance or production rate. Production rate has been identified as a variable that influences employers' ratings of successful versus unsuccessful employees. There are several ways in which production rate can be measured. One method for assessing production rate is to identify countable production units that can be reliably measured. Countable production units could include number of dishes washed, number of assemblies completed, number of computer cards punched, number of rooms cleaned, etc. Once a measurable unit of production has been identified, a recording form should be developed. Essential information on this form would

include time work started, number of units completed, and time work ended. From this basic information, production rate per minute can be calculated by dividing the number of units completed by the total number of minutes worked.

Production Quality Assessment

Another aspect of work proficiency is the quality of production. Work quality refers to how accurately the vocational task is completed according to the employer's standards. Employer's standards for accuracy may include a minimal number of errors (e.g., 95% of assemblies completed without defects) and neatness in job performance (e.g., all trash is removed from floor after sweeping). As with production rate, employers' standards for quality may differ from one situation to another. These standards may also vary within the same job from supervisor to supervisor.

To measure production quality, the criterion for accurate performance needs to be specified. This must be done in conjunction with community employers and on-the-job supervisors. Once this is specified, a worker's performance can be assessed daily and evaluated in relation to these quality standards. Quality standards could be objective (e.g., percentage of carburetors assembled without error) and/or subjective (e.g., employer's rating of quality in cleaning a motel room).

Summary

A critical factor in the development of more appropriate vocational education programs in the public schools will be the nature of the assessment data that are collected. Relying solely on traditional assessment methods will not result in an efficient and productive vocational evaluation. Teachers need to use alternative evaluation methods for developing each student's vocational education plan. Vocational assessment should begin with an identification of the criteria behaviors required for successful vocational performance across a variety of occupational clusters. Once these criteria are established, students can be observed in a variety of different ways to determine their performance level in relation to these standards. Ongoing student assessment data should be collected to determine and influence the environmental conditions under which the student performs optimally.

Moreover, the effectiveness of a vocational training program needs to be assessed in relation to the social importance of the results. Potential measures of the social importance of results include student and parent satisfaction with the job, employer acceptance of the student, co-worker attitudes, long-term employment status, dollars earned, decreases in disability payments, and cost-effectiveness of the training program. Also, student and parent attitudes toward the vocational training program may significantly influence long-term effectiveness. If the student or his or her parents are dissatisfied with a particular job, long-term retention is unlikely. The best policy for collecting this information would be to constantly assess student and parental interest and satisfaction with the various job experiences to which students are exposed. Assessment information from the community employers who supervise student job experiences is also very important. Frequent assessment of supervisor and co-worker satisfaction with a student's performance on the job is essential. Retraining or correction techniques to improve the student's skill can then occur. The result of this total assessment process is the development of an appropriate vocational education for all students in the public school.

Educational Suggestions for Students with Vocational Difficulties

The training and preparation of students for work assignments is crucial to the success of vocational programming endeavors. The suggestions that follow can assist teachers in their effort.

At times students are assessed as having attending difficulties. Such students should receive training in attending to task prior to intensive vocational job training.

Many students are assessed as having low motivation while on a vocational assignment. It is important that training supervisors incorporate motivational procedures to encourage students to produce while on an on-the-job assignment.

Students with identified vocational skills for a particular task learn better if simulated job training experiences use the same materials and equipment as are present at the job site.

When students' vocational difficulties are assessed as being due to limited cognitive ability, training may produce better results when vocational instruction stresses step-by-step training. Also, training is more effective when spaced learning is used rather than massed learning.

At times students are assessed as having deficits in the ability to transfer job skill training from one activity to another. For these students training in generalization and incidental learning is beneficial.

Sometimes vocational clients are assessed as performing consistently but not well enough to meet the vocational objectives of an assignment. For such clients a change in the reward system for their productivity is in order.

When students fail on a community vocational assignment, teachers should assess whether the work provided in the training environment has too little a relationship with the work required in the community assignment.

Study Questions

1. List five vocational employment areas that form a continuum of a most to least dependent option.
2. Describe the primary differences between static and dynamic assessment procedures.
3. Describe the McCarron-Dial, the Singer, and the TOWER evaluation systems.
4. List four variables that should be evaluated during a criterion-referenced assessment.
5. Describe social validation procedures.
6. List the advantages and disadvantages of the work sample approach to vocational assessment.
7. Make a task analysis checklist of skills to assess the duties of a chambermaid in cleaning motel bedrooms.

Suggested Readings

Brolin, D. (1973). Vocational evaluation: Special education's responsibility. *Education and Training of the Mentally Retarded, 39*, 619–624.

Mithaug, D., Mar, D., & Stewart, O. (1978). *Prevocational assessment and curriculum guide*. Seattle: Exceptional Education Press.

Rusch, F. R., & Mithaug, D. (1980). *Vocational training for mentally retarded adults*. Champaign, IL: Research Press.

Wehman, P. (1981). *Competitive employment*. Baltimore: Paul H. Brookes.

References

Bates, P., Renzaglia, A., & Clees, T. (1980). Improving the work performance of severely/profoundly retarded young adults: The use of a changing criterion procedure design. *Education and Training for the Mentally Retarded, 15*, 95–106.

Bellamy, G. T., Horner, R. H., & Inman, D. P. (1979). *Vocational habilitation of severely retarded adults: A direct service technology.* Austin, TX: PRO-ED.

Belmore, K., & Brown, L. (1978). A job skill inventory strategy designed for severely handicapped potential workers. In N. Haring & D. Bricker (Eds.), *Teaching the severely handicapped* (Vol. 3, pp. 223–262). Columbus, OH: Special Press.

Brolin, D. E. (1976). *Vocational preparation of retarded citizens.* Columbus, OH: Charles E. Merrill.

Brolin, D. E., & Kokaska, C. J. (1979). *Career education for handicapped children and youth.* Columbus, OH: Charles E. Merrill.

Botterbusch, K. F. (1978). *Psychological testing in vocational evaluation.* Menomonie, WI: Materials Development Center, Stout Vocational Rehabilitation Institute, University of Wisconsin-Stout.

Botterbusch, K. F. (1980). *A comparison of commercial vocational evaluation systems.* Menomonie, WI: Materials Development Center, Stout Vocational Rehabilitation Institute, University of Wisconsin-Stout.

Boyer, E. (1978). Position statement on comprehensive vocational education for handicapped persons. *Federal Register,* September 25. Washington, DC: Department of Health, Education, and Welfare, Office of Education.

Browning, P., & Irvin, L. K. (1981). Vocational evaluation, training, and placement of mentally retarded persons. *Rehabilitation Counseling Bulletin, 25,* 374–409.

Durand, J., & Neufeldt, A. H. (1980). Comprehensive vocational services. In R. J. Flynn & K. E. Nitsch (Eds.), *Normalization, social integration, and community services* (pp. 283–298). Austin, TX: PRO-ED.

Forness, S. R. (1971). Educational prescription for the school psychologist. *Journal of School Psychology, 8*(2), 96–98.

Gold, M. W. (1973). Research on the vocational habilation of the retarded: The present, the future. In N. Ellis (Ed.), *International review of research in mental retardation* (Vol. 6, pp. 97–147). New York: Academic Press.

Gold, M. W. (1980). *Marc Gold: "Did I say that": Articles and commentary on the try another way system.* Champaign, IL: Research Press.

Kerr, C., & Rosow, J. M. (1979). *Work in America: The decade ahead.* New York: Von Nostrand Reinhold.

Kuder, G. (1966). *Kuder occupational interest survey* (KOIS). Chicago: Science Research Associates.

Miller, S. R. (1979). Career education: Lifelong planning for the handicapped. In D. A. Sabatino & T. L. Miller (Eds.), *Describing learner characteristics of handicapped children and youth* (pp. 567–589). New York: Grune & Stratton.

Mithaug, D. E., & Hagmeier, L. D. (1978). The development of procedures to assess prevocational competencies of severely handicapped young adults. *AAESPH Review, 3,* 94–115.

Neff, W. (1968). *Work and human behavior.* New York: Aldine-Atherton.

Neff, W. (1970). Vocational assessment: Theory and models. *Journal of Rehabilitation, 36*(1), 27–29.

Pinkard, C. M., Gilmore, A. S., Ricker, L. H., & Williams, C. P. (1963). *Predicting vocational capacity of retarded young adults.* Tampa, FL: Research Division, MacDonald Training Center Foundation.

Revell, W. G., Kriloff, L. J., & Sarkees, M. D. (1980). Vocational evaluation. In P. Wehman & P. J. McLaughlin (Eds.), *Vocational curriculum for developmentally disabled persons* (pp. 73–94). Baltimore: University Park Press.

Revell, G., & Wehman, P. (1978). Vocational evaluation of severely and profoundly retarded clients. *Rehabilitation Literature, 39,* 226–231.

Rusch, F. R., & Mithaug, D. E. (1980). *Vocational training for mentally retarded adults: A behavior analytic approach.* Champaign, IL: Research Press.

Sawyer, S. (1980). Job skill inventory of a motel chambermaid position. Unpublished paper, Department of Special Education, Southern Illinois University, Carbondale, Illinois.

Schalock, R. L., & Karan, O. C. (1979). Relevant assessment: The interaction between evaluation and training. In G. T. Bellamy, G. O'Connor, & O. C. Karan (Eds.), *Vocational rehabilitation of severely handicapped persons: Contemporary service strategies.* Austin, TX: PRO-ED.

Tenth Institute on Rehabilitation Services. (1975). *Vocational evaluation project final report.* Washington, DC: Office of Human Development, Rehabilitation Services Administration.

U. S. Department of Labor. 1977. *Dictionary of Occupational Titles: Vol. 4.* Washington, DC: U.S. Government Printing Office.

U. S. Training and Employment Services. (1969). *Non-reading aptitude test battery.* Washington, DC: U.S. Government Printing Office.

Wehman, P. (1981). *Competitive employment: New horizons for severely disabled individuals.* Baltimore: Paul H. Brookes.

Wolf, M. M. (1978). Social validity: The case for subjective measurement or how applied behavior analysis is finding its heart. *Journal of Applied Behavior Analysis, 11,* 203–214.

13

Assessment of Visually Handicapped Students

Toni Heinze

OBJECTIVES

After completing this chapter the teacher should be able to:

1. Provide examples of the heterogeneity of visually handicapped youngsters.
2. Describe some of the modifications that are made to tests and testing procedures when the visually handicapped student is involved and then discuss possible results of such modifications.
3. Outline areas in which assessment is especially important to the visually handicapped student and provide examples of evaluative procedures for each.
4. Discuss several general guidelines to consider when assessing the visually handicapped youngster.
5. Discuss the role of functional vision in the assessment process.

Definitions

The term *visually handicapped* refers to a relatively small group of individuals with a wide range of characteristics. This range of characteristics is evident in the variety and degree of the visual impairment itself. Few visually handicapped youngsters are actually totally blind. Rather, the majority of them have some remaining useful vision. This remaining vision can vary greatly as to the types of things the youngster can or cannot see, and it can change over time and under different conditions. Some examples are:

1. Central loss—what the child looks at directly is affected (blurred, distorted, color changes, etc.); affects reading, eye-hand coordination, writing, picking up fine details; magnification is often helpful; positioning and/or eccentric viewing techniques often help because information is received by a more efficient part of the retina.
2. Peripheral loss—child can see what he or she looks directly at, but information to the side, top, and bottom is affected (tunnel vision); affects safety and mobility, playground and team activities, continuity of reading, finding place on board and in books, gathering incidental information.
3. Total field loss—entire field may be blurred or contain distortions; child may not see details, may seem unaware of much information, may need to get very close to pictures or print; effects vary depending on the severity of the condition; lighting may be very important, aids may be helpful, familiarity training may also be helpful.

The evaluator will want to consider what kind of visual impairment the student has and its degree of severity so as to better know its role in the learning and assessment process.

In recent years, there has been an emphasis on an educational definition of the visually handicapped. Barraga (1976, p. 16) provides a fairly comprehensive educational definition: "a visually handicapped child is one whose visual impairment interferes with his optimal learning and achievement, unless adaptations are made in the methods of presenting learning experiences, the nature of the materials used, and/or in the learning environment." This type of definition has two advantages: (1) it does not use rigid numbers (e.g., 20/200) as criteria, and (2) it requires that the child's functioning be evaluated on a wide range of tasks, within a wide range of environments, in order to arrive at such a classification. Such an educational definition would include both low-vision children who have some useful remaining vision and blind children who must learn through their other senses (Orlansky & Rhyne, 1981).

CASE STUDY

Part I

Name: Tony
Date of Birth: March 5, 1971
Date of Evaluation: February 5,
    1981

Age: 9 years, 11 months
Grade: 4

Background and Referral

Tony is a 9-year-old boy attending fourth grade in a public day school. He was referred for testing and observation to provide information relative to receiving special education services and to provide assistance to his current classroom teachers.

Tony wears glasses which, according to the ocular report, correct his vision to 20/200. Tony's ocular condition is macular degeneration, a progressive condition resulting in a central loss. No definite time frame regarding future degree of vision loss can be forecasted. While Tony is eligible for vision services, no vision teacher has been available in the school district; however, the school district plans to begin an itinerant vision program during the following fall.

During the previous fall semester, Tony's teachers and mother noted a change in his general performance, school work, handwriting, and attitude. Tony's mother felt that Tony's vision was deteriorating, while his teachers were more aware of his difficulties in school work. According to Tony's mother, a recent ophthalmological exam had shown no measurable visual change, but the doctor had reminded her that Tony's eye condition was progressive and that changes could take place unpredictably in the future. According to his teachers, difficulties in schoolwork and handwriting noted during the fall seemed to be slowly improving during the last couple of months prior to the evaluator's visit.

Past Testing

Previous test results from the *Wechsler Intelligence Scale for Children—Revised/* Verbal showed normal intelligence with the only area of difficulty being immediate recall for specific sequence. Performance tasks, although not scored, demonstrated difficulty in noting details and spatial organization.

Screening

In most cases, teachers themselves are not responsible for screening procedures to detect visual impairments in children. However, the classroom teacher may often be the one who notices that a child is having difficulty seeing in the classroom or on the playground. Therefore, it is appropriate to outline here the basic steps in determining the presence of a visual problem and the teacher's role in these steps.

First, the classroom teacher observes behaviors that may suggest that the child cannot see normally. Some of these behaviors are listed in Table 13.1. While the presence of some of these behaviors does not always mean the child actually has a visual problem, it does warrant at least careful observation and referral for screening (Rotatori & Kapperman, 1980).

Second, a formal screening procedure is carried out, usually by a school nurse or by a group of trained volunteers. Here screeners use instruments and activities that provide gross information about the child's near acuity, distant acuity, muscle balance, color vision, depth perception, and possibly width of field. Instruments that are used (sometimes in combination) include the Titmus Vision Screener, the Keystone Telebinocular, the Snellen Chart (distant acuity), picture or reading cards (near acuity), the Worth Four Dot (muscle balance), the Stereo Fly (stereopsis) and the Ishihara Plates (color vision). If the child fails this screening, he or she may be retested. If the child fails again, referral for a thorough ocular examination is made.

Third, an ophthalmologist or optometrist can determine refractive errors and prescribe glasses, contacts, or low vision aids. If a condition other than refractive errors is involved, an ophthalmologist, who has a medical degree, is the appropriate choice. The ophthalmologist can prescribe glasses, contact lenses, and aids and can also prescribe drugs and perform surgery.

Areas Requiring Assessment

Level of Functioning

One of the first areas to assess is that of visual functioning. Here the evaluator attempts to determine (1) the child's present level of visual efficiency; (2) the variables that influence this efficiency; and (3) the types of visual skills that need attention (Longo, Rotatori, Heinze & Kapperman, 1982). Visual functioning should be examined early in the assessment process so that the evaluator can use this information in selecting appropriate tests, materials, and environmental conditions for assessment in other areas (Warren, 1981).

The type and scope of information about the child's visual functioning is typically gathered through a variety of sources. These sources include (1) the ophthalmological report (ocular), which outlines the severity, history, stability, prescription, low vision aids, and sometimes information regarding physical requirements necessitated by the visual condition; (2) the low vision clinic, which provides acuity measures, some functional applications to daily tasks, environmental conditions that may be influential, and prescribed low

TABLE 13.1 Observable Behavior That May Indicate a Visual Problem[a]

1. One eye turns out either continuously or intermittently
2. Eyelids are red and/or swollen
3. Eyes tear excessively
4. Eyelids are encrusted
5. Styes appear frequently on eyelids
6. Child complains of seeing double while engaged in near or distant vision tasks
7. Child complains of headaches, especially in forehead or temples
8. Child complains of burning or itching of eyes after close visual tasks
9. Child complains of nausea or dizziness after close visual tasks
10. Child complains of blurring of print after reading for short periods
11. Child's head turns while reading across page
12. Child loses place on page easily while reading
13. Child requires use of finger or marker while reading
14. Child displays short attention span while reading or copying
15. Child omits words while reading
16. Child rereads or skips lines unknowingly
17. Child's comprehension decreases as reading continues
18. Child mispronounces similar words as reading continues
19. Child repeats letters within words
20. Child has difficulty with printing and/or handwriting
21. Child orients drawings poorly on a page
22. Child misaligns digits in columns of numbers
23. Child squints, closes, or covers one eye while engaged in close visual tasks
24. Child positions head eccentrically while engaged in close visual tasks
25. Child shows gross postural deviations while engaged in visual tasks
26. Child blinks excessively while engaged in close visual tasks
27. Child brings materials extremely close to face while working
28. Child rubs eyes excessively during or after periods of close visual tasks
29. Child attempts to avoid near-centered tasks
30. Child makes errors in copying from blackboard
31. Child squints or otherwise shows difficulty viewing item on the blackboard, bulletin board, etc., unless he or she moves closer
32. Child "misses" during eye-hand coordination activities
33. Child bumps into obstacles on the floor, door jambs, table corners, etc.
34. Child has difficulty keeping track of his or her role in team games
35. Child seems unaware of materials to be used unless they are located in a particular place
36. Child seems to miss much incidental information (signs, social gestures, etc.)

[a]Adapted from Kapperman (1979)

vision aids and training tips for their use; (3) observational and historical information from parents and other teachers; and (4) the functional vision assessment, which examines the youngster's use of remaining vision in classroom, play, social, daily living, and mobility tasks. The following are some of the techniques that the teacher of visually handicapped students may employ to collect such data.

Barraga's *Visual Efficiency Scale* (1970) was designed as a simple scale for teachers of visually impaired students (especially those in primary grades) to assist them in evaluating several visual skills such as size, shape, and letter discrimination, closure, attention to detail, and differences in position in space. The student responds by marking or somehow identifying his or her choice from among a group of stimuli. After a number of years, feedback from the field has led to the development of a more comprehensive evaluative tool, the *Program to Develop Efficiency in Visual Functioning* (Barraga, 1980) as shown in Figure 13.1. The program consists of two parts: the diagnostic assessment procedure and the design for instruction. The diagnostic assessment procedure includes reaction to light, tracking skills, directing body movements to visual stimuli, matching on various attributes, manipulation of objects to reproduce a spatial setup, reproduction of block designs, matching pictures with outlines, matching words with pictures, matching letters in various type styles and sizes, and noting inner detail. The training kit for the program includes numerous sequential lessons in the areas tapped by the assessment and also some of the materials required for teaching these lessons. A source book is also included to provide the teacher with philosophical and practical suggestions as well as many resources for teaching materials. One of the limitations of this assessment/training program is its occasional shortage of functional items. Therefore, the *Program to Develop Efficiency in Visual Functioning* is best used in conjunction with careful observation of the visually impaired child's daily visual-motor behaviors with a variety of functional tasks and in everyday settings. These behaviors should include noting changes in visual efficiency under different environmental conditions, a greater sampling of the child's eye-body coordination, the use of a systematic search pattern for locating visual information, and the identification and use of environmental landmarks and other visual clues (Yarnell & Carlton, 1981).

Another instrument, the *Visual Functioning Assessment Tool* (Costello, Pinkney, & Scheffers, 1980) was developed by a group of professionals serving low vision students in California. It was intended to be used by vision teachers, orientation and mobility specialists, or eye specialists and is appropriate for youngsters from preschool through most grades if age-appropriate materials are used. The following areas are included in the assessment: basic ocular appearances and reflexes, attention to light and environment, tracking/

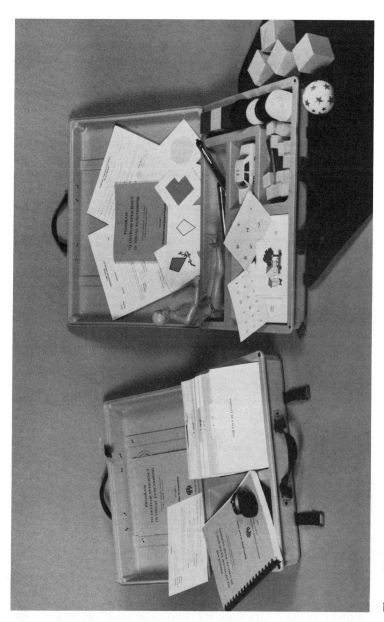

Figure 13.1 Program to Develop Efficiency in Visual Functioning (Barraga, 1980).

scanning, visual field, depth perception, eye-hand and eye-foot co-ordination, visual imitation and memory, and visual discrimination for color, size, shape, outline, and category. Detailed administrative and recording formats are provided. The assessment makes use of a task analysis approach and provides some practical implication of students' responses. It is intended as part of a battery of techniques that can provide information about a youngster's basic visual and visual perceptual skills.

It is important that the vision teacher combine a variety of visual functioning scales with a collection of informal observational information. The child's participation in daily tasks and use of materials provide many relevant opportunities to gather such observational information. For example, the teacher working with grade school children will want to check on the youngster's ability to handle the following: textbooks and supplementary materials with different type styles and sizes, page contrast, and figure-ground variations, board-work (locating information, reading, copying), legibility of hand-writing, and use of low vision aids.

Additionally, the teacher would want to assess the child's visual functioning in the following mobility and daily living skills: gathering information from social gestures, functioning under different lighting and weather conditions, and locating landmarks, obstacles, surface changes, and signs. When data from a variety of visual efficiency scales, checklists, and informal observations have been collected, the evaluator can then (1) outline an appropriate training program to assist the youngster in increasing his or her flexibility in getting and using visual information; (2) aid in selecting an appropriate battery of assessment tools in a variety of other developmental, academic, or special skills areas; and (3) communicate to the child's classroom teachers and parents about the child's level of visual functioning and their joint roles in improving his or her visual skills.

Achievement

A variety of general achievement tests (e.g., *Stanford Achievement Tests, Iowa Tests of Basic Skills, Cooperative Sequential Tests of Educational Progress*) are used with visually handicapped students since they have been made available in large print and braille. The *Stanford Achievement Test*, in addition to being available in large print and braille, is the only group achievement test that included visually handicapped students in its standardization procedures (Morris, 1974). Therefore, despite its lengthy administration, it might well be the most appropriate choice of the group achievement tests available. For purposes of program planning, however, more analytical information is needed.

The *KeyMath Diagnostic Arithmetic Test* (Connolly, Nachtman, & Pritchett, 1976) has several characteristics that make it appropriate for a large number of low-vision students: (1) an easel kit presenting many stimuli in a vertical manner, often a more efficient angle for low-vision readers; (2) large bold type; and (3) relatively simple pictures and diagrams having little detail, bold color, and high contrast. A recent adaptation of the KeyMath by the American Printing House for the Blind (1981) offers the evaluator an opportunity to use this test with blind children as well. The adapted Braille Edition provides the same items as are on the original KeyMath but uses (1) raised line drawings for tactual examination, (2) simpler representations for some of the pictures, and (3) braille rather than print for items that the student would read along with the evaluator. Computation problems are also presented in braille. The Braille Edition is coded so that the score sheets and profiles used with the original KeyMath can easily be used with the adapted version. The standardization population of the original KeyMath did not include visually impaired children, so strict use of the norms are of questionable value. However, the greatest strength of this test is its criterion-referenced scope of tasks as well as profile of strengths and weaknesses, which provides useful information about several important math skills and concepts.

Since braille reading is a major avenue of communication for blind students, teachers of the visually handicapped are interested in techniques for predicting a child's potential. One test that attempts to do this is the *Roughness Discrimination Test* (RDT; Nolan & Morris, 1965). The test consists of a series of cards, each of which has four squares of sandpaper. Three of the squares are an identical grade of coarseness, while the fourth is different. The child is asked to tactually examine all four squares and determine which square is different. Some items are grossly different while others require a much finer discrimination ability. This ability to discriminate differences in texture grade is then interpreted as an indicator of potential tactual ability to read braille. The test's authors found that the RDT accurately predicted whether a child would be in the upper or lower half of his or her reading group 70% of the time with reading errors as the criterion, and 75% of the time when reading speed was the criterion. Predictability was increased somewhat when RDT performance and IQ were used as joint indicators of success.

Orientation and Mobility Skills

Orientation and mobility skills are considered "survival" skills for the visually handicapped youngster. Orientation refers to being able to figure out where one is in one's environment using a variety of sensory, environmental, and organizational clues. Mobility refers to being able to travel from one place to another efficiently and safely. Skills in this area critically affect self-concept, opportunities for having a wide range of experiences and social contacts, one's control over the environment, and eventually the ability to live independently. Important components in this area include body image, basic positional and environmental concepts, motor skills, posture and gait, sensory training, self-familiarization techniques, judgment of time and distance, movement and exploration, search systems, sighted guide techniques, protective skills, cane techniques, use of public transportation, and possible use of low vision aids or electronic aids (Lord, 1969).

An area of great importance in orientation and mobility and yet one with which a number of young blind children have difficulty is that of body image. Since the body is our first and most basic reference system, it is a very important area to assess early. *The Body Image of Blind Children* (BIBC; Cratty & Sams, 1968) is an informal tool for evaluating a child's familiarity with body parts, body planes, and left-right discrimination on one's own body as well as another's body. On the BIBC the child is asked to move his or her own body in a variety of ways in order to respond to specific tasks as well as determine specific movements made by another person with whom the child is in contact. The test is made up of five sections. Section 1 (Body Planes) asks the child to touch the top of his or her head, to move so that one side is touching the wall, or to place a box so that it touches his or her back. Section 2 (Body Parts) directs the child to touch his or her leg, ear, thigh, and other parts ranging from simple to more advanced. In Section 3 (Body Movements), concepts such as forward, backward, to the side, toward the examiner, high in the air, and so on are used to direct the child's movements. Section 4 (Laterality) asks the child to touch his or her right knee, hold the box with the right hand, or to use both left and right simultaneously as in "with your left hand touch your right ear." Section 5 (Directionality) examines left-right discrimination on other people or objects with tasks like "tap my [evaluator's] right shoulder," "touch the right side of the box," or asking the child to determine the direction of the evaluator's movements as he or she faces the child. The recording form groups items according to the above areas but requires only a pass-fail grading system. Therefore, the evaluator must be careful to observe the types of errors or confusions the child has and record these for more specific information. While the test covers a range of types of items, not just body parts, it also invites some confusion as to several concepts that are evaluated simultaneously (body part, direction, type of movement). Therefore, if the child has difficulty with such an item, the evaluator may not be sure which concept is the problem unless he or she breaks down the task (Hill, 1980). Also, in some cases, a task at an earlier level requires a skill not evaluated until a later level, causing some question as to sequencing. Validity and reliability information is inconclusive since complete standardization and statistical data was only available for a fraction of the total subjects in the original study. The accompanying manual discusses implications for programming from the test results.

The *Hill Test of Selected Positional Concepts* (Hill, 1980) was designed to examine specific positional or spatial concepts in visually impaired children. These concepts are evaluated by performance tasks that ask the child (1) to identify positional relationships of body parts ("touch the bottom of your foot"); (2) to demonstrate positional concepts by moving various body parts in relationship to another ("put feet above head"); (3) to demonstrate positional concepts by moving the body in relationship to objects ("put the chair so it is to your left"); and (4) to form object-to-object relationships ("put the cup on top of the block"). Many blind and low-vision children have difficulty with concepts that describe relations between objects in space. These concepts are very important organizers of our world. Usually when a youngster hears "in the box" or "under the table," he or she also sees some action or objects that show that particular relationship. This information is available from a wide range of distances and directions and is reinforced through incidental learning. To the blind or severely visually handicapped child, however, this information is only available if he or she is actually involved in the handling or placement of body parts and/or objects. Therefore, the child may be slower to develop a functional understanding of such spatial concepts. On Hill's test the child demonstrates an understanding of these concepts by manipulating his or her own body and/or a selected number of concrete objects as directed. The evaluator rates the student's response according to described criteria for each item. Norms have been developed on several hundred visually handicapped children, including braille and print readers from residential and day school programs. Content validity on Hill's test was determined by having a group of professionals known for their expertise in the field of concept development sort the items according to appropriate constructs. The professionals matched items on Hill's test between 94% and 100% of the time. Reliability coefficients for the national field testing were .95 and .97 for the total test, with slightly lower reliability for the individual parts of the test.

The *Peabody Mobility Kit* (Harley, Marble, & Wood, 1981) was designed as a program for the assessment and training of basic mobility skills in the visually handicapped youngster who may have mild to moderate additional handicaps. It consists of two versions: one for low-vision students and one for blind students. Each version includes an assessment scale and training booklet in the areas of motor, mobility, concept, and sensory skills. While the program provides clear descriptions of the activities involved, there remain several limitations. In some cases, especially in the area of sensory skills, the types of abilities sampled are limited and often not very functional, particularly for the multihandicapped youngster. The *Peabody Mobility Kit* could best be used by the teacher/evaluator as part of an overall assessment of basic mobility-related skills, with the realization that additional functional problem-solving situations involving more active interaction with the environment will also be necessary.

CASE STUDY

Part II

Present Testing

On two visits, the evaluator observed Tony in his fourth grade class and in various other environments, talked with his teachers, and administered several instruments.

Visual Functioning/Formal

Tony's performance on Barraga's *Diagnostic Assessment* showed satisfactory visual skills in most areas examined. His errors lay in the areas of spatial discrimination and perspective, part-whole relationships, and failure to note fine detail.

Visual Functioning/Informal

The evaluator took reading samples from a variety of text and supplementary materials. Tony had little difficulty with most type styles and sizes typical of fourth- and fifth-grade reading materials. He did, however, have difficulty with light print, some italics, and with pages having distracting backgrounds to the print (figure-ground). Perception of pictures depended greatly on degree of contrast and amount of detail and clutter. Further observation indicated that Tony operates at about 6 inches from most reading materials and views these materials from a variety of positions to compensate for his central visual loss. Tony is able to see board work if allowed to go up and examine it closely, provided there is no glare on the board; however, he has difficulty with copying from and reorienting himself to board work. He often missed punctuation marks in his English writing lessons and decimal points and other small notations in arithmetic. Tony was able to get information from several type styles and sizes, but appeared to work most efficiently from bold 14- to 16-point type. He had most difficulty with books utilizing small charts, diagrams, and map keys. Very lightly-inked worksheets also presented a problem. He presently uses no low vision aids; however, when he was offered a magnifying aid by the evaluator for several tasks, he seemed interested in the additional details he could pick up.

Academic Achievement

Tony's grade equivalents on the *Woodcock Reading Mastery Tests* included:

Subtest	Easy	Instructional	Failure
Letter Identification	3.1	3.8	4.8
Word Identification	2.4	2.7	3.0
Word Attack	1.9	2.5	2.0
Word Comprehension	2.3	2.9	3.9
Passage Comprehension	2.4	2.8	3.5
Total Reading	2.7	3.0	3.6

Considering Tony's placement of 4.6, he is underachieving by approximately 1.5 grades. While Tony's score on Letter Identification was several months below grade level, all other skills range from 1.5 to 2.0 grades below his present grade placement. Word attack and identification skills seem to present the greatest difficulty.

On the *KeyMath Diagnostic Arithmetic Test*, Tony obtained the following grade equivalents:

Numeration	3.1	Mental Computation	0.9
Fractions	3.7	Numerical Reasoning	3.9
Geometry/Symbols	3.3	Word Problems	3.5
Addition	3.7	Missing Elements	4.8
Subtraction	3.7	Money	5.2
Multiplication	5.9	Measurement	3.9
Division	5.3	Time	4.5

Total Grade Score   4.0

Again, considering Tony's present grade placement of 4.6, his overall performance in arithmetic is about one half grade below expectation. Tony's intratest scores show wide variation, with the majority of his arithmetic skills falling in the first and second halves of third grade. His poorest performance was on the subtest Mental Computation, where he achieved at a pre-first-grade level. In contrast, his best score was on the subtest Multiplication, on which he obtained a grade score of 5.9. Tony answered very quickly, appearing not to think through the entire problem in many cases. On addition and subtraction, Tony failed to write in several decimals, which his visual difficulty and lack of expectancy skills may have caused him to miss in the original problem.

Mobility/Informal

The evaluator observed Tony in a variety of mobility situations in his fourth-grade classroom, several other classrooms, and on the playground. She also had Tony travel to various areas of the school building and accompany her on a short route to a neighborhood store. The following observations were made: (1) Tony picked out a variety of useful visual landmarks in both familiar and unfamiliar areas; (2) he seemed more aware of incidental information in familiar areas since he knew where things might be going on and to check them out; (3) he avoided obstacles well, unless small and directly in front of him, and moved confidently except in unfamiliar areas that were dimly lit; (4) he maintained good orientation and seemed aware of auditory information as he traveled; (5) his posture and gait were normal; (6) he had difficulty when provided several verbal directions in a sequence; and (7) in his own classroom he located areas and materials easily, but in other unfamiliar classrooms he lacked a systematic search pattern for scanning or close examination.

Recommendations

Based on tests administered and observations made, the following recommendations seem appropriate:

1. Tony would benefit from the special services provided by an itinerant vision teacher, especially in the areas of visual efficiency skills and listening skills. Visual skills would include expecting and noticing details, position in space and part-whole relationships, and developing a systematic search pattern to decrease his chances of missing important information. Reinforcement for this training can be carried out in the regular classroom. Possible benefits of a magnifying aid and training in its use should be explored. Large print materials in areas that involve small detailed diagrams, maps, tables, or special symbols could be used as reference books only as Tony needs them. Listening skills, especially those involving comprehension and memory for sequence, should be emphasized. In mobility Tony can improve his scanning and search techniques in the environment. He should also benefit from carrying out tasks and locating goals based upon a series of sequential directions. Techniques of eccentric viewing in some close work situations could be helpful. Typing skills should be considered as an alternative to sometimes inefficient handwriting and the instability of Tony's visual condition.

2. Tony would benefit from individual assistance in the areas of reading and math. Emphasis on word attack skills, use of context clues, and careful checking of comprehension would seem appropriate. In math, problem-solving situations that involve mental computation can be stressed. These might take the form of oral word problems, which would also assist in listening for comprehension and auditory sequential memory. Tony's attention should be directed toward appropriate expecting of operational signs, decimals, and other important symbols.

3. Some suggestions for the classroom teacher include calling Tony's attention to special marks that he is not now noticing (e.g., punctuation and decimals); providing Tony with a model for cursive writing to assist him in monitoring his own handwriting; assessing Tony's knowledge through several well-chosen problems rather than a large number of redundant problems; and flexibility of time limits for reading and completing assignments. The additional effort required for visual tasks may also necessitate presenting such tasks in short periods. When board work is involved, Tony should be able to move as close as necessary; copies of problems to be copied from the board might be given to Tony at his desk. Careful verbalization of problems and other pertinent information and examples that are being written on the board will also be very helpful. It is suggested that the teacher use clear, well-constructed mimeographed sheets and supplementary materials that eliminate unnecessary detail. An adjustable reading stand should be available to Tony to allow him to be as close as necessary to his materials without undue strain on neck and shoulder muscles. Tony should be provided the opportunity to use a magnifying aid in the classroom for reading supplementary and reference materials that may be in small print, as well as for spot-checking or confirming special symbols, charts, and maps. The vision teacher, once available, can assist the classroom teacher in these areas.

4. Teachers working with Tony should be alert to functional changes in his visual skills, since his is a progressive condition that may warrant adjustments in his educational needs.

Assessment of the Very Young

One approach for examining the visual functioning of visually handicapped infants and multihandicapped children is outlined by Langley
and DuBose (1976). Their approach involves an informal checklist that
assesses basic visual reflexes and responses (awareness and attention
to light, range of field and field preference, muscle imbalance, ability
to track light and objects, ability to shift visual attention). Early
matching, eye-hand coordination, imitating, attention to pictures, and
object permanence tasks are also included. A similar approach is
advocated by Jose, Smith, and Shane (1980). They also provide visual
stimulation activities for youngsters who are inconsistent in even their
most basic visual responses. Efron and Dubose (1975) present still
another informal approach to assessment of visual functioning in
multihandicapped youngsters in their *Vision Guide for Teachers of
Deaf-Blind Children*. The *Functional Vision Inventory for the Multiply
and Severely Handicapped* from the Peabody Model Vision Program
(Langley, 1980) provides still another, if more structured, approach to
evaluating basic visual functioning. Areas assessed include basic
reflexes, fixation, attention, field preference, tracking skills, reaching
and grasping, avoiding obstacles, eye-hand coordination, and early
perceptual skills. A very detailed administration and recording format
is provided, as are suggested training activities based on results from
the assessment (Langley, 1979). Three additional tools that provide
less comprehensive information but may serve as effective screeners
include (1) the *New York Flashcard Vision Test* (Faye, 1968), (2) the
HOTV matching format for nonreaders, and (3) the Miniature Toys
Test and Rolling Balls Test from the *Stycar Vision Tests* (Langley &
DuBose, 1976). When assessing the infant's or multihandicapped
child's use of remaining vision, special attention must be paid to
distant vision; gross eye-body coordination; reactions to people,
movement, and obstacles; and ability to note environmental changes
(Chase, 1975).

Assessment/Intervention Batteries

One of the more structured tools is the *Guide: Early Childhood
Integrated Education System for the Handicapped* (Croft & Robinson,
1980). This system includes both assessment and curriculum programming. This assessment provides evaluator and parent, or other
caregiver, the opportunity to examine the child's functioning level in
motor, intellectual, language, self-help, and social-personal areas. A
fairly detailed profile results with direct reference to the programming
guidelines provided. The system is behaviorally oriented and provides

specific formats for recorded data. The *Guide* system was developed from an earlier project, *Project Vision Up* (Croft & Robinson, 1976), which was designed primarily for young visually handicapped children from infancy to 6 years of age. Another fairly structured program is the *Oregon Project for Visually Impaired and Blind Preschool Children* (Brown, Simmons, & Methvin, 1978). It is a program involving both assessment and programming guidelines. The Skills Inventory covers self-help, motor, language, cognitive, and socialization areas and uses a checklist format. The role of parents in a cooperative partnership is stressed. In some cases, items on the checklist are not quite as specifically described as on the *Guide* system. Results from the Skills Inventory can be directly related to teaching activities provided. Lastly, recommendations for supportive data via selected formal tools and content reading are provided.

The *Social Maturity Scale for Blind Preschool Children* (Maxfield & Bucholz, 1958), has been used with a number of visually handicapped youngsters in the assessment of early adaptive/social skills. The scale was developed from the *Vineland Social Maturity Scale* (Doll, 1947); however, differences include (1) elimination of items specifically requiring vision; (2) elimination of the self-direction category; and (3) age scales extending only through 5 years of age. As with the Vineland, the Maxfield-Bucholz scale depends on someone who knows the child and on careful observational skills to complete it.

The *Callier-Azuza Scale* (Stillman, 1975) was developed especially for deaf-blind children and employs a checklist format. It covers such developmental areas as motor, perception, daily living, language, and socialization. The Callier-Azuza has been used with a variety of multihandicapped children with varying degrees of success. Examples of tasks that will demonstrate specified skills are provided for some items, but much judgment is still required of the evaluator. The recording format of the scale is not as specific as some of the other tools mentioned above, and the evaluator must provide his or her own teaching strategies. The evaluator is encouraged to assess the desired skills through observation in functional settings rather than by setting up artificial activities (Edris, Rotatori, Kapperman, & Heinze, 1983).

A program designed especially for visually impaired multihandicapped youngsters that includes assessment as one of its components is the *Peabody Model Vision Project* (Langley, 1980). The program contains two assessment tools: one for visual functioning and another for other developmental areas including prevocational skills. The visual functioning component provides guidelines for choosing appropriate evaluative approaches. This is accomplished through (1) sample cases with recommended tools; (2) a compilation of formal tools that may be appropriately used for specific skills; (3) suggested informal tasks that may also tap specific skills; (4) questions for gathering pertinent observational data; and (5) teaching activities. This component of the *Peabody Model Vision Project* can serve as a useful resource to the evaluator by increasing awareness of his or her own choices when selecting evaluative measures for multihandicapped children.

Summary

All children vary in their experiences, abilities, and limitations. The visually handicapped youngster varies in these regards as well in type and severity of visual loss and its effect on learning style, experiences, and developing concepts and skills. Assessment of the visually handicapped child must consider a wide range of variables, and information must be interpreted on the basis of (1) relevance to the child's educational and life needs and (2) specific strengths and problem areas that will assist in program planning. Additionally, the conditions of assessment must represent realistic classroom/play/ work settings to ensure the functional application of the test results. When assessing visual functioning, the evaluator must consider the child's abilities under both ideal conditions (e.g., best lighting, contrast, figure-ground, size, distance) and a variety of more realistic conditions in order to modify or control the environment and to set goals that can eventually increase the child's flexibility for the types of environments in which he or she can function. In other areas, attention to testing conditions can help to discriminate between the child's actual ability and the effects of the visual impairment on performance. Some of the variables to be considered are (1) lighting and illumination, (2) background contrast, (3) orientation to the task, spatial layout, and relevant materials, (4) choices for responding, and (5) applicability of testing environment to realistic environments.

Frequently it is necessary for the evaluator to adapt assessment instruments so that the student can handle the test items. Adaptations that are helpful include (1) changing the manner of administering the test; (2) changing the materials or equipment used in the test; and (3) changing the norms if comparisons are to be made. Changing or deleting test items usually involves leaving out items requiring vision (pictures, printed symbols, visual memory) or modifying the task by using concrete objects, tactual symbols, or raised line drawings. In some cases, the task itself may be changed to a "comparable" task assessing the same skill or concept. In some instances, changing the size of a stimulus may not appreciably change the skill being evaluated. On the other hand, substituting a related task or using concrete models instead of more abstract representations may actually be tapping a different skill or process. Changing the manner in which the test is administered can involve altering directions, extending time limits, and providing special orientation to the spatial layout and materials. Also, the way of presenting the task to the student may be modified (print and pictures enlarged, low vision aids used, questions brailled). Similarly, modifications may be made in the way the student responds to the task (orally, braille, recorded, use of coded tickets for multiple choice or yes/no questions).

The assessment process must be comprehensive and specific because of the nature of the student's deficit. However, if the above factors are incorporated, the assessment information should be reliable and valid. This ultimately leads to the correct implementation of an educational program that is educationally realistic.

Educational Suggestions for Visually Impaired Students

Visually impaired students tend to rely on the senses of hearing and touch to compensate for the lack of information received through the visual channel. Descriptive, verbal explanations are often inadequate for teaching practical skills to the visually impaired. Hands-on, touching experience with actual objects and procedures is vital if visually impaired students are to comprehend abstract terms and concepts. Also, it must be remembered that visually impaired students may have some residual visual ability, which they should be encouraged to use. The following suggestions are intended primarily to facilitate and capitalize on the senses of hearing, touch, and residual vision as aids to information processing in the instructional or assessment situation.

Before instruction or assessment procedures begin, teachers should consult with each visually impaired student about specific adaptive aids that will be helpful to him or her.

Teachers can arrange for a peer teaching approach that pairs visually impaired students with nondisabled students for completing classroom assignments.

Teachers should become familiar with aids such as the braille system, large-print materials, and optical reading aids. The teacher should encourage visually impaired students to use such aids, and make advance arrangements to provide those that are feasible in the instructional or assessment situation.

Adjustable lighting should be available in all work, study, or laboratory areas, allowing either increased or decreased light intensity depending upon the student's assessed need.

Teachers should prepare embossed or three-dimensional models and diagrams to explain concepts or procedures that visually impaired students cannot clearly understand by verbal communication.

Since virtually all specially aided reading takes more time than normal nondisabled reading, teachers should allow sufficient time for visually impaired students to complete assigned readings or tests.

The teacher's class presentation should emphasize auditory communication.

Teachers can emphasize physical handling of equipment and hands-on experience. Also, it is best to progress from concrete experience to theoretical concepts.

Teachers should ensure that each visually impaired student is individually oriented to the layout of the instructional and assessment rooms as well as materials or equipment to be used in them.

Any visual materials to be handed out in class should be given to visually impaired students well in advance, allowing them to become familiar with these materials ahead of time.

Visual materials, especially those that may be legible to partially sighted students, should be simple in design and should not be cluttered with detail or elaborate background.

All visual materials used for instruction or assessment should be explained in detail by the teacher or tester as they are presented.

Adequate periods of visual rest should be allowed during instruction or testing those students likely to experience eye fatigue as they use residual visual abilities.

During group instruction or testing teachers should always address visually impaired students by name.

During instruction or testing the terms *right* and *left* should always refer to the student's right and left side, rather than the teacher's or tester's.

Teachers should consult with each visually impaired student to arrange to seat the student optimally in the classroom or testing room in regards to his or her unique condition.

As a rule, a partially sighted student will not wish to be seated so as to face into his or her own shadow.

Study Questions

1. Provide an example of (1) a test that is designed for sighted students and that is used, as is, with visually handicapped students; (2) a test that is designed for sighted students but has been adapted for visually handicapped students; and (3) a test that is specially designed for visually handicapped students.
2. Why is it so necessary to include performance tasks in the assessment of visually handicapped youngsters?

3. Why is it often recommended that the evaluator use clinical interpretations of test results rather than just normed scores?
4. Why is it recommended that the child's level of visual functioning be assessed early in the evaluative process?
5. What are three areas in which assessment would be pertinent for the visually handicapped child? Give an example of a test or assessment approach appropriate for each area.
6. Describe two assessment devices that are used with visually impaired preschoolers. What are the major advantages of these devices?
7. Discuss why blind and low-vision children have difficulty with concepts that describe relations between objects in space.

Suggested Readings

Convey, T. E. (1976). Standardized tests for visually handicapped children: A review of the research. *New Outlook for the Blind, 70,* 232–236.

Diebold, M., Curtis, W., & Dubose, R. (1978). Developmental scales versus observational measures for deaf-blind children. *Exceptional Children, 44,* 275–278.

Swallow, R. (1977). *Assessment for visually handicapped children and youth.* New York: American Foundation for the Blind.

VanderKolk, C. J. (1981). *Assessment and planning with the visually impaired.* Austin, TX: PRO-ED.

References

American Printing House for the Blind. (1981). *Catalog of educational and other aids.* Louisville, KY: American Printing House for the Blind.

Barraga, N. C. (1980). *Program to develop efficiency in visual functioning.* Louisville, KY: American Printing House for the Blind.

Barraga, N. C. (1970). *Teacher's guide for development of visual learning abilities and utilization of low vision.* Louisville, KY: American Printing House for the Blind.

Barraga, N. C. (1976). *Visual handicaps and learning.* Belmont, CA: Wadsworth.

Brown, D., Simmons, V., & Methvin, J. (1978). *The Oregon project for visually impaired and blind preschool children.* Medford, OR: Jackson County Education Service District.

Chase, J. (1975). Developmental assessment of handicapped infants and children: With special attention to the visually impaired. *The New Outlook for the Blind, 8,* 341–347.

Connolly, A. J., Nachtman, W., & Pritchett, E. M., 1976. *KeyMath Diagnostic Arithmetic Test.* Circle Pines, MN: American Guidance Service.

Costello, K., Pinkney, P., & Scheffers, W. (1980). *Visual functioning assessment tool.* Chicago: Stoelting Co.

Cratty, B., & Sams, T. (1968). *Body image of blind children.* New York: American Foundation for the Blind.

Croft, N., & Robinson, L. (1980). *GUIDE: Early childhood integrated education system for the handicapped.* Idaho Falls, ID: Worldwide Achievements Corporation.

Croft, N., & Robinson, L. (1976). *Project vision-up curriculum handbook.* Boise, ID: Educational Products Training Foundation.

Doll, E. A. (1947). *Vineland social maturity scale.* Minneapolis: American Guidance Service.

Edris, S., Rotatori, A. F., Kapperman, G., & Heinze, T. (1983). A survey of assessment devices administered to deaf-blind children. *ICEC Quarterly, 32,* 24–28.

Efron, M., & DuBose, B. (1975). *A vision guide for teachers of deaf-blind children.* Raleigh, NC: North Carolina State Department of Public Instruction.

Faye, E. E. (1968). A new visual acuity test for the partially-sighted non-readers. *Journal of Pediatric Opthalmology, 5,* 210–212.

Harley, R. K., Marble, J. B., & Wood, T. A. (1981). *Peabody Mobility Kit.* Chicago: Stoelting Co.

Hill, E. (1980). *Hill performance test of selected positional concepts.* Chicago: Stoelting Co.

Jose, R., Smith, A., & Shane, K. (1980). Evaluating and stimulating vision in the multiply handicapped. *Journal of Visual Impairment and Blindness, 1,* 2–8.

Kapperman, G. (1979). Assessment of the visually handicapped. In D. Sabatino & T. Miller (Eds.), *Describing learner characteristics of handicapped children and youth.* New York: Grune and Stratten.

Langley, M. B. (1980). *Functional Vision Inventory for the Multiply and Severely Handicapped/Model Vision Project.* Chicago: Stoelting Co.

Langley, M. (1979). Psychoeducational assessment of the multiply handicapped blind child: Issues and methods. *Education of the Visually Handicapped, 11,* 97–113.

Langley, B., & DuBose, R. (1976). Functional vision screening for severely handicapped children. *The New Outlook for the Blind, 8,* 346–350.

Longo, J. Rotatori, A. F., Heinze, T., & Kapperman, G. (1982). Technology as an aide in assessing visual acuity in severely and profoundly retarded children. *Education of the Visually Handicapped, 14,* 21–27.

Lord, F. E. (1969). Development of scales for the measurement of orientation and mobility skills of young blind children. *Exceptional Children, 36,* 2.

Maxfield, K. E., & Bucholz, S. (1958). *A social maturity scale for blind preschool children: A guide to its use.* New York: American Foundation for the Blind.

Morris, J. (1974). The 1973 Stanford achievement test series as adapted for use by the visually handicapped. *Education of the Visually Handicapped, 6,* 33–40.

Nolan, C. Y., & Morris, J. (1965). Development and validation of the roughness discrimination test. *International Journal for the Education of the Blind, 15,* 1–6.

Orlansky, M., & Rhyne, J. (1981). Special adaptations necessitated by visual impairments. In J. M. Kauffman & D. P. Hallahan (Eds.), *Handbook of special education.* Englewood Cliffs, NJ: Prentice-Hall.

Rotatori, A. F., & Kapperman, G. (1980). An instructional interaction observation system for use with low functioning visually impaired students. *Education of the Visually Handicapped, 12*, 47–52.

Stillman, R. (Ed.). (1975). *The Callier-Azuza Scale*. Dallas: Callier Center for Communication Disorders, University of Texas, Dallas.

Warren, D. (1981). Visual impairments. In J. M. Kauffman & D. P. Hallahan (Eds.), *Handbook of special education*. Englewood Cliffs, NJ: Prentice-Hall.

Yarnell, G., & Carlton, G. (1981). *Guidelines and manual of tests for educators interested in the assessment of handicapped children*. Austin, TX: International Research Institute.

14

Assessment of Hearing-Impaired Students

Shirin Antia

OBJECTIVES

After completing this chapter the teacher should be able to:

1. Describe the effect of language and communication difficulties on the assessment of hearing-impaired students.
2. Identify the areas in which assessment information is needed.
3. Identify assessment instruments that can be used with hearing-impaired students.
4. Describe some modifications that may need to be made when using standardized assessment tools with hearing-impaired students.
5. Describe the roles of the different professionals assessing the hearing-impaired student.

Nancy's parents described their child's birth as difficult. The pregnancy failed to progress, the fetal monitor indicated that the baby was experiencing distress, and an emergency C-section was performed. The doctors later told the parents that the umbilical cord had been wrapped around Nancy's neck and that she was probably deprived of oxygen for an undetermined length of time. Following the birth, Nancy's parents watched her early development very carefully for any possible signs of trouble. They were relieved when Nancy was able to sit at 6 months and could walk at 13 months. Her fine-motor skills appeared to be developing well, and the pediatrician felt that her development would be normal. Nancy continued to grow and develop with the only difficulty being in the speech area; she was somewhat difficult to understand, although she herself appeared to understand others around her. The parents felt this speech problem was temporary and would be something that would improve with age. Nancy began a preschool class when she was 4 years old, and the teacher felt that someone should look into Nancy's poor articulation.

The parents contacted a psychologist who tested Nancy. He found her overall intelligence to be normal but found that her performance on a test of receptive vocabulary was significantly below her intellectual potential. The psychologist referred Nancy to an audiologist for a hearing assessment. Although the parents felt that Nancy could hear just fine, they agreed to the assessment. The audiologist found that Nancy had significant hearing loss (40–60%) in both ears, especially at high-frequently levels. Nancy was given hearing aides, and within a short period of time her speech gradually began improving.

The preceding scenario offers a good introduction to the topic of assessing the hearing impaired. While most of us take our hearing ability for granted, the impact of a hearing loss on one's overall functioning can be very dramatic. Clearly both the extent of a hearing loss and the time in development at which the loss occurs will influence its effect on the individual. The earlier that hearing loss can be detected, the less damaging the outcome. As the preceding case description illustrates, early detection may be difficult even when relatively extensive hearing loss is present.

This chapter describes the assessment of the hearing impaired student. The instruments discussed in this chapter were chosen because they have been commonly used successfully with hearing impaired students (Bess & McConnell, 1981; Moores, 1981). The list of instruments is not meant to be exhaustive, but merely a representative sample of available instruments.

Terms relating to hearing loss have been defined as follows by the Conference of Executives of American Schools for the Deaf (1975). *Hearing impairment* is a generic term indicating a hearing disability that may range in severity from mild to profound. It includes the subsets of deaf and hard of hearing. A *deaf* person is one whose hearing disability precludes the successful processing of linguistic information through audition, with or without a hearing aid. A *hard of hearing* person is one who, generally with the use of a hearing aid, has residual hearing sufficient to enable successful processing of linguistic information through audition.

The major handicap resulting from a hearing loss is that of acquiring the spoken language of the community and the subsequent difficulties in communication. The severity of language delay is dependent on the degree of hearing loss and the age of onset of the hearing loss. Children with prelingual hearing impairment who were deaf from birth or before 18 months of age are likely to have the most severe language delays.

Difficulties in Assessing the Hearing-Impaired Student

An assessment of the hearing-impaired student must take into account the communication and language difficulties resulting from the hearing loss. A teacher who uses a mode of communication that the child does not understand, or who cannot understand the mode used by the child, is likely to reach conclusions that are not valid. A verbal scale of intelligence may give a measure of the hearing-impaired student's language delay but is hardly likely to yield a valid overall IQ score. The following sections discuss the language and communication problems that need to be considered when assessing hearing-impaired students.

Mode of Communication

When an assessment requires communication between the teacher and the student, the mode of communication used must be one with which the student is most familiar. Levine (1974) found that, although a majority of the hearing-impaired students being tested used a combination of modes predominated by signs, 90% of the psychologists who tested these students were unable to communicate effectively using sign language in the testing situations. In some cases an interpreter may be used, although the presence of an interpreter may in itself interfere with the child's performance and test standardization. The teacher must also be aware that different sign systems exist; therefore, the student who is fluent in American Sign Language may not understand Signed English and vice versa.

Language Complexity

Even though the teacher and the hearing-impaired student use the same mode of communication, it cannot be assumed that all the communication problems have been solved. Because of the language delay, the vocabulary and syntax (language structure) used in a test may be too difficult for the hearing-impaired student. The student who is told to put pictures "in order" may fail the task because he or she does not understand the phrase "in order." In many standardized tests the directions are given in language that is too complex for the student to understand. Assessments that require verbal responses from a student (e.g., defining a word or responding verbally to a question) pose problems in both receptive and expressive language. The student may not understand the question because of his or her unfamiliarity with the vocabulary and the question form. The question may not be answered because of the student's problems in expressive language. Thus, most tests used with hearing-impaired students modify the vocabulary and syntax of the test directions and the language used within the test itself.

CASE STUDY

Part I

Name: John Brown   Age: 8 years, 3 months
Date of Birth: January 26, 1973   Grade: 3
Date of Evaluation: May 1, 1981

Background Information

John, a congenitally hearing-impaired child, was 8 years and 3 months old at the time of the assessment. His hearing impairment was caused by maternal rubella. He began wearing a hearing aid at 2 years of age. He attended a regular preschool for 6 months from January 7, 1977. He was admitted to the school for the deaf in August, 1977. John's communication skills and academic skills were evaluated to assess the appropriateness of his current educational placement. The options available were to continue attending the school for the deaf or attend a public school with a resource room program.

Past Test Results

Test	Date	Results
Wechsler Intelligence Scale for Children—Revised	1/79	Performance IQ: 106
Wide Range Achievement Test	6/79	Reading Grade Level: 2.7
Gates-MacGinitie Test of Reading Comprehension	6/79	Grade Level: 3.4

Peabody Picture Vocabulary Test	6/79 Mental Age: 5 years, 3 months
Test of Auditory Comprehension	7/80 Age Equivalent: 6 years, 10 months
of Language	(Test was given using total
	communication)

Auditory Assessment

An auditory assessment is done for two purposes. One purpose is to identify students who have a hearing loss and to specify the extent of the loss. The second purpose is to assess the ability of the hearing-impaired student to use his or her residual hearing. Identification of the student's loss and the extent of the loss is assessed by measuring the student's hearing sensitivity. The student's use of residual hearing is assessed by evaluating his or her ability to discriminate, identify, and comprehend speech and environmental sounds.

Auditory Sensitivity

When testing auditory sensitivity, the audiologist is interested in finding the threshold of the student's hearing ability by identifying the softest sounds that the individual can hear. This is done by a procedure known as pure tone audiometry. The student is required to respond to a series of tones presented at varying frequency (pitch) and intensity (loudness) levels. Frequency is measured in hertz (Hz), while intensity is measured in decibels (dB). The tones presented to the child vary in frequency from 250 Hz, which is a low-pitched sound, to 8,000 Hz, which is an extremely high-pitched sound. They vary in intensity from 0 dB, which can be heard by a normal ear, to 110 dB, which is generally the loudest sound the audiometer can produce. The audiologist systematically varies the intensity of the sounds at each frequency until the child's threshold level at that frequency is found. If a student's threshold level at 500 Hz is 45 dB, this means that the student cannot hear a sound presented at 500 Hz and 30 dB. At the frequency of 500 Hz the student cannot hear sounds softer than 45 dB.

The result of pure tone testing is a pure tone audiogram, which is a graph that charts the student's hearing sensitivity to pure tones. Figure 14.1 shows a pure tone audiogram of a student with normal hearing. It can be seen that the student responded at 0 dB at all the frequency levels shown on the audiogram. Figure 14.2 is the audiogram of a student with a mild hearing loss. At 500 Hz the tone has to be given at

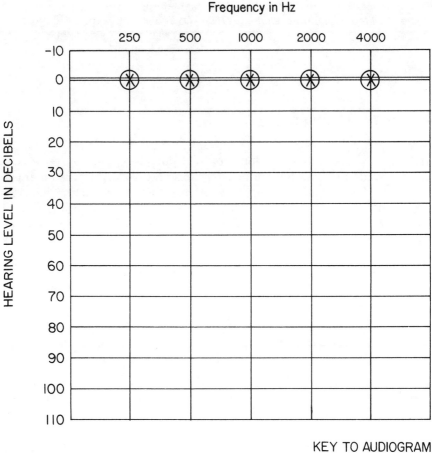

Figure 14.1. Audiogram of a student with normal hearing.

25 dB before this child can hear it. Tones that are softer than the intensity levels marked on the audiogram cannot be heard by this student. Figure 14.3 shows a student with a severe hearing loss. One can see that sounds have to be much louder than those in Figure 14.2 in order for the student to hear them.

The audiologist also needs to measure the student's sensitivity to speech sounds by obtaining a Speech Reception Threshold (SRT). The SRT is obtained by having the student listen to a standardized word list and noting the intensity level at which the child can repeat 50% of the words correctly (Newby, 1972). There may be some problems involved

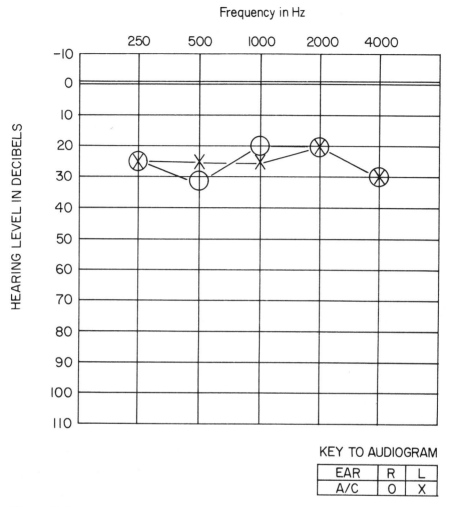

Figure 14.2. Audiogram of a student with mild hearing loss.

in obtaining an SRT with hearing-impaired students. If the words used are not in the student's receptive vocabulary, he or she may not be able to understand them and therefore not repeat them. If the student can repeat the words, his or her speech may not be intelligible enough for the audiologist to understand. Therefore, for hearing-impaired students the test may become one of receptive language ability or speech intelligibility rather than speech discrimination (Maxon, 1980). In these cases the tester may obtain a Speech Awareness Threshold (SAT). The SAT is the level at which the person can detect speech without necessarily being able to identify what is said.

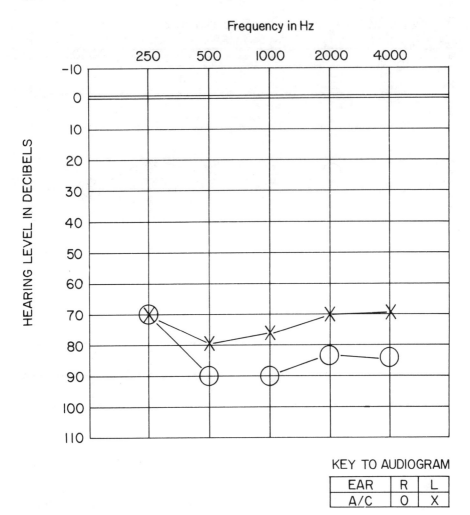

Figure 14.3. Audiogram of a student with a severe hearing loss.

Auditory Identification

An auditory identification task requires that the student name or label the stimulus in some way (Erber, 1979). Thus, the student may be required to say or write a word or point to a picture after having heard the word. The language and vocabulary used in the test must be familiar to the student (Matkin, 1980), and the mode of response (e.g., speech, writing, and picture identification) should not penalize the student.

An auditory identification test designed for hearing-impaired children is the test of *Word Intelligibility by Picture Identification* (Ross

& Lerman, 1970). The test consists of simple monosyllabic words that are judged to be within the receptive vocabulary of a 5-year-old hearing-impaired student. The student is required to choose the correct picture from a set of four possible pictures. The test has been found to discriminate between the auditory identification abilities of students with moderate and profound hearing losses. The response is a simple pointing response and should be well within the ability of most young students.

Cramer and Erber (1974) have devised a set of 10 bisyllabic words to evaluate auditory identification of hearing-impaired students. The words were chosen on the basis of their familiarity to the hearing-impaired children and contain a wide variety of speech sounds. Pictures representing the 10 words are displayed in front of the student, who is expected to identify the stimulus words by pointing to the correct picture.

Older hearing-impaired students or students with mild losses can be given the *Phonetically Balanced Kindergarten* (PB-K) word lists developed by Haskins (1949). The student is required to write or repeat the stimulus words. Writing or repeating words is a more different response, and care must be taken that spelling ability and speech intelligibility do not influence the results.

Although most auditory identification tasks use speech sounds as stimuli, it may also be valuable to obtain information on student's ability to identify environmental sounds (Matkin, 1980). The ability to identify environmental sounds may be necessary for a student to be able to function efficiently within his or her environment (Ling, 1976). Thus the child may need to identify the sound of a car horn, an ambulance siren, a doorbell, or a telephone. The teacher can tape such sounds and require the student to identify them by pointing to pictures depicting objects that make the sounds. Again, information obtained from such a test can be used when planning the student's auditory training program.

Auditory Comprehension

Auditory comprehension refers to the student's ability to understand the meaning of a speech stimulus and requires a knowledge of language (Erber, 1977). One of the few tests available to assess auditory comprehension in hearing-impaired children is the *Test of Auditory Comprehension* (TAC; Trammell, 1976). The TAC consists of 10 subtests arranged in hierarchical order of difficulty. The first 4 subtests are really tests of auditory discrimination and identification that require the student to discriminate between speech sounds (words, phrases), nonspeech sounds (laughing, crying), and environmental sounds, and to identify simple words. The remainder of the subtests assess the student's ability to recall two to four critical elements in the sentence (e.g., "Show me the *baby crying*," "Show me the *big table* and the *open book*"), to sequence events in a short story presented auditorily, and to recall details about a short story presented auditorily. The final subtest assesses the student's ability to comprehend auditorily presented material in a background of noise. The TAC has separate norms for mildly hearing impaired, severely hearing impaired, and normal hearing children. Since the subtests are in increasing order of difficulty, the TAC can also be used as a criterion-referenced test. The TAC is based on a program of auditory training, namely the Auditory Skills Curriculum (Trammell, 1976), and can be used to assess the child's progress through this program.

Tests of Speech Intelligibility

Speech intelligibility is a global measure of speech and does not give diagnostic information for remediation purposes. One way to measure speech intelligibility is to have the listener rate the student's speech production on a rating scale. A widely used rating scale was developed at the National Technical Institute for the Deaf (Jenson, 1975). The student's speech is taped and rated on the following 5-point rating scale:

1. Speech cannot be understood.
2. Speech is difficult to understand; only isolated words and phrases are intelligible.
3. Speech is difficult to understand; only the gist of content can be understood.
4. Speech is intelligible with the exception of a few words or phrases.
5. Speech is completely intelligible.

The rating scale can be used for any kind of speech sample obtained from the student. The speech sample may be obtained by having the student read a passage aloud, engage in a conversation with another person, or tell a story from pictures.

Another method of judging speech intelligibility is to have the listener write down the words that he or she understood from the speech sample. This format is used in the *Clark School Speech Intelligibility Test* (Magner, 1972). The test consists of 600 sentences divided into sets of 6 sentences. Each sentence consists of 10 syllables. The sentences contain only words judged to be in the vocabulary of a third-grade hearing-impaired student. The student is asked to read the sentences aloud. The teacher tapes the speech, and speech intelligibility is judged by a listener, who is asked to write down what he or she hears. The student is given credit for each syllable correctly understood by the listener.

There are a number of problems involved in assessing speech intelligibility of which the teacher should be aware. Since it is common for the student's speech to be taped, care must be taken that the quality of the tape does not affect the intelligibility rating. If the child's speech is not taped but rated "live," there is a danger that the listener will use visual cues such as lip or facial movements to help understand what the child is saying. Also, since the response has to be made immediately, there is no way to resolve listener disagreement unless the student takes the test again. Differences among listeners themselves have been found to influence speech intelligibility scores. In general, listeners who are familiar with the speech of deaf persons are more likely to give higher intelligibility ratings than those unfamiliar with "deaf" speech (McGarr, 1980).

Language context cues are another factor that may influence the listener's ratings of intelligibility. McGarr (1980) found that words that can be easily deduced from context are more likely to be understood by the listener; however, this may reflect the listener's knowledge of language rather than the intelligibility of the word spoken. Thus, in the sentence "Cows give milk," the listener will fill in the word "milk" not necessarily because the word was intelligible but because it is the most likely word to fill the slot. Magner (1972) has taken care to reduce such clues in the sentences chosen for the *Clarke School Intelligibility Test.*

Language Assessment

Some language assessment instruments have been developed specifically for hearing-impaired students. The choice of such an instrument will depend on several factors, one of the most important being the aspect of language that the teacher needs to assess.

Generally three areas of linguistic knowledge should be assessed: (1) semantics (the meaning of language); (2) syntax (the form of language); and (3) pragmatics (the use of language in communication situations). These areas are not separate entities but overlap each other considerably.

The mode of communication used by the teacher and the student can affect the language assessment. For example, when assessing the language of a hearing-impaired student who uses speech reading and speech as modes of communication, the teacher must be aware that the final *s* on plurals (hats) may not be visible on the lips; thus the child may have difficulty distinguishing *hat* from *hats*. Similarly, the absence of the final *s* in the child's expressive language may be a reflection of a speech deficiency and not a linguistic deficiency. For this reason many tests for use with hearing-impaired students use a written format for both expressive and receptive language assessment. The written word serves to lessen some of the ambiguities that are present when communicating with the hearing-impaired student.

Another factor to be considered when assessing the language of the hearing-impaired student is the effect of a visual form of communication on the learning of English grammatical forms. The most obvious case is the student whose mother tongue is American Sign Language (ASL). Since ASL has a syntax quite distinct from English, instruments testing English proficiency are likely to underestimate the student's linguistic knowledge. A more subtle problem emerges with the student who is taught English using a sign system that is meant to follow English structure as closely as possible. The visual spatial features of a sign system cannot reproduce the auditory linear features of the spoken system. Thus, certain aspects of language may be learned differently and at different rates by hearing and hearing-impaired children.

Instruments developed specifically to assess the language of hearing-impaired students are the *Test of Syntactic Abilities* (Quigley, Steinkamp, Power, & Jones, 1978), the Grammatical Analysis of Elicited Language (Moog & Geers, 1980), and the *Original Written Language Inventory* (Craig, 1977).

The *Test of Syntactic Abilities* (TSA) is a test designed to measure the student's knowledge of English syntax. It is both a criterion-referenced and a norm-referenced test and has been standardized on a sample of prelingually profoundly deaf children of average intelligence ranging from 10 to 18 years of age. The test measures nine syntactical structures: negation, conjunction, determiners, question formation, verb processes, pronominalization, relativization, complementation, and nominalization. The TSA is a paper-and-pencil test with a multiple-choice format. The subtests are fairly lengthy and are meant to explore the student's syntactical knowledge in some depth. The total test takes about 10 hours to administer and is generally given to students over a few sittings. First a screening test is given to obtain an overall picture of the student's abilities. The results of the screening test are then used to select a subtest for more intensive assessment of specific structures. The authors suggest that the TSA can be used for three major purposes: (1) diagnosis of syntactic knowledge; (2) assessment of status and growth; and (3) evaluation of language development programs to pinpoint specific kinds of problems within each area.

The TSA test items require the student to make a judgment of grammatical correctness. The distractors used in the test are errors that are commonly made by deaf students in their written language. The TSA manual provides substantial normative data for hearing-impaired students by geographical region and type of school program. For comparative purposes scores of hearing students are also included in the tables.

The TSA is a test of receptive language ability and can only be given to students with at least a first-grade vocabulary and some reading ability. It assesses the deaf student's knowledge of syntax in depth, but gives no information on the student's expressive language, or his or her knowledge of semantics and pragmatics.

The *Grammatical Analysis of Elicited Language* (GAEL) primarily assesses expressive oral language of hearing-impaired students. Two levels are available, the GAEL Simple Sentence Level for students 5 to 8 years of age and the GAEL Complex Sentence Level for students 8 to 11 years of age. The test is meant to elicit certain language forms by contriving situations where the language might occur. The teacher first models the expected language and then provides the student with an opportunity to use the same language form. In order to elicit a specific question form the teacher hides an object within a block and asks, "What is in the blue block?" After the student responds and is familiar with the activity, he or she is given an opportunity to hide the object and ask the teacher the appropriate question. The language forms elicited through the activity are considered to be "prompted" productions. After the student has attempted the target language form when cued by the activity, he or she is then asked to imitate the teacher's production of the target language. Thus, for each language form assessed the student receives a prompted and imitative score.

Norms for the GAEL are available for both hearing and hearing-impaired children. The advanced level contains separate norms for severely hearing-impaired and profoundly deaf students. The norms are based entirely on hearing-impaired students educated and tested in an oral method. As yet no procedures or norms are available for students using total communication.

The *Original Written Language Inventory* (OWL) primarily assesses the written language production of hearing-impaired students. The written language is elicited through a set of pictures depicting a story. Four sets of picture stories are provided, two suitable for use with young students and two with older students. However, the authors suggest that any sequence of pictures could be used to elicit language. Two scoring procedures are described in the manual. One procedure yields a composite score for the number of different kinds of words, phrases, and sentences used by the student. The second scoring procedure provides detailed diagnostic information that the teacher can use for future language planning. This scoring procedure involves an analysis of the kinds of basic sentences and transformations used by the student and a detailed analysis of the kinds of errors made. A thorough knowledge of language structure is required to score the test. No normative data are available on the OWL.

The scoring procedures described in the OWL may be used to analyze an oral language sample as well as a written language sample. The advantage of a written sample is that ambiguities due to unintelligible speech, or use of ASL instead of manual English, are absent. The written language of young students, however, may not accurately reflect their linguistic knowledge, and the teacher may find it advisable to supplement the written language sample with a spontaneous oral (or signed) language sample.

CASE STUDY

Part II

Present Test Results

Auditory Assessment
Results of John's aided *pure tone audiogram* are given below. His aided speech reception threshold is 20 dB. John was given the *Word Intelligibility by Picture Identification Test* (WIPI) and was able to correctly identify 40% of the words through audition alone. When lipreading was added to audition he identified 72% of the words correctly. The audiologist noted that John made excellent use of his residual hearing and appeared to get maximum benefit from his hearing aid.

Aided pure tone audiogram: (better ear only)

Hz:	250	500	1000	2000	4000
dB:	20	15	15	25	25

Speech Assessment
John received a rating of 4 on the *NTID Speech Intelligibility Rating Scale*. This score was based on his spontaneous speech in the classroom as observed by the classroom teacher. A rating of 4 indicates that John's speech is intelligible with the exception of a few words or phrases.

Results of *Ling's Phonetic Level Speech Evaluation* indicate that John has control over the duration, intensity, and pitch of his voice. He can produce most vowels correctly in single and repeated syllables. He can produce most consonants in single and repeated syllables. The consonants with which he has most trouble are /s-/, /z-/, and /th-/. John has problems correctly producing consonant blends in initial, medial, and final positions.

Language Assessment
On the *Test of Syntactic Abilities Screening Form* John's scores are as follows:

Structure	Percentage Correct
Negation	44%
Conjunction	72%
Determiners	57%

Question Formation	90%
Verb Processes	80%
Pronominalization	50%
Relativization	53%
Complementation	56%
Nominalization	66%

Analysis of a spontaneous language sample taken by the teacher indicates that John uses all basic sentence patterns correctly but does not use complex sentences often. Analysis of the Noun Phrase indicates that all structures are present and correctly used, except for possessive pronouns. Analysis of the Verb Phrase indicates that John has some problems in using the present and past forms of the copula and auxiliary correctly and makes several errors in subject-verb agreement.

Achievement Test Results

John took the SAT-HI Intermediate Level 1 and received the following scores.

Subtest	Raw Score	Grade Equivalency
Reading Comprehension	24	3.8
Spelling	29	5.2
Language	28	3.9
Social Science	24	4.4
Science	18	3.5

Speechreading

John's speechreading ability was rated by the teacher based on classroom observation. John was found to speechread complex phrases and sentences spoken by well-known friends and teachers but could only speechread simple phrases spoken by strangers.

A second measure of speechreading ability was obtained by administering two different forms of the *Peabody Picture Vocabulary Test* (PPVT) with and without sign and comparing the results. When administered in aural/oral form, John attained an age equivalent of 4 years, 11 months, whereas he scored at 6-0 years on the total communication administration. The difference in results indicates the difficulty John has when asked to rely solely on an aural/oral method of communication.

Summary and Recommendations

Results of the assessment data indicate that John's communication skills are below what would be expected of a child his age. Though the audiologist noted that he made good use of his residual hearing, scores on the aural/oral administration of the PPVT indicate that John depends on the use of sign to supplement oral receptive communication. The latter is supported by the fact that John can speechread only simple phrases when communicating with strangers.

John's expressive speech is intelligible, and his language structure, though less complex than that of other children his age, is sufficiently intelligible to allow him to communicate with peers and teachers. Results on the Test of Syntactic Abilities indicate that John has considerable difficulties with several sentence transformations, which may pose problems in reading comprehension when reading material becomes more complex.

Academic testing reveal that John is currently achieving at or above grade level in all areas assessed. (It should be remembered that the language subtest on the SAT is a test of punctuation, not language structure.) Thus, despite some communication difficulties John may be able to keep up with his peers in several academic areas.

Based on the assessment information available, it is recommended by the assessment team that John be placed in public school with a resource room program. He will need the support of the resource room teacher to help him further develop and make efficient use of his aural/oral communication skills and to provide language instruction. With such support he should be able to function satisfactorily in a regular classroom in several academic areas.

Speechreading (Lipreading) Assessment

Lipreading involves obtaining spoken information through lip movements alone. Speechreading implies that the listener is "reading" speech by lip movements as well as using facial expressions, body language, and other cues to interpret the message. Speechreading can be defined as reception of oral language through a visual mode. One of the major difficulties involved in speechreading is that visibility of speech is very poor since many speech sounds (phonemes) look alike on the lips and some phonemes are invisible. In fact, only 16 out of 40 English phonemes are visible (Erber, 1977). However, since speechreading is a means for language reception, the speechreader usually uses a knowledge of language and the context in which communication is taking place to fill in the gaps and reconstruct the entire message. For example, the words "mama" and "papa" look identical to the speechreader. However, the student listening to a story of the three bears is able to decide when the teacher refers to "mama bear" and when the teacher refers to "papa bear" by using information from the pictures being shown, from the repetitive nature of the story (where papa bear always speaks first) and perhaps by the teacher's different facial expressions when depicting mama and papa bear. The student will use these clues to help distinguish between the two words.

Several tests are available to assess speechreading ability. Tests commonly used with young students are the *Craig Lipreading Inventory* (Craig, 1969) and the *Children's Speechreading Test* (Butt & Chreist, 1968). Tests used with older students and adults are *CID Everyday Sentences* (Jeffers & Barley, 1971) and the *Utley Filmed Test of Speechreading* (Utley, 1946).

The *Craig Lipreading Inventory* is designed to test the lipreading ability of young deaf students. It consists of two parts, a word recognition subtest and a sentence recognition subtest. The vocabulary words used in the test were selected because they were highly familiar in American English, were within a second-grade reading level, and were representative of all the sounds in American English. A multiple-choice response format is used, and the student's response consists merely of pointing to the correct item on the response sheet. The response sheet contains the written words and sentences as well as pictures depicting the words and sentences. This inventory has been widely used in research studies (Craig, 1964; Stuckless & Birch, 1966) and has been found to differentiate good from poor lipreaders. It has also been found to correlate highly with teacher's estimates of lipreading skills. The advantages of the inventory are the controlled language and syntax and the simple response format. Another positive feature is the availability of contextual cues provided by the written language and pictures on the response sheet. Two equivalent forms of the test are available. The test is also available on film.

The *Children's Speech Reading Test* evaluates speechreading ability in young children who have not yet learned to read. The test items and responses are designed to be appropriate for children 1 to 5 years of age. The authors report that the test has also been useful in assessing the speechreading skills of multiply handicapped children.

The vocabulary items used on the test were chosen from children's early learned vocabulary and are representative of all sounds in English. The test requires the child to identify objects, numbers, pictures, colors, actions, foods, some common adjectives, parts of the body, animal names, and items of clothing. It also requires the child to follow simple directions (e.g., "Put the spoon in the cup," "Walk to the door"). Identification of objects, pictures, and colors have a multiple-choice format. Three or four samples (objects or pictures) are placed in front of the child, who is expected merely to select the correct object or picture. Identification of action requires that the child answer several questions about a single picture. The variety of activities and response formats together with the use of objects that can be manipulated allows the teacher to obtain and keep the interest of the young child.

The *Barley Speechreading Test* is for adolescents and adults. It consists of two sets of 22 sentences selected from a list of 100 sentences known as the CID everyday sentences. The original CID sentences chosen: (1) contain vocabulary appropriate to adults, (2) occur with high frequency in American English, and (3) vary in grammatical length and sentence structure. The following examples demonstrate the kinds of sentences on the test:

"Pass the bread and butter, please."
"It's time to go."
"Hurry up."
"Let's get a cup of coffee."

The student is expected to write down the sentence after it has been spoken by the teacher. Credit is given for each correct word in the sentence.

The *Utley Film Test* is suitable only for older students and adults. The Utley contains three subtests: a word recognition subtest, a sentence subtest, and a story subtest. The word subtest consists of 36 words judged to be at approximately a third-grade reading level chosen from Thorndike's list of 1,000 most commonly used words. The sentence subtests consists of 31 sentences containing common phrases and idiomatic expressions. The story subtest consists of six short stories built around themes judged to be of interest to adolescents. Each story is followed by five questions. The sentence subtest is the most commonly used and has been found to be a more reliable measure of speechreading ability than the other subtests (DiCarlo & Kataja, 1976).

The student writes down what he or she thinks the speaker has said. There are two ways of scoring the test: one is to give credit for every word read correctly; the second is to score a sentence as correct if the content has been perceived with reasonable accuracy. The second method of scoring seems preferable because it gives the student credit for using linguistic and contextual closure.

The Barley (Forms A and B) and the Utley sentence tests have been found to have a high correlation ($r = .79$ for Form A and $r = .83$ for Form B) and could therefore be used interchangeably since the format for administration and mode of response is very similar.

Summary

The key people in the assessment of the hearing-impaired student are the audiologist, the psychologist, the speech and hearing specialist, and the teacher of the hearing-impaired student. It is important that all four professionals be familiar with the problems of deafness and that they have previous experience with hearing-impaired students.

The audiologist's responsibility is to obtain a pure tone threshold, both with and without the hearing aid, and to perform the speech audiometry assessments. An audiologist will obtain appropriate measures of speech discrimination and speech comprehension under various conditions of noise. The audiologist will also help the teacher monitor the amplification system used by the student and the acoustic environment in which the student is expected to function.

The psychologist will be expected to administer psychological and intellectual tests to the hearing-impaired child. It is necessary that the psychologist be easily able to communicate with the student either orally or through sign and fingerspelling. The psychologist also needs to be aware of the language demands of the tests being administered and to adapt them accordingly.

The speech and language pathologist may be needed to assist the teacher in a thorough assessment of the speech and language abilities of the hearing-impaired child. The pathologist may administer lip-reading or language tests. He or she must be aware of the problems involved in assessing the oral language of hearing-impaired students and must be able to separate speech problems from language problems.

The teacher of the hearing-impaired student is responsible for achievement testing, planning, and implementing educational goals and for obtaining from the other professionals the information needed to help plan for the child. For instance, the teacher may request from the audiologist a pure tone threshold obtained while the child is wearing a hearing aid, since the aided threshold gives information on the student's ability to hear certain speech sounds and may aid the teacher in planning speech and auditory training programs. The teacher may also help the other professionals in adapting the language and communication requirements of a test. The teacher's observations should supplement the results obtained by the speech and language specialist, especially in the area of language assessment.

It is, of course, very important that all the professionals share information not only with the teacher but with each other. The psychologist's assessment of the student's behavior and functioning may help the audiologist, who has to decide what kind of a response test (pointing to pictures, reading, writing) will be appropriate for an auditory comprehension assessment. Similarly, the language specialist's or the teacher's assessment of the student's communicative behavior will help the psychologist in selecting and/or adapting an intelligence test.

Educational Suggestions for Hearing-Impaired Students

Generally, the most serious educational consequence of hearing disabilities is the lack of information from auditory stimuli. Students with hearing disabilities tend to emphasize visual information processing as an aid to learning. Most of the suggestions mentioned below are intended to facilitate or capitalize on visual ability as an aid to information processing in the instructional or assessment situation.

Before instruction or assessment procedures begin, teachers should consult with each hearing-impaired student about adaptive aids that will be helpful to him or her.

Teachers should learn or develop a set of simple signs, in consultation with hearing-impaired students, which cover basic terms, concepts, or procedures relevant to instruction or assessment.

Teachers should arrange for a non impaired student to provide copies of his or her notes to hearing-impaired students. Speechreaders will not be able to look at the instructor and write notes at the same time. This can be done with carbon paper or a xerox copy.

Teachers should emphasize the use of visual aids during instruction and assessment.

Teachers can prepare and distribute a glossary of all special or technical terms for instructional or assessment procedures beforehand for the student to review.

If records or tapes are to be used in class, teachers should provide hearing-impaired students with written scripts.

When new words or terms are introduced in class, teachers should spell them out on the chalkboard.

Teachers should emphasize practical demonstrations and hands-on experience. It is best to precede concepts with concrete experience.

Before giving a demonstration, teachers should always go through it verbally first, as speechreading students cannot watch the teacher's or tester's face and hands at the same time.

Teachers should always repeat in full all questions raised by class members.

Speaking a bit slower than normal may aid speechreading students. However, excessive loudness or exaggerated facial or mouth gestures are not helpful.

When vital material is covered, teachers should make sure that hearing-impaired students grasp it by including them in direct questioning on content.

Teachers should never face away from the class (e.g., toward the chalkboard) when speaking.

Teachers should never stand in front of a window or other light source when instructing or testing, as the light may interfere with lipreading.

Always have the interpreter stand close enough to the teacher or tester so that both can be seen at the same time.

Confer with the interpreter ahead of time if new words or terms are to be introduced. Allow time during instruction or testing for fingerspelling these words.

Teachers should individually consult with hearing-impaired students and hearing-aid wearers to find the seating that is acoustically best for them.

Teachers should seat speechreading students near the front of the class and remove visual obstructions between them and the teacher.

Teachers should remember that sudden changes in the environment (e.g., smells, temperature, vibrations) may be distracting to the hearing-impaired student.

Study Questions

1. How is assessment of a hearing-impaired student affected by (1) mode of communication and (2) delay in receptive and expressive language?
2. What is the difference between auditory sensitivity, auditory discrimination, auditory identification, and auditory comprehension? Which areas are likely to be affected by communication and language difficulties?
3. Why are speech intelligibility tests not useful for diagnostic and remediation purposes?
4. What factors affect ratings of speech intelligiblity?
5. Identify and describe three language instruments developed specifically for hearing-impaired students.
6. Explain the terms *linguistic closure* and *contextual closure*. How do these aid in speechreading?
7. Why is it important to give a hearing-impaired student a screening test before administering a standardization achievement test battery?
8. What is the difference between a nonverbal intelligence test and a nonlanguage intelligence test? Which would be more suitable for use with a hearing-impaired student with severe language difficulties?

Suggested Readings

Bess, F. H., & McConnell, F. (1981). *Audiology, education, the hearing impaired child*. St. Louis: C. V. Mosby.
Jeffers, J., & Barley, M. (1971). *Speechreading*. Springfield, IL: Charles C Thomas.
Ling, D. (1976). *Speech and the hearing impaired child: Theory and practice*. Washington, DC: Alexander Graham Bell Association.
Skinner, D. H., & Shelton, R. Z. (1985). *Speech, language, and learning: Normal processes and disorders*. New York: John Wiley & Sons.

References

Bess, F. H., & McConnell, F. (1981). *Audiology, education, the hearing impaired child*. St. Louis: C. V. Mosby.
Butt, D. S., & Chreist, F. M. (1968). A speechreading test for young children. *Volta Review, 70*, 225–239.

Cramer, K. D., & Erber, N. P. (1974). A spondee recognition test for young hearing-impaired children. *Journal of Speech and Hearing Disorders, 39,* 304–311.

Craig, H. (1977). *Original Written Language Inventory.* Pittsburgh, PA: Western Pennsylvania School for the Deaf.

Craig, W. N. (1969). *The Craig Lipreading Inventory.* Pittsburgh, PA: University of Pittsburgh.

Craig, W. N. (1964). The effects of preschool training on the development of reading and lipreading skills of deaf children. *American Annals of the Deaf, 109,* 280–289.

DiCarlo, L. M., & Kataja, R. (1976). An analysis of the Utley lipreading test. *Journal of Speech and Hearing Disorders, 16,* 226–240.

Erber, N. P. (1979). An approach to evaluating auditory speech perception ability. *Volta Review, 81,* 17–24.

Erber, N. P. (1977). Developing materials for lipreading evaluation and instruction. *Volta Review, 79,* 35–42.

Haskins, H. A. (1949). *Phonetically Balanced Test of Speech Discrimination for children.* Unpublished Master's thesis. Northwestern University, Evanston, IL.

Jeffers, J., & Barley, M. (1971). *Speechreading.* Springfield, IL: Charles C Thomas.

Jenson, D. (1975). Communication characteristics of NTID students. *Journal of Rehabilitative Audiology, 8,* 17–32.

Levine, E. S. (1974). Psychological tests and practices with the deaf: A survey of the state of the art. *Volta Review, 76,* 298–319.

Ling, D. (1976). *Speech and the hearing impaired child: Theory and practice.* Washington, DC: Alexander Graham Bell Association.

McGarr, N. S. (1980). Evaluation of speech in intermediate school-age deaf children. In J. D. Subtelny (Ed.). *Speech assessment and speech improvement for hearing impaired* (pp. 45–56). Washington, DC: Alexander Graham Bell Association.

Magner, M. E. (1972). *A Speech Intelligibility Test for Deaf Children.* Northampton, MA: Clarke School for the Deaf.

Matkin, N. (1980). Audiologic management. In J. Subtelny (Ed.), *Speech assessment and speech improvement for the hearing impaired* (pp. 82–91). Washington, DC: Alexander Graham Bell Association.

Maxon, A. B. (1980). Audiological evaluation directions. *Topics in Language Disorders, 1,* 39–45.

Moog, J. S., & Geers, A. E. (1980). *Grammatical analysis of elicited language.* St. Louis: Central Institute for the Deaf.

Moores, D. F. (1981). *Educating the deaf: Psychology, principles and practices.* Boston: Houghton Mifflin.

Newby, H. A. (1972). *Audiology.* New York: Appleton-Century-Crofts.

Quigley, S. P., Steinkamp, M. W., Power, J. P., & Jones, B. W. (1978). *Test of syntactic abilities: Guide to administration and interpretation.* Beaverton, OR: Dormac Inc.

Report of the ad hoc committee to define deaf and hard of hearing. (1975). *American Annals of the Deaf, 120,* 509–512.

Ross, M., & Lerman, J. (1970). A picture identification test for hearing-impaired children. *Journal of Speech and Hearing Research, 13,* 44–53.

Stuckless, E. R., & Birch, J. W. (1966). The influence of early manual communication on the linguistic development of deaf children. *American Annals of the Deaf, 111,* 452–460, 499–504.

Trammell, J. L. (1976). *Test of auditory comprehension.* Hollywood, CA: Foreworks.

Utley, J. (1946). A test of lip reading ability. *Journal of Speech and Hearing Disorders, 11,* 109–116.

15

Assessment of Giftedness, Talent, and Creativity

John O. Schwenn

OBJECTIVES

After completing this chapter, the teacher should be able to:

1. Define the terms *gifted, talented,* and *creative.*
2. Identify characteristics of gifted children.
3. Identify concerns of testing the gifted.
4. Know the procedures used to identify the gifted, talented, and creative.
5. Identify standardized tests used for the gifted, talented, and creative.

Identifying children whom we label gifted and separating them from the general population has been considered by many through the centuries. Over 2,000 years ago, Plato described males with superior intelligence as "men of gold" as compared to those of "silver," "iron," or "brass." These boys, of course, came from the select patrician class and not from the general population. Their special education was geared toward increasing their leadership capacity (Freeman, 1979). Some societies did choose children showing promise and potential from the common masses, rather than just the elite, and provided them with a special education. A good example is Emperor Charlemagne, who in 800 A.D. urged education at state expense for children who belonged to the common masses but showed good potential (Whitmore, 1980).

In the early history of the United States, the gifted were highly valued as leadership ability was needed and desired. In the early eighteenth century, Thomas Jefferson proposed a bill entitled "The Diffusion of Education," which was to provide a university education for all promising youth. As the United States became a "melting pot" for all people, sentiment arose against any elitism, and programs favoring this suffered (Whitmore, 1980).

U.S. public schools began providing formal programs for the gifted during the mid-nineteenth century. The first large-scale educational program for academically talented students was instituted in St. Louis in 1868, whereas identifying the programming for the gifted began in the twentieth century (Passow, Goldberg, Tannenbaum, & French, 1955). The early 1900s brought the establishment of more programs for gifted students, with acceleration and ability grouping or tracking the most common practice (Whitmore, 1980).

In the early 1920s, Terman began a systematic, longitudinal study of gifted children from 3 to 19 years of age. After exhaustive studies of 1,528 subjects with IQs of 140 or higher, he reported characteristics of giftedness that contradicted earlier beliefs. He found the gifted were superior in all areas of development—mental, social, emotional, and physical (Sellin & Birch, 1980).

In 1960, the U.S. Office of Education established a "project talent" program that emphasized discovery and development of human resources (Rice, 1970). A 1977 survey of each state and the District of Columbia reported that 37 states and the District of Columbia had definitions of giftedness, creativity, and talent (Grossi, 1980). Mitchell (1980) surveyed all state departments of education in the fall of 1978 and found that all states except 5 had program assessment guidelines for giftedness and creativity. There is no uniformity in definitions and placement criteria. However, most employ components of the 1972 U.S. Office of Education definition (Grossi, 1980):

Gifted and talented children are those identified by professionally qualified persons who, by virtue of outstanding abilities, are capable of high performance. These are children who require differentiated educational programs in order to realize their contribution to self and society. Children capable of high performance include those with demonstrated achievement and/or potential ability in any of the following areas, singly or in combination:

1. General intellectual ability
2. Specific academic aptitude
3. Creative or productive thinking
4. Leadership ability
5. Visual and peforming arts

(Marland, 1972, p. 2).

General intellectual ability refers to all academic disciplines where the child is performing at a significantly higher level than expected by his or her age level and experiences. Specific academic aptitude refers to the student who excels significantly in one or more major curriculum areas. Creative thinking refers to the student who produces both tangible and nontangible end products and integrates what appears to be unrelated material to formulate new solutions or to produce unique outcomes. Leadership ability means an "individual who regularly provides motivation, guidance, direction, and assistance in crises situations" (Grossi, 1980, p. 24). Artistic ability concerns the creation of any visual art or performing art via a painting, a sculpture, a composition, a musical performance, or a dramatic production.

Characteristics of the Gifted

As in any other category of exceptionality, no singular characteristic separates a gifted, talented, or creative child from the general population (Passow, 1980). The most useful and detailed list of characteristics has been compiled by Ehrlich (1981). A listing of these characteristics appears in Table 15.1.

Considerations in Testing Giftedness, Creativity, and Talent

The percentage of students placed in programs for the gifted, creative, and talented range from the top 1% to the top 20% of the school population. The number of accepted participants and the cutoff score

TABLE 15.1 Characteristics of the Gifted

Characteristic	Description
Learning	Child learns quickly, efficiently, and easily
Thinking	Clear and logical abstract reasoning is frequently demonstrated
Math	Capable of symbolic thought; number work is easily mastered
Reading	Level at least two grades above grade placement
Creativity and imagination	Child can generate large numbers of solutions to problems and questions
Planning and organization	Work is well-planned and organized
Memory	Things are remembered in detail
Flexibility of thought	
Insight	Relationships are seen among apparently unrelated ideas
Vocabulary	Well beyond the child's year
Verbal	Expresses self well
Writing	Obviously advanced for child's age
Knowledge	Wide range of general knowledge with specialized knowledge in a particular area
Leadership	Child leads and influences peers
Originality	Problems are subdued by ingenious methods
Curiousity	Child is inquisitive and investigative
Attention to detail	Child is impatient with detail
Attention and concentration	Attention span is long, distractibility low, and concentration intense
Discipline	Self-disciplined, strives for perfection
Cooperation	Child is congenial and works well with peers
Common sense	Child makes good judgements
Energy	Energetic and physically well-coordinated
Persistence	Little external motivation is needed
Responsiveness	Child is alert, keenly observant, and responsive to environment
Dependability	Reliable and responsible
Popularity	Well-liked and sociable, preference for older playmates
Emotional stability	Not easily upset, patient with peers, highly self-confident
Early development	Obviously advanced in comparison with peers

are dependent upon the school's ability to accommodate students for special programs (Morgan, Tennant, & Gold, 1980). However, the critical issue should not be the percentage of students placed in a program, but rather which students have needs not met by the regular curriculum (Vermilyea, 1981).

Some programs for the gifted are enrichment in nature while others stress academic acceleration. An enrichment program broadens the scope of the child's cultural, social, and academic experiences. In contrast, an acceleration program allows the child to progress more rapidly in an area of concentration such as mathematics. Accelerated programs are generally associated with universities and allow the student to participate in university classes.

Programs developed to identify gifted, creative, or talented students use a limited number of standardized tests. The most commonly used identifier is an IQ score from an intelligence test. A minimum accepted uniform IQ score does not exist for identifying the intellectually gifted. Many states employ an IQ score of 2 standard deviations above the mean on the test administered (e.g., on the WISC–R: 130, on the Stanford-Binet: 132). Other states have IQ cutoff points as low as 120 or as high as 140.

As early as the 1960s, the reliance on IQ scores as unquestionable proof of giftedness was being challenged. Anderson (1961) cautioned that "the IQ is a symptom of a child's learning potential, but is neither a complete nor an entirely reliable measure of the child's true potential" (p. 12). Vernon, Adamson, and Vernon (1977) stressed that it is unwise to rely on tests before the age of 5 or 6. Furthermore, these authors recommended that it is better to wait until the child has completed 1 year of school before testing.

Fox (1976) urged more consideration in selecting tests for the identification of gifted children. The foremost consideration is whether the test can validly identify students who will benefit the most from the type of program offered. Ability and personality must also be considered together in relationship to the program. The author concluded that a global, general estimate of intelligence provided by an intelligence test is simply not enough. Knowing only the child's IQ score, a teacher cannot adequately decide whether a child is ready for a gifted program. Interests and achievement levels must also be known.

Consistent high scores on standardized aptitude and achievement tests are the single best indicator of high potential according to Stanley (1976). However, he also indicates tests must be of "appropriate" difficulty and must match the child's ability. For example, if a third-grade child obtains a grade equivalent of 7.5 on a vocabulary test, a teacher may assume the child has good vocabulary skills. However, if a third-grade child has a perfect score and the test has a low ceiling, the teacher cannot determine how good the child's skills are and a different vocabulary test should be administered.

CASE STUDY

Part I

Name: Steven T.   Age: 8 years
Date of Birth: September 27,   Grade: 3
   1973
Date of Evaluation: October 3,
   1981

Background Information

Steven T. is a handsome, strong, 8-year-old boy. He is above average height and weight for a third-grader. Fine- and gross-motor coordination is good. Steven does well in sports and plays on T-ball and pee-wee basketball teams.

Steven comes from a middle-class family. Mr. T. is a foreman for a local company, and Mrs. T. is a high school English teacher. Both parents have bachelor's degrees, and Mrs. T. is working toward a master's degree. Steven has a 7-year-old brother and a 4-year-old sister.

The parents report that Steven is an excellent, well-behaved child. He remembers everything he learns at school and supplies trivia facts to other children in the neighborhood and anyone else who will listen. Steven spends much of his free time reading rather than watching television. He has a small library of his own. Steven is definitely the leader of neighborhood children.

Steven is at the top of his third-grade class in math, science, and reading. Classroom tests are nearly always perfect. Writing skills are excellent. He usually finishes his work before everyone else in the class and frequently asks for more to do.

Referral

Steven's school began a program for the intellectually gifted. His parents called his teacher to discuss the possibility of referring him for the program. The parents were asked to complete the parent nomination form.

Identifying Giftedness, Creativity, and Talent

Screening

There are several techniques used to screen for giftedness. Teacher nomination is a widely used technique because teachers are familiar with students' work and with "normal" performance at a grade level. Unfortunately, most research (Martinson, 1981; Jacobs, 1971; Pegnato

& Bush, 1959) shows that teacher nomination is an ineffective means of identifying gifted children because teachers tend to nominate only a fraction of those later identified as gifted.

Using teacher nomination as a screening technique may be improved upon if an anecdotal recording method described by Miller and Ford (1980) is utilized. In this method teachers, during inservice and preservice training, are requested to focus on student behavior to identify gifted, talented, and creative students. Through feedback the teachers learn the characteristics of gifted, talented, and creative students.

Rather than relying on a teacher to refer or nominate children, it may be beneficial to ask the teacher to identify children with particular characteristics. This could be completed in questionnaire form and passed to all teachers in a school district. The more often a child's name appears on the list, the greater likelihood the child may be gifted. A sampling of such items could include:

1. Name the most intelligent child in your classroom.
2. Name the child with the largest vocabulary.
3. Name the child earning the highest grade.
4. Name the child who most often correctly completes his or her work first.
5. Name the child who retains what he or she learns without much drill.
6. Name the most motivated child.
7. Name the classroom leader.
8. Name the most popular child.
9. Name the most creative child.
10. Name the child with the most talent.

Parents are sometimes asked to nominate gifted children because of their familiarity with their child's development, attitudes, interests, and skills. Their referrals should be accepted as long as the assessment procedures employed are valid. Questions on a parent nomination form should cover some of the characteristics of gifted, talented, and creative children (see table 15.1). The parent should compare the child in question to other children of similar chronological age.

Some school systems include peer nominations as a segment of the screening process because peers are familiar with each other's work and may be aware of interests or abilities of which the teacher is unaware. Whitmore (1980) reports children are inclined to nominate striving, high conforming, high achievers and discount the "not so good" peer. However, they may be influenced by their like or dislike of a peer. To combat this, a questionnaire format could be used where the student nominates other students in the class. Students whose names appear most frequently could be referred for further evaluation. A sampling of items could include:

1. Who in the class would you most want to help you with your school work if you were having difficulty?
2. Who in the class uses the biggest words?
3. Who in the class most frequently answers the teacher's questions correctly?
4. Which student in the class is most frequently deciding what other members of the class will do?
5. With whom in the class would you prefer to spend the most time?
6. The best musician in the class is _____.
7. The best artist in the class is _____.
8. The best actor/actress in the class is _____.
9. Which student in the class comes up with the most original ideas?
10. Who in the class understands things most easily?
11. Who in the class has the best ideas for games and other interesting things to do?

Of these three groups of nominators, the teacher's judgment is considered the most reliable and should be included in the screening process. When teacher judgment is combined with other methods, there is greater likelihood that students who have gifted, talented, or creative characteristics will be referred (Martinson, 1981).

Rating Scales

Characteristics of giftedness, talent, and creativity are most commonly developed into rating scales based upon the student's own particular needs. Rating scales should measure direct behavior that can be easily observed. An excellent rating scale to guide teachers' ratings of potentially gifted students is the *Scales for Rating Behavioral Characteristics of Superior Students* (Renzulli, Smith, White, Callahan, & Hartman, 1976). The teacher responds to each item by rating the child "seldom or never," "occasionally," "considerably," or "almost always." The scale includes: 8 Learning Characteristics related to the student's learning behavior; 9 Motivational Characteristics; 11 Artistic Characteristics; 7 Musical Characteristics; 10 Dramatic Characteristics; 11 Precision Communication Characteristics; 4 Expressiveness Communication Characteristics; and 15 Planning Characteristics. The "almost always" option is the desired rating for those exhibiting gifted behavior. High scores on any one scale should be interpreted as exhibiting gifted or creative behavior. The authors state that only the scales relevant for a particular educational program are to be used.

The Learning, Motivation, and Creativity scales are most consistent with the objectives of the majority of state and local programs. Student responses should be analyzed separately on each scale. A different set of characteristics is represented on each scale, so no attempt should be made to add scores together to form a total score. No predetermined cutoff scores are available, but a mean score can be computed on each dimension. Students deviating markedly upward from the mean should be considered for further evaluation.

Standardized Tests

Group Achievement Tests
Many schools employ group achievement tests as a screening measure. If a student scores at or above a particular percentile or scores a set number of grades above grade placement, he or she is referred for further evaluation. Percentile cutoff points vary from the 80th to the 99th percentile. Grade levels are usually set at two grade levels above grade placement. Two commonly used group achievement tests are described below.

The *SRA Assessment Survey* (Naslund, Thorpe, & Lefever, 1975) consists of two forms and five levels. It covers basic academic skills from grades 1 through 9 in reading, mathematics, and language arts. Social students, work-study skills, and science are also covered from grades 4 through 9. This test, unlike most other achievement tests, employs no time limits. The median reliability coefficient is .90. The standard error of measurement rises in the upper grade levels. SRA score correlations average .75. Content validity is rated high (Bauerfeind, 1978; Buros, 1978).

The 1971 *College Board Scholastic Aptitudes Test* is a college entrance exam administered throughout the country six times per year. A mathematics score covering only mathematics skills and a verbal score covering social, political, scientific, artistic, philosophical, and literary areas are obtained. This test would be especially suited for students being identified for accelerated programs in math. A child obtaining a score of 700 or higher on math should be further evaluated for giftedness (Rosser, 1981). Estimated internal consistency reliabilities are .91 for the verbal score and .90 for the mathematics score. Multiple validity correlations are near .62. Numerous studies show high validity (Buros, 1974; DuBois, 1974).

Individually Administered Achievement Tests
Students scoring high on group achievement tests may be administered individual achievement tests. Some school systems routinely administer individual achievement tests to all students referred for giftedness, talent, or creativity. Cutoff points vary from the 80th to the

99th percentile or for grade levels at least two years above grade placement. It is important that teachers select individual achievement tests that have adequate reliability and validity. Two tests that are frequently used are reported below.

The *Peabody Individual Achievement Test* (Dunn & Markwardt, 1970) contains norms for children in kindergarten through grade 12 and between the ages of 5 years, 3 months and 18 years, 3 months. Subtests administered are Mathematics, Reading Recognition, Reading Comprehension, Spelling, and General Information. A total test score is also computed. Grade equivalents, age equivalents, percentile scores, and standard scores are obtained. The median reliability coefficient is .78. Content validity is considered high. Concurrent validity studies with the *Peabody Picture Vocabulary Test* report mean correlations in the .50 to .60 range (Dunn & Markwardt, 1970).

The *Woodcock-Johnson Psycho-Educational Battery* (W-J; Woodcock & Johnson, 1977) is a comprehensive battery of tests that measures cognitive abilities, scholastic aptitudes, achievement, and interests. The battery contains 27 subtests. Selected subtests can be administered to attain scores on the major areas mentioned above. Scores derived from the test battery include grade equivalents, age equivalents, percentile ranks, and normal curve equivalents for each individual subtest.

There are 12 cognitive ability subtests ranging in complexity from tasks of visual matching and auditory blending to tasks of concept formation and reasoning with analogies. Scores based on performances from specified combinations of these subtests provide information about a student's general cognitive ability, four cognitive factors, and four achievement aptitudes. Ten subtests measure achievement ability. The basic achievement areas are covered as well as science, social studies, and humanities. Finally, there are five subtests that assess a student's level of preference for participating in scholastic or nonscholastic activities. The reliability and validity for the *Woodcock-Johnson Psycho-Educational Battery* are reported in the technical manual. The figures reported give adequate evidence for its reliability and validity.

Group Intelligence Tests
Group intelligence tests are administered as a screening device. Martinson (1981) cites evidence that if accepted cutoff points on group intelligence tests such as 125 or 130 were utilized, up to one-half of those later qualifying for gifted programs on individual intelligence tests would be eliminated. As Whitmore (1980) points out, the underachiever is frequently overlooked on group intelligence tests because these tests rely most heavily on verbal skills such as reading and following directions. Those who are strongest on performance skills are thus penalized. Other children may have excellent verbal ability

but poor performance skills. Many of these children may erroneously qualify for gifted programs. Group intelligence tests that are frequently used by teachers include the *California Test of Mental Maturity* (Sullivan, Clark, & Tiegs, 1970), the *Goodenough-Harris Drawing Test* (Goodenough & Harris, 1963), the *Lorge-Thorndike Intelligence Test* (Lorge, Thorndike, & Hagan, 1966) and the *Otis-Lennon Mental Ability Test* (Otis & Lennon, 1972).

Individually Administered Intelligence Tests
Individually administered intelligence tests are the most commonly used measure to determine eligibility for gifted programs. Of all the individual intelligence tests, the *Stanford-Binet Intelligence Scale* and the Wechsler scales, which include the WISC–R, WPPSI, and WAIS–R, are the most frequently used and the most reliable and valid. Students must obtain a minimum score that is set by a state education department or school system. Eligibility IQ cutoff scores begin at 120.

CASE STUDY

Part II

Observations

Steven is a nice-looking, friendly boy with whom rapport was easily established. He was very verbal throughout the psychoeducational evaluation. Steven asked questions about the testing and added personal anecdotes that were related to the activities in which he was participating. His good sense of humor was evident in his responses. Verbal answers were of high quality. Steven obtained the highest allowable scores on performance activities as he completed tasks within the fastest time limits. Steven worked hard at the tasks presented. The results of the evaluation are a valid indication of his ability.

Parent Nomination

Mr. and Mrs. T. completed a parent nomination form. In comparing Steven to other 8-year-old children, they found their son displayed many gifted characteristics. The only "no" rating they gave Steven was in asking "why" questions, as they feel he asks no more questions of this type than other 8-year-olds.

Teacher Nomination

The teacher completed the *Scales for Rating the Behavioral Characteristics of Superior Students*. She rated Steven on the Learning Characteristics, Motivational Characteristics, Creativity Characteristics, Leadership Characteristics, Communication Characteristics—Precision, Communication Characteristics—Expressive, and Planning Characteristics. In all areas, the most frequent response was "almost always." Items not rated "almost always" were rated "consistently." Overall, Steven obtained the highest ratings in the classroom on each scale. The teacher then referred Steven for a complete standardized assessment for placement in the gifted program.

Academic Assessment

The results of the previous spring's California Achievement Test indicated Steven is functioning at the 95th percentile, or better than 95 out of every 100 students his chronological age. The teacher wanted a more current assessment and thus administered the achievement tests of the *Woodcock-Johnson Psycho-Educational Battery*. He attained the following scores:

Subtests	Reading Grade Level
Letter-Word Identification	7.8
Word Attack	7.5
Passage Comprehension	7.5
Calculation	8.0
Applied Problems	7.5
Dictation	7.3
Proofing	7.5
Science	8.0
Social Studies	8.1
Humanities	7.1

Steven's grade placement was 3.1. His scores are in the seventh- to eighth-grade range, which is approximately four to five grades above grade placement.

Intellectual Assessment

The school psychologist then administered a *Wechsler Intelligence Scale for Children—Revised*. Steven obtained a Verbal IQ score of 124, a Performance IQ score of 135, and a Full Scale IQ score of 133.

Verbal Subtests	Scaled Scores	Performance Subtests	Scaled Scores
Information	13	Picture Completion	17
Similarities	15	Picture Arrangement	15
Arithmetic	12	Block Design	14
Vocabulary	16	Object Assembly	16
Comprehension	14	Coding	13
Digit Span	15	Mates	14

Summary

Both Steven's parents and his teacher noted characteristics of gifted children. His parents answered "yes" to most questions on a parent nomination form. The teacher scored "almost always" on the *Scales for Rating Behavioral Characteristics of Superior Students*. On the *California Achievement Test*, Steven scored at the 95th percentile. The school requires a score of at least the 90th percentile. On the Woodcock, Steven is functioning four to five grades above his grade placement. Steven obtained a Full Scale IQ score of 133 on the WISC-R, which places him within the gifted range. Steven's school system requires a cutoff score of 125. The information, taken together, shows Steven is eligible for placement in his school system's gifted program.

Assessing Creativity

The term *creativity* is associated with artists, musicians, dramatists, scientists, and inventors whose work is so outstanding and shows such originality that it wins considerable acclaim or recognition. Definitions of creativity abound (Torrance, 1974; Vernon, Adamson, & Vernon, 1977), but no totally satisfactory definition of creativity is available. One has even more difficulty with the measurement of creativity. Traditional measurement devices are frequently too rigid, as most sum one's abilities into one score. Unconventional, original thinking and other types of creativity are not tapped by traditional assessment devices because they cannot be measured with one single correct answer. In fact, many believe creativity is highly individual and thus not measurable (Goldberg, 1965).

A number of assessment procedures are used to measure creativity. Many of the procedures stress the ability of the child to grasp relationships between ideas and the production of effective solutions to problems.

Guilford and his associates used Guilford's "structure of intellect" model to define various categories of thinking from divergent productions and transformations to convergent productions. Simple tests were developed for each factor. A number of these tests were developed by Thurstone, the United States Air Force, and Educational Testing Service (Torrance, 1974). A sample of some factors and their tests are described in Table 15.2.

The *Ross Test of Higher Cognitive Processes* (Ross & Ross, 1976) is designed to measure eight levels of higher cognitive thinking based on Bloom's Taxonomy of Educational Objectives. The test can be administered to children in grades 4 through 6. Section I contains 14 Analogies and measures the child's ability to determine the relationship of two words to each other. Section II, Deductive Reasoning, consists of 18 items designed to measure an analysis of statements in logic. Section III, Missing Premises, contains 8 items of one premise and one conclusion. The student must supply the missing premise to reach the correct conclusion. Abstract Relations, Section IV, consists of 14 items measuring a child's ability to synthesize a series of words to form a conceptual structure. Section V, Sequential Synthesis,

TABLE 15.2 Creativity Factors and Tests to Measure Them

Factor	Test and Description
Sensitivity to problems	*Apparatus Test*—suggest two improvements for a common appliance
Word fluency	*Suffixes W-1*—write words ending with a specified suffix
Expressional fluency	*Word Arrangements*—write sentences containing four specified words
Ideational fluency	*Theme If-2*—write as many words as possible about a given topic
Semantic spontaneous flexibility	*Brick Uses*—write a variety of uses for a brick
Associational fluency	*Controlled Associations*—write as many synonyms as possible for each given word
Originality	*Plot Titles*—write clever titles for story plots
Figural redefinition	*Hidden Pictures*—Find a human or animal picture hidden in a scene
Symbolic redefinition	*Camouflaged Words*—find the name of the sport or game concealed in a sentence
Semantic redefinition	*Object Synthesis*—name an object that could be made by combining two specified objects

contains 10 statements that must be placed in the correct order. Section VI, Questioning Strategies, measures the child's ability to identify one item out of five by using three groups of three questions. The child selects the best method of producing the desired data. Section VII, Analysis of Relevant and Irrelevant Information, consists of 14 math problems that may contain insufficient, irrelevant, or extraneous information. The student must analyze figures, determine their critical elements, form a hypothesis, and then use the hypothesis to identify new figures. Test-retest and split-half reliability procedures produced coefficients significant beyond the .001 level of confidence. The Ross test was compared to the Lorge-Thorndike Intelligence Test. Statistical significance was not obtained, indicating this test is not a test of general intelligence (Ross & Ross, 1976).

Thinking Creatively in Action and Movement (Torrance, 1981) can be administered individually to children 3 to 8 years of age. The testing time is 10 to 30 minutes. The student responds physically or verbally to four different activities. "How Many Ways?" samples the child's ability to produce alternative ways of moving. "Can You Move Like?" asks the child to pretend he is six different animals or objects. "What Other Ways?" has the child see objects or tasks in new ways. "What

Might It Be?'' has the child find unusual uses for common objects. The test is culturally unbiased and is based on the premise that preschool children best express themselves through the kinesthetic modality (Torrance, 1981).

The *Torrance Tests of Creative Thinking*, a revision of the *Minnesota Tests of Creative Thinking* (Torrance, 1974), are appropriate for use with students from kindergarten through graduate school. The verbal and figural aspects of creativity are assessed in the four areas of fluency, flexibility, originality, and elaboration. Verbal components number five. The Ask-and-Guess subtest is based on a presented drawing. The child writes all the questions he or she can about the picture, writes as many causes of the action in the drawing as he or she can, and finally lists possible results of the action in the picture. On Product Improvement, the child lists clever, interesting, and unusual ways to change a stuffed animal to make it more fun to play with. The child is required to list as many different and interesting things he or she can for common, everyday objects on Unusual Uses. The object of Unusual Questions is to list as many questions as possible about the item in Unusual Uses. The last verbal activity is Just Suppose. Here the child is given an improbable situation and must predict the outcome. The figural segment of the tests consists of three tasks. The first is Picture Construction, where the child thinks of a picture in which a shape, made of colored paper, is an integral part. In Incomplete Figures, the child is given a number of incomplete figures requiring the production of an original response. The last task is Repeated Figures. Here the student is given 30 parallel lines or 40 circles to make multiple associations to a single stimulus. Reliability has been consistently above .90. The manual reports adequate validity in a number of comparisons (Torrance, 1974).

Assessing Giftedness, Talent, and Creativity in the Performing Arts

The performing arts are frequently overlooked in traditional programs for the gifted, talented, and creative. Few assessment instruments are available, and historically there has been an unwillingness to measure talent objectively. Systematically and objectively testing for achievement in the performing arts is not an easy task. The wide range of abilities and the diversity of talent make it difficult to identify children with a high degree of potential. Setting and defining criteria for outstanding performance is also difficult (Renzulli et al., 1976).

The opinion of "expert" raters is frequently used to place children in a program for giftedness in the performing arts. However, nominations are most frequently made by teachers. Typically teacher nominations are based upon specific characteristics exhibited by their students. For example, a young child with artistic talent may display the following characteristics:

1. The child takes a strong interest in visual activities.
2. The child shows an interest in others' artwork whether they are peers or professionals.
3. Details are remembered explicitly. These may be recited to others or represented in artworks.
4. When given a choice, the child spends free time drawing, painting, making collages, sculpturing, and building.
5. The child works seriously on art projects and finds great satisfaction in them.
6. Technical skill in art production is advanced. Art tools and supplies are used proficiently.
7. Familiar art materials are often used in unusual ways.
8. Artwork is superior in design and composition, which includes balance, space, unity, and color.
9. Details are added to drawings, paintings, sculptures, and designs.
10. The child develops a distinctive artistic style that is recognized by others (Karnes, Strong, Anderson, & Kemp, 1978).

A young child with musical talent may display the following characteristics:

1. The child is unusually interested in music and chooses musical activities when given a choice. This child may suggest the class sing during free time or may volunteer to sing or play an instrument for the class.
2. The child often makes up original tunes or original words to familiar tunes.
3. The child becomes sensitive to the music's mood or character. If the music is slow, he or she may sit quietly and keep time to the selection, or if it is fast, he or she may dance to it. Comments about the mood of the music are expressed.
4. Rhythmic patterns are easily repeated or made up.
5. The child sings in tune or nearly in tune.
6. Rhythmic patterns are identified as the same or different.
7. Familiar songs are identified as the same or different.
8. The child identifies the higher or lower of two notes.
9. Short melodies are identified as the same or different (Karnes et al., 1978).

Ellison, Clifford, Fox, Coray, and Taylor (1976) suggest using biographical characteristics as part of the process of selecting those with artistic and musical abilities. The procedure involves the teacher collecting life history information from students who describe them-

selves and their backgrounds. The rationale for gathering this information is that past behavior, experiences, and self-descriptions are
indicators of future performance. The correlation between this procedure and the actual identification of artistic performers is high
(Ellison et al., 1976).

The *Art Vocabulary* test (Silverman, Hoepfner, & Hendricks, 1969)
can be administered to children in grades 6 through 12. However,
norms are available for grade 7 only. This test measures art vocabulary
and achievement in art and related concepts. This test consists of 96
items presented in four images. The student selects the image that best
portrays the presented art term. The test takes approximately 20
minutes to administer. Raw scores are converted to percentile ranks,
but no interpretation data is provided. Reliability ranges from .67 to
.88 depending on whether an answer sheet or test booklet is used
(Burchett, 1978).

The *Horn Art Aptitude Inventory* (Horn & Smith, 1945) can be
administered to students in grades 12–16 and to adults. The test has
two parts. The first part involves scribbling and doodling. The student
is asked to sketch 10 familiar objects such as a house, book, or
corkscrew in small scale on an 18 1/2-by-11-inch page as fast as he or
she can. Each of the 20 exercises is timed and highly speeded. The
second part is imagery. The student uses 12 rectangles containing key
lines that he or she must incorporate into a picture within a time limit.
Rating scales and examples are included. Intercorrelations vary from
.83 to .86. Alternate form reliability is .76 (Palmer, 1959).

The *Baldwin-Mills Singing Achievement Test* (Corbin, 1971) can be
administered to students in grade 5 through 16. This is an individually
administered sight-singing, standardized, objective achievement test.
The test consists of 14 eight-measure melodies that vary in difficulty
from a simple two-pitch exercise to a major-ninth exercise. All are
presented in conventional rhythmic configurations. Of the 14 melodies, 11 are considered easy. No norms are presented. A qualified
examiner is needed to administer this test (Colwell, 1978).

The *Drake Musical Aptitude Tests* (Drake, 1957) can be administered to groups of children 8 years old and over as well as to adults.
These tests provide an objective measure of musical memory and
rhythm. Practice exercises are provided. On the music memory test,
recorded melodies played on a piano are compared as either being
identical or having a change in notation, key, or tempo. The rhythm
test measures the ability to keep time. A beat ceases and the listener is
told to keep counting. When told to stop, the listener writes down the
number he or she has reached. Reliabilities range from the .80s to the
.90s. Validity coefficients vary from .31 to .91, with the median
coefficient .59 (Lundin, 1959).

The *Primary Measures of Music Audition* is a series of tape-recorded group tests for children 5 to 8 years of age. Short musical phrases that vary in tonal patterns and rhythm are presented. The child draws a circle around two identical faces if the selections are the same and around two different faces if the selections are different. The listening time is 12 minutes. The purposes of the test are twofold. First, the test is used to identify musically gifted children who could possibly benefit from special or additional musical instruction. Second, the test may be used to diagnose comparative tonal and rhythmic strengths and weaknesses of all children. Good test-retest ability and good validity are reported with musically gifted children (Gordon, 1980).

The *Seashore Measures of Musical Talents, Revised Edition* (Seashore, 1960) can be administered to assess students' skills in six areas. In Pitch, the student is presented with two notes and must indicate whether the second is higher or lower than the first. In Loudness, the same note is sounded twice and the student indicates whether the second note is stronger or weaker than the first. Two tapped patterns are sounded in Rhythm. The student indicates whether they are the same or different. In Time, the same note is sounded twice, and the student states whether the second is longer or shorter than the first. Two notes are sounded consecutively in Timbre, and the student indicates whether the quality is the same or different. A number of consecutive notes that form no particular melody are sounded in Memory. One note is changed in a second presentation. The student then gives the number of the altered note. The test can be given to students in grades 4–16 and to adults. Percentile scores are presented with a higher score indicating a better ability. Reliabilities vary from .62 to .79 (Wing, 1963).

Summary

The identification of gifted, talented, and creative students is a difficult task due to the lack of agreed-upon definitions and specific singular characteristics. However, identification can be successful if the assessment of the gifted, talented, and creative follows a series of steps involving screening procedures, the completion of rating scales, and the administration of standardized tests. The assessment process should also be continuous so that children initially showing little promise can be reconsidered if superior abilities become apparent later. The latter may occur more often with children from different cultural or low socioeconomic backgrounds. To protect against the latter it is important to use some identification procedures that are not language dependent.

The assessment process should always be comprehensive in nature, covering intellectual, academic, and social-emotional areas.

Routinely, the teacher should seek out information from other teachers, the student's classmates, and parents because of their social-interactional experiences with the gifted student. Although teacher identification procedures are the most reliable, it is suggested that a variety of other information be collected.

The total assessment data gathered must be reviewed in regard to the advantages and limitations described in this chapter. It is recommended that the data be gathered as early as possible so that appropriate learning experiences be scheduled to enhance the gifted student's abilities. This is vitally important because these children are our greatest resource and potential leaders of our country.

Educational Suggestions for Students with Gifted Abilities

Before allowing advanced placement for students who are assessed as intellectually gifted, teachers should determine whether these students have met valid program criteria for mastery levels to advance.

At times, students who are assessed as gifted in an academic area are placed for part of the day in a higher grade. The teacher of such students should inform the other teacher of any socioemotional provisions that are necessary for the successful experience of these younger students in that advanced grade.

For students who are identified as gifted in junior high school, teachers should make contact with local college or university personnel to seek their assistance in advising, counseling, and arranging for early-admission programming.

After identifying a primary-grade student as gifted, it is imperative that a teacher seek out local resources for programmatic instructional assistance.

After identifying students as gifted, teachers must understand that they have to change their patterns of teaching temporarily to accommodate specific instructional procedures with the gifted students.

Teachers must assess whether gifted students need reassurance in a gifted program that stresses pupil-teacher planning. Initially, gifted students feel somewhat uneasy in this type of situation because they are used to teacher-dominated instruction. If this is the case, the teacher must reassure the students to help strengthen their self-confidence in their skills and abilities.

Once a teacher has assessed a gifted student as being ready for self-directed study, it is essential that the teacher have the competency to conduct guided independent study.

Study Questions

1. Discuss the various components or categories of giftedness that comprise the 1972 U.S. Office of Education's definition of "gifted."
2. Discuss the difficulty involved in using strict cutoff points on two tests to identify gifted children.
3. Discuss the advantages of using a number of tests to identify the gifted student.
4. If you were going to identify all the gifted children in your school system, indicate which sources of referral you would use and why. What screening techniques would you use and why?
5. Identify the tests you would choose to use with the various categories of gifted students.
6. Discuss three assessment procedures to measure creativity. Delineate the differences between the procedures.
7. List specific characteristics that a young child with artistic talent may display.

Suggested Readings

Barron, F. (1969). *Creative person and creative process*. New York: Holt, Rinehart and Winston.
Bruch, C. B. (1971). Modification of procedures for identification of the disadvantaged gifted. *Gifted Child Quarterly, 15*, 267–272.
Clark, B. (1979). *Growing up gifted*. Columbus, OH: Charles E. Merrill.
Rubenzer, R. (1979). Identification and evaluation procedures for gifted and talented program. *Gifted Child Quarterly, 23*, 304–316.

References

Alvino, J., & Wiler, J. (1979). How standardized testing fails to identify the gifted and what teachers can do about it. *Phi Delta Kappan, 61*, 106–109.
Anderson, K. E. (Ed.). (1961). *Research on the academically talented student*. Washington, DC: Education Project on the Academically Talented Student.
Bauerfeind, A. (1978). Review of SRA assessment survey. In O. K. Buros (Ed.), *The eighth mental measurements yearbook*. Highland Park, NJ: Gryphon Press.
Burchett, K. E. (1978). Review of Art vocabulary test. In O. K. Buros (Ed.), *The eighth mental measurements yearbook*. Highland Park, NJ: Gryphon Press.
Buros, O. K. (1974). *Tests in print II*. Highland Park, NJ: Gryphon Press.
Buros, O. K. (1978). *The eighth mental measurements yearbook*. Highland Park, NJ: Gryphon Press.
Colwell, R. (1978). Review of Baldwin-Mills singing achievement test. In O. K.

Buros (Ed.), *The eighth mental measurements yearbook*. Highland Park, NJ: Gryphon Press.

Drake, R. M. (1957). *Drake musical aptitude tests, grades 3 through college*. Chicago: Science Research Associates.

DuBois, P. H. (1974). Review of college board scholastic aptitudes test. In O. K. Buros (Ed.), *The eighth mental measurements yearbook*. Highland Park, NJ: Gryphon Press.

Dunn, L. M., & Markwardt, F. C. (1970). *Peabody Individual Achievement Test*. Circle Pines, MN: American Guidance Service.

Ehrlich, V. Z. (1981). *A guide for parents and teachers*. Englewood Cliffs, NJ: Prentice-Hall, Ion Press.

Ellison, R. L., Clifford, A., Fox, D. G., Coray, K. E., & Taylor, C. W. (1976). Using biographical information in identifying artistic talent. *Gifted Child Quarterly, 20*, 402–413.

Fox, L. H. (1976). Identification and program planning: Models and methods. In D. P. Keating (Ed.), *Intellectual talent: Research and development*. Baltimore: Johns Hopkins University Press.

Freeman, J. (1979). *Gifted children*. Austin, TX: PRO-ED.

Goldberg, M. L. (1965). *Research on the gifted*. New York: Bureau of Publications, Teachers College.

Goodenough, F., & Harris, D. B. (1963). *Goodenough-Harris Drawing Test*. New York: Harcourt, Brace & World.

Gordon, E. E. (1980). The assessment of music aptitude of very young children. *Gifted Child Quarterly, 24*, 107–111.

Grossi, J. A. (1980). *Model state policy, legislation, and state plan toward the education of gifted and talented students*. Reston, VA: Council for Exceptional Children.

Horn, C. C., & Smith, L. F. (1945). The Horn Art Aptitude Inventory. *Journal of Applied Psychology, 29*, 350–355.

Jacobs, C. (1971). Effectiveness of teacher and parent identification of gifted children as a function of school level. *Psychology in the Schools, 8*, 140–142.

Karnes, M. B., Strong, D. S., Anderson, S., & Kemp, P. (1978). *Nurturing talent in the visual and performing arts in early childhood*. Urbana, IL: Institute for Child Behavior and Development.

Lorge, I., Thorndike, R. L., & Hagan, E. (1966). *Lorge-Thorndike Intelligence Tests*. Boston: Houghton-Mifflin.

Lundin, R. W. (1959). Review of Drake musical aptitude tests. In O. K. Buros (Ed.), *The fifth mental measurements yearbook*. Highland Park, NJ: Gryphon Press.

Marland, S., Jr. (1972). *Education of the gifted and talented*. Report to Congress by the U.S. Commissioner of Education. Washington, DC: U.S. Government Printing Office.

Martinson, R. A. (1981). *The identification of the gifted and talented*. Reston, VA: Council for Exceptional Children.

Miller, P., & Ford, B. G. (1980). A new way to identify G/C/T children: The anecdotal approach. *Gifted/Creative/Talented, 14*, 14–16.

Mitchell, B. M. (1980). What's happening to gifted education in the United States today? *Phi Delta Kappan, 61*, 563–564.

Morgan, H. J., Tennant, C. G., & Gold, M. J. (1980). *Elementary and secondary level programs for the gifted and talented.* New York: Teachers College Press.

Otis, A. S., & Lennon, R. T. (1972). *Otis-Lennon Mental Ability Test.* New York: Harcourt, Brace & World.

Palmer, O. (1959). Review of Horn art aptitude inventory. In O. K. Buros (Ed.), *The fifth mental measurements yearbook.* Highland Park, NJ: Gryphon Press.

Passow, A. H. (1980). The nature of giftedness and talent. *Gifted Child Quarterly, 25,* 5-9.

Passow, A. H., Goldberg, M., Tannenbaum, A. J., & French, W. (1955). *Planning for talented youth.* New York: Teachers College, Bureau of Publications.

Pegnato, C. W., & Bush, J. W. (1959). Locating gifted children in junior high schools: A comparison of methods. *Exceptional Children, 25,* 300-304.

Renzulli, J. S., Smith, L., White, A. J., Callahan, C. M., & Hartman, R. K. (1976). *Scales for Rating Behavioral Characteristics of Superior Students.* Mansfield Center, CT: Creative Learning Press.

Renzulli, J. S. (1973). Talent potential in minority group students. *Exceptional Children, 39,* 437-444.

Rice, J. R. (1970). *The gifted: Developing total talent.* Springfield, IL: Charles C Thomas.

Ross, J. D., & Ross, C. M. (1976). *Ross Test of Higher Cognitive Processes.* Navaro, CA: Academic Therapy Publications.

Rosser, P. (1981). What to do about the IQ problem. *Gifted Children Newsletter, 2*(14).

Seashore, C. E. (1960). *Seashore Measures of Musical Talents.* New York: The Psychological Corporation.

Sellin, D. F., & Birch, J. W. (1980). *Educating gifted and talented learners.* Rockville, MD: Aspen Publications.

Stanley, J. C. (1976). Use of tests to discover talent. In D. P. Keating (Ed.), *Intellectual talent: Research and development.* Baltimore: Johns Hopkins University Press.

Sullivan, E. T., Clark, W. W., & Tiegs, E. W. (1970). *California Test of Mental Maturity.* Monterey, CA: CTB/McGraw-Hill.

Torrance, E. P. (1981). *Thinking Creatively in Action and Movement* (TCAM). Bensenville, IL: Scholastic Testing Service.

Torrance, E. P. (1974). *Norms and Technical Manual for Torrance Tests of Creative Thinking.* Lexington, MA: Ginn and Company.

Vermilyea, J. (1981). Common sense in the identification of gifted and talented students who need alternative programming. *Gifted/Creative/Talented, 16,* 11-14.

Vernon, P. E., Adamson, G., & Vernon, D. F. (1977). *The psychology and education of gifted children.* Boulder, CO: Westerview Press.

Whitmore, J. R. (1980). *Giftedness, conflict, and underachievement.* Boston: Allyn & Bacon.

Wing, P. (1963). Review of Seashore measures of musical talent. In O. K. Buros (Ed.), *The sixth mental measurements yearbook.* Highland Park, NJ: Gryphon Press.

Woodcock, R. W., & Johnson, M. C. (1977). *Woodcock-Johnson Psycho-Educational Battery.* Hingham, MA: Teaching Resources Corporation.

Index